Refugee Rights and Realities
Evolving International Concepts and Regimes

This volume on international refugee law and policy assesses the rights of refugees and asylum seekers and the often contrasting reality of state practice. It brings together contributions from seventeen experts, drawn from a variety of professions and disciplines, including lawyers, NGO advisors and political scientists. The first part of the book concerns the evolving refugee definition and some of its key conceptual elements, with chapters variously considering matters of theory as well as jurisprudential and treaty law developments, both historical and current. Later parts of the book are concerned with asylum regimes, in particular the roles of key actors in the refugee discourse, the Office of the United Nations High Commissioner for Refugees, nation states, and the embryonic regional asylum regime of the European Union. Permeating the latter parts is the relationship, and sometimes the gulf, between the reality of institutional and state action and the rights of refugees.

FRANCES NICHOLSON is a freelance researcher and editorial consultant based in Cambridge and was Airey Neave Research Fellow (1996–7) at the Human Rights Law Centre, University of Nottingham. PATRICK TWOMEY is Lecturer in Law and Deputy Director of the Human Rights Law Centre, University of Nottingham.

Refugee Rights and Realities

Evolving International Concepts and Regimes

edited by
Frances Nicholson
and
Patrick Twomey

CAMBRIDGE
UNIVERSITY PRESS

PUBLISHED BY THE PRESS SYNDICATE OF THE UNIVERSITY OF CAMBRIDGE
The Pitt Building, Trumpington Street, Cambridge CB2 1RP, United Kingdom

CAMBRIDGE UNIVERSITY PRESS
The Edinburgh Building, Cambridge CB2 2RU, UK http://www.cup.cam.ac.uk
40 West 20th Street, New York, NY 10011-4211, USA http://www.cup.org
10 Stamford Road, Oakleigh, Melbourne 3166, Australia

First published 1999

Printed in the United Kingdom at the University Press, Cambridge

Typeset in Plantin 10/12 pt in QuarkXPress™   [SE]

A catalogue record for this book is available from the British Library

Library of Congress Cataloguing in Publication data

Refugee rights and realities: evolving international concepts and
regimes / edited by Frances Nicholson and Patrick Twomey.
   p. cm.
ISBN 0 521 63282 X (hb)
1. Political refugees – Legal status, laws, etc.   2. Asylum, Right
of. I. Nicholson, Frances. II. Twomey, Patrick M.
K3230.R45R442   1999
341.4′86 – dc21   98-43632   CIP

ISBN 0 521 63282 X hardback

Contents

Tables

Notes on contributors

Howard Adelman
Howard Adelman is a Professor of Philosophy at York University in Toronto and was the founder and director of the Centre for Refugee Studies at the same university for twelve years until the end of 1993. He was also editor of Canada's international periodical on refugees, *Refuge*. He is the author or editor of twelve books, over seventy-five articles in books and refereed journals, and many special studies. He co-authored a report with Astri Suhrke of the Chr. Michelsen Institute in Norway for a consortium of nineteen countries, seven international agencies and twelve international NGOs, and is entitled *Early Warning and Conflict Management: Genocide in Rwanda* (DANIDA, Copenhagen, 1996). An edited book also resulted from that study: *The Path of a Genocide: The Rwanda Crisis from Uganda to Zaire* (Transaction Books, 1999).

Jean-Yves Carlier
Jean-Yves Carlier is a barrister and Professor at the Faculty of Law of the Université catholique de Louvain, Belgium, where he teaches migration law, European law and international private law. His latest publications in refugee law are *Who is a Refugee? A Comparative Case Law Study* and *Europe and Refugees: A Challenge*, edited with Dirk Vanheule (Kluwer, The Hague, 1997). Carlier is also a practising lawyer, a member of the European Legal Network on Asylum (ELENA) and a member of the editorial board of the *International Journal of Refugee Law*.

S. Alex Cunliffe
Alex Cunliffe is a principal lecturer in the Department of Politics at the University of Plymouth. His current research interest focusing upon the international treatment of refugees springs from an honorary research post at the University of Hong Kong analysing the plight of the Vietnamese Boat People. Previous publications in the field include articles in *Political Studies* and *The Pacific Review*, together with articles with Michael Pugh in the *Journal of Refugee Studies* and *Security Dialogue*.

Cornelis D. de Jong

Between 1 June 1996 and 31 July 1998 Cornelis D. de Jong was Justice Counsellor of the Permanent Mission of the Netherlands to the European Union in Brussels. In this capacity he chaired a number of working groups on asylum and immigration under the Dutch Presidency during the first half of 1997. For three years before that he worked for the European Commission, first as national expert, later as adviser to the Head of the Justice and Home Affairs Task Force. From 1979 to 1993 he worked for the Netherlands Ministries of Foreign Affairs, of Social Affairs and Employment, and of Justice respectively. Since 1987 he has participated in the negotiations on the formulation of a common European asylum and immigration policy. From August 1998 until April 1999 he worked at the Netherlands Foreign Office as General Co-ordinator for the EUROMED-conference on 'Migration and Human Exchanges'. He is also currently finishing his doctoral thesis on *Freedom of Thought, Conscience and Religion in the United Nations (1946–92)*.

Guy S. Goodwin-Gill

Guy S. Goodwin-Gill is Professor of International Refugee Law and Rubin Director of Research at the Institute of European Studies, University of Oxford, and Professor of Asylum Law at the University of Amsterdam. From 1976 to 1988 he served with UNHCR in various posts, and has been editor-in-chief of the *International Journal of Refugee Law* since its first issue in 1989. His publications include *The Refugee in International Law*, 2nd edition (Clarendon Press, Oxford, 1996); *Codes of Conduct for Elections* (Inter-Parliamentary Union, Geneva, 1998); *Free and Fair Elections: International Law and Practice* (Inter-Parliamentary Union, 1994); *Child Soldiers*, with Ilene Cohn (Clarendon Press, Oxford, 1994), as well as many articles on these and related international law issues.

Elspeth Guild

Elspeth Guild is a partner in Kingsley Napley Solicitors, London, and specialises in immigration and asylum law with particular reference to the European Union. She is the author of *The Developing Immigration and Asylum Policies of the European Union* (Kluwer, The Hague, 1996) and joint author with Denis Martin of *Free Movement of Persons in the European Union* (Butterworths, London, 1996). She is convenor of the European Group of the Immigration Law Practitioners' Association which comprises over 700 lawyers and academics in the UK and 400 in continental Europe, and is co-ordinator of the Centre for Migration Law at the University of Nijmegen.

Danièle Joly
Danièle Joly is Director of the Centre for Research in Ethnic Relations at the University of Warwick. She has a *Licence ès Lettres* (University of Nanterre), an MA in industrial relations (Sorbonne) and a doctorate (University of Aston). She has published articles on Muslim populations in Britain and on refugees in Europe. Her main publications are *Immigrant Associations in Europe* (edited with J. Rex and C. Wilpert); *Reluctant Host: Europe and its Refugees* (edited with Robin Cohen); *Refugees in Europe: The Hostile New Agenda* (with Lynette Kelly and Clive Nettleton); *Britannia's Crescent: Making a Place for Muslims in British Society*; *Haven or Hell? Asylum Policies and Refugees in Europe*; and *Scapegoats or Social Actors*.

Claire Messina
Claire Messina is Humanitarian Affairs Officer in the Office for the Co-ordination of Humanitarian Affairs at the United Nations Secretariat in New York. She was the International Organisation for Migration Conference Officer in the joint UNHCR/IOM/OSCE Secretariat responsible for preparing and organising the Commonwealth of Independent States conference on refugees and migrants. She conducts research on migration and displacement problems in the CIS countries.

Nuala Mole
Nuala Mole read law at Oxford followed by European law at the College of Europe, Bruges. She has for many years advised on the rights of individuals in international law and particularly under European Community law. She is the rapporteur to the EC on the UK's compliance with the law on the free movement of people and is the founder director of the AIRE Centre (Advice on Individual Rights in Europe), the European citizens' rights bureau for the UK. The Centre also litigates on behalf of individuals before the European Commission and Court of Human Rights in Strasbourg.

Erin D. Mooney
Erin D. Mooney is a human rights officer in the Office of the United Nations High Commissioner for Human Rights, and, in that capacity, the assistant of the Representative of the UN Secretary-General on Internally Displaced Persons, Dr. Francis M. Deng. At the time of presenting the paper on which her chapter is based, she was pursuing doctoral studies full-time at the University of Cambridge.

Richard Plender
Richard Plender was called to the bar in 1974 and became a QC in 1989. At the bar he has concentrated on international law and European Community law. He took the case of *Vilvarajah* to the House of Lords for

the UNHCR and to the European Court of Human Rights for the applicant. Among his appointments are that of legal adviser to the UNHCR, *référendaire* at the Court of Justice of the European Communities, director of the Centre of European Law, King's College, London, and visiting professor at City University, London. He has also published widely on European Community and international law.

Michael Pugh

Michael Pugh is reader in international relations at the University of Plymouth and edits *International Peacekeeping*, a quarterly refereed journal. His previous publications in the field include articles with Alex Cunliffe in *Security Dialogue* and the *Journal of Refugee Studies*. He has also published *Maritime Security and Peacekeeping* (Manchester University Press), *The Armed Protection of Humanitarian Activity* for the International Committee of the Red Cross, 'The Withering of UN Humanitarian Reform: A Rejoinder', 29 *Security Dialogue*, 1998, p. 167, and 'Military Intervention and Humanitarian Action: Trends and Issues', 22 *Disasters*, 1998, p. 339.

Prakash Shah

Prakash Shah graduated from the London School of Economics with an LLB in 1991 and the following year gained his Masters in Law from London University. He is currently a temporary lecturer teaching immigration and nationality law, and ethnic minorities and the law, at the School of Oriental and African Studies (SOAS) in London. In 1991 he submitted his doctorate at SOAS entitled 'Refugees, Race and the Legal Concept of Asylum in Britain'.

Daniel J. Steinbock

Daniel J. Steinbock is Anderson Professor of Law and Values at the University of Toledo College of Law, Ohio, USA. He received his undergraduate and law degrees from Yale University. He is co-author of *Unaccompanied Children: Care and Protection in Wars, Natural Disasters and Refugee Movements* (Oxford University Press, 1988) and has written about unaccompanied children and refugee law. He has worked with Cambodian refugees in Thailand and Rwandan refugees in Zaire.

Jerzy Sztucki

Jerzy Sztucki was Head of the Department of International Law at the Polish Institute of International Affairs, Warsaw, from 1955 and then served as Scientific Secretary from 1962 to 1968. He was Associate Professor of International Law at the University of Lund, Sweden, from 1970 to 1983 and Professor of International Law at the University of

Uppsala from 1983 to 1992. Since his retirement he has been associated with the Raoul Wallenberg Institute of Human Rights and Humanitarian Law at the University of Lund, Sweden.

Patricia Tuitt

Patricia Tuitt is a lecturer in the Department of Law, Birkbeck College, University of London, having moved there from the University of East London in 1998. She has written several articles on refugee law and policy. Her book *False Images: The Law's Construction of the Refugee* (Pluto Press, London) was published in 1996.

Volker Türk

Volker Türk is currently Assistant Chief of Mission (Protection) for the UNHCR in Bosnia-Herzegovina. From 1995 to 1997 he was legal adviser in the Division of International Protection, UNHCR, Geneva; from 1993 to 1995 regional legal adviser for Central and Eastern Europe (Europe Bureau, UNHCR, Geneva); and from 1991 to 1993 protection officer (UNHCR, Kuwait). Before that he worked as a university assistant at the Institute of International Law at the University of Vienna where he finished his doctoral thesis on UNHCR and its mandate (published in German by Duncker & Humblot, Berlin, 1992). From 1985 to 1988 he was research assistant at the Institute of Criminal Law at the University of Linz, Austria.

Jens Vedsted-Hansen

Jens Vedsted-Hansen is Associate Professor at the Institute of Legal Science, University of Copenhagen. He has published a book on *Residence Rights and Maintenance* (*Opholdsret og forsørgelse* in Danish) (Copenhagen, 1997), as well as articles and book contributions on immigration and refugee law. He has previously worked at the University of Aarhus and at the Danish Centre for Human Rights. From 1987 until 1994 he was a member of the Danish Refugee Appeals Board. He co-ordinated the legal sub-study of the Nordic Comparative Studies on Temporary Protection for Refugees from 1995 to 1998.

Daniel Warner

Daniel Warner is deputy to the Director for External Relations and Special Programmes at the Graduate Institute of International Studies, Geneva, Switzerland. He has served as a consultant to UNHCR and is on the editorial boards of the *International Journal of Refugee Law* and *Refugee Survey Quarterly*. His articles on refugee issues have appeared in the *Journal of Refugee Studies*, the *International Journal of Refugee Law* and the *Peace Review*.

Acknowledgments

The editors wish to thank the many people who helped make the publication of this book possible. It resulted from a conference on *Refugee Rights and Realities: Approaches to Law and Policy Reform* which was organised by the Human Rights Law Centre (http://www.nottingham.ac.uk/law/hrlc.htm) and held at the University of Nottingham in November 1996. The financial backing of the Airey Neave Trust and a contribution from the London Office of the United Nations High Commissioner for Refugees made it possible to bring together the broad spectrum of people who participated in the conference. Organisational support for the latter was afforded by Leysa Day in the School of Law and a conference committee composed of members of the Students Human Rights Centre and LLM students taking the Refugee Protection LLM module in 1996/97.

  With regard to this collection, our thanks go to Claire Jennings and Catherine Phuong in the School of Law for their assistance, to Finola O'Sullivan of Cambridge University Press for her enthusiasm for this project from the outset and to the anonymous reviewers. Finally, our thanks to the contributors, without whose forbearance and congenial revision of their contributions, this collection would never have reached a format in which it will it is hoped contribute to a legal, political and ultimately moral debate.

Table of cases

European Court of Justice

Table of treaties and other international instruments

The most up-to-date status of ratifications of international instruments deposited with the UN can be found at the UN Treaty Collection at http://www.un.org/Depts/Treaty/ and at RefWorld at http://www.unhcr.ch/refworld

Abbreviations

AALCC	Asian–African Legal Consultative Committee
All ER	*All England Law Reports*
APC	armoured personnel carrier
ARRVS	Afdeling Rechtspraak Raad van State (Netherlands Council of State, Judicial Section)
BBTG	Broad-Based Transitional Government (Rwanda)
BIA	Board of Immigration Appeals (USA)
CA	Court of Appeal (UK)
CAHAR	Committee of Experts on the Legal Aspects of Territorial Asylum, Refugees and Stateless Persons (Council of Europe)
CDR	Centre for Documentation and Research (of UNHCR, formerly called Centre for Documentation on Refugees)
CDR	Coalition for the Defence of the Republic (Rwanda)
CFSP	Common Foreign and Security Policy (EU Council of Ministers)
CICR	Comité international de la croix-rouge
CIPPDD	International Centre for Rights of the Person and of Democratic Development (Montreal)
CIREA	Centre for Information, Discussion and Exchange on Asylum (within EU)
CIREFI	Centre for Information, Discussion and Exchange on the Crossing of Frontiers and Immigration (with EU)
CIS	Commonwealth of Independent States
CLADHO	Liaison Committee of Associations in Defence of Human Rights in Rwanda
CLR	*Commonwealth Law Reports*
CMG	Change Management Group (within UNHCR)
CMLR	*Common Market Law Reports*

CPRR	Commission permanente de recours des réfugiés (French-speaking refugee appeal board in Belgium)
CRA	Commission suisse de recours en matière d'asile (Swiss asylum appeals board)
CRR	Commission française de recours des réfugiés (French refugee appeals board)
CSCE	Conference on Security and Co-operation in Europe
DAC	Development Assistance Committee (of OECD)
DANIDA	Danish International Development Agency
DHA	Department of Humanitarian Affairs (within UN)
DLR	*Dominion Law Reports*
DPA	Department of Political Affairs (within UN)
DPKO	Department of Peace-Keeping Operations (within UN)
EC	European Community/European Communities
ECHO	European Community Humanitarian Office
ECHR	European Convention for the Protection of Human Rights and Fundamental Freedoms
ECOSOC	Economic and Social Council (of United Nations)
ECR	*European Court Reports*
ECRE	European Council on Refugees and Exiles
EEC	European Economic Community
EHRR	*European Human Rights Reports*
ERC	Emergency Relief Co-ordinator
ETS	*European Treaty Series*
EU	European Union
EURODAC	European Automated Fingerprinting Recognition System
EXCOM	Executive Committee of UNHCR
FCA	Federal Court of Appeal (Canada)
FIDH	Fédération internationale des droits de l'homme
FIS	Islamic Salvation Front (Algeria)
G8	Group of Eight industrialised countries
GA	General Assembly
GAO	General Accounting Office (USA)
GAOR	General Assembly Official Records
GIA	Armed Islamic Group (Algeria)
IASC	Inter-Agency Standing Committee (within UN)
IAT	Immigration Appeal Tribunal (UK)
ICCPR	International Covenant on Civil and Political Rights
ICJ	International Court of Justice
ICRC	International Committee of the Red Cross

IDP	internally displaced person
IFA	internal flight alternative
IFOR	Implementation Force (NATO-led force in the former Yugoslavia)
IFRC	International Federation of Red Cross and Red Crescent Societies
IGC	Inter-governmental Consultations on Asylum, Refugee and Migration Policies in Europe, North America and Australia
IHRR	*International Human Rights Reports*
IIDH-ACNUR	Instituto Interamericano de Derechos Humanos (Inter-American Institute of Human Rights)/Alto Comisionado de Naciones Unidas para los Refugiados (UNHCR)
IISS	International Institute for Strategic Studies (London)
ILC	International Law Commission
ILM	*International Legal Materials*
ILO	International Labour Organisation
ILPA	Immigration Law Practitioners' Association (UK)
Inter-Am CHR	Inter-American Commission for Human Rights
IOM	International Organisation for Migration
IRIN	UN Integrated Regional Information Network
IRO	International Refugee Organisation
IRP	involuntarily relocating person
IRR	Institute of Race Relations (UK)
IUSSP	International Union for the Scientific Study of Population
JHA	Justice and Home Affairs (EU Council of Ministers)
JICRA	Jurisprudence et informations de la Commision suisse de recours en matière d'asile
LNTS	*League of Nations Treaty Series*
LTTE	Liberation Tigers of Tamil Eelam (Sri Lanka)
MRNDD	National Republican Movement for Democracy and Development (Rwanda)
MSF	Médecins sans frontières
NATO	North Atlantic Treaty Organisation
NGO	non-governmental organisation
NIF	neutral international force (in Rwanda)
OAS	Organisation of American States
OAU	Organisation of African Unity

OCHA	Office for the Co-ordination of Humanitarian Affairs (within UN)
OECD	Organisation for Economic Co-operation and Development
OERC	Office of the Emergency Relief Co-ordinator (within UN)
OFPRA	Office français de protection des réfugiés et apatrides (France)
OJ	*Official Journal of the European Communities*
ONG	Organisation non-gouvernementale (NGO)
ONU	Organisation des nations unies (UN)
OSCE	Organisation for Security and Co-operation in Europe
P100M	Interdisciplinary Research Programme on Root Causes of Human Rights Violation (Leiden, Netherlands)
PKK	Kurdistan Workers' Party (Turkey)
PLO	Palestine Liberation Organisation
RAB	Refugee Appeals Board (Denmark)
RFE/RL	Radio Free Europe/Radio Liberty
RPF	Rwandese Patriotic Front
RSC	*Revised Statutes of Canada*
SCR	*Supreme Court Reports (Canada)*
SFOR	Stabilisation Force (in former Yugoslavia)
SFRY	Socialist Federal Republic of Yugoslavia
SFS	Swedish Code of Statutes
SHAEF	Supreme Headquarters, Allied Expeditionary Force
TEU	Treaty on European Union
UDHR	Universal Declaration of Human Rights
UIDH	Inter-African Union of Human Rights (Ouagadougou)
UN	United Nations
UNAMIR	UN Assistance Mission to Rwanda
UNCITRAL	United Nations Commission on International Trade Law
UNDP	United Nations Development Programme
UNDRO	United Nations Disaster Relief Organisation
UNECE	United Nations Economic Commission for Europe
UNESCO	United Nations Educational, Scientific and Cultural Organisation
UNFPA	United Nations Population Fund
UNHCR	United Nations High Commissioner for Refugees
UNHRFOR	United Nations Human Rights Field Operation for Rwanda

UNICEF   United Nations Children's Emergency Fund
UNPA   United Nations Protected Areas
UNPREDEP   United Nations Preventive Deployment Force (in
             the former Yugoslav republic of Macedonia)
UNPROFOR   United Nations Protection Force in the former
             Yugoslavia
UNREO   United Nations Rwanda Emergency Operation
UNTS   *United Nations Treaty Series*
USSR   Union of Soviet Socialist Republics
VBC   Vaste   Beroepscommissie   voor   Vluchtelingen
             (Flemish refugee appeals board in Belgium)
WFP   World Food Programme
WHO   World Health Organisation

Introduction

Patrick Twomey and Frances Nicholson

This collection had its origins in a conference entitled *Refugee Rights and Realities: Approaches to Law and Policy Reform* which was held at the University of Nottingham in November 1996 and was organised by the Human Rights Law Centre as part of a research project funded by the Airey Neave Trust. The conference considered the rights of refugees and asylum seekers and the often contrasting reality of the practice of states and other actors in this area. It brought together some 200 people from over a dozen countries, representing a cross-section of refugee expertise, for an inter-disciplinary dialogue on strategies to address various legal and social aspects of refugee matters.

Papers presented at the conference plenary sessions and the ten workshops were revised in light of debate at the conference, culminating in the seventeen chapters presented in this collection. Other papers, with a more specific United Kingdom focus, were revised and published as *Current Issues of UK Asylum Law and Policy* (Ashgate, 1998). The primarily UK and European focus of the conference was determined by budget and logistical factors rather than any lack of appreciation that the issue of refugees is a global concern (particularly as only a small percentage of the world's refugees actually seeks or finds protection in Europe). While this specific geographical scope is reflected in this collection, the individual chapters nevertheless have an application beyond any national or regional context.

The collection is divided into four sections. Part 1 concerns the evolving refugee definition and some of its key conceptual elements, with chapters variously considering matters of theory as well as jurisprudential and treaty law developments, both historical and current. Parts 2, 3 and 4 are concerned with asylum regimes, in particular the roles of key actors in the refugee discourse, the Office of the United Nations High Commissioner for Refugees (UNHCR), nation states, and the embryonic regional asylum regime of the European Union. Permeating the latter three parts is the relationship, and sometimes the gulf, between the reality of institutional and state action and the rights of refugees. The contributions are as

1

diverse as the authors themselves and in this they reflect the conference debate and refugee discourse generally. The authors come from a variety of disciplines (including law, international relations and philosophy), backgrounds (academic, practitioners or *fonctionnaire*) and ideological standpoints (classical liberal, feminist etc.).

At the end of the twentieth century, with the global map studded with localised conflicts, internecine strife, fractured states and associated forced migration, the upward trend in refugee numbers has produced a tangible sense of compassion fatigue on the part of many states. Hence the language speaks of refugees as a 'tide' or 'burden' to be passed on by or, at best, shared between states, and as including the 'bogus' who 'abuse the system'. All the while, states insist they wish to keep this system free for the 'genuine' refugee. Yet, before we hark back to some supposed halcyon days of refugee protection, sight should not be lost of the long-standing, intrinsically statist nature of the international refugee protection regime, as perpetuated in its regional and national derivatives. With its emphasis on territory, jurisdiction, admission/departure etc., asylum has been inextricably linked, from its inception through the era of the Cold War and the latter's proxy conflicts, to general principles of public international law, with ultimate control over decision-making resting with individual states.

Thus, state concerns not to write 'blank cheques' or forfeit control over entry to territory saw them withdraw by the middle of the century from a proposed *right of asylum* in favour of a right to *seek and enjoy* it. In contrast, the language of general human rights obligations, at least the rights of the so-called first generation, emphatically provides that 'everyone has the right to . . .' and 'states shall' etc. It is this primary control over the recognition of the status, linked to the absence of an accompanying international judicial supervisory body, which impairs the 1951 Geneva Convention Relating to the Status of Refugees as a human rights document and, in a sense, isolates refugee rights from their general human rights foundation. Yet, refugees, no less than prisoners, women, minorities etc., are a category of human rights bearers, the uniqueness of whose situation requires particular solutions.

That the Convention is a human rights document is incontestably borne out by its contents. Taking as its starting point the Universal Declaration of Human Rights, it details extensive rights concerning non-discrimination, religion, property, association, court access, employment, welfare, housing, education, free movement, documentation etc. In essence it is a catalogue of rights assured to the successful claimant of the status of refugee though the tenor of their formulation might be unfortunate. For example, the term 'human rights' only finds explicit expression in the preamble, while some substantive rights are included under the heading 'administrative measures'. More fundamentally, so long as state concerns about control of entry and sovereignty prevail, and required solutions are premised on defining the refugee and identifying an offending and responsible state, the refugee phenomenon, while indisputably a matter of individual rights, continues to be viewed in political and security terms.

As the sovereignty–human rights scales slowly tip in favour of the latter, with the revolution in international law that recognises rights as deriving from the individual's humanity as opposed to their citizenship or nationality, the refugee remains problematic. Real or imagined threats to states of origin and receiving states (which are reflected in the prominence afforded in article 2 of the Geneva Convention to refugee duties towards the receiving country) remain the dominant refrain in refugee discourse, whether in terms of altering political balances or ethnic/racial homogeneity, depleting financial and skills resources, or otherwise destabilising state and societal infrastructures.

Contrary to twentieth-century trends in human rights protection generally, the principal obligation of states to refugees is framed in negative, as opposed to positive, terms, that is, as an obligation not to return (*refouler*) an individual to persecution rather than as a duty to admit those fearing persecution. A combination of this narrowly drawn obligation and the legal and ideological malleability discovered within the refugee definition allows ample scope for states to select and prioritise their 'favourite refugees', who are often protected for the political capital gained by affording the refugee label to those fleeing the territory of ideological foes. The level of refugee rights protection has owed as much to the vagaries of the ideological posturing of states as to any sense of individual dignity or of asylum seekers or refugees as bearers of rights *per se*. At the same time, the primacy of the economic interests of states has seen refugees being subsumed within general migration at times when labour is needed. In large part refugees have been consigned to a passive role in the relationship between states.

Nevertheless, it goes without saying that the 'reality' of the refugees' experiences is a tale of individual human rights. This extends from the rights abuses and failures which first prompt movement, the human rights obligations of states in light of such movement, experiences in receiving states and refugee camps (often the scene of new and continued violations of rights), to the rights necessary to establish themselves in countries of asylum or, on return, in their country of origin.

Tapping the wider human rights structures and theoretical analysis does not offer an absolute panacea for the refugee predicament. Indeed there are inherent dangers for refugees in 'rights talk'. For instance, when the right to return/remain is not voluntarily assumed, return or containment can be to, or within, 'areas' which prove to be anything but safe. Resort to the underlying rights base does, however, provide an escape route from the sometimes tautological, but nevertheless critically important, debates which have developed around the refugee definition, particularly on the meaning of persecution, the recognised grounds, and social group membership. Equally, the fundamental quandary remains in that it presupposes the identification of a rights hierarchy that would activate the duty of states to uphold the principle of *non-refoulement* and other obligations of protection. In part this involves no more than a rephrasing of the question, 'Is this persecution?' Yet, as some commentators, notably James Hathaway, have illustrated, there is a pre-existing international human rights law foundation upon which such an exercise can draw, notably non-derogable rights, where, in the words of UNHCR's training manual, 'their violation is of such a character as to render the person's continued stay in the home country intolerable'.

Such an approach still presupposes the crossing of frontiers and that refugees can reach a point where they can activate such rights. Once again human rights obligations offer a more useful framework, within which practices and mechanisms such as interdiction, carrier sanctions and 'buffer zones' might be challenged.

An associated advantage of a wider human rights perspective is that it allows domestic courts and tribunals to tap the vast resource of international human rights instruments, most of which post-date the Geneva Convention, and the resulting jurisprudence in their deliberations. More generally, it offers the appeal of moving the parameters of the refugee debate so that the language of 'cost' and 'burden' less readily provides states with a political escape route from what would clearly be understood as their international human rights obligations.

The refugee definition

Much energy has been invested in analysis of the refugee definition. It is unlikely that the Convention drafters envisaged the extent to which it would become a standard feature of courtroom dispute or generate so prolific a body of work amongst legal academics. In the absence of expansive *travaux préparatoires* accompanying the Convention, this analysis is an exercise deeply rooted both in the social and political thinking of the time of its formulation and the time and circumstances of its interpretation. The chapters in Part 1 of this collection reflect the scope and diversity of this exercise.

In chapter 1, in a classical legal analysis of the Convention refugee definition, both in terms of how it has and ought to be interpreted, Daniel Steinbock considers the definition's 'ordinary meaning', a more purposive approach and the more recent moves towards a wider human rights perspective. His endorsement of the purposive approach is qualified by the acknowledgment that the utility of such an approach is nevertheless dependent on the purpose actually inferred. Subsequent chapters echo this dilemma.

Jean-Yves Carlier offers in chapter 2 an analytical model, based on a teleological analysis of case law concerning the Convention definition, in his 'Theory of the Three Scales'. This comprises an assessment of risk (in terms of fear being well founded), persecution (according to a test based on what the author identifies as 'basic' human rights) and proof (of risk of mistreatment). Through such a model and the reasoned, interpretative judicial function, he argues that the Convention definition can have a continuing relevance. Most fundamentally, the author notes that such a model can only meet the protective intent of the Convention when 'appropriate' presumptions underpin the questions posed.

The question of contemporaneous relevance also permeates chapter 3 by Jerzy Sztucki, a contemporary of the drafting process. Tracing the historical and regional development of the definition he notes the underlying tension within the quest for precision and universality of application, which has variously produced 'Convention fundamentalism' and more 'comprehensive' approaches towards the refugee definition. Ultimately, the author opines that the refugee cannot be authoritatively defined and that the reality of the refugee situation can only be addressed through a purposive reading of the Convention.

Chapter 4 by Richard Plender and Nuala Mole moves from the 1951 Convention to the wider panoply of international human rights instruments, reflecting the authors' practical involvement in some of the seminal asylum decisions before both UK and European courts. These instruments have in many respects widened the protection available to asylum seekers and refugees. Analysing the various rights involved in the quest for protection, from return to persecution, they concentrate on the prohibition of torture, rights relating to detention, due process and family life through which the Human Rights Committee and the European Commission and Court of Human Rights have, against a backdrop of a restrictive definitional approach, established a web of protection not dependent on the question, 'Who is a refugee?'

In chapter 5 Patricia Tuitt returns to the question, 'Who is a refugee?' She contends that the reality of refugee discourse, with its focus on space, mobility and a classic conceptualisation of the refugee as political dissident or religious leader, means that it is fundamentally premised on a socio-political construct which is intrinsically adult and male.

Echoing one of the key definitional elements identified in Steinbock's opening chapter and acknowledging one of Tuitt's central theses, the critical issue of the 'political' refugee is explored in chapter 6 by Prakash Shah. The pliant refugee definition as used by Western states during the Cold War to open their arms to their ideological kin has, in more recent times, continued to reflect the political reality behind the grant or refusal of refugee status. Related to the age-old freedom fighter–terrorist dilemma, the desire not to alienate certain countries of origin, whether political ally or economic benefactor, by affording protection to those they persecute, increasingly means that the 'political' is redefined as 'criminal' and legitimate voices are placed in peril or admitted at the price of being muzzled.

In the 1990s the European refugee paradigm changed forever as the clear East–West political polarity disintegrated and, with the falling of the Berlin Wall, millions long-presumed persecuted were redefined as undeserving of protection. Equally, the redrawing of the European political map involved the fracturing of old states, creating new boundaries and new refugees. Claire Messina's final chapter in this part focuses on a much under-researched general migration situation, that of the countries of the Commonwealth of Independent States (CIS). The range of motivations for population movement in this region, variously part of a legacy of historic, forced and voluntary migration as well as more recent conflicts and human rights abuses, has seen a variety of labels applied. These include internally displaced persons, repatriants and formerly deported persons. Moreover, the narrower label of 'refugee' is 'politically loaded' for the CIS states, in some respects in the inverse of the Western states' Cold War refugee construct, in that the archetypal Soviet bloc refugee was the communist activist fleeing right-wing regimes. As Messina observes, this categorisation exercise is a vivid illustration, both of the inadequacy of the central international refugee definition in complex migratory situations and of the difficulties associated with finding consensus on the creation of broader categories, notably that of 'forced migrant'.

The role of UNHCR

Part 2 of the collection, which addresses a central institutional aspect of the refugee debate, opens with chapter 8 by Volker Türk. UNHCR, from its mandate extending beyond concern for the Convention refugee to the elucidation offered by its *Handbook* guidelines and involvement in the drafting of national asylum legislation, has played a central role in matters of definition. Equally, despite problems stemming from some interpretations of UNHCR's 'humanitarian' role and 'non-political character', UNHCR's broader human rights obligations permeate its mandate even in the context of the shifting sands of the refugee debate.

Türk advances both an historical and current analysis of UNHCR's legal mandate and competence, extended beyond the Convention to encompass refugees, asylum seekers, returnees, internally displaced persons and persons threatened with displacement or otherwise at risk. Acknowledging abortive attempts to codify the law relating to the right of asylum, he details UNHCR's input into regional and other legal developments concerning refugees, stressing its fundamental importance in any future quest for consolidation of necessarily diverse developments and trends.

In chapter 9 Alex Cunliffe and Michael Pugh focus on a distinct aspect of UNHCR's extended mandate, its humanitarian co-ordination role in the former Yugoslavia, which they identify as representing 'a triumph of politics over law'. Raising questions that have arisen prior and subsequent to the Balkan conflagration, the 'lead agency' role is criticised as being but a cover for impotency in other quarters. Moreover, it is identified as an example of the consequences of an inappropriate institutional response and the absence of a clear mandate or, worse, the allocation of an inappropriate one.

In chapter 10, Erin Mooney elaborates on this issue in an analysis of the phenomenon of 'in-country' protection, both in terms of UNHCR's role in the former Yugoslavia and in other regions such as the Caucasus. This shift, from the primarily exilic orthodoxy of the international refugee protection regime to one variously described as one of security, containment, pre-emptive or palliative protection, has drawn withering criticism. Such arguments, which are based on mandate, donor influence and an inability to deliver such protection, are accepted in part, but challenged in detail in this chapter.

Guy Goodwin-Gill returns to the issue of UNHCR's mandate in chapter 11, which criticises the drift from 'protection' towards 'humanitarian action' and situates this development in the context of institutional reform, both of the United Nations and UNHCR, and of the specific failures in the former Yugoslavia, Rwanda and the Great Lakes. He argues that a combination of pragmatic solutions and the growth in 'negative responsibility', whereby doing nothing is construed as the greatest wrong, ultimately means that the principle of protection and the humanitarian 'ideal' of return not only deny refugees their rights, but their very identity. Yet, rather like rights and realities, the author concludes that pragmatism and protection are not by definition irreconcilable.

State responses and individual rights

After the question of institutional responsibility, the three chapters in Part 3 of this collection focus on state responses and responsibilities. In traditional refugee law terms, responsibility has meant the obligations of potential asylum states towards asylum seekers who reach their frontiers. As outlined above, the situation of the refugee within a general rights paradigm, however, fundamentally expands this. State responsibility comes to be viewed as encompassing inaction as well as action and applying to the refugee-generating state and the refugee-receiving state alike. This part of the collection addresses some of these issues, offering a theoretical approach to examining the state–individual relationship and, more specifically, an account of state actions to exclude potential claimants from the asylum process and the individual and collective inaction of states in the lead-up to the 1994 genocide in Rwanda.

Daniel Warner draws upon social, anthropological, international relations and legal theory to seek to reconcile schools of thought that variously see the state as the problem and the solution to the refugee's predicament. From the primacy of citizenship in the state–individual relationship and what the author labels the 'state–territory–citizenship trinity' stem the marginalisation of the refugee whereby the refugee is constituted, not simply as victimised or unprotected, but as subversive of the established primacy of the nation-state. It is this complexity, of the refugee as the *inter* in international, which leads Warner to contend that human rights and state responsibility alone are an inadequate basis on which to examine the relationship between the refugee and the state.

Jens Vedsted-Hansen follows with a more classical legal perspective that explores the advent of substantive and procedural barriers to accessing the asylum process against the backdrop of the international human rights obligations of states and the asserted 'right' of refugees to choose their country of asylum. The distortion of the reference to 'coming *directly* from a territory where [the refugee's] life or freedom [is] threatened' in article 31 of the Convention into an insistence by states on direct flight and the use of constructs such as that of safe third country, stand in the way of the proposed right to choose one's country of asylum. Acknowledging that the Convention is unclear on both counts, the author draws upon its text, on various Conclusions of UNHCR's Executive Committee and on general human rights principles to question the legitimacy of such trends in state practice.

In chapter 14 Howard Adelman is concerned with the reality of collective, in the sense of the UN and otherwise, state failure in the context of the Rwandan genocide. In a forceful critique of institutional structural weaknesses and, most fundamentally, of the absence of political resolve and rationality, the author offers a reality check to the sometimes facile assumptions made about early warning and preventive action. Ultimately, Rwanda and the Great Lakes were not about the weaknesses of legal definitions, mandates or applicable norms, but about the refusal of states to honour pledges of 'never again' and to convert 'paper' rights into protective reality.

The European regime

Sovereignty concerns might mean that European Union member states baulk at the use of the word 'regime' to describe asylum developments within the EU and other European mechanisms, such as the Schengen Convention on the abolition of checks at common borders, yet in this final part a legal practitioner, an ethnic relations academic and a diplomat clearly identify such a developing regime. If it can be described as a regime then it is certainly one in flux. Treaty revision, the planned expansion of EU membership, the modalities of an ever-changing refugee phenomenon and perennial sovereignty concerns mean that the quest for an EU asylum policy has proved, and remains, a fraught exercise.

In chapter 15, in her analysis of the trend towards asylum harmonisation, Elspeth Guild takes as her starting point the fundamental divergence of opinion, traceable back to the Treaty of Rome and its goal of economic integration, as to the intent lying behind the expression, an 'ever closer union'. In addition to criticisms of EU asylum issues, such as institutional deficiencies and the use of soft law, her more fundamental objection relates to the downward harmonisation trend which, she contends, amounts to a quasi-territorial limitation on member states' obligations and a deviation from the accepted interpretation of the Geneva Convention.

Equally critical, Danièle Joly examines in chapter 16 a fundamental shift in approach to asylum on the part of western European states which is linked to the economic downturn of the 1970s and the demise of the ideological enemy in the form of the Soviet bloc. The new regime, according to the author, represents a change of culture and norms marked by features such as restriction, non-integration, selective harmonisation and the introduction of the concept of temporary protection.

In a more positive assessment than the preceding two chapters, the collection's final chapter by Cornelis de Jong traces the historical evolution of European harmonisation in this area, from the adoption of the European Commission's 1991 work programme on asylum and immigration to the new asylum and immigration provisions of the Amsterdam

Treaty. He identifies the merits and weaknesses of developments under this programme, in terms of rights protection, but generally refutes the assertion that harmonisation is downward in direction. He nevertheless exposes the slow pace of progress, as well as the dilution of the emphasis on harmonisation, the resort to non-binding instruments and so on, in the quest for a European asylum policy.

Part 1

The evolving refugee definition

1   The refugee definition as law: issues of interpretation

Daniel J. Steinbock[1]

Which foreign victims of oppression or hardship in their homelands should we shelter? For the last forty years the world's basic answer has been: those outside their country with a 'well-founded fear of being perse-cuted for reasons of race, religion, nationality, membership of a particular social group or political opinion'. Developed in the years immediately fol-lowing the Second World War and first embodied in the 1951 Convention Relating to the Status of Refugees,[2] this definition of a 'refugee' has formed the cornerstone of the international response to forced migration for the past four decades.[3] Now adhered to – at least formally – by 133 nations, the Convention definition is one of the most widely accepted international norms, and probably one of the very few to have penetrated the public consciousness. Though the Convention and its 1967 Protocol[4] do not so require, it has inspired many states to employ the definition in their domestic asylum systems.[5]

---

[1] A longer version of this chapter was originally published in 45 *UCLA Law Review*, 1998, p. 733.

[2] Convention Relating to the Status of Refugees, 189 UNTS 137 (hereinafter the Geneva Convention), article 1(A)(2). The entire paragraph of the Convention definition reads:

Article 1. Definition of the term 'Refugee'
A. For the purposes of the present Convention, the term 'refugee' shall apply to any person who . . .
   (2) As a result of events occurring before 1 January 1951 and owing to well-founded fear of being persecuted for reasons of race, religion, nationality, membership of a particular social group or political opinion, is outside the country of his nationality and is unable or, owing to such fear, is unwilling to avail himself of the protection of that country; or who, not having a nationality and being outside the country of his former habitual residence as a result of such events, is unable or, owing to such fear, is unwilling to return to it . . .

Parties to the Protocol Relating to the Status of Refugees (see note 4 below) agree to the omission of the words 'as a result of events occurring before 1 January 1951' and the words 'as a result of such events'.

[3] Ivor Jackson, 'The 1951 Convention Relating to the Status of Refugees: A Universal Basis for Protection', 3 *International Journal of Refugee Law*, 1991, p. 403.

[4] Protocol Relating to the Status of Refugees, 31 January 1967, 606 UNTS 267 (hereinafter the 1967 Protocol).

[5] James C. Hathaway, 'A Reconsideration of the Underlying Premises of Refugee Law', 31

Coupled in international law with the protection against *refoulement*, or return, to the country of persecution,[6] satisfaction of the refugee definition has been the salvation of millions of people compelled, often in the most dire circumstances, to flee their native lands. The refugee definition and the instruments in which it is contained, conceived in a desire to avoid repetition of the worst excesses of the Second World War era, have added a substantial measure of humanity to the post-war period. Indeed, by providing tangible redress from certain basic human rights violations, the Convention and its Protocol can be seen as two of the foremost international human rights instruments.

As a result of its great practical impact, virtually every word of the core phrase of the refugee definition has been subject to interpretative dispute. Some aspects of the definition have acquired a fairly well-settled gloss. The meaning of 'well-founded fear' of persecution, for example, has been decided by the highest courts of the United States, the United Kingdom and other states, and these decisions and their aftermath have been widely accepted as a fair resolution of the issue of the necessary likelihood of persecution. The central question of what it means to be persecuted 'for reasons of race, religion, nationality, membership in a particular social group, or political opinion' remains, however, a contested one. What does it mean to be 'persecuted' and that the persecution be 'for reasons of race, religion, nationality, membership of a particular social group or political opinion'?

This chapter explores the manner in which the Convention definition has been, and ought to be, interpreted. Applying traditional methods of treaty and statutory interpretation, the chapter first examines briefly the textual meaning and the drafting history of the refugee definition. Purely textual approaches employed in some states have had unanticipated effects, with both restrictive and expansive results. As for the drafting history, a review of the *travaux préparatoires* adds surprisingly little to an understanding of the content of the refugee definition, though the larger historical context provides important lessons. An approach based on the object and purpose of the refugee definition is probably the most appropriate interpretative method. The chapter proposes that, assuming a sufficiently serious threat to life, bodily integrity or liberty, application of the refugee definition should centre around principles of non-discrimination, condemnation of collective guilt and protection of freedom of

footnote 5 (*cont.*)
Harvard International Law Journal, 1990, p. 129; David Martin, 'The Refugee Concept: On Definitions, Politics, and the Careful Use of a Scarce Resource', in *Refugee Policy: Canada and the United States* (ed. Howard Adelman, Centre for Refugee Studies, York University, Toronto, 1991), p. 32.
[6] Geneva Convention, article 33(1), and customary international law.

thought and expression, finding that these purposes are truest to the Convention's language and history. It then considers several other possible formulations of the refugee definition's object and purpose. Finally, some implications and limits of these principles in the application of the refugee definition are discussed.

The ordinary meaning of the refugee definition

The point of departure for interpretation of the refugee definition, in international and many domestic legal systems, is the 'ordinary' or 'plain' meaning of its terms. On the international level, this textual approach is embodied in both the jurisprudence of the International Court of Justice[7] and in the Vienna Convention on the Law of Treaties.[8] Article 31 of the Convention directs that '[a] treaty shall be interpreted in good faith in accordance with the ordinary meaning to be given to the terms of the treaty in their context and in the light of its object and purpose'.[9] The Vienna Convention is 'clearly based on the view that the text of a treaty must be presumed to be the authentic expression of the intentions of the parties'.[10] The *travaux préparatoires* play a subsidiary role in the interpretative process.[11] The drafting history thus may be resorted to only to 'confirm' the ordinary meaning of the text, or when the textual approach leaves the meaning 'ambiguous or obscure' or leads to a patently absurd or unreasonable result.[12]

Although the Geneva Convention provides for disputes relating to its interpretation or application to be referred to the International Court of Justice (ICJ) at the request of any state party to the dispute, this mechanism has never been invoked. The ICJ thus has never had occasion to construe any portion of the Convention. In their domestic application of the Convention, states party have employed the textual approach in varying degrees. On the other hand the Office of the United Nations High Commissioner for Refugees (UNHCR), with which states are obliged to co-operate,[13] has adopted a less literal approach in its *Handbook*.[14]

[7] Ian Brownlie, *Principles of Public International Law* (5th edn, Oxford University Press, 1998), p. 632.
[8] UN Doc. A/Conf. 39/27, concluded at Vienna on 23 May 1969, 1155 UNTS 331, entered into force 27 January 1990 (hereinafter the Vienna Convention).
[9] Vienna Convention, article 31(1). Rather than connoting a wide range of background, practice or history, 'context' under the Vienna Convention means merely the text, preamble, annexes and related instruments. Vienna Convention, article 31(2).
[10] Ian Sinclair, *The Vienna Convention on the Law of Treaties* (2nd edn, Manchester University Press, 1984), p. 115.   [11] Sinclair, *Law of Treaties*, p. 141.
[12] Vienna Convention, article 32.   [13] Geneva Convention, article 35.
[14] UNHCR, *Handbook on Procedures and Criteria for Determining Refugee Status* (Geneva, 1979, revised 1992).

There is insufficient space here to make more than a few remarks about the limits of the so-called 'ordinary meaning' or 'plain meaning' approach to the Convention. In the United States, the Supreme Court has had four occasions to interpret the Convention, all of which ostensibly have employed the textual method. In my opinion, two of those cases have reached incorrectly narrow results, one egregiously so. In *Immigration and Naturalization Service* v. *Stevic*,[15] the Supreme Court concluded that a person who establishes a well-founded fear of persecution may (at least in theory) be returned to a country of persecution unless he or she can establish that persecution is more probable than not. The Supreme Court reached this result by considering the language of article 33 and its domestic law analogue[16] in total isolation both from the other provisions of the Convention and from its history and purpose. The other case, *Sale* v. *Haitian Centers Council, Inc.*,[17] also purported to use the plain meaning of the Convention. In reality it distorted that meaning to reach the tragic – and in my opinion, totally incorrect – conclusion that the maritime interdiction and the return of Haitian asylum seekers did not offend the basic *non-refoulement* guarantee of the Convention.[18]

In a third case, *Immigration and Naturalization Service* v. *Elias-Zacarias*,[19] the Supreme Court decided that a refugee claimant must produce at least 'some evidence' that the feared harm is 'for reasons of' one of the five specified grounds. This result has been heavily criticised,[20] but I believe some connection between 'persecution' and the reason for it to be supported, if not compelled, by the text of the definition. In addition to the cases in which 'ordinary meaning' has produced unduly restrictive interpretations, there have been some cases in which it has also led to results that can hardly be said to have been contemplated by the Convention's drafters. Examples would include giving refugee status to

---

[15] 467 US 407 (1989).   [16] Refugee Act of 1980, Pub.L. No. 96–212.

[17] 509 US 155 (1993).

[18] Indeed the Inter-American Human Rights Commission ruled in October 1996 that these US interdiction policies violated articles of the American Convention on Human Rights as well as the prohibition of *refoulement* set out in article 33 of the Geneva Convention. Inter-American Human Rights Commission, *Haitian Refugee Cases*, Case No. 10.675, Inter-Am CHR OEA/Ser/L/V/II.93, Doc. 36 (17 October 1996); revised and adopted as a final report on 13 March 1997, see 5 IHRR, 1998, pp. 120–65.

[19] 502 US 478 (1992). The fourth case was *Immigration and Naturalization Service* v. *Cardoza-Fonseca*, 480 US 421 (1986) concerning the meaning of 'well-founded fear of persecution'.

[20] Deborah Anker *et al.*, 'The Supreme Court's Decision in *Immigration and Naturalization Service* v. *Elias-Zacarias*: Is There Any "There" in There?', 69 *Interpreter Releases*, 1992, p. 285 at p. 286; Joan Fitzpatrick, 'Revitalizing the 1951 Refugee Convention', 9 *Harvard Human Rights Journal*, 1996, p. 229 at p. 237; and Karen Musalo, 'Irreconcilable Differences? Divorcing Refugee Protections from Human Rights Norms', 15 *Michigan Journal of International Law*, 1994, p. 1179.

victims of harms directed particularly at women, such as genital mutilation, who, while arguably falling within the term 'membership of a particular social group' were almost certainly outside the scope of the refugee definition as originally conceived.[21]

In short, the text of the refugee definition constitutes what might be described as the boundary of its application. Within those limits textual analysis can only take us so far towards a workable interpretation of the refugee definition. Quite apart from the question of whether the plain meaning is true to either the intentions of the drafters or the values they sought to serve, such textual analysis is simply inadequate to respond to the myriad circumstances that bring asylum seekers to invoke refugee status. For practical reasons alone, we must look elsewhere for guidance.

Significance of the *travaux préparatoires*

According to the Vienna Convention on the Law of Treaties, the *travaux préparatoires* of a treaty are a subsidiary tool of interpretation, used only to 'confirm' the ordinary meaning or if a term is 'ambiguous or obscure'. What do the *travaux préparatoires* of the Geneva Convention and its Protocol tell us about persecution and the reasons for it? First, there is no definitive treatment in the drafting process of either 'persecution', 'race', 'religion', 'nationality', 'membership of a particular social group' or 'political opinion', or of the connection between those grounds and the feared persecution implied by the term 'for reasons of'. While the deliberations were heavily weighted toward consideration and establishment of the refugee definition, they rarely reached any level of specificity concerning its terms, despite several observations about the need for clarity in the description of those to whom the Convention would apply. Instead, other more structural issues occupied the attention of the participants: whether to enumerate categories or describe criteria; what temporal and geographic restrictions, if any, to impose; and which other potentially eligible groups should be barred.

However, the drafters were, at all stages, concerned about the content of the definition, including the non-categorical bases for refugee status. They repeatedly emphasised the need for clarity regarding the scope of the Convention's coverage. They rejected more general terms for the definition in favour of a well-founded fear of being persecuted for reasons of race, religion, nationality and political opinion. Although it was accomplished with very little discussion or elaboration, the conference of plenipotentiaries added an additional ground – membership of a particular social

---

[21] See p. 29 below.

group – to the prohibited reasons for persecution, an amendment which suggests that the former grounds were not thought to be all-encompassing. The end result is that the words 'persecution for reasons of race, religion, nationality, membership of a particular social group, or political opinion' mean something other than some unspecified illegitimate governmental action. Indeed, the focus on the terms of the Convention definition of 'refugee' and, particularly, the fact that the enumerated reasons for persecution were supplemented by the conference of plenipotentiaries, supports the argument that the conference representatives may have regarded the original grounds as being restricted to something like their literal meaning. In short, much of the evidence from the drafting process is consistent with the conclusion that the phrase 'for reasons of race, religion, nationality, membership of a particular social group or political opinion' was believed to add meaning to, or indeed to qualify, the concept of 'persecution'.

In its final form, the Convention encompassed persons who had fled, or might flee, as a result of events that had already taken place.[22] While the precise number of refugees who would eventually present themselves to states party was unknown, the nature, and indeed the circumstances, of the precipitating events were matters of historical record.[23] The drafters thus must have had in mind the groups of refugees to which the Convention alluded in its general definitional language.

The primary events influencing the Convention's drafters were, of course, the Nazi persecutions of 1933–45.[24] The Convention's inclusion of persecution for reasons of race, religion and nationality speaks most directly to that experience. The treatment of Jews for reasons of their religion and perceived 'race' was the paradigm condition the drafters meant to encompass.[25] In addition, while the period before and during the Second World War had certainly seen its share of persecution of individuals, the immediate post-war period prior to the conference witnessed a new wave, consisting mostly of those in flight from increasingly repressive communist regimes in central and eastern Europe.[26] These refugees,

[22] Guy S. Goodwin-Gill, 'Refugees: The Functions and Limits of the Existing Protection System', in *Human Rights and the Protection of Refugees under International Law* (ed. Alan E. Nash, Canadian Human Rights Foundation, Quebec, 1988), p. 165.

[23] In that sense the drafters had avoided creating the 'blank cheque' which was at the head of the parade of unacceptable scenarios advanced by states which participated in the Convention's formulation.

[24] Jack Garvey, 'Toward a Reformulation of International Refugee Law', 26 *Harvard Journal of International Law*, 1985, p. 483.

[25] *Sale* v. *Haitian Centers Council, Inc.*, 509 US 155 (1993), at 207 ('The Convention . . . was enacted largely in response to the experience of Jewish refugees in Europe during the period of World War II') (Blackmun J dissenting).

[26] Michael R. Marrus, *The Unwanted: European Refugees in the Twentieth Century* (Oxford

and other groups of similarly displaced persons who refused to repatriate on the basis of feared political persecution, also were clearly of concern to the drafters of the Convention. As with other post-war international legislation, its authors were to a great extent legislating about past events.

There is very little in the events of the Second World War and its immediate aftermath to override the language used in the Convention restricting refugee status to those with a well-founded fear of persecution on one of the five specified grounds. That is, the refugees of the era were those who had been harmed because of their personal characteristics (race, religion, nationality) or because of their beliefs (religion or political opinion) or social class (social group). These post-war refugees included those who had not yet been targeted but who might be, as well as those who simply objected on political grounds to the new central and eastern European governments, fleeing from conditions they found intolerable. There is no indication in the *travaux préparatoires* or the historical conditions of the period that the Convention was designed to cover other forms of social suffering existing in Europe or elsewhere.

Purposes of the refugee definition

For a number of reasons, interpretation of the refugee definition needs to look to the Convention and Protocol's object and purpose. One is that the text cannot otherwise be fully understood, as the Vienna Convention recognises and as case law illustrates. Secondly, an exclusively textual interpretation may undermine the important normative concerns embodied in the refugee definition. Thirdly, the Convention refugee definition is both a product and a part of the history of the twentieth century, and an excessively literal textual approach runs the risk of ignoring that history.

As noted above, the Vienna Convention directs that a treaty be interpreted in good faith in accordance with the ordinary meaning of its terms in their context and 'in light of its object and purpose'.[27] Although the 'ordinary meaning' is the primary source of a treaty's meaning, 'every text, however clear on its face, requires to be scrutinised in its context and in light of the object and purpose which it is designed to serve'.[28] As Brownlie states: 'A corollary of the principle of ordinary meaning is the principle of integration: the meaning must emerge in the context of the treaty as a whole and in light of its objects and purposes.'[29] Therefore, while 'the initial search is for the "ordinary meaning" to be given to the

University Press, Oxford, 1985), pp. 348–54; Jacques Vernant, *The Refugee in the Post-War World* (Yale University Press, New Haven, 1953), pp. 66–7, 70, 74–5 and 79.
[27] See p. 15 above.   [28] Sinclair, *Law of Treaties*, p. 116.
[29] Brownlie, *Public International Law*, p. 634.

terms of the treaty in their "context"; it is *in light of* the object and purpose of the treaty that the initial and preliminary conclusion must be tested and either confirmed or modified'.[30] This is especially so when the textual approach leaves the decision-maker with a choice of possible meanings.

The basic source for discerning the object and purpose of a treaty is its preamble and text.[31] These may be understood in light of the prior relations and agreements between the parties,[32] but the object and purpose must be grounded in the terms of the treaty itself. This limitation may be contrasted with a 'teleological approach', which, after discovering the treaty's overall purpose, may use this purpose to infer results unsupported by the text.[33] The teleological approach is rejected by the Vienna Convention, which, as noted above, employs the treaty's object and purpose only as a means of explicating the text.

Protection of the innocent

This section proposes that interpretation of the refugee definition centres around three related purposes which can be inferred from its text, history and context. One such purpose is protection against serious harm inflicted for reasons of personal status – what might be called 'the persecution of difference'. This principle serves a second, related, purpose: protection from measures based upon the attribution of collective guilt. The third purpose of the refugee definition is the privileging of individual belief and expression. These purposes are not unrelated, and the discussion which follows will address some of their connections. One common thread is that the persecution of either difference or belief may be seen as harm to persons who are innocent of any wrongdoing.

Traditionally, some societies have conceived of both personal status and/or political expression as bases for criminal sanctions or other less formal punishments. The Geneva Convention and many other post-war international instruments, however, firmly reject both as grounds for the imposition of punishment or other harm. The aims of the refugee definition concern the two great paradigms of the post-war period: the rights of non-discrimination and free expression. They thereby serve to safeguard two essential attributes of the human personality, at least for

---

[30] Sinclair, *Law of Treaties*, p. 130.
[31] Francis G. Jacobs, 'Varieties of Approach to Treaty Interpretation', 18 *International and Comparative Law Quarterly*, 1969, p. 318; *Case Concerning Rights of Nationals of the United States of America in Morocco* (*US Nationals v. Morocco*), *ICJ Reports*, 1952, p. 196.
[32] *US Nationals v. Morocco, ibid.*
[33] See, e.g., Sinclair, *Law of Treaties*, pp. 130–4; Jacobs, 'Treaty Interpretation', pp. 323–5.

those, who as Patricia Tuitt points out, can physically reach a place to invoke refugee protection.[34]

The next three subsections will pursue these themes in greater detail, while the last section will consider other possible formulations of the purposes of the refugee definition.

The persecution of difference

The core concept of the refugee definition is protection against the infliction of harm on the basis of differences in personal status or characteristics. This idea is implicit in the very notion of 'persecution' and is made explicit by the linking of 'persecution' with the first four of the five cognisable grounds: race, nationality, religion and social group membership. Race, religion, nationality and social group membership are primarily – if not exclusively – matters of status, as opposed to individual action. Refugee law says, in effect, that harm cannot legitimately be premised on an individual's personal characteristics or status. That is the clear message of the text, supported by its background. By implication, refugee law only contemplates the imposition of punishment on the basis of an individual's wrongful acts.

Persecution for reasons of personal characteristics or status fits squarely within what is probably the most prevalent theme of post-1945 human rights law: non-discrimination. Others have reviewed the growth and development of this principle in international legislation,[35] so I will not do so here. Their findings may be summed up in the following terms:

Mere inspection of the basic international human rights documents demonstrates that racial, sexual, and religious discrimination are, certainly in terms of attention paid on the face of the agreements, the overarching human rights concern of the international community . . . [T]he UN charter, the Universal Declaration, the international covenants, and the various conventions devote more attention to preventing discrimination than to any other single category of human rights. [36]

Interestingly, neither of the cited sources summarising the relevant international documents on non-discrimination mentions the Geneva Convention and Protocol. Strictly speaking, of course, these two instruments do not create new non-discrimination rights, but they do embody

---

[34] See chapter 5 of this volume.

[35] See, e.g., Warwick McKean, *Equality and Discrimination under International Law* (Clarendon Press, Oxford, 1983); and Jack Greenberg, 'Race, Sex and Religious Discrimination in International Law' in *Human Rights in International Law*, (ed. Theodor Meron, Clarendon Press, Oxford, 1984), vol. II, p. 307.

[36] Greenberg, 'Religious Discrimination', p. 309.

protection from the practices condemned directly in much other international legislation. In that sense they are part and parcel of the central post-war human rights concern. Indeed, the Convention protection from racial, religious, national or social group *persecution* may be seen to fit in the middle of a continuum between *discrimination* and *genocide*. Persecution is generally thought of as an especially severe form of discrimination, but as less serious than genocide, which entails the attempted destruction of a whole people or group.[37]

Like other mid-century international law, these developments are a direct response to the Second World War and its surrounding era. They also mark a coming of age of what might be called the 'anti-caste principle': the idea that some people must not be treated arbitrarily as second-class citizens. Cass Sunstein has described the justification for this principle as follows:

> The motivating idea behind an anticaste principle is, broadly speaking, Rawlsian in character. It holds that without very good reasons, social and legal structures ought not to turn morally-irrelevant differences into social disadvantages, and certainly not if the disadvantage is systemic. A difference is morally irrelevant if it has no relationship to individual entitlement or desert. Race and sex are certainly morally irrelevant characteristics in this sense; the bare fact of skin color or gender does not entitle one to social superiority.[38]

Similarly, a 1949 United Nations report described discrimination as 'any conduct based on a distinction made on grounds of natural or social categories, which have no relation either to individual capacities or merits, or to the concrete behaviour of the individual person'.[39]

As with race and gender, religion, nationality and social group membership are also regarded as morally irrelevant, at least as bases for the severe conditions that persecution entails. That is, while religion, nationality and social group membership may be the basis for social and other minor distinctions, they are not valid grounds for physical harm, death or imprisonment. These are basic axioms of post-1945 moral, legal and political thought. Historically, however, recognition of the non-discrimination principle was not always the norm, as Warwick McKean succinctly explains:

---

[37] For a poignant illustration of these distinctions, see Toby F. Sonneman, 'Buried in the Holocaust', *New York Times*, 2 May 1992, p. 23 (complaining that the US Holocaust Memorial Council 'refers to the Romany ordeal as persecution, while the Jewish experience is treated as attempted racial extermination').

[38] Cass R. Sunstein, 'Words, Conduct, Caste', 60 *University of Chicago Law Review*, 1993, p. 795 at p. 800.

[39] United Nations, *The Main Types and Causes of Discrimination*, UN Doc. E/CN. 4/Sub. 2/40 Rev. 19, 1949, p. 9.

One of the most constant themes underlying the great historical struggles for social justice has been the demand for equality. Maine pointed out that ancient law was largely a jurisprudence of personal inequalities in which every individual possessed a status imposed upon him independently of his own will and as a result of circumstances beyond his control, so that his legal position depended on whether he was a freeman or a slave, a noble or a commoner, a native or a foreigner, male or female. Most differences in status were 'natural inequalities' in that they depended upon birth or other unalterable circumstances. A status was the condition of belonging to a class to which the law assigned certain legal capacities or incapacities.[40]

The refugee definition is an integral part of this movement toward equality and away from status, a development which, of course, is not yet complete as a matter of practice.

Collective guilt

Viewed from a different perspective, the refugee definition provides protection from the imposition of collective guilt and punishment, from the infliction of harm on individuals for real or suspected wrongs by others of similar background or otherwise associated with the victims. Much 'persecution' is the result of retaliation for alleged 'crimes' by other persons of the victims' racial, religious, national or social group. Such reprisals can result from grievances which have been felt over many years – or even centuries. Almost every instance of civil strife in the twentieth century has been motivated and/or accompanied by attributions of collective guilt. Moreover, collective attack by one side often begets collective retaliation by the other. The problem is compounded in civil wars, where military strikes by one side often trigger reprisals against civilians believed to be associated with the enemy combatants. When the dividing lines in a civil war correspond to ethnic divisions, the attacks are even more likely to be directed indiscriminately at members of the other side's ethnic group, whether combatants or not.

International law in the post-1945 era has rightly condemned attributions of group guilt, collective punishment and attacks on civilians. It has insisted instead that punishment be imposed on the basis of individual responsibility assessed in formal judicial proceedings. Condemnation of collective punishment has been expressed most directly in international humanitarian law. Article 33 of the Fourth Geneva Convention, for example, states:

[40] McKean, *Equality and Discrimination*, p. 1.

No protected person may be punished for an offence he or she has not personally committed. Collective penalties and likewise all measures of intimidation or of terrorism are prohibited.[41]

Reprisals against protected persons and their property are likewise prohibited. Prohibition of attacks on civilians and others not participating in hostilities – one of the most fundamental principles of humanitarian law – expresses the same sentiment: the avoidance of harm to civilians as a group in response to action by their armed forces.

Condemnation of collective guilt and the insistence on formal findings of guilt, individually determined, are implicit in basic international human rights law as well. Thus, everyone has the right of life, liberty and security of person,[42] the right to recognition before the law,[43] and the right to be free of arbitrary arrest, detention or execution.[44] Moreover, everyone has the right to a judicial determination of 'his rights and obligations and any criminal charge against him'.[45] This means that '[n]o one shall be deprived of his liberty except on such grounds and in accordance with such procedures as are established by law'.[46] All of these rights assume – and help ensure – that loss of life or liberty will be premised only on individual wrongdoing. Collective responsibility and punishment, especially when imposed summarily, are antithetical to the foregoing human rights guarantees. In recent years the connection between legality and punishment has been made explicit. Thus, Protocol II to the Geneva Conventions declares that '[n]o sentence shall be executed on a person found guilty of an offence' except after a fair trial, and 'no one shall be convicted of an offence except on the basis of individual penal responsibility'.[47]

---

41 Convention Relative to the Protection of Civilian Persons in Time of War (Fourth Geneva Convention), 12 August 1949, 75 UNTS 287. See also Protocol I, article 75(2)(d) (collective punishment of persons in the power of a party to a conflict prohibited, whether committed by civilian or military agents) and Protocol II, article 4(2)(b) (collective punishments of persons not, or no longer, taking part in hostilities), Protocols Additional to the Geneva Conventions of 12 August 1949, 8 June 1977, 1125 UNTS 3 and 1125 UNTS 609. International Law Commission (43rd Session), *Draft Report of the International Law Commission on the Work of its Forty-Third Session*, 15 July 1991, UN Doc. A/CN, 4/L464, Annex A, article 22(2) (including collective punishment among exceptionally serious war crimes); United Nations Sub-Commission on Protection of Minorities, Draft Declaration on Minimum Humanitarian Standards, article 3(2)(b), Resolution 1994/126 (prohibiting collective punishments against persons and their property).

42 Universal Declaration of Human Rights, General Assembly Resolution 217 A (III) (10 December 1948) (hereinafter UDHR), article 3.

43 UDHR, article 6, International Covenant on Civil and Political Rights, General Assembly Resolution 2200 A (XXI) (16 December 1966), entered into force 23 March 1976 (hereinafter ICCPR), article 16.   44 UDHR, article 9; ICCPR, articles 6 and 9.

45 UDHR, article 10.   46 ICCPR, article 9(1).

47 Protocol II, articles 6(2) and 2(b). See also Minimum Humanitarian Standards, articles 9 and 9(b).

Attribution of group guilt, and measures based upon that premise, are thus condemned in humanitarian and human rights law. The same sentiments animate refugee law and the Convention refugee definition, the formative stages of which coincided almost exactly with the drafting of the Universal Declaration of Human Rights and the Geneva Conventions of 1949. Indeed, given the relative infrequency with which violations of international humanitarian and human rights law result in meaningful sanctions, refugee law may currently provide the international legal regime's most effective remedy for collective punishment. Its history and language, along with contemporaneous developments in international human rights protection, clearly evince a purpose to provide protection for victims of this kind of group-based harm.

Political opinion and expression

Protection from persecution for reasons of political opinion can be seen to serve two separate but related purposes. One is that persecution for this reason stands in the same position as persecution for reason of race, religion, nationality or social group membership: it is an irrelevant criterion for the infliction of harm. In that sense political opinion is most analogous to religious opinion. Implicit in this approach is the assumption that political opinion *per se* is not a sufficient indicator of seditious or other punishable behaviour to warrant a pre-emptive strike by the authorities, in contrast, for example, to conspiracy, attempted anti-government activity, or even advocacy of such activity. Political opinion is treated as too inchoate a threat to subject its holder to governmental sanctions. Like the other aspects of personal status – or, in the case of religion, belief – it is thus morally irrelevant to the infliction of harm. This justification explains why wrongly imputed political opinion falls within the refugee definition. Persecution for reason of a political opinion the victim does not hold, but is incorrectly believed to hold, does not protect the victim's free conscience or expression rights because, in this situation, the victim does not have the imputed political opinion. What justifies refugee protection is that the assumed political opinion which is attributed to the victim by the persecutors is an irrelevant ground for punishment, whether the persecutor is correct or not.

Protection against persecution premised on the victim's political opinion can be seen to serve an additional purpose: enhancement of the individual's freedom of conscience and expression in his or her homeland. Affirmative recognition of these rights can be found elsewhere in 'the network of international conventions and declarations governing freedom of opinion and expression'.[48] For instance, article 19 of the Universal Declaration of Human Rights states: 'Everyone has the right to freedom of opinion and expression; this right includes freedom to hold opinions without interference and to seek, receive and impart information and ideas through any media and regardless of frontiers.' Refugee status 'for reasons of' political opinion has come to include behaviour that is, at the least, co-extensive with the rights contained in article 19. Thus, persecution for reasons of political *opinion* also includes persecution for reasons of political *expression*.[49] The entire concept represents a privileging of a particular human right – freedom of conscience and expression – just as the other elements of the refugee definition embody a form of the anti-discrimination principle.

The main explanation for this preference for free expression and non-discrimination is probably historical. As discussed above, the drafters were responding to recent known events.[50] With respect to persecution for reasons of political opinion, they knew only too well that the totalitarian regimes from which refugees had fled before, during and after the Second World War tolerated no dissent. Severe persecution for reasons of 'political opinion', even unexpressed opinion, was a hallmark of these regimes.

Free speech is, of course, antithetical to dictatorship, and in providing sanctuary to those who voiced their opposition the drafters of the Convention were, to some degree, aiming to undermine the oppressors' authority. While free speech does not ensure democracy, it is a necessary precondition. In a limited way, then, the Convention serves the purpose of encouraging and facilitating the larger project of democracy. This, in turn, may eventually diminish the flow of refugees, as free speech and democracy reduce the incidence of persecution in the country of origin.

More problematic is the question of whether the refugee definition also covers action (as opposed to expression) motivated by political aims. In other words, do governmental responses to acts which violate laws of general application constitute persecution? This subject has generated more case law and scholarly commentary than can be reviewed here.[51] Examples of politically motivated acts include conscientious refusal to serve in a government's armed forces, emigration which violates laws

[48] Richard Plender, *International Migration Law* (2nd edn, Martinus Nijhoff, Dordrecht, 1988), p. 423.
[49] Guy S. Goodwin-Gill, *The Refugee in International Law* (2nd edn, Clarendon Press, Oxford, 1996), p. 49.   [50] See p. 18 above.
[51] See, e.g., Goodwin-Gill, *The Refugee in International Law*, pp. 52–66; James C. Hathaway, *The Law of Refugee Status* (Butterworths, Toronto, 1991), pp. 152–7 and 169–85; *Rodriguez-Roman* v. *Immigration and Naturalization Service*, 98 F. 3d 416 (9th Cir. 1996).

against unlawful departure, and armed resistance to an undemocratic government.

Other possible purposes

This section describes two other views of the purposes of the refugee definition and their implications, along with a critical analysis of these approaches.

Politically motivated opposition to oppressive regimes

It has been argued that the purpose of the Convention and its refugee definition is to provide shelter for those who are politically opposed – in thought, word or deed – to oppressive regimes in their country of origin. In his treatise, *The Status of Refugees in International Law*, Grahl-Madsen contends that the historical origins of the refugee definition justify affording refugee status to those who violate the laws of general application of oppressive regimes, particularly where those laws are part of its oppressive apparatus.[52] For Grahl-Madsen 'active resistance, evasion of military duties, unauthorised departure or absence from the home country' may qualify the person for refugee status if the offence is 'in some way a reflection of his true, alleged or implied political opinion'.[53]

The words persecution 'for reason of political opinion' may be read so as to imply that the Convention is designed to meet the needs of persons fleeing from a country where people are persecuted because of their beliefs, where opposition is not tolerated. The fact that anyone has taken up resistance or committed other acts for political motives against an oppressive government and thereby become liable to sanctions, shall not disqualify him from gaining refugee status. It is our assertion that this is, in a nutshell, the meaning of the provision just discussed.[54]

The UNHCR *Handbook* adopts a modified version of this position, and to some degree it parallels that taken by some courts.[55]

Grahl-Madsen grounds his conclusions in the Convention (rather than in the *Handbook*, which post-dates his treatise) or free-floating conceptions of wise policy. In the main, his argument extrapolates from pre-Convention history. During the Second World War, the Supreme Headquarters, Allied Expeditionary Force (SHAEF) expressly sheltered persons who were persecuted 'because of their activities in favour of the

---

[52] Atle Grahl-Madsen, *The Status of Refugees in International Law* (A. W. Sijthoff, Leyden, 1966), vol. I, pp. 220–5.
[53] In this connection, he contends: 'The struggle for a certain political conviction is not to be regarded as a fault but as a right founded in the law of Nature'. Grahl-Madsen, *Status of Refugees*, p. 232.   [54] *Ibid.*, p. 253.   [55] See UNHCR, *Handbook*, paras. 80–6.

United Nations', that is, the Allies.[56] In practice, this policy continued in the post-war period with respect to refugees from the Soviet Union and other countries in the Soviet bloc under the terms not of a special ideological exemption as in the SHAEF Memorandum quoted above, but of the political opinion language of the Convention itself. After acknowledging that the interpretation most in keeping with the wording of article 1A(2) of the Convention would require that the political opinion of the person in question be 'decisive' for the nature and severity of the punishment for a politically motivated act,[57] Grahl-Madsen continues:

> However, the Refugee Convention does not exist *in vacuo*. It is a link in a historical development, and there is a direct line from Paragraph 32 of SHAEF Administrative Memorandum Number 39, *via* Part I, section C, paragraph I, of the Annex I to the IRO [International Refugee Organisation] Constitution, to Article I A(2) of the Refugee Convention, and those who profess the liberal doctrine, according to which a person expecting punishment for a politically motivated act may benefit from the Convention, are consciously or subconsciously aware of this historical relationship. The French Commission des Recours and the German Bundesverwaltungsgericht both adhere to the latter doctrine, and even if their decisions should be based on instinct rather than a linguistic analysis of the text of the Convention, we think they rest on solid ground.[58]

This historically grounded interpretative move potentially brings within the definition's coverage politically motivated conduct such as unauthorised departure, conscientious objection to military service, or acts of resistance. Coupling this approach with reliance on evolving human rights norms, others have also argued for the inclusion of these acts within the refugee concept.[59]

While an approach based in the history of the Convention may cover those whom a textual method of interpretation would omit, it may also exclude others who arguably fall within the literal terms of the refugee definition. For example, potential victims of female genital mutilation (FGM) may qualify as victims of social group persecution, with the relevant social group being young women of a tribe practising FGM who have not yet been subjected to it.[60] It is hard to justify the application of the refugee definition to this practice or other gender-based harms on the basis of the historical background of the Convention, however. There is

---

[56] SHAEF Administrative Memorandum No. 19, quoted in Grahl-Madsen, *Status of Refugees*, p. 228, where he writes: 'The Allied military authorities thus came to the aid of persons who, viewed from the "other side of the hill", were guilty of political (or military) offences (treason).'   [57] Grahl-Madsen, *Status of Refugees*, pp. 220 and 238–40.
[58] *Ibid.*, p. 249 (citations omitted).
[59] See, e.g., Goodwin-Gill, *The Refugee in International Law*, pp. 49–66.
[60] See *Re Kasinga*, A 73476–695 (BIA 1996), 35 ILM 1998, p. 1145, especially concurring opinion of Board Member Filuppu.

no evidence that the drafters or practitioners of refugee law in the post-war period intended to encompass known, traditional gender-based inequalities, however severe. The incremental trend towards defining women as a social group (of which the FGM issue is only part) was most likely not contemplated by the drafters of the Convention. Indeed, if history is to be the guide then the whole concept of 'social group' perse-cution in general probably ought not be extended much beyond the sense of 'social class'.[61]

Furthermore, as Grahl-Madsen forthrightly recognised, interpreta-tions premised in the events of the Second World War era may conflict with the literal terms of the refugee definition. Some have attempted to circumvent this problem by contending that the drafters were speaking and writing in a kind of code in order to avoid undue offence to the nations whose citizens in a sense were the true objects of their concern.[62] That is, the Western states which authored the Convention definition con-structed a refugee protection system 'consistent with their own desire to give international legitimacy to their efforts to shelter self-exiles from the socialist states'.[63] In this view, its terms were a cover for an ideologically based attempt to embarrass communist regimes. Under the protection of the new Convention, the Western countries often treated flight from com-munism, without further evidence, as sufficient to establish well-founded fear of persecution.[64] Practice at the time then becomes the key to unlock-ing the code, but it may produce some murky answers as the debate shifts to examine just what behaviour, by persecuting states or by victims, this code is meant to reflect. This approach requires that objects and purposes be inferred, not from the language of the refugee definition, but from its history, and then overriding the text with that object and purpose.

Human rights protection

Several writers have argued that the refugee definition protects against violations of recognised human rights, regardless of whether the threat-ened harm is premised on the victim's race, nationality, religion, social group membership or political opinion.[65] Under these theories, the rele-vant question is whether a human rights violation will occur, and whether it will result in harm sufficiently serious to amount, 'quantitatively', to persecution. Jean-Yves Carlier's contribution to this volume, 'The Geneva Refugee Definition and the "Theory of the Three Scales"', is one example of this approach.[66]

---

[61] Plender, *International Migration Law*, p. 421.
[62] Hathaway, 'Underlying Premises'.   [63] *Ibid.*, p. 151.   [64] *Ibid.*, p. 150.
[65] See pp. 30–1 below.   [66] See chapter 2 of this volume.

A human rights-based interpretation marks a shift from causes to effects as the focus of refugee law. There are, to be sure, some convincing policy reasons for doing so. A refugee standard focusing on the most basic human rights – freedom from slavery, torture, arbitrary execution or imprisonment – would ensure some sanctuary from what are regarded internationally as the most abhorrent forms of harm. It would also assure a more equal response to what are perceived as morally equivalent threats.[67] Focusing on the effects rather than the causes also serves to eliminate, in most cases, the need to enquire into the reasons for the harm.

Perhaps the most unequivocal statement of the human rights theory is that of Aleinikoff.[68] He begins with the contention that the term 'persecution' has a meaning separate and independent from any identifiable ground on which it is imposed. In his view, persecution is linked to the specific grounds only to connote the 'unacceptable, unjustified, abhorrent' or 'intolerable' infliction of harm.[69] In other words, the drafters used the phrase 'for reasons of race, religion, nationality, political opinion, or membership of a particular social group' not to qualify or define persecution but only as examples of unacceptable acts, and these examples were not meant to be exhaustive. Extracting this larger purpose from the history and language of the Convention, Aleinikoff suggests that: 'Persecution might well be given a free-standing meaning, that requires judgments about both the degree of and justifications for the harm, but not one that necessarily invokes the five grounds as the test of the qualitative aspect.'[70] The notion that the infliction of any serious and unacceptable harm constitutes 'persecution' lurks in other critiques as well.[71]

Separating 'persecution' from its causes may broaden its reach, but it also raises new conceptual difficulties. In Aleinikoff's formulation, for example, persecution is unacceptable, unjustified, abhorrent or intolerable harm, but just what circumstances reach that level of illegitimacy? The most logical source of content for a free-standing definition of persecution is international human rights law, and several commentators have suggested that persecution equates with human rights violations. One

---

[67] See, e.g., Andrew Shacknove, 'Who is a Refugee?', 95 *Ethics*, 1985, p. 274 at p. 276; Astri Suhrke, 'Global Refugee Movements and Strategies of Response', in *US Immigration and Refugee Policy: Global and Domestic Issues* (ed. M. Kritz, D. C. Heath and Co., 1983), pp. 159–60.

[68] T. Alexander Aleinikoff, 'The Meaning of "Persecution" in United States Asylum Law', 3 *International Journal of Refugee Law*, 1991, p. 5.

[69] *Ibid.*, p. 12. This he describes as the 'qualitative' aspect of the refugee definition.

[70] *Ibid.*, p. 13.

[71] See, e.g., Donald P. Gagliardi, 'The Inadequacy of Cognizable Grounds of Persecution as a Criterion for According Refugee Status', 24 *Stanford Journal of International Law*, 1987, p. 259 at pp. 271–2.

potential practical difficulty with this approach is that the relatively broad range of human rights enunciated internationally would make many millions of people potential refugees in today's world.

In perhaps the most sophisticated attempt to relate persecution to human rights norms, Hathaway attempts to identify certain basic rights 'which all states are found to respect as a minimum condition of legitimacy'.[72] He thus defines 'persecution' as the sustained systematic violation of basic human rights demonstrative of a failure of state protection.[73] Remediation of the failure of state protection is, in this view, the central purpose of the refugee definition and the larger refugee law regime. Hathaway's analysis derives a hierarchy of rights based upon a combination of their presence in various international human rights instruments and the degree to which derogation of the rights is permitted in emergency situations.[74] Conceptually, this catalogue of rights could serve as a working definition of the kinds of deprivation which, by themselves, constitute 'persecution' without any need to show a prohibited reason for the human rights infringement.[75] However, even this formulation demonstrates the necessity of choice among the types of harm which would satisfy a free-standing definition of persecution.[76]

The question remains, though, whether the Convention definition of a refugee is meant to encompass all persons exposed to serious human rights violations. Despite their valiant efforts, neither Aleinikoff, Hathaway nor other writers provide a convincing fit between their proposed purposes and the text of the definition. Rather, to one degree or another, they attempt to extract a purpose from the language and then subordinate the language to the discovered purpose, a process which finds little support in accepted methods of treaty and statutory interpretation.[77]

Furthermore, the theory that the refugee definition incorporates all serious human rights violations must address the fact that the definition makes no mention of many human rights that, at the time of its drafting, had just been enunciated in the 1948 Universal Declaration of Human Rights (UDHR). These include the right to life, liberty and security of

---

[72] Hathaway, *The Law of Refugee Status*, p. 106.   [73] *Ibid.*, p. 112.

[74] *Ibid.*, pp. 106–12.

[75] Hathaway does not contend that this is the case under the refugee definition as written. While describing the use of civil and political categories as perhaps 'unduly anchored in a particular era', he stops short of recommending the abandonment of the linkage of such civil or political status with 'persecution'. *Ibid.*, pp. 137–9.

[76] In addition to this question of policy preference, there is a related issue of which institution (executive, administrative, legislative or judicial) would be given the role of filling in the content of such a definition.

[77] See, e.g., Sinclair, *Law of Treaties*, pp. 118 and 130–1.

person; freedom from slavery; freedom from torture and other cruel, inhuman or degrading punishment; rights of equal access to the courts; freedom of movement and departure; the right of property ownership; rights to work and leisure; rights of democratic participation; and others.[78] Instead, the preamble of the Convention simply refers to the United Nations Charter and the UDHR as affirming 'the principle that human beings shall enjoy fundamental rights and freedoms without discrimination',[79] and the bulk of the Convention is aimed at putting recognised refugees on a more (but not totally) equal footing with host country nationals.[80] The human rights embodied in the refugee definition itself centre around non-discrimination and freedom of thought and expression. That said, violation of many of the UDHR's provisions can constitute persecution if inflicted for discriminatory or political opinion reasons, but that is a significant qualification.

If the drafters intended to cover the imposition of serious harms in the absence of such reasons, why did they not say so? Certainly the existence and importance of the UDHR were well known to the parties responsible for drafting the Convention. The *Ad Hoc* Committee on Statelessness and Related Problems, whose work initiated the drafting process, began its deliberations a little more than a year after the adoption of the UDHR. In this context it is hard to conclude either that the particular wording of the refugee definition was meant only to be illustrative, or, even further, that despite its specific language and the omission of then recently announced international human rights it nevertheless intended to encompass them.

On at least one occasion the international community has by treaty explicitly expanded *non-refoulement* to human rights violations unrelated to persecution. That instrument is the United Nations Convention Against Torture, which was opened for signature in 1984 and entered into force in 1987.[81] It is now ratified by 112 states. The main thrust of the Convention is to outlaw and prevent acts of torture. Article 3(1) sets out a right to *non-refoulement* for those threatened with torture if returned. It states: 'No State Party shall expel, return (*"refouler"*) or extradite a person to another State where there are substantial grounds for believing that he

---

[78] UDHR, articles 3–10, 13–14, 17, 21 and 23–4.
[79] UDHR, preamble, para. 1.
[80] Thus, if the preamble's reference to the UDHR has any significance at all, it is most likely the implication that recognised refugees should receive treatment that is more equal to that afforded the host country's nationals.
[81] Convention Against Torture and Other Cruel, Inhuman or Degrading Treatment or Punishment, General Assembly Res. 39/46, 39 UN GAOR, Annex, Supplement No. 51, at 197, UN Doc. A/39/51 (1984).

would be in danger of being subjected to torture.'[82] There is no requirement, obviously, that the feared treatment would be inflicted for any particular reason. In that respect, the Convention Against Torture expands
significantly the reach of *non-refoulement*.[83]

Implications

An understanding of the purposes of the refugee definition can aid its
interpretation and application in a number of ways, but the results will
depend, of course, on which purpose is inferred. For the reasons given
above, the text and history of the definition most firmly support, I believe,
the conclusion that the refugee definition serves to protect people against
three related kinds of harm: harsh discrimination, attribution of collective
guilt, and punishment for the exercise of rights of free expression and
belief. The following sections explore briefly some of the implications of
this approach.

Social group persecution

Consideration of objects and purposes is especially useful in interpreting and applying the concept of social group persecution. It may be that
there is no clear ordinary meaning of 'membership of a particular social
group', and there is a plausible argument that the drafters of the Geneva
Convention intended this phrase to have the 'special meaning'[84] of persecution for reasons of 'social class'.[85] While the drafting history may be
taken into account either to confirm this 'special meaning' or to clarify
terms which are otherwise ambiguous or obscure,[86] the *travaux préparatoires* are quite cryptic on the meaning of 'social group'. The better
approach is to employ the definition's object and purpose to elucidate

---

[82] Article 3(2) of the Torture Convention provides:

> For the purpose of determining whether there are such grounds, the competent author-
> ities shall take into account all relevant considerations including, where applicable, the
> existence in the State concerned of a consistent pattern of gross, flagrant or mass viola-
> tions of human rights.

[83] See J. Herman Burgers and Hans Danelius, *The United Nations Convention Against
Torture: A Handbook on the Convention Against Torture and Other Cruel, Inhuman, and
Degrading Treatment of Punishment* (Martinus Nijhoff, Boston, 1988), p. 125: '[T]he
scope of the two provisions is different. In the *Geneva Convention*, protection is given to
refugees, i.e. to persons who are persecuted in their country of origin for a special reason,
whereas article 3 of the present *Convention* applies to any person who, for whatever
reason, is in danger of being subjected to torture if handed over to another country.' See
also pp. 86–7 below.

[84] See Vienna Convention, article 31(4): 'A special meaning shall be given to a term if it is
established that the parties so intended.'   [85] See p. 29 above.

[86] Vienna Convention, article 32(a).

the textual reference to social group persecution. Like the other cognisable grounds mentioned in the refugee definition, 'social group membership' is a status or characteristic of an individual that is an irrelevant basis for the infliction of harm. With this purpose in mind, 'social group' can be applied to a wide variety of social statuses and affiliations on which persecution may be premised. Analysed this way, the social group need not be 'immutable' as some courts have held, nor should associational ties among the members be a prerequisite.[87] Such an approach protects against the attribution of group guilt, an object implicit in the Convention. So construed, the refugee definition is capable of responding to evolving forms of oppression, and more fully implements the human rights guarantees of non-discrimination inherent in its text.

Proof and presumptions

One of the major developments of the past few decades has been the greater incidence of refugee claims arising from civil wars, communal violence and civil disorder. In these circumstances the reasons for the infliction of harm may be less than clear. The dynamics of civil conflict, particularly, may obscure the boundaries between combat, crime and persecution. Refugee claimants fleeing such situations may be unable to establish the reasons for the harm they have experienced, or of which they have a well-founded fear. Indeed, at a deeper level these reasons may be virtually unfathomable at all.[88]

Here, too, attention to the objects and purposes of the Convention definition may have something to contribute. Its overall aim seems to be protection of those who would be harmed for who they are or what they believe rather than for what they have done. The problems of proof might be solved through the use of certain presumptions. Certainly, as a general matter, attacks on women, children, the sick, the disabled and the elderly can be presumed to be for reasons of their status – as relatives or as members of the same ethnic group as the combatants, for example – rather than for their own actions. The same presumption might be applied to violence directed at civilians in general. Given their inclusion in the core area of the refugee definition's concern, they ought not to have to show that the 'persecution' they face is 'for reasons of' any particular motive. The same principle might apply to the disproportionate punish-

---

[87] See Goodwin-Gill, *The Refugee in International Law*, pp. 358–66; and Hathaway, *The Law of Refugee Status*, pp. 157–61.

[88] Hans Magnus Enzensberger, *Civil Wars: From LA to Bosnia* (New Press, New York, 1994).

ment of actual civil war participants.[89] The likelihood that the harm is for a prohibited reason is high enough that the need for proof, taken in light of the difficulties in gathering such evidence, should be dispensed with, and there should thus be a *presumption* in favour of the claimant.

Core meaning

One other effect of focusing on the purposes of the refugee definition is a renewed attention to its core meaning. While this is not the place to consider the issue fully, one might wonder whether those refugees whose protection is the central concern of the definition might have a greater claim to refugee status than others who fall closer to the periphery. The Convention, of course, does not distinguish among those who come within its bounds, but at a time of *de facto* restriction it might be sensible to be especially careful to give priority to those people who unquestionably are covered by the Convention's text and purpose. The objects and purposes approach described above helps to identify those people. By implication, it also influences where the outer boundaries of the definition might lie. While the identified purposes clearly serve to protect important human rights, it is also clear that they are not co-extensive with the entire body of human rights law.

Nevertheless, the core meaning of the refugee definition is as important today as it was fifty years ago. A recent report of Human Rights Watch, for example, begins: 'The current epidemic of communal violence – violence involving groups that define themselves by their differences of religion, ethnicity, language or race – is today's paramount human rights problem.'[90] Victims of communal violence fall squarely within the purposes of the refugee definition, a fact which may be obvious but is worth remembering at a time when too many countries are more than willing to impede or reject their claims.

Bibliography

Aleinikoff, T. Alexander, 'The Meaning of "Persecution" in United States Asylum Law', 3 *International Journal of Refugee Law*, 1991, p. 5

Burgers, J. Herman and Hans Danelius, *The United Nations Convention Against Torture: A Handbook on the Convention Against Torture and Other Cruel, Inhuman, and Degrading Treatment or Punishment* (Martinus Nijhoff, Boston, 1988)

---

[89] Walter Kälin, 'Refugees and Civil Wars: Only a Matter of Interpretation', 3 *International Journal of Refugee Law*, 1991, p. 435.

[90] Human Rights Watch, *Slaughter Among Neighbors: The Political Origins of Communal Violence* (Yale University Press, New Haven, 1995), p. 1.

Gagliardi, Donald P., 'The Inadequacy of Cognizable Grounds of Persecution as a Criterion for According Refugee Status', 24 *Stanford Journal of International Law*, 1987, p. 259

Garvey, Jack, 'Toward a Reformulation of International Refugee Law', 26 *Harvard Journal of International Law* 1985, p. 483

Goodwin-Gill, Guy S., 'Refugees: The Functions and Limits of the Existing Protection System', in *Human Rights and the Protection of Refugees under International Law* (ed. Alan E. Nash, Canadian Human Rights Foundation, Quebec, 1988), p. 165

Greenberg, Jack, 'Race, Sex and Religious Discrimination in International Law', in *Human Rights in International Law* (ed. Theodor Meron, Clarendon Press, Oxford, 1984), vol. II, p. 323

Hathaway, James C., 'A Reconsideration of the Underlying Premises of Refugee Law', 31 *Harvard International Law Journal*, 1990, p. 129

Human Rights Watch, *Slaughter Among Neighbors: The Political Origins of Communal Violence* (Yale University Press, New Haven, 1995)

Jackson, Ivor, 'The 1951 Convention Relating to the Status of Refugees: A Universal Basis for Protection', 3 *International Journal of Refugee Law*, 1991, p. 403

Jacobs, Francis G., 'Varieties of Approach to Treaty Interpretation', 18 *International and Comparative Law Quarterly*, 1969, p. 318

Kälin, Walter, 'Refugees and Civil Wars: Only a Matter of Interpretation', 3 *International Journal of Refugee Law*, 1991, p. 435

Marrus, Michael R., *The Unwanted: European Refugees in the Twentieth Century* (Oxford University Press, Oxford, 1985)

Martin, David, 'The Refugee Concept: On Definitions, Politics, and the Careful Use of a Scarce Resource', in *Refugee Policy: Canada and the United States* (ed. Howard Adelman, Centre for Refugee Studies, York University, Toronto, 1991)

McKean, Warwick, *Equality and Discrimination under International Law* (Clarendon Press, Oxford, 1983)

Shacknove, Andrew, 'Who is a Refugee?', 95 *Ethics*, 1985, p. 274

Sonneman, Toby F., 'Buried in the Holocaust', *New York Times*, 2 May 1992, p. 23

Suhrke, Astri, 'Global Refugee Movements and Strategies of Response', in *US Immigration and Refugee Policy: Global and Domestic Issues* (ed. M. Kritz, D. C. Heath and Co., 1983)

Sunstein, Cass R., 'Words, Conduct, Caste', 60 *University of Chicago Law Review*, 1993, p. 795

Vernant, Jacques, *The Refugee in the Post-War World* (Yale University Press, New Haven, 1953)

2 The Geneva refugee definition and the 'theory of the three scales'

Jean-Yves Carlier

This chapter[1] has one principal objective: to propose an analysis of the definition of 'refugee' as found in the 1951 Geneva Convention Relating to the Status of Refugees[2] which can lead to clearer reasoning being applied whenever decisions have to be made on the recognition or refusal of refugee status. This analysis is summarised below in the section entitled 'The Theory of the Three Scales'. Before outlining this theory, it is useful first of all to ask whether the definition of refugee as enshrined in the Convention still holds good today.

Does the Convention definition still hold good today?

Article 1 of the Convention defines a refugee as 'any person who . . . owing to well-founded fear of being persecuted for reasons of race, religion, nationality, membership of a particular social group or political opinion is outside the country of his nationality and is unable or, owing to such fear, is unwilling to avail himself of the protection of that country'.

This definition is frequently judged to be out of date because it was written at a point in time (1951) in which conditions were very different from what they are today. As the title of the present volume suggests, what we have is a divorce between rights and reality. Other contributions in Part 1 of this volume look more broadly at definitional issues beyond the Convention itself.[3] Nonetheless, we still need to answer briefly this question: is the Convention itself out of date?[4] If the answer is indeed yes, it would appear pointless to propose a new analysis of its definition. My response is 'no', for two main reasons, one of form and the other of substance.

The reason of form is quite simple: the Convention remains the sole, legally binding, international instrument providing specific protection to

---

[1] Translation by Michael Lomax.   [2] 189 UNTS 137 (hereinafter the Convention).
[3] See also François Crépeau, *Droit d'asile: De l'hospitalité aux contrôles migratoires* (Bruylant, Brussels, 1995); Société française pour le droit international, *Droit d'asile et des réfugiés* (Colloque de Caen, Pedone, Paris, 1997).   [4] See chapter 3 of this volume.

refugees. The very large number of states which have ratified it are required to respect it.[5] It is remarkable to note that regional instruments, ranging from the binding 1969 Convention of the Organisation of African Unity (OAU),[6] to the non-binding 1996 Joint Position of the European Union (EU) on the harmonised application of the definition of the term refugee,[7] make direct reference to the Geneva Convention definition, albeit in the former to extend its content, and in the latter to restrict its interpretation.

To the reason of form we must add a reason of substance. It is wrong to believe that the definition of refugee as enshrined in the Convention no longer covers contemporary situations. It is now commonly asserted, first, that this definition should be seen as intended to cover only the individual examination of a small number of cases and not mass flows; and, secondly, that the reasons for exile have changed. The fact is that the drafters of the Convention already had mass flows in mind, in the form of war refugees, before, during and after the Second World War. At the same time, the Convention, 'considering that it is desirable to revise and consolidate previous international agreements relating to the status of refugees and to extend the scope of . . . such instruments',[8] was particularly concerned to provide a general and abstract definition of the notion of refugee as part of the general corpus of texts covering the protection of human rights.[9] The first recital of the Convention reminds us that 'the Charter of the United Nations and the Universal Declaration of Human Rights . . . affirmed the principle that human beings shall enjoy fundamental rights and freedoms without discrimination'.

From this we can rightfully deduce that the Convention and its definition of refugee can be interpreted, teleologically, in the light of those texts which protect and develop human rights.[10] Hence, just as standards

[5] As of 4 February 1999, 133 states had ratified the Convention.
[6] OAU Convention Governing the Specific Aspects of Refugee Problems in Africa, 1001 UNTS 46.
[7] Joint Position 96/196/JHA defined by the Council on the basis of article K.3 of the Treaty on European Union on the harmonised application of the definition of the term 'refugee' in article 1 of the Geneva Convention of 28 July 1951 Relating to the Status of Refugees, Council of Ministers, OJ, 4 March 1996, L63/2.
[8] Geneva Convention, preamble, third recital.
[9] UNHCR, *Handbook on Procedures and Criteria for Determining Refugee Status* (Geneva, 1979, re-edited 1992), para. 5: 'there was a call for an instrument containing a *general* definition of who is to be considered as a refugee' (emphasis in original).
[10] This position simply repeats the direction of the work of James C. Hathaway, *The Law of Refugee Status* (Butterworths, Toronto, 1991). This position corresponds to the objective pursued by the writers of the Geneva Convention in 'cette période . . . marquée par le désir très fort de concrétiser et développer les libertés fondamentales et les droits essentiels de l'homme' ('this period . . . marked by the very strong desire to give concrete form to and extend fundamental freedoms and essential human rights'): I. C. Jackson, 'Evolution historique de la protection internationale des réfugiés: défis de la situation

concerning the content and level of protection of human rights have evolved, equally the causes of exile included in the concept of persecution within the meaning of the Convention can change and still be included within this definition. One single example can illustrate this: gender-based discrimination. Even though condemned in the basic human rights texts, gender-based discrimination was more widely tolerated in 1950 than it is today. From this we can deduce that, in the case of refugees, important discriminations against women which, in 1950, appeared 'acceptable' are no longer so, and fall into the category of persecution by reason of membership of a social group, i.e. that of women. The adoption in different countries, including Canada and the USA, of 'Guidelines for Women's Asylum Claims', is one illustration of this.[11]

Although the Convention only covers persecution based on five types of violation of fundamental rights rather than each violation of every fundamental right, and although its protection is limited to persons who have crossed an international border, it remains an effective legal instrument for protecting refugees. 'Forty-five years after its introduction, the Convention refugee definition does a surprisingly good job of stretching us between ground and sky, of maintaining the healthy tension between criticality and feasibility.'[12] In this respect, it is significant to note that texts envisaging temporary protection for displaced persons are intended as a supplement and not as a substitute to the Convention.[13] The correct application of the Convention definition is all the more important. One may not include, under complementary and temporary protection instruments, persons who would erroneously be excluded from the protection of the Convention.[14] The Convention itself gives temporary protection in so far as its terms cease to apply in certain circumstances.[15]

actuelle', in *Asile, violence, exclusion en Europe* (ed. M. C. Caloz-Tschopp, Université de Genève et Groupe de Genève, Geneva, 1994), p. 245.

[11] Nancy Kelly, 'Guidelines for Women's Asylum Claims', 6 *International Journal of Refugee Law*, 1994, p. 517; Isabelle Daoust and Kristina Folkelius, 'UNHCR Symposium on Gender-Based Persecution', 8 *International Journal of Refugee Law*, 1996, p. 180; Valerie L. Osterveld, 'The Canadian Guidelines on Gender-Related Persecution: An Evaluation', 8 *International Journal of Refugee Law*, 1996, p. 569; Deborah E. Anker, 'Women Refugees: Forgotten No Longer?', in *Europe and Refugees: A Challenge?* (ed. Jean-Yves Carlier and Dirk Vanheule, Kluwer Law International, The Hague, 1997), p. 125.

[12] James C. Hathaway, 'Is Refugee Status Really Elitist? An Answer to the Ethical Challenge', in *Europe and Refugees* (ed. Carlier and Vanheule), p. 88.

[13] Proposal presented by the Commission of the European Communities to the Council for a Joint Action concerning temporary protection of displaced persons, 5 March 1997, COM(97)93.

[14] Cristina J. Gortázar Rotaeche, *Derecho de asilo y 'no rechazo' del refugiado* (Dykinson, Madrid, 1997), p. 135: 'muchos de los supuestos de "refugiados de la violencia" les sería aplicable del todo la Convención de Ginebra si los Estados la interpretarán adecuadamente.' [15] These circumstances are set out in article 1C.

Let us not be mistaken. The Convention does not suffer from any legal or conceptual weakness. It suffers from a political weakness: the absence of management of the phenomenon of migration is leading to a confusion that links the right of asylum to migration.[16] In a period where there is a need for migrants, not only do a large number of people not need to claim refugee status because they benefit from entitlement to residence and work outside their country of origin, but the authorities tolerate a liberal interpretation of the Convention, open to the protection of human rights. In a period when there is a desire to stem immigration, the trend reverses, with the attitude towards the right of asylum changing from one of hospitality to one of controlling migration.[17] This provides a partial explanation for a higher degree of recognition of refugee status in Canada than in Europe. However, it is not the only factor. To this must be added stronger procedural guarantees, including the need to give clear grounds of judgment in decisions relating to the refugee definition, linked to the protection of fundamental rights. This is the objective pursued by the 'theory of the three scales'.

The 'theory of the three scales'[18]

A comparative study of case law on the application of the Convention refugee definition in fifteen states has led to the observation that the reasoning for decisions relating to refugee status is poor or non-existent. Too often, the grounds for a decision to recognise or reject refugee status, if given at all, are limited to general considerations which can be summarised as follows: the interested party does not establish, and/or his file or his hearing does not demonstrate, that he or she has a well-founded fear of persecution within the meaning of the Convention. These considerations are generally accompanied by certain factual items concerning the personal situation of the party concerned and/or the general situation in the country of origin. The impression gained is one of a high degree of subjectivity as to whether or not the applicant has succeeded or not in convincing the decision-maker. With a few notable but rare exceptions, decisions make little reference to other cases or to doctrine. More funda-

[16] Item 4 of the explanatory memorandum to the Joint Action concerning temporary protection of displaced persons confirms this observation: 'Although the Geneva Convention does *ipso facto* not exclude recognition of refugee status for whole groups of persons, Western European States have been reluctant to make use of this possibility.'
[17] Crépeau, *Droit d'asile*.
[18] See Jean-Yves Carlier, Dirk Vanheule, Klaus Hullmann and Carlos Peña Galiano, *Who is a Refugee?* (Kluwer Law International, The Hague, 1997). The 'theory of the three scales', set out for the first time in this work, is picked up again and adapted in the present text.

mentally, the decisions do not set out the legal reasoning which has guided the application of the law, in this case article 1 of the Convention.[19] Moreover, even though relating to a subject directly linked to human rights, decisions rarely mention the principle of proportionality or the balancing test of interest which would permit an assessment of the alleged persecution. Such lack of reasoned arguments would be a cause for disquiet in other legal areas. More detailed reasoning is produced in the event of a road accident, when it is a question of evaluating liability and assigning damages. Is danger to the life or freedom of a human being of less importance?

It is to remedy this gap that we propose a mechanism, the 'theory of the three scales', which seeks to provide more adequate reasoning for decisions relating to refugee status. What is offered is not so much a new interpretation of the refugee definition as a new formulation of the decisions relating to refugee status. This mechanism is centred on the main question in the determination of refugee status: is there a risk of persecution in case of return to the country of origin?[20] This central question can be subdivided into three questions:

1. At what point does risk exist? This is the level of Risk ('R').
2. At what point does persecution exist? This is the level of Persecution ('P').
3. At what point is the risk of persecution sufficiently established? This is the level of proof ('P').

These three central questions ('R', 'P', 'P') can be brought together in what we would call in French a *théorie des trois échelles* (theory of three scales) or *des trois niveaux* (theory of three levels) with each level (scale) corresponding to a question.

These three levels or questions – the risk, the persecution, and the proof – are now considered separately before the theory combining the three scales is itself outlined.

The level of risk (When is there well-founded fear?) ('R')

For the applicant to have a well-founded fear of being persecuted, there must be a risk of persecution. What degree or level of risk is necessary?

---

[19] Guy S. Goodwin-Gill, *The Refugee in International Law* (2nd edn, Clarendon, Oxford, 1996), p. 350: 'Even where decisions are felt to be correct, lack of confidence can result from systematically basing oneself on subjective assessment and failing to articulate clearly the various steps which lead to particular conclusions and the reasons which justify each stage.'

[20] '[T]he key question is whether there are sufficient facts to permit the finding that, if returned to his or her country of origin, the claimant would face a serious risk of harm.' *Ibid.*, p. 349.

Often, the question is not addressed in the case law, which, without being more specific, simply acknowledges the existence of a serious risk or of a risk of concrete and individualised persecution. Spanish and Portuguese case law is more precise, and refers to a 'reasonable likelihood'.[21] German case law refers to a 'considerable likelihood', but also to situations where 'the risk of persecution upon return cannot be excluded with certainty'.[22] Swiss case law speaks of a 'strong probability'[23] but also of risk 'not without foundation'.[24] French case law says, in one single decision, that it must be taken as certain or sufficiently probable that the person would be subject to persecution.[25]

In the leading Australian case on the interpretation of article 1A(2), the High Court of Australia has stated: 'The Convention necessarily contemplates that there is a real chance that the applicant will suffer some serious punishment or penalty or some significant detriment or disadvantage if he returns.'[26] This approach is incorrect. To put it simply, as soon as there is risk, the risk is sufficient. It cannot be required that it be serious. A minimum risk is enough.

US case law, followed by that of England and Canada, has certainly addressed the degree of risk in the greatest detail, beginning with the

---

[21] Spain, Tribunal Supremo, 29 January 1988, *Repertorio de jurisprudencia Aranzadi*, No. 514, p. 520; Portugal, Supremo Tribunal Administrativo, 1° secçâo, Acordâo, 23 June 1983, *Acordâos Doutrinais do Supremo Tribunal Administrativo*, No. 262, p. 1165.

[22] Verwaltungsgericht (Administrative Court) Stuttgart (4th division), 5 October 1992, A4K 7766/91: protection against expulsion for a Baptist woman from Romania.

[23] Commission suisse de recours en matière d'asile (CRA – Swiss Asylum Appeal Board), 19 January 1993, *Jurisprudence et informations de la Commission suisse de recours en matière d'asile* (JICRA), 1993, No. 11: a Turk, persecuted because he belonged to a party, had 'objective reasons for fear more significant than someone who was in contact with the State security services for the first time'. In this sense, 'there is a strong probability that the feared measures of persecution will occur in the near future'.

[24] CRA, 28 September 1993, 2nd Ch., No. 225 117. A Turkish asylum seeker who, after entering Switzerland, publicly worked for the cause of the 'Kurdish cultural circle', which was considered to be a 'reason for persecution subsequent to flight of a subjective nature' (*subjektiver Nachfluchtgrund*), risked being exposed to torture on his return to Turkey. It was certain that the Turkish authorities possessed his address because the Swiss authorities had sent his driving licence to the Turkish general consulate in Zürich to verify its authenticity, which constituted a deviation from the obligation to secrecy. In the light of the Amnesty International 1992 annual report, the behaviour of the asylum seeker and the actions of the Swiss authorities, the risk of torture on the return of the asylum seeker to Turkey was 'not without foundation'. Provisional entry as a refugee therefore had to be granted.

[25] Commission française de recours des réfugiés (CRR – French Refugee Appeals Board), 13 December 1982, 17.796, in Frédéric Tiberghien, *La protection des réfugiés en France* (Economica, Paris, 1988), p. 327.

[26] *Chen Yee Kin v. Minister for Immigration and Ethnic Affairs* (1989) 169 CLR 379, quoted by Martin Tsamenyi and M. Bliss, 'The Australian Approach to "Persecution" under the Refugee Convention' (paper for Refugee, Rights and Realities Conference, University of Nottingham, 30 November 1996), p. 4.

Cardoza-Fonseca case in the US Supreme Court, in which the Supreme Court ruled: '[O]ne can certainly have a well-founded fear of an event happening when there is less than a 50 per cent chance of the occurrence taking place.'[27] Does this criterion, qualified as the 'reasonable person test' require more than a 'minimal likelihood'? On several occasions, US case law has made clear that a risk of around 10 per cent can be sufficient.[28] Canadian case law has held that the degree of 'reasonable chance' is located '[in] the field between upper and lower limits; it is less than a 50 per cent chance (i.e. a probability) but more than a minimal or mere possibility'.[29] If the risk is such 'that a reasonable person would find it credible', it seems certain that a reasonable person, with 'common sense' (*'eine mit Vernunft begabte Person'*)[30] would seek to protect himself or herself and his or her family from the moment that there is the slightest risk of persecution.

The subjective element of the fear is frequently put forward,[31] though the detailed examination of this element does not seem necessary when evaluating the risk of persecution. Very often, the flight from the country of origin in difficult conditions and the application for asylum are enough to establish an applicant's subjective fear.

In other words, for the first scale a reasonable risk of persecution, even if minimal, will suffice.

The level of violation of basic human rights (What constitutes persecution?) ('P')

Just as a well-founded fear of persecution is assessed by the level of reasonable risk, the notion of persecution itself is assessed by the level of the violation of basic human rights. The nature of the persecution can vary: physical, psychological or economic. Regardless of the nature of the persecution, it is the degree, that is, the quantitative and qualitative level of the violation of basic human rights which determines when the threshold of persecution is reached. In this connection, reference is frequently made to the 'cumulative nature' of persecution.[32]

---

[27] *Immigration and Naturalization Service* v. *Cardoza-Fonseca*, 107 S. Ct 1207, 1213 (1987) (Nicaragua).

[28] *Montecino* v. *Immigration and Naturalization Service*, 915 F. 2d 518, 520 (9th Cir. 1990): 'We are holding only that fear of reprisal from guerrillas on the part of an ex-soldier [in El Salvador] is a type of political persecution and that if such a soldier, on the basis of objective circumstances personally known to him, believes that he has at least a one in ten chance of being killed by the guerrillas, he meets the statutory test of eligibility.'

[29] *Adjei* v. *Canada* (1989) 57 DLR (4th) 153, 155 (FCA) (Ghana).

[30] Verwaltungsgerichtshof (Administrative Court), Germany, 15 December 1993, 93/01/0285.   [31] UNHCR, *Handbook*, para. 37.   [32] *Ibid.*, para. 201.

Since the drafters of the Convention did not wish to attribute a specific meaning to the term *persecution*, it is possible to refer to the ordinary meaning of the term.[33] The term derives from the Latin *persequi*, 'to follow with hostile intent, pursue', which has become 'to prosecute to the end', probably itself deriving from Roman actions against Christians.[34] The question of knowing when 'prosecution' becomes 'persecution' is a contemporary one.[35] In French, persecution is defined as a '*traitement injuste et cruel infligé avec acharnement*' (unjust and cruel treatment relentlessly imposed)[36] which can be rephrased as '*poursuites injustes et violentes*' (unjust and violent prosecution)[37] or as '*importunité continuelle*' (continuous harassment).[38] Likewise, in English, persecution can be 'the actions of persecuting or pursuing with enmity and malignity' or 'persistent or continued injury or annoyance',[39] while to persecute can be 'to afflict or harass constantly so as to injure or distress, to oppress cruelly; to trouble or annoy constantly'.[40] The terms '*Verfolgung*' in German,[41] '*vervolging*' in Dutch[42] and '*persecución*' in Spanish[43] similarly lay emphasis on prosecution. Without doubt the *Petit Robert* definition of the French term best reflects the required qualitative (unjust and cruel) and quantitative (relentless) nature of the action, as well as the level of seriousness and level of harassment.[44]

---

[33] Vienna Convention on the Law of Treaties, article 31(1). *R* v. *Immigration Appeal Tribunal, ex parte Jonah* (UK) [1985] *Immigration Appeals Reports* 7, in which Nolan J held that 'the proper approach must be to apply to the word persecution its ordinary meaning as found in the dictionary'.   [34] *Encyclopædia Universalis* (Paris, 1989), vol. 17, p. 918.

[35] See some cases from the Danish Flygtningenœvnet (RAB – Refugee Appeal Board), 29 June 1988, No. 21–0185 (F-status). Excessive punishment may also indicate that the actions of the authorities are persecutory. A computer specialist who possessed state secrets from a Hungarian company visited Denmark. On his return to Hungary, he risked being subjected to a punishment of three years' imprisonment subject to s. 217 of the Hungarian Penal Code. The Board found this to be disproportionate and granted him *de facto* refugee status (F-status), which differs from Convention refugee status (K-status), under Danish law. In RAB, 4 May 1994, No. 21–1199 (K-status), following the departure from Serbia, an ethnic Albanian from Kosovo was sentenced to six years' imprisonment for politically motivated violence against two Serbs. Considering the length of the imprisonment and the substance of the sentence, the Board granted the applicant asylum. In RAB, 22 December 1989, No. 21–0103 (F-status) the Board decided that punishment for desertion from the Jordanian army may be so excessive and disproportionate that it constitutes persecution. In RAB, 5 October 1987, No. 21–3920 (Turkey) and RAB, 9 September 1994, No. 21–1284 (Algeria), the Board decided that where a deserter who may, in some cases, be punished by an obligation to do alternative service, nevertheless this did not constitute persecution.   [36] *Petit Robert* dictionary.

[37] *Littré* dictionary.   [38] *Petit Larousse* dictionary.   [39] *Oxford English Dictionary*.

[40] *Webster's New Twentieth Century Dictionary*.

[41] *Wörterbuch der deutschen Gegenwartssprache*.

[42] Van Daele, *Groot Woordenboek der Nederlandse Taal*.

[43] *Diccionario del español*, Credos.

[44] Vaste Beroepscommissie voor Vluchtelingen (VBC – Flemish Refugee Appeals Board in Belgium) (2nd ch.), 17 July 1993, W 973, refusing refugee status for a Bulgarian.

It would appear that the only essential criterion applied in case law, either expressly or implicitly, to determine whether an excessive violation of basic human rights has occurred, is disproportionality. The proportionality criterion allows measurement of the results or the objectives against the means used. When the means, albeit legal and legitimate, to achieve an end are disproportionate to the end itself, human dignity is violated and the threshold of persecution is crossed, thus constituting a 'serious limitation of the means of existence'.[45] In general, the disproportionate nature will be a function of the quantitative and qualitative severity of the treatment, on the one hand, and of the basic human right that the treatment violates, on the other. The more fundamental the right in question is (life, physical integrity, freedom), the less quantitatively and qualitatively severe the treatment need be.[46] The lower the priority attributed to the violated freedom (economic, social or cultural rights), the more quantitatively and qualitatively severe the treatment must be.

The persecutory nature of an action will be reinforced when accompanied by a discrimination between the applicant and other persons or between the category of persons to which the applicant belongs and another category of persons in a similar situation. When the different treatment inflicted upon these categories of persons is disproportionate and without objective justification, it constitutes discrimination. It seems to me incorrect to consider, as some case law does, that there is no discrimination when the entire category of persons to which the claimant belongs receives the same treatment.[47] It is also necessary to examine if

Quoting Hathaway, *The Law of Refugee Status*, p. 101, the Belgian Board indicated that persecution is 'a constant or systemic violation of basic human rights implying a serious assault on human dignity against which the state cannot or will not protect'.

[45] Afdeling Rechtspraak Raad van State (ARRVS – Council of State, Judicial Section, Netherlands), 2 February 1984, *Gids Vreemdelingenrecht*, D12–93.

[46] *Fatin* v. *Immigration and Naturalization Service* (USA), 12 F.3d 1233 (3rd Cir. 1993). '[T]he concept of persecution is broad enough to include governmental measures that compel an individual to engage in conduct that is . . . abhorrent to that individual's deepest beliefs.' Further, the court stated in this case that 'the petitioner's testimony in this case simply does not show that for her the requirement of wearing the *chador* or complying with Iran's other gender-specific laws would be so profoundly abhorrent that it could aptly be called persecution'.

[47] *Gomez* v. *Immigration and Naturalization Service* (USA), 947 F. 2d 660 (2nd Cir. 1991). Gomez was a Salvadoran woman who had been the victim of rape and molestation by guerrillas between the ages of 12 and 14. When she was 18, she left El Salvador and fled to the USA. After being arrested for drug-related offences, she faced deportation and applied for asylum. Gomez argued that, by virtue of her prior rape by Salvadoran guerrillas, she had become a member of a social group, that is, women who have been previously battered and raped by Salvadoran guerrillas. Drawing on this she asserted that this discrete group is subject to, and targeted for, persecution in her country of origin. The Board of Immigration Appeals (BIA) and the Court of Appeals, without excluding that brutalised women can assert a well-founded fear of persecution, rejected Gomez's claim on the basis of the lack of proof of a well-founded fear of persecution. As the BIA noted:

the treatment suffered by this category of persons is discriminatory in relation to that suffered by another category of persons in a similar situation. The comparison between persons in the same category is more a question of the targeted nature of the persecution as it relates to the applicant, in the light of the general conditions in the country of origin.

Be this as it may, discrimination only reinforces persecution, without being a necessary condition for its existence. Persecution exists as soon as the treatment inflicted disproportionately violates a basic human right. This 'non-comparative' approach was developed in the Canadian 'Guidelines on Civilian Non-Combatants Fearing Persecution in Civil War Situations',[48] which also influenced the Board of Immigration Appeals in the USA in its determinations of refugee status in civil war situations. This approach 'focuses not on whether the asylum seeker is more at risk than anyone else in the country, but on whether the claimant has established a link between serious harm and a refugee ground'.[49]

The evaluation of proportionality will be more easily established if the decision expressly refers to the fundamental freedom or basic human right which has been violated. Certain decisions, mainly in the Netherlands and Canada, make direct reference to human rights provisions. Other decisions refer to the 1950 European Convention for the Protection of Human Rights and Fundamental Freedoms[50] or to the Geneva Convention to assert the general level of respect for fundamental rights in the country of origin, or to evaluate the persecution in terms of the Geneva Convention, or to evaluate the risk of inhuman treatment which argue against the *refoulement* (return) of a person not granted

---

footnote 47 (*cont.*)

'Gomez failed to produce evidence that women who have previously been abused by the guerrillas possess common characteristics – other than gender and youth – such that would-be persecutors could identify them as members of the purported group. Indeed, there is no indication that Gomez will be singled out for further brutalisation on this basis. Certainly, we do not discount the physical and emotional pain that has been wantonly inflicted on these Salvadoran women. Moreover, we do not suggest that women who have been repeatedly and systematically brutalised by particular attackers cannot assert a well-founded fear of persecution. *We cannot, however, find that Gomez has demonstrated that she is more likely to be persecuted than any other young woman.* Accordingly, because Gomez has not presented evidence that she has a fear of persecution on account of her race, religion, nationality, political opinion or membership in a particular social group, that she has not proven her status as a refugee.' (emphasis added).

[48] Immigration and Refugee Board, Ottawa, Canada, March 1996.

[49] Mark R. von Sternberg, 'The Plight of the Non-Combatant in Civil War and the New Criteria for Refugee Status', 9 *International Journal of Refugee Law*, 1997, p. 169, quoting at p. 170 *Matter of H.*, Interim Decision 3276 (BIA 1996) in which the Board found that a member of the Darood clan and of the Marehan sub-clan who had been beaten and tortured by members of the United Somali Congress had been persecuted on account of a statutory ground (membership in a particular social group) and was not simply the victim of inter-clan warfare.   [50] 213 UNTS 221.

refugee status. As can be seen from the case law, cases relating to discrimination are important for women and deserters.

In my opinion, for cases related to discrimination against women, such as the compulsory sterilisation of Chinese women, the scale of degrees test may demonstrate the cumulation of the seriousness of the right violated and the severity of the treatment inflicted. The same would apply to rape and sexual violence. Such treatment is a disproportionate violation of physical integrity which must be considered as persecution even if applied to all women.

The degree of seriousness of the right violated and of the inflicted treatment is also evident in the case law relating to the refugee status of deserters. Almost unanimously, the courts raise two questions: (i) whether the applicants have deserted a war condemned by official international bodies (United Nations) or by unofficial bodies whose expertise is generally recognised (Amnesty International); and (ii) whether the punishment imposed on these deserters is disproportionate. One of those two conditions seems enough to decide that the deserter is facing persecution. If the war in question is condemned by international bodies, any punishment, even as light as a fine, is unacceptable. In the absence of such condemnation, disproportionate punishment is unacceptable. The same applies for conscientious objectors in situations where no alternative civil service is proposed, when one considers that the United Nations is founded on a search for peace. Only after this initial analysis is it appropriate to consider whether, in the case in question, the reason for the desertion or objection or the reason for the persecution falls within one of the motives set out in the Geneva Convention, such as religious or political opinion.

With regard to the question of the agent of persecution, case law is consistent in recognising that the agent of persecution is not necessarily a constituent part of the state but that persecution can also be indirect. Case law, however, adopts differing positions when it comes to examining the extent of the responsibility of the state when the persecution is the act of a third party, private parties or entities. A restrictive view considers that it is necessary to prove that the state 'tolerates or encourages' such persecution,[51]

---

[51] This is the case in Austria, Switzerland, and France. In CRR, 19 March 1991, 112.948, the French Appeals Board rejected the request of a Turk who, since his arrival on French territory, has been the victim of threats and attacks by Turkish compatriots who were members of a 'fascist' organisation, on the grounds that the Geneva Convention makes refugee status subject to 'the existence of persecution by the authorities of the asylum-seeker's country of origin or committed with the complicity of these authorities'. Such complicity was not proven in that case. This question is particularly pertinent for Algerian asylum seekers in France, CRR, 22 July 1994, No. 237.939, *Actualité juridique – Droit administratif*, 1995, p. 52, note by F. Maillol, and more recently, in the Conseil d'Etat (Council of State), 19 June 1996, No. 165.276, 6 *Dalloz*, 1997, p. 43, note by François Julien-Laferrière.

at least by passive tolerance. This position was adopted by the member states of the EU in the Joint Position on the harmonised application of the term 'refugee', on 4 March 1996. Paragraph 5.2 states that persecution by third parties is only accepted as an argument in favour of recognising refugee status if 'it is encouraged or permitted by the authorities'.[52] A more expansive view holds that it is sufficient for the state to be unable to assure protection.[53] An isolated decision in Germany clearly expresses this point when the Verwaltungsgericht ruled: '[F]rom the point of view of the refugee, it is of no importance that the feared persecution depends on the state, state authorities or uncontrollable groups. It suffices to establish that the state cannot, or will not, offer the necessary protection.'[54] In any case, the applicant must have tried to secure the protection of the authorities of his or her country as long as such an attempt would appear reasonable under the circumstances. This expansive view is justified from the standpoint of the protective function of international refugee law, which substitutes international protection for that which is lacking in the home state.

In my view, the Convention definition makes no reference to the agent of persecution; it is enough that the victim of persecution cannot, or no longer wishes to, claim the protection of the authorities of the country of origin. It would therefore appear that, whoever the agent of persecution may be and whatever the situation of the authorities in the country of origin, it is sufficient, once the risk of persecution has been established, to conclude that no adequate national protection exists in order to substitute international protection. 'Security of nationals is after all the essence of sovereignty.'[55] The role of the international community, through the

[52] Nevertheless, three reservations are made as regards this position. First, a state's failure to act should give rise 'to individual examination of each application . . . *in accordance with national judicial practice*, in the light *in particular* of whether or not the failure to act was deliberate'. In other words, in accordance with the formal principle of respect of national judicial practice as mentioned at the beginning of the Joint Position, anything is possible. Secondly, persons who are the victim of third party persecution 'may be eligible *in any event* for appropriate forms of protection under national law'. The phrase 'in any event' indicates that the minimum requirement is that of protection, and that nothing prevents this protection from being offered by Convention refugee status. Thirdly, the Danish and Swedish delegations made, in an annex, an express statement considering that persecution by third parties 'may also fall within the scope of the Convention in other cases, when the authorities prove unable to offer protection'.

[53] This is or was the case in Belgium, Canada, Denmark, the Netherlands, the UK and the USA. In Canada, the Supreme Court in *Canada* v. *Ward* [1993] 2 SCR 689 ruled: 'Persecution under the Convention includes situations where the state is not in strictness an accomplice to the persecution, but is simply unable to protect its citizens.'

[54] Verwaltungsgericht (Administrative Court) Frankfurt/Main (9th Division), 28 March 1994 (9 E 11871/93.A LV) (Sri Lanka). Higher courts in Germany have not, however, upheld this ruling. See Bundesverwaltungsgericht (Federal Administrative Court) of 15 April 1997 (9 C 38.96) and of 2 September 1997 (9 C 40.96).

[55] *Canada* v. *Ward* [1993] 2 SCR 689 at 724.

action of the receiving state, is not – according to international refugee law – to condemn the country of origin, but to protect a refugee.

The link between persecution and the five causes mentioned in the Convention does not need to be developed here, as it is seen elsewhere in the jurisprudence and in this book.[56] Let us state here simply that for the five causes – race, religion, nationality, membership of a particular social group or political opinion – the link between persecution and its cause can be either internal or external. It is internal when it is the attitude of the refugee himself which leads to persecution, as a result of positive acts, for example affirming his opinions or his membership of a social group. The connection is external when it is the persecutor who attributes or imputes to the person the characteristics which this person possesses, but which he or she does not actively put forward (for example, the persecution of any Jew, woman or homosexual), or even which this person does not possess (for example, a political opinion imputed to a person who simply refuses to state a position). In this respect, it is of little importance whether the agent of persecution is the state or a private individual in so far as the external link is to be examined with respect to the persecutor and not necessarily to the state when the latter is not the persecutor. Hence, if members of one religion who do not publicly express their convictions are persecuted by the members of another religion, it is enough to examine whether the latter attribute a religious cause to their attitude and whether the state is incapable of protecting those persecuted.

The link between persecution and its cause should not therefore be examined exclusively from the viewpoint of the persecutor or the persecuted, nor by a combination of the two viewpoints, but each should be examined in turn. It is enough that a link be established between the persecution and one of the five causes, in terms of either the persecuted party or the persecutor, for the condition of persecution to be fulfilled, within the meaning of the Convention.[57]

In summary, the second of the three scales measures the quantitative and qualitative level of the severity of the treatment inflicted and the importance accorded to the fundamental right violated, in order to judge

[56] Or the 'nexus' to use Hathaway's terminology in *The Law of Refugee Status*, p. 135. See also chapter 1, pp. 17–19 above.
[57] For an example in this direction in the USA, see *Matter of S. P.*, Interim Decision 3287 (BIA 1996), quoted by von Sternberg in 'The Plight of the Non-Combatant in Civil War', p. 171. In this case, the Board recognised as a refugee a young Tamil in Sri Lanka, who was kidnapped from a refugee camp by members of the LTTE (Liberation Tigers of Tamil Eelam), forcing him to work as a welder at one of their camps. When the camp was overrun by the Sri Lankan army, the applicant was taken to prison, tortured and threatened with imminent death for being a member of the LTTE. In affording refugee status, the Board looked at the persecutors' intent and at the disproportionality of the treatment inflicted.

if the threshold of persecution has been reached. Whilst, in principle, the level of severity of treatment must be high, this requirement can be relaxed according to the importance attributed to the violated right. In any event, contrary to the first level (risk), the level of 'reasonableness' to be reached here is no longer minimal but serious. This does not mean, however, that the treatment must be more severe than the treatment inflicted on persons in the same category as a whole, insofar as a qualitatively severe treatment, constituting persecution, can be meted out to an entire category of persons. Indeed the reverse can be true: the quantitative extension of this treatment could only reinforce its 'persecution' quality.

The level of proof (What constitutes sufficient proof of well-founded fear of being persecuted?) ('P')

The third level complements the other two. This level relates to the examination of proof of the risk and of the persecution. In reality, this level is implicitly included in the first two levels. It is nevertheless interesting to consider proof as a separate level in order to require decision-makers to rationalise their decisions more precisely by distinguishing considerations about proof from considerations about risk and persecution.

According to the rules of civil procedure, it is for the plaintiff to present evidence of the allegations underlying his or her claim. Apart from the fact that refugee status is seldom recognised as a civil right (in itself a debatable issue), it is recognised that the special nature of asylum leads to a kind of shared burden of proof. It is up to the applicant to give a credible and coherent account, free from contradictions on essential points. This system favours the educated, articulate person, such that it is appropriate to 'take into account the very low level of education'[58] of some applicants and in such cases to accept certain inconsistencies and contradictions. The applicant must where feasible support his or her account with evidence, though this is commonly impracticable.[59] It falls to the authorities

---

[58] Commission permanente de recours des réfugiés (CPRR – French-speaking Refugee Appeals Board in Belgium) (2nd ch.), 24 February 1992, R 064.

[59] *Aguilera-Cota* v. *Immigration and Naturalization Service* (USA), 914 F. 2d 1375 (9th Cir. 1990). *Aguilera-Cota* concerned a politically neutral Salvadoran who had worked for the Central Board of Elections. He was pressured in a threatening note by unknown persons to give up his job. The immigration judge did not believe that the note should be accorded much weight because the claimant did not know who wrote it and had not retained it. The Court of Appeal ruled: '[There is] nothing novel about the concept that persecutors cannot be expected to conform to arbitrary evidentiary rules established by the Immigration and Naturalization Service; neither Salvadoran leftists nor Middle Eastern terrorists, such as members of the PLO [Palestine Liberation Organisation] or the Hezbollah, have been given adequate notice that our government expects them to

of the country where the individual is seeking asylum to seek the truth, both of the general conditions in the country of origin and of the facts claimed by the applicant. This information may be obtained through a diplomatic mission, from the United Nations High Commissioner for Refugees (UNHCR), from a non-governmental organisation (NGO), or from experts on the country in question.

The authority must question the applicant on a specific item before concluding that he or she 'cannot give any information'. The assessment must be adversarial, both with respect to the applicant, who must accept cross-examination concerning his or her claims, and to the administrative authority, which must notify the applicant of its findings and allow rebuttal or comment on documents and information in the file.

The benefit of the doubt must generally be granted to the applicant both in matters relating to his or her personal condition (psychological, health, education), and in matters relating to objective elements which give rise to sufficient 'presumptions' or 'indications'.

In summary, the third scale, that is, the level or the degree of proof, is a 'balancing test of probabilities' which should provide reasonable proof attesting to the risk of persecution. The reasonableness test is stricter than for the first level. With respect to its credibility, the account should appear more credible than incredible, with resort to the benefit of the doubt in case of uncertainty.

Having considered case law relevant to the theory of the three scales – risk, persecution and proof – it remains to be summarised in a theory.

The theory of the three scales ('R', 'P', 'P')

The theory of the three scales (levels) is a gauge of the question central to recognition of refugee status, that is, whether there is a risk of persecution in the case of return to the country of origin. This question falls into three parts:

sign their names and reveal their individual identities when they deliver threatening messages. We have previously tried to make it clear that asylum applicants are not required to produce documentary evidence of events such as those involved here. As we have said, "persecutors are hardly likely to provide their victims with affidavits attesting to their acts of persecution." . . . Moreover, the fact that the petitioner did not possess the note for the immigration judge to read was irrelevant. As we have noted, "refugees sometimes are in no position to gather documentary evidence establishing specific or individual persecution or a threat of persecution." . . . The last thing a victim may want to do is to carry around a threatening note with him. Doing so could cause extended detention, questioning or even torture or death, whichever side happened by chance to stop and search him. When the correct legal standard is applied, it is clear that Aguilera's testimony concerning the note strongly supports his objective fear of persecution.'

1. Is there Risk? ('R')
2. Is there Persecution? ('P')
3. Is there Proof of risk of persecution? ('P')

Each question corresponds to a certain level (or scale) which makes it possible to measure the degree to be reached in order to consider respectively whether there is risk, persecution and sufficient proof. When these three levels (or scales), taken together, reach a certain overall level, the applicant reaches the threshold of refugee status. As with three-runged ladders (the French word *échelle* translates as both 'scale' and 'ladder'), the theory of the three scales is comprised of three independent levels (or scales), each indicating the specific threshold for a particular question. At the same time they are also interdependent and when taken together function as a ladder, making it possible to reach a certain point, that is, the minimum threshold for recognition of refugee status. This interdependence also means that if there is a minimum threshold which must be met for each scale, the overall threshold level is reached by the cumulation of the three scales. To use an image from the vocabulary of refugee support groups, the ladder must be long enough to scale the walls of the 'fortress' Europe or of the 'fortress' of the state in which asylum is being sought.

The three scales are:

1. The level of risk (At what point is there well-founded fear?) ('R').
2. The level of violation of basic human rights (At what point is there persecution?) ('R').
3. The level of proof (At what point have the risk and the mistreatment been sufficiently established?) ('P').

Each scale puts a distinct question, so that the required level for each scale is different:

1. A *minimal* risk is sufficient.
2. The violation of basic human rights must be *serious*.
3. The level of proof must be *reasonable* and allow the benefit of doubt.

In assessing whether the overall minimum threshold for recognition of refugee status is reached, the necessary length of each single scale is dependent on that of the other two scales. Thus, when the level of violation of basic human rights is very high, for instance in cases of persecution such as an attack on a person's life, it can be agreed that the level of risk and of proof can be reduced accordingly, since the combined level of the three scales allows the recognition threshold to be reached.

A mathematical formula can illustrate this reasoning, assuming that a minimum score of 65 out of a maximum of 100 is necessary for refugee recognition. See Table 2.1. To combine the three scales the 'minimum' total for refugee recognition has to be 65, which is higher than the sum of the individual minima on each scale (45). To achieve the minimum total

Table 2.1 *The theory of the three scales as a mathematical formula*

For the	maximum is	minimum is
Risk (R)	30	5
Persecution (P)	30	20
Proof (P)	40	20

of 65 the score on certain scales has to be higher than the minimum. It is this which enables us to play on the three scales. An assessment reaching 65 is achieved just as much with a high risk (20) of serious persecution (25), little proven (20), as with a low risk (5) of not quite as serious persecution (20), established with certainty, because proven in the past (40). This mathematical formula is just one illustration of the flexibility of the 'theory of the three scales'. It is not intended as an obligatory formula as this could, under the guise of figures, contribute to dehumanising the procedure of recognising refugee status.

This 'theory of the three scales' may appear overly abstract and mechanical, in particular when it is illustrated by a mathematical example. However, I share the opinion that 'the determination of refugee status is by no means a mechanical and routine process'.[60] The objective is not to create a routine which is negative in that it dehumanises refugee status but, on the contrary, to establish a positive habit of focusing the discussion on the three questions that require detailed and sensitive analysis in the light of the facts and of the law before any decision is taken with regard to refugee status.

It is important to acknowledge that the Convention and its refugee definition aim to protect refugees and not to condemn the country of origin or to protect the country of asylum. A teleological interpretation, based on the protective nature of the Convention, requires the following questions to be put to the authorities responsible for implementing the Convention:

1. Why do you say that the level of risk is not *minimal*?
2. Why do you say that the violation of basic human rights is not *serious*?
3. Why do you say that the *reasonable* level of proof, allowing doubt, is not reached?

The objective of the 'theory of the three scales' is precisely to bring the decision-making authorities and courts to rationalise their decisions more adequately with regard to these three questions.

[60] UNHCR *Handbook*, para. 222.

Bibliography

Basso Sekretariat Berlin (Hrsg), *Festung Europa auf der Anklagebank* (Dokumentation des Basso-Tribunals zum Asylrecht in Europa, Westfälisches Dampfboot, Münster, 1995)

Carlier, Jean-Yves, Dirk Vanheule, Klaus Hullmann and Carlos Peña Galiano, *Who is a Refugee?* (Kluwer Law International, The Hague, 1997); and in French as *Qu'est-ce qu'un réfugié?* (Bruylant, Brussels, 1998)

Carlier, Jean-Yves and Dirk Vanheule (eds.), *L'Europe et les réfugiés: un défi?, Europe and Refugees: A Challenge* (Kluwer Law International, The Hague, 1997)

Crépeau, François, *Droit d'asile: De l'hospitalité aux contrôles migratoires* (Bruylant, Brussels, 1995)

Goodwin-Gill, Guy S., *The Refugee in International Law* (2nd edn, Clarendon Press, Oxford, 1996)

Gortázar Rotaeche, Cristina J., *Derecho de asilo y 'no rechazo' del refugiado* (Universitad Pontificia Comillas, Dykinson, Madrid, 1997)

Grahl-Madsen, Atle, *The Status of Refugees in International Law* (A. W. Sijthoff, Leyden, 1966–72)

Hailbronner, Kay, *Asyl- und Einwanderungsrecht im europäischen Vergleich. Comparative Law of Asylum and Immigration in Europe. Droit comparé de l'asile et de l'immigration en Europe* (Schriftenreihe der Europäischen Rechtsakademie Trier, Bundesanzeiger, Cologne, 1992)

Hathaway, James C., *The Law of Refugee Status* (Butterworths, Toronto, 1991) *Reconceiving International Refugee Law* (Martinus Nijhoff, The Hague, 1997)

Hathaway, James C. and John A. Dent, *Refugee Rights: Report on a Comparative Survey* (York Lanes Press, Toronto, 1995)

Kälin, Walter, 'Refugees and Civil Wars: Only a Matter of Interpretation?', 3 *International Journal of Refugee Law*, 1991, p. 435

Société française pour le droit international, *Droit d'asile et des réfugiés* (Colloque de Caen, Pedone, Paris, 1997)

UNHCR, *Symposium on Gender-Based Persecution*, 9 *International Journal of Refugee Law*, Special Issue, autumn 1997.

3 Who is a refugee? The Convention definition: universal or obsolete?

Jerzy Sztucki

Introduction: the original concept

The definition of 'refugee' appears to be central to any discussion of 'refugee rights and realities', but it is, at the same time, one of the most awkward aspects of such debate. The *travaux préparatoires* at various levels, concerning article 1 of the 1951 Convention Relating to the Status of Refugees,[1] amount to approximately one-quarter of their total volume, and the representative of Venezuela in the Third Committee of the UN General Assembly probably reflected general sentiments when he expressed the opinion that 'the definition of the term "refugee" was the most difficult problem to be settled'.[2]

The discussion of that question is, of course, dominated by the definition in article 1 of the Convention, which is widely regarded as 'universal'.[3] At the same time, the Convention with its definition is sometimes described as a Cold War product, 'Eurocentric' and, if only for these reasons, obsolete.

At its inception, the Convention certainly was a Cold War product. The Cold War atmosphere permeates the *travaux préparatoires* of the Convention, and is also reflected in the fact that no communist country participated in the Conference of the Plenipotentiaries of 1951 or (with the exception of Yugoslavia and China) became a party to the Convention and/or the 1967 Protocol Relating to the Status of Refugees before 1989.[4]

---

[1] 189 UNTS 137, in force 22 April 1954 (hereinafter the Convention). Note that because of space limitations, references to literature in the footnotes are dispensed with.

[2] GAOR, 5th Session, 3rd Committee, p. 338, UN Doc. A/C.3/325 (Summary Record of the 325th meeting, 24 November 1950, para. 40).

[3] See, e.g., para. 9 of the preamble to the Convention of the Organisation of African Unity (OAU) Governing the Specific Aspects of Refugee Problems in Africa, 1969 (1001 UNTS 46 at p. 47), in force 20 June 1974 (hereinafter the OAU Convention); UN Doc. A/AC.96/830, 7 September 1994, *Note on International Protection*, submitted to the Executive Committee of the UNHCR Programme by the High Commissioner, para. 10 (hereinafter *Note on International Protection*).

[4] 606 UNTS 267 (hereinafter the Protocol), in force 4 October 1967. Yugoslavia became a party to the Convention in 1959 and to the Protocol in 1968; China became a party to both instruments in 1982; Hungary in 1989; and all other former Communist states in

The Convention and the admission of refugees from the communist countries served as an element of psychological warfare, and it was in this spirit that the Convention was generously applied in the 1950s and 1960s. The economies of the prospective receiving countries, which were able to absorb the thus available manpower, were an important concurrent factor.

The Convention was certainly also 'Eurocentric' at its inception, as the problem of refugees, at the time of its adoption, was primarily if not exclusively European, since the persons in question were of European origin and had been displaced within Europe. However, in the course of time the Convention has lost its primarily Cold War and Eurocentric character. The main flow of refugees has shifted from the Cold War adversaries to non-aligned countries, and the Cold War is over. Only a minority of the total refugee population lives in Europe and refugees of European origin account for only a part of it.[5] The 1967 Protocol responded to the globalisation of the refugee problem by waiving the temporal limitation of the events to which the Convention applies and by providing for its applicability without geographical limitations.[6] By February 1999, 137 states (only approximately 30 per cent of them European) were parties to the Convention and/or the Protocol. Thus, from a formal point of view, the Convention definition can be, by now, regarded as 'universalised'.

From the substantive point of view, however, the universality of the Convention definition is open to discussion. It can be regarded as 'universal', if this term is understood as synonymous with 'general', in contradistinction to the selective definitions in the inter-war instruments on refugees,[7] or to the long enumeration of persons qualifying as 'refugees' in the Annex to the Constitution of the International Refugee Organisation (IRO).[8] Indeed, some states were perturbed by the general character of the initial draft definition. For example, the French represen-

footnote 4 (cont.)
Europe in the 1990s. Cuba and North Korea are still not parties. *Multilateral Treaties Deposited with the Secretary-General*, status as at 31 December 1997 (UN, New York, 1998), pp. 234–5 and 256–7.
[5] UNHCR, *The State of World's Refugees: In Search of Solutions* (Oxford University Press, Oxford, 1995), pp. 247 and 248; and UNHCR, *UNHCR by Numbers 1997* (Geneva, 1997), p. 5. Figures published by different sources are not identical.
[6] However, earlier declarations of limitation to events in Europe have been left intact. As at 4 February 1999 five states applied that limitation: Congo (Brazzaville), Madagascar, Malta, Monaco and Turkey (Hungary lifted its earlier limitation on 8 January 1998).
[7] Those referred to in article 1A(1) of the Convention are the Arrangements of 12 May 1926 Relating to the Issue of Identity Certificates to Russian and Armenian Refugees, 89 LNTS 47; the Arrangement of 30 June 1928 Concerning the Extension to Other Categories of Refugees of Certain Measures Taken in Favour of Russian and Armenian Refugees, 89 LNTS 63; the Convention of 28 October 1933 Relating to the International Status of Refugees Coming from Germany, 192 LNTS 59; and the Protocol of 14 September 1939, 198 LNTS 141.   [8] 18 UNTS 3, Annex, pp. 18, 19–20.

tative in the Economic and Social Council (ECOSOC) declared: 'Never before had a definition so wide and generous, but also so dangerous for the receiving countries, been put forward for signature of governments. The obligations flowing from the Convention were such that the day might come when certain countries might find it impossible to honour them.'[9]

Ultimately, the applicability of the Convention was limited to the events prior to 1 January 1951 and, optionally, also to the events in Europe before that date. Thus, states did not contemplate the universal applicability of the Convention definition and one hardly needs to argue that the quality of 'refugee' does not depend on the date or place of events which caused the flight. Indeed, the Final Act of the Conference of Plenipotentiaries of 1951 comprises, *inter alia*, Recommendation E relating to 'refugees . . . who would not be covered by the terms of the Convention'.[10] At least one such category already existed then, namely Palestinian refugees, so termed in the relevant resolutions of the UN General Assembly.[11] They were already taken care of by the United Nations Relief and Works Agency for Palestine Refugees in the Near East (UNRWA) and thus did not fall under the Convention in accordance with the exclusion clause in article 1D of the Convention. Furthermore, the definition of 'refugee' in the Statute of the Office of the UNHCR, adopted in the same period and against the same background as the Convention, is in a sense broader than that in the Convention, insofar as it has no geographical limitations and also includes persons who for 'reasons other than personal convenience', that is, not only because of a 'well-founded fear of being persecuted' on some specific grounds, are outside their countries of origin, etc.[12]

The Convention definition was tailored to fit an approximately foreseeable number of prospective beneficiaries who fell within acceptable categories. Indeed, at the time of the adoption of the Convention, the overwhelming majority were already outside their countries of origin. The definition has been premised on what may be called peacetime persecution inherent in the 'normal' functioning of oppressive regimes as they were known and perceived at the time of the adoption of the Convention. Other conditions which can generate refugee flows, which

[9] ECOSOC, Official Record, 11th Session, p. 278, UN Doc. E/SR.406 (Summary Record of the 406th meeting, 11 August 1950, paras. 55–7).
[10] 189 UNTS 137 at p. 148.
[11] UN General Assembly Resolutions 212 (III) of 19 November 1948 and 302 (IV) of December 1949, GAOR, 3rd Session, *Resolutions*, p. 66 and 4th Session, *Resolutions*, p. 23, respectively.
[12] Article 6.A(ii) of the Annex to General Assembly Resolution 428 (V) of 14 December 1950, GAOR, 5th Session, Supplement No. 20, p. 47.

have developed subsequently to the adoption of the Convention, are not specified in its definition.

'Flexibility' and ambiguity of the Convention definition

It is arguable that a definition claiming universality can be neither too detailed nor very precise. It is also arguable that its drafters eventually abandoned efforts to be more precise, because they already had a clear understanding of whom they had in mind. However this might be, the Convention definition is, for better and for worse, 'flexible'. Its otherwise fundamental elements of 'well-founded fear' and 'persecution' are open to a wide range of interpretations. An authoritative interpretation of these concepts was given for the first time by UNHCR in 1979.[13] Although occasionally invoked in judicial decisions in refugee matters and referred to in official documents,[14] this interpretation is not binding on states parties to the Convention. Furthermore, practice demonstrates not only differences of interpretation as between states, but also different interpretations by the same state in application to specific situations.[15]

Another element of the Convention definition, which is uncertain because not mentioned in the text, is that of the agents of persecution, who are sometimes sponsored by governments. Victims of such persecution (on one or more of the Convention grounds) are recognised by UNHCR as Convention refugees, if the state concerned is unable or unwilling to curb such persecutions,[16] but, in practice, states parties to the Convention have often interpreted 'persecution' as related exclusively to state organs. It may be mentioned in this context that persecution, independently of its agents (if local authorities do not provide protection), has been formally included for the first time in the definition of 'refugee' in Swedish legislation by the 1996 amendment to the Aliens Act (chapter 3, paragraph 2).[17]

Still another question not reflected in the Convention definition and open to a variety of interpretations is that of the status of family members. The principle of family unity is not incorporated in the Convention, but instead forms the subject matter of Recommendation B, included in the Final Act of the Conference of Plenipotentiaries of 1951[18] – an indication

---

[13] UNHCR, *Handbook on Procedures and Criteria for Determining Refugee Status under the 1951 Convention and the 1967 Protocol Relating to the Status of Refugees* (Geneva, re-edited 1992), pp. 11–16.

[14] See, for example, Part II.D of the *Declaration and Comprehensive Plan of Action* adopted by the International Conference on Indo-Chinese Refugees, UN Doc. A/CONF.148/2, 26 April 1989.   [15] See chapter 2 above.   [16] UNHCR, *Handbook*, p. 17.

[17] See *Lag om ändring i utlänningslagen* (Act on Amendment to Aliens' Act) 1989:529, Svensk forfattningssamling (Swedish Code of Statutes – SFS), 1996:1379.

[18] 189 UNTS 137, at p. 146.

of the wish of the signatories to retain freedom in these matters. The Executive Committee of the UNHCR Programme (EXCOM) has at least three times, in its Conclusions, emphasised the fundamental importance of the principle of family unity and stressed the need to ensure the reunification of separated refugee families.[19] Leaving aside the non-binding character of the Conclusions, EXCOM has not thus far defined the concept of 'family'. It suffices to compare, for example, the 'Principles Concerning Treatment of Refugees' adopted by the Asian-African Legal Consultative Committee (AALCC) in 1966,[20] which generally define the 'dependants' of a refugee as refugees, with the very limited definition of 'family' in article 4 of the 1990 Dublin Convention,[21] in order to realise the range of possibilities and, consequently, the vague delineation of the concept of 'family' in the refugee context.

Also, the concept of 'membership of a particular social group', which recently acquired some topicality in connection with the question of gender-based persecution, is fairly vague.

If the cessation and exclusion clauses, including especially article 1C(5) and (6) and article 1F, are to be regarded as forming a part of the Convention definition, as for example they are in Canadian legislation,[22] the list of debatable questions is extended further.

However, whatever the problems might be in interpreting the Convention definition, the problem of the definition of 'refugee' in general is another one,[23] as implied already in Recommendation E of the Conference of Plenipotentiaries of 1951. Perhaps regarded then as some remote and obscure hypothesis, it soon acquired relevance when the Convention definition turned out to be inapplicable, for example with respect to Chinese 'refugees' in Hong Kong or Angolan 'refugees' in the Congo (Leopoldville), so termed in the relevant resolutions which the UN General Assembly adopted specially with respect to them.[24] Thus, the beginning of the expansion in practice of the notion of 'refugee' was already evident then, while a general definition was lacking. This process of expansion was dramatically accentuated in the 1960s and 1970s, as a consequence of the changing character of refugee flows.

---

[19] Executive Committee of the UNHCR Programme (EXCOM), Conclusions No. 9 (XXVIII), 1977, No. 24 (XXXII), 1981 and No. 84 (XLVIII), 1997.
[20] Text in UNHCR, *Collection of International Instruments and Other Legal Texts Concerning Refugees and Displaced Persons* (Geneva, 1995), vol. II, p. 10; see also p. 62.
[21] 30 ILM 1991, p. 432.
[22] Immigration Act, RSC 1985 (4th Supplement), chapter 1–2.
[23] See chapter 1 above.
[24] See UN General Assembly Resolutions 1167 (XII), 26 November 1957, and 1671 (XVI), 18 December 1961, respectively, GAOR, 12th Session, Supplement No. 18, p. 20, and 16th Session, Supplement No. 17, vol. I, p. 27, respectively.

Subsequent developments and regional responses of developing countries

While oppressive regimes have not disappeared from the surface of the globe, it is not their peacetime persecution which in recent decades has become the main cause of the accelerating flow of victims of persecution – not infrequently on one or more of the Convention grounds. Today the causes and context of persecution have changed. Increasingly frequently they occur amidst, or form an integral element of, armed conflicts which are mostly of an internal character. It is symptomatic of these developments that, on several occasions in the 1990s, 'refugees', so termed in the relevant resolutions, have become of concern not only to the UN General Assembly, but also to the Security Council, which on some occasions has explicitly regarded refugee problems as an aspect of the 'threat to the peace' as set out in Chapter VII of the UN Charter.[25]

As a result of these developments, the Convention definition, as initially conceived and interpreted, has been confronted with generically different categories of people in need of international protection. Moreover, these categories outnumber those whom the drafters of the Convention had in mind. This has given rise to the question of paramount importance, which is not reflected in the language of the Convention definition, namely, its applicability to situations of armed conflict, for the Protocol has only formally extended the applicability of the Convention: the substance of the Convention definition of 'refugee' has remained the same.

The challenges of these new developments have been met, in substance, in the first place, at a regional level. The OAU Convention, while reproducing almost verbatim the Convention definition in its article 1(1), adds in article 1(2):

The term 'refugee' shall also apply to every person who, owing to external aggression, occupation, foreign domination or events seriously disturbing public order *in either part or the whole* of his country of origin or nationality, is compelled to leave his place of habitual residence in order to seek refuge in another place outside his country of origin and nationality.[26]

By 4 November 1996, forty-three African states were parties to the OAU Convention which in spite of scarce resources available has been generously applied. However, as the recent cases of Liberia and of central Africa have demonstrated and as has been acknowledged by UNHCR,

---

[25] See, for example, UN Security Council Resolutions 688 (1991) (Iraqi Kurds), 752 (1992) (Bosnia and Herzegovina) and 897 (1994) (Somalia) in Security Council Official Records, *Resolutions and Decisions*, 46th year, p. 31; 47th year, p. 13; and 49th year, p. 55, respectively.   [26] 1001 UNTS 46, at p. 47 (emphasis added).

'even the proverbial African generosity towards refugees had become strained'.[27]

In a similar vein, in the context of central America, the 1984 Cartagena Declaration on Refugees proclaims in paragraph 3 of its 'conclusions' that 'it is necessary to consider *enlarging* of the concept of a refugee' and that:

the definition or concept of a refugee to be recommended for use in the region [that is, central America] is one which, in addition to containing the elements of the 1951 Convention and the 1967 Protocol, *includes* among refugees persons who have fled their country because their lives, safety or freedom have been threatened by generalized violence, foreign aggression, internal conflicts, massive violation of human rights or other circumstances which have seriously disturbed public order.[28]

Although not formally binding, the Cartegena Declaration has been successfully applied and has been accepted, in practice, throughout Latin America.[29]

The specific grounds warranting the status of refugee are different in the two above-quoted documents. One also notes that in the OAU Convention, article 1(2) appears to be a kind of 'addition' to the Convention definition, which is independent of its other elements (fear of persecution on specific grounds, lack of national protection), while the Cartagena Declaration, despite using the phrase 'in addition', gives the impression that the 'addition' is 'built in' in the Convention definition ('includes'), leaving its other elements unaffected. In reality, however, none of these other elements is required for the complementary categories of refugees. The basic concept of both documents is the same.

Arab experts, assembled at the UNHCR sponsored Fourth Arab Seminar on 'Asylum and Refugee Law in the Arab World' in Cairo in 1992, went a step further, recommending that:

in situations which may not be covered by the 1951 Convention, the 1967 Protocol, or any other relevant instrument in force or United Nations General Assembly resolutions, refugees [so termed, although not covered by *any* instrument] . . . shall nevertheless be protected.[30]

---

27 UN Doc. A/AC.96/860, 23 October 1995, Report of 46th session of EXCOM, p. 31.
28 UNHCR, *Collection*, p. 208 (emphasis added) (hereinafter the Cartagena Declaration).
29 See UN Doc. A/AC.96/830, 7 September 1994, *Note on International Protection*, p. 18; and GAOR, 51st Session, Supplement No. 12, Report of the UNHCR, 1996, p. 3. See also Declaración de San José sobre Refugiados y Personas Desplazadas (Declaration of San José on Refugees and Displaced Persons), text in IIDH-ACNUR, *10 Años de la Declaración de Cartagena sobre Refugiados*, San José, 5–7 December 1994, pp. 415–28.
30 UNHCR, *Collection*, p. 118, article 5 of the Declaration on the Protection of Refugees and Displaced Persons in the Arab World, 19 November 1992.

The above-quoted definitions have only regional application.[31] Otherwise they reaffirm the 'basic and universal' character of the Convention definition. Furthermore, while in some cases they are formulated in legally non-binding documents, the fact remains that states subscribing to these documents together constitute more than half of the total number of states, and, moreover, that this majority is *responding to real situations*, which cannot remain without impact outside the regions in question.

The impact of new developments and of regional definitions at the global level

One has to distinguish between the impact of such regional definitions at the global level, that is, on international institutions, especially UNHCR, and their impact on individual states, or groups of states, outside the said regions, that is, mainly on industrialised countries.

At the global level one can observe cautious but progressive yielding to the pressure of the realities of the refugee situation. The relevant passage of the UNHCR *Handbook* reads:

> Persons compelled to leave their country of origin as a result of international or *national* armed conflicts are not normally considered refugees *under the 1951 Convention or 1967 Protocol* . . . However, *foreign invasion or occupation of all or part of a country* can result – and occasionally has resulted – in persecution for one or more of the reasons enumerated in the 1951 Convention.[32]

Leaving aside the apparent inconsistency between the references to both international and national conflicts in the first paragraph, and to international ones only in the second, one notes that both appear under the heading '*War refugees*'.

The 1985 Report of UNHCR, while recognising the 'complexity of the causes of *refugee* movements', still makes a distinction between 'refugees *and* victims of man-made disasters'.[33] In the subsequent annual reports, this distinction is progressively played down.[34] In the *Note on International Protection* submitted in 1994, UNHCR, while admitting that, however liberally the Convention definition is applied, 'some *refugees* fleeing civil wars and other forms of armed conflict . . . fall outside the letter of the Convention', expresses the opinion that the Convention definition 'has

[31] The complexity of the mass population movements which have taken place since the collapse of the Soviet Union in late 1991 have also spawned a host of new broader definitions and categories which are outlined in greater detail in chapter 7 below.
[32] UNHCR, *Handbook*, p. 39, paras. 164–5 (emphasis added).
[33] GAOR, 40th Session, Supplement No. 12, p. 1 (emphasis added).
[34] See, e.g., Report 1986, GAOR, 41st Session, Supplement No. 12, pp. 1, 4: Report 1987, GAOR, 42nd Session, Supplement No. 12., p. 1; etc.

proved sufficiently flexible to afford international protection to *refugees* fleeing a wide variety of threats to their lives and fundamental rights'. It is described as directly relevant 'to many, perhaps most, contemporary refugee situations'. 'Most States', the *Note on International Protection* continues, 'concur with the UNHCR that the Convention and Protocol apply to *refugees* from civil wars who have good reason to fear being victimized because of their religion, ethnic origin, clan or imputed political opinion'.[35] In the corresponding *Note on International Protection* from 1995, the language is perhaps even plainer: 'Persons fleeing or remaining outside a country *for reasons pertinent to refugee status qualify as Convention refugees, regardless of whether those grounds have arisen during conflict.*'[36] Indeed, UNHCR, referring to the definition of 'refugee' in '[r]egional refugee instruments in other parts of the world', has declared unequivocally: 'This is also the definition favoured by UNHCR.'[37]

Still, from the conceptual point of view, UNHCR's position seems to differ from that reflected in the regional instruments in question. The regional instruments provide for an extended concept or definition of 'refugee', whereas UNHCR's position is that of extensive interpretation of the Convention definition. At first glance this position has perhaps a flavour of 'Convention fundamentalism'. However, in a situation where there is no realistic possibility of revising the Convention definition, the UNHCR, in order to rest on solid legal ground, must rely on that definition, while advocating its extensive interpretation, as is consistent with the text which is silent as to the circumstances (peacetime or wartime) in which Convention requirements for eligibility for refugee status are met.

Certainly, international refugee law was initially conceived as being applicable, in principle, to peacetime conditions in order to 'assure refugees the widest possible exercise of . . . fundamental rights and freedoms'.[38] Yet fundamental human rights principles are to be respected in all situations, including those of armed conflicts, even if certain human rights may be suspended in time of war or emergency. Since the end of the 1980s, there has been a growing awareness that there are no impenetrable boundaries between human rights law, humanitarian law and refugee law. The UNHCR training manual declares: 'The international refugee law, like humanitarian law, is in fact a branch of human rights law.'[39]

---

[35] UN Doc. A/AC.96/830, paras. 30 and 20–2 (emphasis added).
[36] UN Doc. A/AC.96/850, 1 September 1995, *Note on International Protection*, para. 4 (emphasis added).
[37] UNHCR, *The State of the World's Refugees: A Humanitarian Agenda* (Oxford University Press, Oxford, 1997), p. 52.   [38] Para. 2, preamble to the Convention.
[39] UNHCR, *Introduction à la protection internationale des réfugiés* (Module de formation, Geneva, June 1992), p. 19.

The eroding contours of the 'refugee' definition

Yet, the more extensive the interpretation of the Convention definition is, the more diffuse is the boundary between Convention and other *refugees*. For example, in the light of the aforesaid, those who have a well-founded fear of persecution on one or more of the Convention grounds are Convention refugees, *if at the hands of the adversary*. By contrast, those who flee abroad because their lives and safety are threatened by the intensity of more or less 'regular' hostilities (which are always more or less indiscriminate with respect to civilians) without the risk of falling into the hands of the adversary, are not.[40] Perhaps they qualify as *mandate* refugees ('reasons other than personal convenience'), for 'it is clear that such victims of conflict require international protection, including asylum on at least a temporary basis'.[41] Even if this is so, there is still an 'intermediate' category of civilians who fled abroad because they, on one or more of the Convention grounds, were made the main targets of military action. The marketplace in Sarajevo is one of many examples of such situations. Needless to add that, according to the above-quoted regional definitions, all these people would qualify as 'refugees'.

A considerable terminological, or conceptual, flora has grown up within which refugee realities confront the language of the Convention and the UNHCR Statute and this does not make the general concept of 'refugee' easier to grasp. One such notion is that of the so-called 'good offices' refugees, introduced in 1957.[42] The concept of 'refugees who do not come within the competence of the United Nations', used for the first time in 1959,[43] appears to be synonymous. Both, at least initially, were related to assistance only, not protection. Then, in 1966, emerged the term 'refugees who are his [that is, the UNHCR's] concern'.[44] Since 1975 the term 'displaced persons' has appeared in a number of official

---

[40] UN Doc. A/AC.96/830, para. 30 ('*at the hands* of one or more of the parties to a conflict', by contrast (emphasis added)). See also p. 21.

[41] *Ibid*. The term 'temporary refuge', as used by EXCOM as early as 1979 and 1980 in the context of large-scale influxes, had another connotation, unrelated to the expected possibility of return in the more or less near future. See EXCOM Conclusions No. 14 (XXX), 1979 and No. 19 (XXXI), 1980.

[42] See, e.g., UN General Assembly Resolution 1167 (XII) of 26 November 1957, GAOR, 12th Session, Supplement No. 18, p. 20; and Resolution 1388 (XIV) of 20 November 1959, GAOR, 14th Session, Supplement No. 16, p. 21; etc.

[43] See, e.g., UN General Assembly Resolution 1388 (XIV) of 20 November 1959, GAOR, 14th Session, Supplement No. 16, p. 21; and Resolution 1499 (XV) of 5 December 1960, GAOR, 15th Session, Supplement No. 16, vol. 1, p. 19, etc.

[44] See, e.g., UN General Assembly Resolutions 2197 (XXI) of 16 December 1966 and 2294 (XXII) of 11 December 1967, GAOR, 21st Session Supplement No. 16, p. 48 and 22nd Session, Supplement No. 16, p. 38, respectively.

texts,[45] while the UNHCR internal training manual clarifies that the term (as then used) applies to *externally* displaced persons who do not fully satisfy the criteria (at least, as then interpreted) for recognition as refugees.[46] Parenthetically it can be added that the same Indo-Chinese, to whom the term was applied in 1975, were subsequently 'elevated' to the status of refugees,[47] although in the Declaration of the International Conference on Indo-Chinese Refugees they are called 'asylum-seekers'.[48] European practice produced still more terms (see below). A curiosity is to be found in paragraph 2 of the Preamble to Resolution 688 (1991) of the UN Security Council, where reference is made to the 'flow of refugees *towards* and across international frontiers',[49] as if the term 'refugee' also could apply to people still within national territory. Further examples of inconsistent terminology from the practice of the UN General Assembly and the ECOSOC are quoted in the *Note on International Protection* of 1994.[50]

The concept of 'temporary protection', which was introduced in European practice against the background of developments in the former Yugoslavia and somewhat earlier in the practice of the United States ('temporary protected status' – TPS) and Australia ('temporary entry permits' – TES) with respect to nationals of specific states tormented by conflicts, blurs further the distinction between Convention refugees and others in need of protection. This temporary protection, which is granted for limited fixed periods with a possibility of prolongation, is different from Convention refugee status which is also temporary in nature by virtue of the cessation clause in article 1C(5) of the Convention, but which is not subject to a pre-set time limit. Resort to the concept of 'temporary protection', which has been 'absorbed' by the UNHCR, implies that the people in question are not regarded as 'genuine' Convention refugees to whom *the Convention cessation clause* would apply.

Another new frontier of the notion of 'refugee' concerns victims fleeing gender-related persecution. In 1985, the EXCOM recognised in paragraph (k) of its Conclusion No. 39 (XXXVI) 'that States . . . are free to adopt the interpretation that women asylum-seekers who face harsh or inhuman treatment due to their having transgressed the social mores of

---

[45] See, e.g., UN General Assembly Resolutions 3455 (XXX) of 9 December 1975 and 31/35 of 30 November 1976, GAOR, 30th Session, Supplement No. 34, p. 93 and 31st Session, Supplement No. 39, p. 94, respectively.

[46] UNHCR, *Introduction*, p. 35.

[47] See, e.g., GAOR, 40th Session, Supplement No. 12, Report of the UNHCR, 1985, p. 1.

[48] See UN Doc. A/CONF. 148/2, Part I, paras. 4, 8 and 9; and Part II.C (on the implications of this term, see below).

[49] See UN Security Council Resolution 688 (1991) of 5 April 1991 (emphasis added).

[50] See UN Doc. A/AC.96/830, p. 16, note 8.

the society in which they live may be considered as a "particular social group" within the meaning of article 1A(2) of the 1951 United Nations Refugee Convention'.[51] However, in 1993 – in paragraph (d) of Conclusion No. 73 (XLIV) – it '[s]upport[ed] the recognition as refugees of persons whose claim to refugee status is based upon a well-founded fear of persecution, *through sexual violence*, for reasons of race, religion, nationality, membership of a particular social group or political opinion'.[52]

The concept of gender-related persecution has thus acquired a double meaning. The first of the two above-quoted Conclusions classifies victims of such persecution as members of a 'particular social group', while the second focuses on sexual violence as a form of persecution giving rise to refugee status *when inflicted for any Convention reason.*

The 1993 Guidelines on gender-related persecution issued by the Canadian Immigration and Refugee Board – the first national quasi-normative instrument of its kind – rely primarily on the linkage of persecution with the five Convention grounds, but refer also to EXCOM Conclusion No. 39 (XXXVI).[53]

The question of gender-related persecution also highlighted the ambiguous meaning of 'particular social group' and the criteria on which people are to be recognised as such. The Gender Guidelines issued by the US Immigration and Naturalization Service in 1995, which represented a research paper rather than a normative instrument, focused on just this question and note different positions taken in the US jurisprudence on the applicability of the criterion of social group membership to gender-based persecution.[54] On the other hand, according to chapter 3 of the earlier mentioned 1996 amendment to the Swedish Aliens Law, victims of gender-related persecution quite unambiguously *do not* qualify as refugees (paragraph 2) but as 'others in need for protection' (paragraph 3), the social-group criterion apparently being regarded as inapplicable in this case.[55]

1994 marked another, almost 'revolutionary', change in approach to the concept of 'refugee'. The 1994 *Note on International Protection*, while

---

[51] See also UNHCR, *Guidelines on the Protection of Refugee Women*, Geneva, July 1991, p. 36, para. 54.

[52] See also para. (g) of Conclusion No. 77 (XLVI), 1995 (second emphasis added).

[53] See Immigration and Refugee Board (Canada), *Guidelines on Women Refugee Claimants Fearing Gender-Related Persecution*, text in 5 *International Journal of Refugee Law*, 1993, pp. 278–97.

[54] See Immigration and Naturalization Service (USA), *Gender Guidelines: Considerations for Asylum Officers Adjudicating Asylum Claims from Women*, text in 7 *International Journal of Refugee Law*, 1995, pp. 700–15. See also UNHCR, *Handbook*, p. 19, paras. 77–9, Refugee Women's Legal Group, *Gender Guidelines for the Determination of Asylum Claims in the UK* (London, 1998).   [55] See Act on Amendment to Aliens' Act (Sweden) SFS, 1996:1379.

maintaining that 'the continuing relevance of the grounds for refugee status contained in 1951 Convention definition is evident',[56] makes a switch from the 'well-founded fear of persecution' on certain grounds, as the basis of refugee status, to the 'need for international protection as a defining concept', for '[i]t is this vital need for international protection that most clearly distinguishes refugees from other aliens'.[57] The causal link is, in a sense, reversed. It is no longer the quality of 'refugee', however defined, which entitles one to protection. It is the need for protection that entitles one to treatment as a refugee. A 'comprehensive approach' is called for and the 'need for protection', whatever its quality in practice, has become a generic 'defining concept'. 'Protection-based comprehensive approaches' are also reflected in the *Notes on International Protection* of 1996 and 1997, which are otherwise focused mainly on practices (often regrettable) rather than on conceptual matters[58] and perhaps culminate in the recent statement by UNHCR which has declared a lack of 'direct concern' with '[s]uch details' as the 'meaning of phrases such as "well-founded fear", "persecution" and "membership of a particular social group"' and 'uses the refugee concept to denote those people who have had to leave or remain outside of their homeland because of serious threats to their life and liberty'.[59]

The 'comprehensive approach' has undermined even such an elementary criterion of refugee status as the requirement of being outside one's country of origin. Recognising that internally displaced persons quite often also need international protection, such protection is being offered in a number of cases, though with varying degrees of success.[60]

It is apparently in the spirit of this 'comprehensive approach' that one of the most recent statistical publications of the UNHCR provides that the term 'refugees' comprises: (i) those recognised as such by states parties to the Convention and/or the Protocol; (ii) those recognised as such under the OAU Convention and the Cartagena Declaration; (iii) those recognised by UNHCR as 'mandate refugees'; (iv) those granted residence on humanitarian grounds; and (v) those granted temporary protection on a group basis.[61]

---

[56] UN Doc. A/AC.96/830, para. 20.   [57] *Ibid.*, paras. 6 and 8.
[58] UN Doc. A/AC.96/863, 1 July 1996, para. 24. See also UN Doc. A/AC.96/882, 2 July 1997, paras. 3, 17 and 35 and the title of Section IV.
[59] UNHCR, *The State of the World's Refugees* (1997), pp. 51–2.
[60] See UNHCR, *UNHCR's Operational Experience with Internally Displaced Persons* (Geneva, September 1994), pp. 12, 28, 31–2, 38, 57 and 78–80; see also para. (g) of EXCOM Conclusion No.75 (XLV), 1994. See also UN Doc. EC/1994/SCP/CR W.P.2, 4 May 1994 (Conference Room Paper on Protection Aspects of UNHCR Activities on Behalf of Internally Displaced Persons).
[61] See UNHCR, *Refugees and Others of Concern to UNHCR: 1996 Statistical Overview* (Geneva, 1997), p. 1.

Is this then the definitive answer to the question of who is a 'refugee' in general? Apparently not, since UNHCR has shifted the boundaries between 'refugees' and 'others of concern'. In the corresponding statistics for the previous year (1995) humanitarian cases (group (iv)) are not classified as 'refugees' but as 'others of concern'.[62] Thus, it turns out that the concept, or definition, of 'refugee' can vary from one year to the next.

'Protection as a defining concept' has also come to be reflected in some national legislation, though without necessarily meaning that state practice has become more liberal. For instance, the amended Swedish Aliens Act already cited above deals in chapter 3 generally with '[p]ersons in need of protection'. Paragraph 2 of the chapter deals with 'refugees', approximately as defined in the Convention, while paragraph 3 deals with 'others in need of protection', namely those who (i) have a well-founded fear of capital or corporal punishment or of torture or other inhuman treatment, on whatever grounds, not only the Convention ones; (ii) cannot return to their countries because of international or national armed conflict or because of natural disaster; or (iii) have a well-founded fear of persecution because of gender or sexual orientation. Residence permits granted for 'humanitarian reasons' are dealt with separately (chapter 2), as being unrelated to 'protection' within the meaning of refugee law. On the other hand, deserters and conscientious objectors, who since 1976 had formally been entitled to asylum in Sweden (though were not regarded as refugees) have been dropped from the list of those in need of protection.

Convention definition in European interpretation

While the concept, or definition, of 'refugee' in Africa and Latin America, as well as on the global level, has tended to expand, the tendency in western Europe has been the opposite.

Western European states have always been 'Convention fundamentalist'. All the European conventions which, in one context or another, refer to 'refugees' explicitly indicate that the term is to be understood in the sense assigned to it in the Convention.[63] The 1990 Dublin Convention and the 1990 Schengen Convention applying the Schengen Agreement of 14 June 1985 also invoke the Convention and the Protocol as their sacrosanct basis.[64] The same is true of the three 1992 London Resolutions of

---

[62] *Ibid.*

[63] See European Treaty Series, No. 12, 1953 (Protocol, article 1); No. 13, 1953 (Protocol, article 1); No. 14, 1953 (Protocol, article 1); No. 31, 1959 (article 1(1)); No. 78, 1972 (article 1(o)); and No. 107, 1980 (article 1(a)).

[64] Convention determining the state responsible for examining applications for asylum lodged in one of the member states of the European Communities (the Dublin

the European Community Council of (Immigration) Ministers.[65] What distinguishes the European 'Convention fundamentalism' from that professed on the global level is that, unlike the latter, it manifests itself in an ever more restrictive interpretation and application of the Convention definition, culminating in the March 1996 Joint Position on the harmonised application of the term 'refugee' in article 1 of the Geneva Convention.[66] This in spite of numerous resolutions of the Council of Europe's Committee of Ministers and, particularly, of its Consultative (later Parliamentary) Assembly calling in various contexts for a liberal asylum policy.[67]

However, in the first post-war decades the 'Convention fundamentalism' of the European states was not perceptibly manifest. People arriving in this part of the world were, by and large, those initially contemplated by the Convention. Refugee situations in other continents were dealt with by separate resolutions of the UN General Assembly as indicated above. In such circumstances there was no need for a specific delineation of the notion of 'refugee' and there was no formal procedure for determining refugee status. The mass influx from Hungary in 1956 and from Czechoslovakia in 1968 did not alter this. The industrialised countries of western Europe were at that period able and willing to admit aliens on various bases, be they political, economic or humanitarian.

The situation began to change rapidly around the middle of the 1970s. Falling rates of economic growth and a consequent reduced demand for labour were one reason. Those in need of social assistance, including refugees, were becoming a burden in this context. Notions of 'B-refugees', 'de facto refugees' and suchlike emerged, which stressed the distinction between them and Convention refugees – the only 'genuine' ones. 'Convention fundamentalism' was thus implicit in the admission policies of the 1970s, which were still relatively liberal though toughening, and such lesser statuses were perceived as going beyond international legal obligations. These developments in western Europe coincided with, and were partly provoked by, 'larger and more complex migratory flows, blurring facile distinction between refugees and migrants', to use the words of UNHCR.[68] The number of arrivals in all industrialised countries was

Convention), 30 ILM 425, 1991; and Convention applying the Schengen Agreement on the gradual abolition of checks at common borders, 30 ILM 84, 1991. See preamble and articles 1(1)(b), 2, 3, 5 and 4 of the former and articles 1, 26, 28 and particularly article 135 of the latter.   [65] See UNHCR, *Collection*, p. 464.
[66] OJ, 1996, L63/2. See also Part 4 of this volume on the European regime.
[67] See *inter alia*, Council of Europe, Committee of Experts on the Legal Aspects of Territorial Asylum, Refugees and Stateless Persons (CAHAR), *Selected Texts Concerning Territorial Asylum and Refugees Adopted Within the Council of Europe* (Strasbourg, 1986); see also UNHCR, *Collection*, pp. 412–41.
[68] UNHCR, *The State of the World's Refugees* (1995), p. 197.

constantly growing and in the decade from 1983 to 1992 climbed from 100,000 to 849,000.[69]

Insofar as the 'complex migratory flows' followed a South–North direction, authorities and public opinion began, more or less reasonably, to assume that some – perhaps a greater part – of those coming from countries otherwise tormented by conflicts were, in fact, seeking economic betterment as opposed to protection. However, in the prevailing economic conditions and constraints on the admission of migrant workers, they tried to present their cases as 'refugees', perhaps not quite unreasonably, given the situations in their respective countries of origin and the apparent 'flexibility' of the refugee definition. Also the politico-psychological factors which in the first post-war decades favoured liberal admission policies worked now in the opposite direction, provoking a rise in xenophobia. Illegal or irregular transboundary movements, which have been perceived and portrayed as getting out of control, have become the main preoccupation of those who determine refugee policy, whose primary goal has become 'simply to keep the number of immigrants down'.[70]

Thus, in the 1970s European countries also introduced formal screening procedures and, as a consequence, a new notion, that of 'asylum seekers', emerged blurring further the delineation of the notion of 'refugee'. It appeared for the first time in the Conclusions of EXCOM in 1977[71] and in a resolution of the UN General Assembly in 1981.[72] 'Asylum seekers', as a category, are distinct from 'refugees', as is sometimes explicitly emphasised by governments.[73] This is thus a kind of position of suspense, subject to the outcome of screening which leads to the recognition or non-recognition as a refugee. Pending the outcome of screening, all 'asylum seekers' (as 'non-refugees') are not formally protected by *any* provision of the Convention which consistently speaks of *refugees*.

Formally, the determination of refugee status is *declaratory*, not constitutive, in character: a person does not become a refugee as a consequence of recognition, but is recognised because he or she is a refugee (according

---

[69] *Ibid.*, p. 196.   [70] *Ibid.*, p. 228.
[71] See Conclusion No. 5 (XXVIII), 1977.
[72] See UN General Assembly Resolution 36/125 of 14 December 1981, GAOR, 36th Session, Supplement No. 51, p. 178. In Resolution 34/60 of 29 November 1979, the term 'those seeking refuge' is used, GAOR, 34th Session, Supplement No. 46, p. 173.
[73] See, e.g., the Australian reservation to the EXCOM Conclusion No. 58 (XL), 1989, in UN Doc. A/AC.96/737, p. 23; see also article 3 of the Turkish *Regulation on Procedures and Principles related to ... [those] Wishing to Seek Asylum*, 14 September 1994 (Decision of the Council of Ministers No. 94/6169), text in 8 *International Journal of Refugee Law*, 1996, pp. 311–18.

to what interpretation of what definition?).[74] For the asylum seeker there is little comfort in this otherwise perfect logic, since unless recognised he or she will be treated, rightly or wrongly, as a 'non-refugee' with all the consequences (perhaps sometimes tragic) of non-recognition. Thus, for all practical purposes a refugee is one who is recognised as such. Indeed this understanding is even implied in some recent publications of UNHCR.[75]

The limitations of space preclude an analysis here of restrictive measures taken by European countries over the last two decades and especially in the 1990s, which were aimed at restricting the admission of aliens including refugees or potential refugees.[76] However, the essence of the attitude which had developed in Europe by the middle of the 1990s can be perhaps conveyed by some references to the 'Summary of Discussion' at the meeting of experts on the refugee problems in Europe held in Zürich in March 1996.[77] The 'protection-based comprehensive approach' was, in a sense, reversed. 'The topic for discussion was *whether or not international protection was required by other people*' than those envisaged (apparently, initially) by the Convention and the Protocol. With reference to the OAU Convention and the Cartagena Declaration, those 'other people' were termed 'externally displaced persons', as distinct from 'refugees' and the opinion was expressed that such persons 'are considered by the UN General Assembly within the overall competence of the High Commissioner for Refugees'.[78] The participants thus disclaimed any international obligation of individual states with respect to those people. However, since UNHCR cannot offer protection on its own premises, it has been realised long ago that 'the ultimate responsibility for refugees within the mandate of the High Commissioner falls in fact upon the countries of residence [or presence]'.[79]

As a result of this attitude, the rate of recognition as Convention refugees in western Europe, which in 1983 stood at 42 per cent, fell to approximately 16 per cent in 1996. For the sake of justice, it has to be added that an additional 10 per cent were allowed to remain on humanitarian

---

[74] UNHCR, *Handbook*, p. 9; also UNHCR, *Détermination du statut de réfugié, Module de formation* (Geneva, 1992), pp. 5–6.

[75] UNHCR, *1996 Statistical Overview*. EXCOM has used a somewhat less 'provocative' term – 'identified', rather than 'recognised' as refugees – for instance in para. (a) of the Conclusion No. 58 (XL), 1989.

[76] See below. See also UNHCR, *The State of the World's Refugees* (1997), pp. 191–4.

[77] Meeting of Experts on the Current Refugee Protection Problems in Europe, Zürich, 21–24 March 1996, *Summary of Discussion* (International Institute of Humanitarian Law, mimeograph). Sixteen countries (including Australia, Canada and the USA) participated. [78] *Ibid.*, paras. 16–18 (emphasis added).

[79] Para. 4 of the preamble to UN General Assembly Resolution 832 (IX) of 21 October 1954, GAOR, 9th Session, Supplement No. 21, p. 19.

grounds.[80] This total of 26 per cent is nevertheless considerably below the rate of formal recognition recorded in 1983. Moreover, the falling rate of admission must be seen against the number of applications, also falling in the great majority of European countries, due *inter alia* to measures aimed at preventing and deterring arrivals, such as the introduction of visa requirements from countries producing, or likely to produce, considerable flows of asylum seekers, the imposition of fines on companies transporting passengers without proper documents, and detention under intentionally protracted screening procedures, often under conditions of separation of families including children.

From this 'fundamentalist' point of view obligations of individual states under the Convention arise only when its potential beneficiaries appear at the border or in the territory of a state. Consequently, the Convention is of no relevance to measures aimed at the prevention of their arrival. Such measures are nevertheless apparently incompatible with 'the object and purpose' of the Convention – to use the language of the law of treaties – and also with the right to seek even if not to enjoy asylum, as proclaimed in article 14 of the Universal Declaration of Human Rights which is invoked in paragraph 2 of the preamble to the Convention. It must also be emphasised that, considerations of 'Convention fundamentalism' apart, the treatment of asylum seekers is subject to human rights law in general. For, even if they can be regarded as formally not having 'entered' the receiving state, they are under its jurisdiction, as a mere consequence of the fact that it is the receiving state which processes their applications and decides on their fate. Needless to add, the not so infrequent summary rejection of asylum seekers at the border and forcible return to the country of origin or sometimes to a rather arbitrarily determined 'safe third country' is, anyway, a violation of article 33 of the Convention.

The concept of 'refugee' in the developed countries outside Europe

Insofar as industrialised countries outside Europe are concerned, it appears that their respective concepts of 'refugee' are somewhat more loosely bound to the Convention definition, even though this definition was embraced by the US Refugee Act 1980,[81] and the Canadian

---

[80] Figures for 1983 from UNHCR, *The State of World's Refugees* (1995), pp. 196–7; figures for 1996 from UNHCR, *The State of the World's Refugees* (1997), pp. 290–2. Other sources provide different figures (see statistical tables in 8 *International Journal of Refugee Law*, 1996, pp. 483–6) but the tendency is the same: a dramatic fall in Europe and a considerable rise in otherwise much lower figures in the USA, Canada and Australia.

[81] Refugee Act 1980, 17 March 1980, Pub. L. No. 96–212, 94 Stat. 102 (1980).

Immigration Act 1985 speaks explicitly of 'Convention refugees'.[82] There are several reasons for such a situation. The USA did not immediately ratify the Convention, and assumed its Convention obligations only in 1968, when it ratified the Protocol. Similarly Canada ratified both the Convention and the Protocol only in 1969. In the meantime both states developed their own concepts of 'refugee' and their own refugee policies.

Another peculiarity of this group of states is that they are typically countries of immigration. In Canada, and especially in Australia and New Zealand, the admission of refugees is more or less a part of their immigration programmes. This situation is accentuated by the fact that a considerable percentage of refugees arrive in these countries within the framework of resettlement programmes: 92 per cent in the case of USA in the years 1987–96; 67 per cent in the case of Canada in the same period; 37 per cent in the case of Australia in the years 1989–96.[83] This means that refugees are selected for admission by national officials according to national criteria for eligibility for refugee status from among people already regarded as 'mandate refugees', with special emphasis on their expected adaptability as immigrants and also, especially in the case of Australia and New Zealand, on humanitarian considerations. The latter aspect also casts conspicuous light on how individual states interpret the Convention definition in apparently different ways. For Canada the rate of recognition as Convention refugees in the years 1987–96 was 62.7 per cent of applications, but the rate of admissions on humanitarian grounds was only 7.4 per cent. By contrast, for Australia the corresponding figures for years 1989–96 were 11 per cent and 81.5 per cent respectively.[84]

Moreover, countries of this group admit applications for asylum or refugee status from outside the country, that is, prior to arrival, which further blurs the distinction between refugees and simple immigrants. Indeed, this procedure, whatever its merits, disregards one of the basic elements of the Convention definition of 'refugee', that of being outside the country of origin.

In the USA, prior to 1980, the concept of 'refugee' was based on the national perception of the world and on Cold War considerations. Consequently, it was related to countries of origin. Persons fleeing communism or certain countries in the Middle East were generally 'presumed' to have valid reasons for flight, and were being admitted as refugees unless falling under one of the exclusion clauses applicable to all

---

[82] See Immigration Act 1976, RSC 1985 (4th Supplement), Chapter 1–2.
[83] UNHCR, *1996 Statistical Overview*, pp. 52 and 55 respectively. No figures are available for New Zealand.   [84] *Ibid.*

immigrants. Refugees from other countries had very small chances of being admitted as such. The Refugee Act of 1980 introduced a uniform worldwide standard and adopted a definition of 'refugee' virtually identical with that of the Convention. Yet, it appears that the earlier approach survived up to the 1990s. Statistics published in 1987 reveal that there were still big disproportions in the recognition rates between for example Poles (49–55 per cent) or Iranians (64–66 per cent) on the one hand, and Guatemalans (approximately 1 per cent) or Salvadorans (2–3 per cent) on the other hand.[85]

That discrimination was remedied in January 1991 by the settlement of *American Baptist Churches* v. *Thornburgh*.[86] The settlement coincided with the adoption of the Immigration Act 1990 which introduced the concept of 'temporary protected status' for victims of armed conflicts, natural disasters or other extraordinary temporary conditions in their home countries. This status is being granted on a group basis, again by selecting individual countries whose nationals are eligible for that status. The plight of Haitians intercepted on the high seas in the 1990s is another example of the application of the country criterion which is not envisaged by the Convention definition, leaving aside other aspects of that practice (prevention of arrivals and rendering the Convention irrelevant).

Indeed, the geographical element, though in much less pronounced form, is also present in the Australian concept of 'refugee', insofar as an applicant must usually fit into one of the five *regional* resettlement programmes.[87] 'Temporary entry permits', also known in Australian law where they are applicable to applicants from countries experiencing political and/or civil upheaval, are based on strict national criteria, for example, the Gulf countries, Lebanon, the former Yugoslavia, and China following the Tiananmen Square incident.

The countries of this group offer wide possibilities of review of decisions on asylum and recognition of refugee status, not only by administrative tribunals but also, under certain conditions, by courts of general jurisdiction. While it is not possible to review their jurisprudence in any detail here, it must be emphasised that, in general, it demonstrates 'Convention fundamentalism' in a much higher degree than in administrative practice. There are also considerable differences in judicial interpretation of Convention clauses not only between countries but even between courts of the same country.

---

[85] US General Accounting Office (GAO), *Asylum: Uniform Application of Standards Uncertain*, 9 January 1987.
[86] Order and Stipulated Settlement Agreement (N.D. Cal.), 31 January 1991.
[87] After D. Campbell and J. Fisher (eds.), *International Immigration and Nationality Law* (Martinus Nijhoff, Dordrecht, 1993), vol. I, AUS-IV-9.

The 'refugee' definition and customary international law

Both the tendency to amplify the Convention definition, be it by additions or by extensive interpretation, and the 'Convention fundamentalism' which, by restrictive interpretation, sometimes reduces its meaning to a mockery, bring us back to the question put at the beginning of this chapter: is the Convention definition universal or obsolete? As noted earlier, its universality, or quasi-universality, in the formal meaning cannot be questioned. However, it is arguable that the substance of the Convention definition is less universal now than it was when the Convention entered into force, or even less universal than could be claimed, say, some fifteen years ago.

Several factors have contributed to these developments. The adoption of the Cartagena Declaration in 1984 and the growing number of accessions to the OAU Convention have resulted in an increase in the number of states which embrace a broader concept or definition of 'refugee' than that of the Convention. The need for protection as a defining concept in distinguishing between refugees and other migrants, introduced by the UNHCR around the middle of the 1990s, has been another factor. Further, numerous amendments to national immigration and refugee legislation, which do not in any case follow the same pattern, have demonstrated the 'flexibility', or rather the *instability*, of the substance of the Convention definition. Accumulated national jurisprudence in refugee matters has revealed a broad range of interpretations of the Convention clauses, as have the opposite tendencies in this respect in the administrative practices in different parts of the world. Various 'refugee-like' categories have emerged in practice in response to pressing realities. As a result of all that, the Convention definition has become very diffuse.

International law recognises the 'dynamic' interpretation of treaties. In particular, according to article 31(3)(b) of the Vienna Convention on the Law of Treaties, 'subsequent practice in the application of the treaty' is an integral element of interpretation. However, the admissibility of such a 'dynamic' interpretation of a treaty presupposes an 'agreement [be it tacit or implicit] of the parties regarding its interpretation'.[88] Yet such an agreement is manifestly lacking in the case of the Convention definition of 'refugee'. On the contrary, 'subsequent practice' demonstrates a wide variety of interpretations and application.

It is certainly true that the Convention is still of 'fundamental importance', to use the words of the EXCOM, and enjoys the position of 'primacy . . . as forming the international legal basis for the protection of

---

[88] 1155 UNTS 331, p. 340.

refugees'.[89] Surely, the Convention definition is still 'fundamental' and 'basic', but not more than that. 'Fundaments' can erode here and there in the course of time. On the other hand, new structures can be erected here and there on the same 'basis'. It appears that this is precisely what has happened, bearing in mind, again, in the words of EXCOM, the 'changing . . . elements of the contemporary refugee problem' and the 'current size and characteristics of the refugee problem [which] necessitate appropriate reassessment of international responses'.[90] It is therefore submitted that the language of the Convention definition has become less adequate. This is indeed indirectly admitted whenever the question is raised about its possible amendment, even if it is at the same time recognised that an amendment is not feasible at present.[91] Nevertheless, inadequacy is not tantamount to obsolescence.

It is in this light that the possible status of a definition of 'refugee' as a norm of general customary international law should be seen. First of all, the question arises: what definition? Apparently not any definition of 'refugee in general', for there is no unambiguous one. Nor can it be any of the regional definitions, for the existence of a norm of customary international law must be evidenced by 'general practice *accepted as law*'.[92] Needless to argue that this is not the case of any regional definition. It remains therefore to consider the status of the Convention definition.

According to the Vienna Convention on the Law of Treaties, '[n]othing . . . precludes a rule set forth in a treaty from becoming binding upon a third State as a customary rule of international law recognised as such',[93] but, as the International Court of Justice (ICJ) indicated in the *North Sea Continental Shelf* case in 1969, 'this result is not lightly to be regarded as having been attained'.[94] Whatever might be said of the ICJ's decision in that particular case, that is, on the ICJ's interpretation of the status of the equidistance principle in article 6 of the Convention on the Continental Shelf of 1958 in customary international law, which was taken by a majority of eleven votes to six,[95] the authority of the general

---

[89] EXCOM Conclusion No. 77 (XLVI), 1995, para. (c). See also Conclusion No. 79 (XLVII), 1996, para. (c).
[90] Paragraph 4 of preamble to EXCOM Conclusion No. 62 (XLI), 1990.
[91] See, e.g., UN Doc. A/AC.96/799, 25 August 1992, *Note on International Protection*, p. 7; UN Doc. A/AC.96/837, 4 October 1994, p. 5 (Report of the Committee of the Whole [of EXCOM] on International Protection); also *Summary of Discussion*.
[92] Article 38(1)(b) of the ICJ Statute.   [93] Article 38, 1155 UNTS 331, p. 341.
[94] *North Sea Continental Shelf* case (Federal Republic of Germany/Denmark; Federal Republic of Germany/The Netherlands), judgment of 20 February 1969, *ICJ Reports*, 1969, p. 42, para. 71.
[95] *Ibid.*, p. 53, para. 101. Six judges from among the majority appended declarations or separate opinions (*ibid.*, pp. 54–6). In the case of *Delimitation of the Continental Shelf* between the UK and France the arbitral tribunal reasoned somewhat differently on this question, 54 ILR 1977, pp. 6, 48.

criteria for acquiring this status which the ICJ has established can hardly by questioned.

The ICJ ruled: 'It would in the first place be necessary that the provision concerned should . . . be of a fundamentally norm-creating character such as could be regarded as forming the basis of a general rule of law.'[96] At first glance, the Convention definition may seem to fulfil this requirement. However, with respect to the equidistance principle then at issue, the ICJ noted that 'controversies as to the exact meaning and scope of this notion, must raise . . . doubts as to the potentially norm-creating character of the rule'.[97] In our case the question is of 'differences' rather than 'controversies', but the differences 'as to the exact meaning and scope' of the notion of 'refugee' are indeed wider than the controversies around the equidistance principle.

The ICJ continued: 'With respect to other elements . . . it might be that . . . a very widespread and representative participation in the convention might suffice of itself, provided it included that of States whose interests were specially affected.'[98] It depends on interpretation whether the participation of 72 per cent of the states of the world in the Convention is to be regarded as 'very widespread', or whether it is sufficiently 'representative'. It should be borne in mind that it comprises only ten out of forty-eight Asian states, or 23 per cent of those states,[99] and that the parties to the Convention and/or the Protocol do not include such big and/or 'specially affected' states with refugee populations of over 100,000, as for example Bangladesh, India, Indonesia, Nepal, Pakistan or Thailand,[100] nor states which have generated mass flows of refugees, such as Afghanistan or Vietnam. One would perhaps hesitate to answer all these questions unequivocally in the positive. Parenthetically, it can be noted in this context that the 1977 Protocols I and II to the 1949 Geneva Conventions, which have gained more accessions than the Convention (146 to Protocol I, 138 to Protocol II) have not been regarded, in contradistinction to the Conventions themselves, as possessing the status of norms of customary international law, apparently because three of the five permanent members of the UN Security Council have not ratified them.[101]

[96] *North Sea Continental Shelf Case* p. 42, para. 72.   [97] *Ibid.*
[98] *Ibid.*, p. 43, para. 73.
[99] The ten states are Cambodia, China, Iran, Israel, Japan, Philippines, Solomon Islands, South Korea, Tuvalu and Yemen: UNHCR, *Multilateral Treaties*.
[100] UNHCR, *The State of World's Refugees* (1995), p. 249.
[101] See commentary to article 1 of Draft Statute of the International Criminal Tribunal for the Former Yugoslavia in the Report of the UN Secretary-General, UN Doc. S/25704, 3 May 1993, p. 9, para. 35; see also Security Council Resolution 827 (1993) of 25 May 1993 approving the report and the draft.

However, the last condition formulated by the ICJ is the most difficult one to be met by the Convention definition of 'refugee', namely, 'State practice . . . should have been both extensive and virtually uniform in the sense of the provision invoked.'[102] In the light of the aforesaid, it appears clear that there is no virtual uniformity of state practice in this sense. 'Varying interpretations of the refugee definition' have been admitted by UNHCR as late as 1994[103] and nothing has changed in this respect since.

It is therefore submitted that the Convention definition of 'refugee' would hardly stand judicial scrutiny of its status as a *norm* of general customary international law governing the *specific conduct* of all states, if the criteria formulated by the ICJ in 1969 were to be applied. This is, however, without prejudice to its authority, its enormous political and psychological impact, and its 'basic' and 'fundamental' character as a general obligation of *principle* (as distinct from a *norm*).

This chapter began with a proposition that the question of 'who is a refugee' appeared to be the key issue in discussing 'refugee rights and realities'. It should perhaps end with a reflection on whether it really is so. The question cannot be answered in an unambiguous manner which might serve as a basis for 'virtually uniform' practice. From the point of view of 'refugee realities' it is perhaps more important that states in practice follow common sense and 'recognise[e] the social and humanitarian nature of the problem of refugees'[104] and apply the Convention definition in accordance with the 'object and purpose' of the Convention, rather than approach it in a legalistic manner.

Bibliography

Documents and official publications

IIDH-ACNUR, *10 Años de la Declaración de Cartagena* (San José, 1995)
OAU/UNHCR, *Commemorative Symposium on Refugees and the Problems of Forced Population Displacements in Africa*, Addis Ababa, 8–10 September 1994, 7 *International Journal of Refugee Law*, Special Issue, 1995
UNHCR, *Collection of International Instruments and other Legal Texts Concerning Refugees and Displaced Persons* (HCR/IP/1/Eng./Rev.1, Geneva, 1995), vol. I and vol. II
    Conclusions on the International Protection of Refugees Adopted by the Executive Committee of the UNHCR Programme (HCR/IP/2/Eng./RV. 1992, Geneva, loose-leaf)

---

[102] *North Sea Continental Shelf*, p. 44, para. 74 (emphasis added).
[103] UN Doc. A/AC.96/830, p. 12.
[104] Para. 5 of the preamble to the Convention.

Handbook on Procedures and Criteria for Determining Refugee Status under the 1951 Convention and the 1967 Protocol Relating to the Status of Refugees (HCR/IP/4/Eng./Rev.2, Geneva, 1979, re-edited 1992)
The State of the World's Refugees: In Search of Solutions (Oxford University Press, 1995)
The State of the World's Refugees: A Humanitarian Agenda (Oxford University Press, 1997)
UN Documents of the Executive Committee of the UNHCR Programme, mimeograph/Series A/AC.96/... and A/AC.96/SR...
United Nations Resolutions and Decisions Relating to the Office of the United Nations High Commissioner for Refugees (5th edn HCR, INF.48/Rev. 4, loose-leaf)

Literature

Bhabha, J. and G. Coll (eds.), *Asylum Law and Practice in Europe and North America* (Federal Publications Inc., Washington DC, 1992)
Carlier, Jean-Yves, *et al.* (eds.), *Who is a Refugee? A Comparative Case Law Study* (Kluwer Law International, The Hague, 1997)
Goodwin-Gill, Guy S., 'Asylum: The Law and Politics of Change', 7 *International Journal of Refugee Law*, 1995, pp. 1–18.
The Refugee in International Law (2nd edn, Oxford University Press, 1996)
Grahl-Madsen, Atle, *The Status of Refugees in International Law* (Sijthof, Leiden, 1966–72)
Gros Espiell, Hector, 'Derechos humanos, derecho internacional humanitario y derecho internacional de los refugiados' in *Studies and Essays on International Humanitarian Law and Red Cross Principles in Honour of Jean Pictet* (ed. Christophe Swinarski, Comité international de la croix-rouge (CICR) and Martinus Nijhoff, Geneva and The Hague, 1984), pp. 699–712
Hathaway, James C., 'Refugee Status Arising from Generalized Oppression' in *The Living Law of Nations, Essays . . . in Memory of Atle Grahl-Madsen* (ed. G. Alfredsson and P. MacAlister-Smith, N. P. Engel, Kehl, Strasbourg and Arlington, 1996), pp. 61–8
The Law of Refugee Status (Butterworths, Toronto, 1991)
Jackson, Ivor C., 'The 1951 Convention Relating to the Status of Refugees: A Universal Basis for Protection', 3 *International Journal of Refugee Law*, 1991, pp. 403–13
Jaeger, Gilbert, 'Les Nations Unies et les réfugiés', *Revue belge de droit international*, 1989, 1, pp. 19–120
'Refugees or Migrants?' in *NGOs and Refugees: Reflections at the Turn of Century* (ed. M. Kjaerum *et al.*, Danish Centre for Human Rights, Copenhagen, 1993), pp. 143–68
Lee, Luke T., 'Progressive Development of Refugee Law and its Codification' in *International Law in Transition: Essays in Memory of Judge Nagendra Singh* (ed. P. S. Pathak and R. P. Dhokalia, Nijhoff, Dordrecht, 1992), pp. 107–66
Meijers, H., 'Refugees in Western Europe: "Schengen" Affects the Entire Refugee Law', 2 *International Journal of Refugee Law*, 1990, pp. 428–41
Melander, Göran, *The Two Refugee Definitions* (Raoul Wallenberg Institute of Human Rights and Humanitarian Law, Report No. 4, Lund, 1987)

Nobel, Peter, 'What Happened to Sweden's Refugee Policies?', 2 *International Journal of Refugee Law*, 1990, pp. 265–73

Patrnogic, Jovica, 'International Protection of Refugees in Armed Conflicts' (reprint from *Annales de droit international médical*, July 1981)

Sieverts, Frank Arne, 'The Refugee Definition and Vulnerable Groups' in *The Living Law of Nations, Essays . . . in Memory of Atle Grahl-Madsen* (eds. G. Alfredsson and P. MacAlister-Smith, N. P. Engel, Kehl, Strasbourg and Arlington, 1996), pp. 83–8

Wolfrum, R. (ed.), *United Nations: Law, Policies and Practice*, Section 107, 'Refugees, Including UNHCR' (C. H. Beck Verlag, Munich, 1995), vol. II, pp. 1025–39

4 Beyond the Geneva Convention: constructing a *de facto* right of asylum from international human rights instruments

Richard Plender and Nuala Mole

Other chapters in Part 1 have focused on issues concerning the refugee definition and refugee rights under the 1951 Geneva Convention Relating to the Status of Refugees[1] and the 1967 New York Protocol.[2] This chapter examines the other international or regional instruments affecting the rights of refugees and asylum seekers. The first section sets out the most relevant international and regional instruments; the second how these apply to the entry of asylum seekers, their detention, their right to family life and their right to an effective remedy.

International instruments in addition to the Geneva Convention

The Universal Declaration of Human Rights

Chief of these other instruments is the Universal Declaration of Human Rights,[3] adopted by the General Assembly of the United Nations as 'a common standard of achievement for all . . . nations, to the end that every . . . organ of society . . . shall strive . . . to secure their universal and effective recognition and observance'.[4] By article 14 of that Declaration, one of these rights is 'the right to seek and to enjoy in other countries asylum from persecution', subject to restrictions in the case of 'prosecutions genuinely arising from non-political crimes and from acts contrary to the purposes and principles of the United Nations'.[5]

Article 14 does not provide for a right to *receive* asylum. Indeed, the word 'receive' was removed from an earlier draft during the course of the negotiations on the text. The omission of that word is significant, but it

---

[1] Geneva, 28 July 1951, 189 UNTS 137, Cmd 9171.
[2] New York, 31 January 1967, 606 UNTS 267, Cmnd 3906.
[3] General Assembly Resolution 217 A (III) of 10 December 1948, 42 *American Journal of International Law*, 1949, Supplement 127. [4] *Ibid*, preamble (emphasis added).
[5] *Ibid.*, article 14(2).

should not lead us to disregard article 14 altogether. The right to *seek and enjoy* asylum is not an empty phrase. For instance, a state may violate the right to seek asylum when it returns an applicant to the country whence he or she came without giving him or her an adequate opportunity to present his or her case and it may violate the right to *enjoy* asylum when it accepts an individual as a refugee but imposes upon him or her excessive restraints such as unreasonable conditions of detention.

The right to seek and enjoy asylum is a universal right. The proclamation of that right in the Universal Declaration inspires and assists in the interpretation of the more specific instruments, concluded at the international level, which may form the basis for individual claims before international tribunals or (where national law so provides) before national courts.

The International Covenant on Civil and Political Rights

No right to receive, or even to seek, asylum was expressly incorporated into the International Covenant on Civil and Political Rights (ICCPR) 1966,[6] even though it had been included in the draft prepared by the Human Rights Commission in 1954. As in the case of the European Convention on Human Rights (discussed in the next section of this chapter), the proposal to include such a right in the ICCPR was rejected as incompatible with the sovereign power of states to decide whether to admit or exclude aliens from their territory.[7]

The UN Human Rights Commission nevertheless incorporated into the Covenant a provision which provides protection for aliens, lawfully in the territory of a member state, from being arbitrarily expelled from that country. Article 13 provides:

An alien lawfully in the territory of a State Party to the present Covenant may be expelled therefrom only in pursuance of a decision reached in accordance with law and shall, except where compelling reasons of national security otherwise require, be allowed to submit the reasons against his expulsion and to have his case reviewed by, and be represented for the purpose before, the competent authority or a person or persons especially designated by the competent authority.

The ICCPR has been ratified by 144 states as of 4 February 1999. Only six states have made reservations or interpretative declarations regarding the rights guaranteed by article 13.[8] They include the United Kingdom

[6] 6 ILM, 1967, p. 368.
[7] See Manfred Nowak, *UNO-Pakt über bürgerliche und politische Rechte und Fakultativprotokoll – CCPR Kommentar* (N. P. Engel Verlag, Kehl, 1989), article 13/3–13/4.
[8] These states are France, Iceland, Malta, Mexico, Monaco and the UK. Finland withdrew a reservation concerning article 13 in 1985 after legislation was amended to conform to

which has entered a general reservation stating that article 13 as well as all other provisions of the Covenant shall not preclude immigration measures.[9]

The Convention Against Torture

The United Nations Convention Against Torture and Other Cruel, Inhuman or Degrading Treatment or Punishment,[10] adopted in 1984 and effective since 1987, contains one provision of interest to asylum seekers. Article 3 provides:

1. No State Party shall expel, return (*'refouler'*) or extradite a person to another State where there are substantial grounds for believing that he would be in danger of being subjected to torture.
2. For the purposes of defining whether there are such grounds, the competent authorities shall take into account all relevant considerations including, where applicable, the existence in the State concerned of a consistent pattern of gross, flagrant or mass violations of human rights.[11]

The European Convention on Human Rights

Like the ICCPR, no right to receive or even to seek asylum was included in the European Convention for the Protection of Human Rights and Fundamental Freedoms in 1950.[12] It was not until 22 November 1984, when the Council of Europe adopted Protocol No. 7 to the European Convention on Human Rights, that the contracting parties undertook the obligation to refrain from the arbitrary expulsion of aliens from the

the ICCPR. See also Human Rights Committee, *General Comment No. 24(52)* on issues relating to reservations made upon ratification or accession to the Covenant or the Optional Protocols thereto, or in relation to declarations under article 41 of the Covenant, 11 November 1994, CCPR/C/21/Rev.1/Add.6.

[9] Nuala Mole, 'Immigration and Freedom of Movement', in *The International Covenant on Civil and Political Rights and United Kingdom Law* (ed. David J. Harris and Sarah Joseph; Clarendon Press, Oxford, 1995).

[10] Adopted by the UN General Assembly and opened for signature on 10 December 1984 (Resolution 39/46); entered into force on 26 June 1987. As of 4 February 1999 there were 112 parties to the Convention.

[11] This provision is not mirrored in the 1987 European Convention for the Prevention of Torture and Inhuman and Degrading Treatment or Punishment (ETS 126), which 'merely' sets up a European Committee for the Prevention of Torture and Inhuman or Degrading Treatment or Punishment which is authorised to visit 'any place within [a party's] jurisdiction where persons are deprived of their liberty by a public authority' (article 2) with a view to strengthening the protection from torture provided *inter alia* by article 3 of the European Convention on Human Rights.

[12] Adopted in Rome on 4 November 1950 and entered into force 3 September 1953, 40 parties as of 4 January 1999, 213 UNTS 221; ETS 5.

territory of a contracting state where they are lawfully resident.[13] As of
4 January 1999 this Protocol had been ratified by twenty-six states.

The European Social Charter

The economic, social and cultural rights set out in the Geneva
Convention have been incorporated into the 1961 European Social
Charter[14] by way of an Appendix entitled 'Scope of the Social Charter in
terms of persons protected'. Paragraph 2 of that Appendix provides:

Each Contracting Party will grant to refugees as defined in the Convention relating to the Status of Refugees, signed at Geneva on 28 July 1951, and lawfully
staying in its territory, treatment as favourable as possible, and in any case not less
favourable than under the obligations accepted by the Contracting Party under
the said Convention and under any other existing international instruments applicable to those refugees.[15]

These rights are therefore, indirectly, subject to the supervisory mechanism set up under the European Social Charter, which includes the
examination of the two-yearly state reports[16] by a Committee of
Independent Experts.[17] In 1996 a Revised European Social Charter[18]
with a comparable Appendix was agreed. It has since been signed by eighteen Council of Europe states and ratified by one but has yet to enter into
force.

Other regional conventions

Unlike the Universal Declaration, the European Convention on Human
Rights and the ICCPR, the two major remaining regional human rights
instruments, the 1969 American Convention on Human Rights[19] and the
1981 African Charter on Human and Peoples' Rights,[20] both contain an

[13] ETS 117, entered into force 1 November 1988. Article 1 reads:
  1. An alien lawfully resident in the territory of a State shall not be expelled therefrom
  except in pursuance of a decision reached in accordance with law and shall be allowed:
  a. to submit reasons against his expulsion;
  b. to have his case reviewed; and
  c. to be represented for these purposes before the competent authority or a person or
  persons designated by that authority.
  2. An alien may be expelled before the exercise of his rights under paragraph 1a, b and c
  of this article, when such expulsion is necessary in the interests of public order or is
  grounded on reasons of national security.
[14] Signed in Turin on 18 October 1961 and entered into force on 26 February 1965.
[15] Article 38 of the European Social Charter stipulates that the Appendix 'shall form an
  integral part of it'.   [16] Ibid., article 21.
[17] Ibid., articles 24 and 25 (as amended by articles 2 and 3 of the Protocol amending the
  European Social Charter of 21 October 1991).   [18] ETS 163.
[19] 9 ILM, 1970, p. 673; OAS Treaty Series 36.   [20] 21 ILM, 1982, p. 58.

express right to seek and be granted or obtain asylum in another territory or country.

Article 22(7) of the former states:

Every person has the right to seek and be granted asylum in a foreign territory, in accordance with the legislation of the state and international conventions, in the event he is being pursued for political offences or related common crimes.[21]

Article 12(3) of the latter states:

Every individual shall have the right, when persecuted, to seek and obtain asylum in other countries in accordance with laws of those countries and international conventions.

Jurisprudence developed by the Inter-American human rights system includes notably the *Haitian Interdiction* v. *United States* case, in which the Inter-American Commission of Human Rights ruled that the US government's policy of interdicting Haitian boat people on the high seas had violated provisions of the American Declaration, including the right to 'seek and receive asylum'.[22]

Asylum seekers' right to enter

The principle of *non-refoulement*

The general instruments governing the protection of human rights characteristically require contracting states to secure the extension of the rights in question to 'everyone within their jurisdiction'[23] or to any person 'within [their] territory and subject to [their] jurisdiction'.[24] Thus the

---

[21] The similarly worded article XXVII of the American Declaration of the Rights and Duties of Man adopted by the Ninth International Conference of American states in Bogotá, Colombia, in 1948 states: 'Every person has the right, in case of pursuit not resulting from ordinary crimes, to seek and receive asylum in foreign territory, in accordance with the laws of each country and with international agreements.' Although originally adopted as a non-binding resolution, the Inter-American Court of Human Rights has subsequently confirmed the American Declaration as an authoritative interpretation of the references to human rights in the Charter of the Organisation of American States (OAS). See also Scott Davidson, 'The Civil and Political Rights Protected in the Inter-American Human Rights System' in *The Inter-American System of Human Rights* (ed. David J. Harris and Stephen Livingstone, Clarendon Press, Oxford, 1998), especially pp. 227–80.

[22] Case 10.675, Report No. 51/96, 13 March 1997, 5 IHRR, 1998, pp. 120–65.

[23] European Convention on Human Rights, article 1. In Application No. 1611/62, *X.* v. *Federal Republic of Germany*, decision of 25 September 1965, 8 *Yearbook of the European Convention on Human Rights*, 1965, p. 158, the Commission stated at p. 168:

Whereas in certain respects, the nationals of a Contracting State are within its 'jurisdiction' even when ... abroad; whereas, in particular, the diplomatic and consular representations of their country of origin perform certain duties with regard to them which may, in certain circumstances, make that country liable in respect of the Convention.

[24] ICCPR, article 2.

state continues to enjoy, subject only to very specific exceptions,[25] the sovereign right to exclude or admit an alien to its territory. In general, the question of a person's human rights arises only once he or she has entered the territory of a contracting party. However, the European Commission and Court of Human Rights have now made it clear that the phrase 'within their jurisdiction' includes responsibility for the acts of visa officials in an overseas embassy,[26] of officials in the international zone of airports[27] and for the acts of their authorities whether performed inside or outside their national boundaries.[28]

Furthermore, aliens unlawfully present enjoy the protection of the international machinery for the protection of human rights, to the extent that this protects them from forcible return to countries where they face the risk of persecution. In the well-known terms of the Geneva Convention, the protection so afforded is expressed in the principle of *non-refoulement*. As will be seen the emerging jurisprudence of the European Commission and Court of Human Rights makes it clear that aliens unlawfully on the territory may also be protected from expulsion if they would face exposure to torture or inhuman or degrading treatment, or if the act of expulsion would itself constitute torture or inhuman or degrading treatment.[29]

The Committee Against Torture

In an early decision upon this issue, following a complaint made against Switzerland, the Committee Against Torture set out the principles to apply when considering whether the expulsion of an asylum seeker would violate article 3 of the Convention Against Torture:

The aim of the determination, however, is to establish whether the individual concerned would be *personally* at risk of being subjected to torture in the country to which he would return. It follows that the existence of a consistent pattern of gross, flagrant or mass violations of human rights in a country does not as such constitute a sufficient ground for determining that a person would be in danger of

---

[25] The rules applicable in those circumstances relate in particular to the right of non-discrimination, the prohibition of inhuman treatment and respect for family life. See UN Human Rights Committee, *General Comment No. 15(27)* (The Position of Aliens under the Covenant) of 22 July 1986, CCPR/C/21/Rev.1/Add. 5, para. 5.

[26] *X. v. Federal Republic of Germany*, judgment, p. 168.

[27] *Amuur* v. *France*, Application No. 19776/92, judgment of 25 June 1996, *Reports of Judgments and Decisions* 1996–III; 22 EHRR, 1996, p. 533.

[28] *Loizidou* v. *Turkey* (Preliminary Objections) Case No. 40/1993/435/514, judgment of 26 June 1995, Series A, No. 310.

[29] See e.g. *H. L. R.* v. *France*, Application No. 11/1996/629/813, judgment of 29 April 1997, *Reports of Judgments and Decisions*, 1997–III; *D.* v. *UK*, Application No. 30240/96, judgment 2 May 1997, Series B, No. 37.

being subjected to torture upon his return to that country; additional grounds must exist that indicate that the individual concerned would be personally at risk. Similarly, the absence of a consistent pattern of gross violations of human rights does not mean that a person cannot be considered to be in danger of being subjected to torture in his specific circumstances.[30]

In finding that there were substantial grounds for believing that the applicant would be in danger of being subjected to torture, the Committee had regard, *inter alia*, to reports on the human rights situation in the applicant's home country (Zaire) prepared by the UN Secretary-General and the UN Special Rapporteur on Extrajudicial, Summary or Arbitrary Executions, the UN Special Rapporteur on Torture and the UN Working Group on Enforced or Involuntary Disappearances.

Moreover, the Committee considers that, in view of the fact that Zaire is not a party to the Convention, the [applicant] would be in danger, in the event of expulsion to Zaire, not only of being subjected to torture but *of no longer having the legal possibility of applying to the Committee for protection.*[31]

Since the decision in *Mutombo*, other important points have emerged from the jurisprudence of the Committee. In particular in the case of *Kisoki v. Sweden*,[32] it noted that it was normal for people who have been tortured to disclose only piecemeal the detailed story of their experiences and suggested that this should not of itself damage an asylum claimant's credibility. In *Ismail Alan v. Switzerland*[33] the Committee considered the question of the feasibility of an internal flight alternative and found that such an alternative was not available to the applicant in Turkey.[34]

The European Convention on Human Rights

A similar protection against *non-refoulement* has been developed by the European Commission and Court of Human Rights in its jurisprudence under article 3 of the European Convention on Human Rights. Article 3 provides: 'No one shall be subjected to torture or to inhuman or degrading treatment or punishment.'

---

[30] *Balabou Mutombo v. Switzerland*, Communication No. 13/1993, decision of 27 April 1994 at para. 9.3.   [31] *Ibid.*, para. 9.6 (emphasis added). (Since this ruling Zaire has become a party to the Convention Against Torture.)

[32] Communication No. 41/1996; 8 *International Journal of Refugee Law*, 1996, p. 651.

[33] Communication No. 21/1995; 8 *International Journal of Refugee Law*, 1996, p. 440.

[34] See also *Tala v. Sweden*, Communication No. 43/1996; 5 IHRR, 1998, p. 113; and *Aemi v. Switzerland*, Communication No. 34/1995. See also the judgment of the European Court of Human Rights on 30 October 1997 in the case of *Paez v. Sweden* (18/1997/802/1005) where the Court took into account the fact that the applicant's brother's complaint had been upheld by the Committee Against Torture.

In its decision in *Soering* v. *UK*,[35] which concerned the extradition of the applicant from the UK to the United States where he could have been subject to the death penalty, the European Court of Human Rights established that, in cases of extradition, states parties have an inherent obligation towards individuals who, if extradited, would face a real risk of being exposed to torture, inhuman or degrading treatment.[36] At that time the UK was not a party to the 6th Protocol[37] of the European Convention (which outlaws the death penalty) so the matter had to be considered in the context of the death row phenomenon. For those states which are parties to the 6th Protocol it seems that an expulsion or extradition to face the death penalty would, *ipso facto*, be a breach of the Protocol.[38] The Commission found admissible under article 2, which protects the right to life, the question of expulsion to face the risk of death in the cases of *D.* v. *UK*[39] and *Bahaddar* v. *Netherlands*[40] but went on to examine the complaints only under article 3. The Commission in its report in *Bahaddar* considered that although there may be circumstances under which it would be appropriate to consider expulsion under article 2, it chose to look only to article 3. The Court reiterated the principle in *Soering* in relation to expulsions not involving extradition in *Cruz Varas* v. *Sweden*[41] and *Vilvarajah* v. *UK*.[42]

For many years respondent governments nevertheless continued to assert that the Convention had no application to expulsion cases. In *Chahal* v. *UK*,[43] the UK government abandoned the objections which it had maintained before the Commission and eventually accepted the applicability of the Convention in its pleadings before the Court. The case concerned the UK's proposal to deport to India an Indian national accused of committing and plotting acts of terrorism, including involvement in a plot to assassinate prime minister Rajiv Gandhi, in support of Sikh separatists

---

[35] *Soering* v. *UK*, judgment of 7 July 1989, Series A, No. 161; 11 EHRR, 1989, p. 439.
[36] *Ibid.*, para. 91.
[37] ETS 114. The UK has since signed the 6th Protocol on 27 January 1999.
[38] *Aylor-Davis* v. *France*, 76A *Decisions and Reports*, p. 164. In that case assurances had been given by the state of Texas that the death penalty would not be sought. See also *Raidl* v. *Austria*, Application No. 25342/94 (1995), 82A *Decisions and Reports*, p. 134.
[39] *D.* v. *UK*, Application No. 30240/96, Commission Report adopted 15 October 1996.
[40] *Bahaddar* v. *Netherlands*, Application No. 25894/94, Commission Report adopted 13 September 1996.
[41] Application No. 46/1990/237/307, judgment of 20 March 1991, Series A, No. 201, 14 EHRR, 1991, p. 1.
[42] Application No. 45/1990/236/302–306, judgment of 30 October 1991, Series A, No. 215, 14 EHRR, 1991, p. 248.
[43] Application No. 22414/93, Commission report adopted 27 June 1995; Court judgment of 15 November 1996, *Reports of Judgments and Decisions*, 1996–V, paras. 72–82; 23 EHRR, 1997, p. 413. For further details of this case as considered in the English courts see chapter 6 below.

in Punjab. In that case, both the Commission[44] and the Court[45] rejected the UK's contention that states parties are liable for torture, inhuman or degrading treatment only if this is inflicted within their own jurisdiction. In its 1996 judgment the Court of Human Rights held:

> The prohibition provided by Article 3 against ill-treatment is equally absolute in expulsion cases. Thus *whenever substantial grounds have been shown for believing that an individual would face a real risk of being subjected to treatment contrary to Article 3 if removed to another State, the responsibility of the Contracting State to safeguard him or her against such treatment is engaged in the event of expulsion* . . . In these circumstances the activities of the individual in question, however undesirable or dangerous, cannot be a material consideration. The protection afforded by Article 3 is thus wider than that provided by Articles 32 and 33 of the United Nations 1951 Convention on the Status of Refugees.[46]

The Court's point requires reiteration. Unlike the 1951 Convention, article 3 of the European Convention does not provide for nor allow any restriction as to who is protected. It is also non-derogable.[47] It is therefore not restricted to those persecuted on grounds of 'race, religion, nationality, membership of a particular social group or political opinion'.[48] Furthermore, there is no provision for the exclusion of those who have committed a 'serious non-political crime outside the country of their refuge'.[49] As the European Court of Human Rights had previously made clear in the *Soering* case, the protection of article 3 applies to everyone, 'however heinous the crime allegedly committed'.[50] Nor is there a provision permitting the exclusion of any person 'whom there are reasonable grounds for regarding as a danger to the security of the country in which he is, or who, having been convicted by a final judgment of a particularly serious crime, constitutes a danger to the community of that country'.[51] On the contrary the European Convention organs have now held in a series of cases[52] that this is not a material consideration.

---

[44] *Ibid.*, para. 101, quoting a passage from *Vilvarajah* v. *UK* at para. 103.
[45] *Chahal* judgment, paras. 72–82.   [46] *Ibid.*, para. 80 (emphasis added).
[47] Article 15 of the European Convention on Human Rights provides:
   1. In time of war or other public emergency threatening the life of the nation, any High Contracting Party may take measures derogating from its obligations under this Convention to the extent strictly required by the exigencies of the situation, provided that such measures are not inconsistent with its other obligations under international law.
   2. No derogation from Article 2, except in relation to deaths resulting from lawful acts of war, or from Articles 3, 4 (paragraph 1) and 7 shall be made under this provision.
[48] Geneva Convention, article 1(A).   [49] *Ibid.*, article 1(F).
[50] *Soering* judgment, para. 88, quoted below; see also *Chahal* judgment, paras. 104–5.
[51] Geneva Convention, article 33(2).
[52] *Ahmed* v. *Austria*, Application No. 25964/94, judgment of 17 December 1996, *Reports of Judgments and Decisions*, 1996–VI; 24 EHRR, 1997, p. 278; *Chahal* v. *UK*; *H. L. R.* v. *France*.

The European Court of Human Rights laid down the test for what constitutes 'a real risk of treatment contrary to Article 3' in *Cruz Varas v. Sweden*. It ruled:

The ill-treatment must attain a minimum level of severity if it is to fall within the scope of Article 3. The assessment of this minimum is, in the nature of things, relative. It depends on all the circumstances of the case, such as the nature and context of the treatment, the manner and method of its execution, its duration, its physical or mental effects and, in some instances, the sex, age and state of health of the victim.[53]

This ill-treatment need not take the form of deliberate persecution at the hands of agents of the state from which the refugee fled. The Commission has had occasion in a number of cases to consider danger which did not emanate from the authorities of the state of origin, but had until recently not found it necessary to rule on the point because of lack of evidence.[54]

In the recent case of *Ahmed v. Austria*[55] the Commission expressly found that the absence of state authority in Somalia was immaterial to the issue which arose under article 3. The judgment of the Court in the same case did not specifically refer to the point but did not dispute the Commission's view and went on to uphold its finding of a violation. In the case of *H.L.R. v. France*,[56] the French government sought to argue before both the Commission and the Court that, as the UN Torture Convention expressly provided that the state authorities must be responsible for the ill-treatment, the European Convention should be interpreted in this way too. The Court in *Chahal* considered the assurances of the Indian government to the effect that the applicant 'would enjoy the same legal protection as any other Indian citizen and that he would have no reason to expect to suffer mistreatment of any kind at the hands of the Indian authorities' but ultimately found that such assurances did not provide Chahal with adequate guarantees of safety. In *H. L. R. v. France*, the Court upheld the Commission's view that the threat did not have to emanate from agents of the state, but found no violation on the facts of the case. The judgment in *D. v. UK* has settled the matter once and for all. It was accepted by all parties that the government of the state of destination could not be held responsible for the destitution that the applicant would face if returned, but the Court nevertheless found that his expulsion would be a violation of article 3.[57]

[53] *Cruz Varas* judgment, paras. 75, 76 and 83; see also *Vilvarajah* judgment, paras.107–8 and the Commission report in *Chahal*, para. 107.
[54] *Nasri v. France*, Application No. 19465/92, judgment of 13 July 1995; Series A, No. 320B; 21 EHRR, 1995, p. 458; *Ahmed v. Austria*; *H. L. R. v. France*; *D. v. UK*.
[55] *Ahmed* judgment, para. 46.   [56] *H. L. R.* judgment, para. 32.
[57] *D. v. UK* judgment, paras. 52–4.

Article 3 also applies to the case of the so-called 'refugee in orbit'. In its report in the case of *Harabi* v. *The Netherlands*,[58] the Commission, following an earlier admissibility decision,[59] held:

that the repeated expulsion of an individual, whose identity was impossible to establish, to a country where his admission is not guaranteed, may raise an issue under Article 3 of the Convention . . . Such an issue may arise, *a fortiori*, if an alien is over a long period of time deported repeatedly from one country to another without any country taking measures to regularise his situation.[60]

Unlike the 1951 Convention which applies only to persons outside their country of nationality,[61] the circle of protected persons under article 3 of the European Convention on Human Rights can include those dependent relatives of the asylum seeker who, in consequence of his or her deportation, are effectively forced into exile and are faced with a serious threat of torture or of inhuman or degrading treatment. In the case of *Fadele* v. *UK*,[62] the Commission declared admissible a complaint under article 3, where the UK denied the Nigerian father of three British children the right to come to the UK to settle with his children. They complained that to make the children change their lifestyle radically by forcing them to join their father in extremely poor living conditions in Nigeria, rather than allow him to settle with them, would result in the UK breaching article 3.[63] No decision on the merits was ever reached as the case was settled through the good offices of the Commission.[64]

The International Covenant on Civil and Political Rights

Article 7 of the Covenant contains a similar prohibition on torture and adds 'cruel' to inhuman or degrading as prohibited treatment or punishment. The Human Rights Committee, like the European Convention organs, has interpreted this to include a prohibition on expulsion to face such treatment. In its second General Comment on article 7, the Committee stated: 'States parties must not expose individuals to the danger of torture or cruel or inhuman or degrading treatment or punishment on return to another country by way of their extradition, expulsion

---

[58] *Harabi* v. *Netherlands*, Application No. 10798/84, 46 *Decisions and Reports*, p. 112.
[59] *Giama* v. *Belgium*, Application No. 7612/76, *Yearbook of the European Convention on Human Rights*, 1980, p. 428; 21 *Decisions and Reports*, p. 73.
[60] *Harabi* v. *Netherlands*, p. 116.   [61] Article 1A(2).
[62] *Fadele* v. *UK*, Application No. 13078/87, 70 *Decisions and Reports*, p. 159.
[63] *Ibid.*, p. 161, para. 8.
[64] The settlement took the form of the father being issued with an entry clearance for settlement and the UK government paying both the air fare for the whole family as well as the legal costs actually and reasonably incurred: *ibid.*, para. 12.

or *refoulement*.'[65] The case law of the Committee under the Optional Protocol on this aspect of article 7 has largely been devoted to extradition issues, and in particular to the situation of an individual facing the imposition of the death penalty if convicted on return. In *Kindler* v. *Canada*,[66] the Committee held: '[A] state party would itself be in violation of the Covenant if it handed over a person to another state in circumstances in which it was foreseeable that torture would take place. The foreseeability of the consequence would mean that there was a present violation by the state party even though the consequence would not occur until later.'

Detention of asylum seekers

The detention of asylum seekers, whether made before a decision to admit the asylum seekers as refugees or under some other status, or prior to expulsion or return, raises a series of issues under international human rights instruments.

The legality of the detention of asylum seekers under the European Convention on Human Rights

Article 5 (1) of the European Convention on Human Rights provides:

No one shall be deprived of his liberty save in the following cases and in accordance with a procedure prescribed by law: . . .
(f.) the lawful arrest or detention of a person to prevent his effecting an unauthorised entry into the country or of a person against whom action is being taken with a view to deportation or extradition.

In *Lynas* v. *Switzerland*,[67] the Commission established that, although there is no right not to be extradited or expelled under the Convention, only the existence of extradition (or deportation) proceedings are capable of justifying the deprivation of liberty under article 5(1)(f).[68] Therefore, where such proceedings are not conducted with 'due diligence' or where the detention results from a misuse of authority the detention ceases to be so justified. These principles were reiterated in the Commission's deci-

---

[65] Human Rights Committee, *General Comment No. 20(44)* (article 7), CCPR/C/21/Rev.1/Add.3, para. 9.
[66] *Kindler* v. *Canada*, Communication No. 470/1991.
[67] Application No. 7317/75, 6 *Decisions and Reports*, p. 141.
[68] In the context of the ICCPR the Human Rights Committee held that detention pending deportation did qualify as deprivation of liberty under article 9(1): see Communication No. 155/1983 *Hammel* v. *Madagascar* and, despite submissions by the Canadian government to the contrary, Communication No. 236/1987, *VMRB* v. *Canada* at paras. 4.4 and 6.3; see Nowak, *CCPR Kommentar*, article 9/23.

sion in *X. v. UK*.[69] In that case, however, it was found that the delay in the deportation proceedings was caused by the applicant's own conduct and the complicated nature of the procedure and that there was, therefore, no lack of diligence which rendered the detention unlawful.

In *Caprino v. UK*,[70] the Commission stated that the term 'prescribed by law' in article 5(1) has to be read as 'lawful under the applicable domestic law', which includes EC law, in that case specifically EC Directive 64/221 'on the co-ordination of special measures concerning the movement and residence of foreign nationals which are justified on grounds of public policy, public security or public health'.[71]

The Commission, however, went on to hold that, having considered whether the detention was 'prescribed by law', it was necessary to determine separately whether the detention was necessary to secure the deportation of the applicant. In doing so it recalled that article 5(1)(f), as an exception to the general right to liberty and security of person, had to be interpreted strictly.[72] However, it was sufficient that 'action is being taken against him with a view to deportation'[73] and the eventual outcome of the deportation proceedings was irrelevant in the determination of whether the detention was 'necessary'. In the instant case the Commission found that the relationship between the detention and the deportation were adequate to justify the detention under article 5(1)(f). This was reiterated in the substantive decision in this case, where the Commission reaffirmed that detention under article 5(1)(f) had to be subject to principles such as necessity and proportionality.[74]

The European Court addressed this issue in its judgment dated 15 November 1996 in *Chahal*.[75] In that case the appellant had been detained for six years: the longest detention ever effected under the immigration laws of the UK. It was not disputed that he had been detained 'as a person against whom action is being taken with a view to deportation' within the meaning of article 5(1)(f). It was, however, contended that his detention had ceased to be 'in accordance with a procedure prescribed by law' because of its excessive duration. The Commission had found that five years was excessive and that the proceedings had not been pursued with the requisite speed. It also noted that there had been no abuse of the judi-

---

[69] Application No. 8081/77, 12 *Decisions and Reports*, p. 207, which concerned a ten-month delay in deportation proceedings before the Immigration Appeal Tribunal.
[70] Application No. 6871/75, 12 *Decisions and Reports*, p. 14. This case concerned the deportation of an Italian national on grounds that it was 'conducive to the public good' under the Immigration Act 1971.   [71] OJ Special Edition, 1963–4, No. 850/64, p. 117.
[72] In this analysis the Commission further relied on article 18 of the Convention which stipulates: 'The restrictions permitted under this Convention to the said rights shall not be applied for any purpose other than those for which they have been prescribed.'
[73] *Caprino v. UK*, Application No. 6871/75, 12 *Decisions and Reports*, p. 14 at p. 20.
[74] *Caprino v. UK*, Application No. 6871/75, 22 *Decisions and Reports*, p. 5.
[75] *Chahal* judgment, paras. 108–17.

cial review process by the applicant in order to delay his deportation. The Court did not uphold the position of the Commission. It noted that Chahal's case involved very serious issues. It was neither in the interests of the individual nor in the general public interest that such decisions should be taken hastily. Bearing in mind the fact that the applicant had availed himself of several legal remedies, including judicial review, appeal and petition to the House of Lords as well as submissions to a special tribunal established to deal with cases of national security, the time taken was not to be considered excessive.

Judicial control of the legality of the detention under the European Convention

Article 5 of the European Convention on Human Rights provides:

(1) No one shall be deprived of his liberty save ... in accordance with a procedure prescribed by law.

. . .

(4) Everyone who is deprived of his liberty by arrest or detention shall be entitled to take proceedings by which the lawfulness of his detention shall be decided speedily by a court and his release ordered if the detention is not lawful.

In *Caprino* v. *UK,* the Commission emphasised that article 5(4) is a provision separate from article 5(1).[76] The same proposition appears from the constant jurisprudence of the European Court of Human Rights.[77] The necessity for a speedy decision by a court is of particular importance where the decision to detain is taken by an administrative body. In declaring the application admissible, the Commission indicated that judicial review proceedings, which enable the applicant to challenge only the legality and not the merits of the decision, may be insufficient for the purposes of article 5(4).[78] In its decision on the substance of that

[76] *Caprino* v. *UK,* Application No. 6871/75, 12 *Decisions and Reports,* p. 21.
[77] *Kolompar* v. *Belgium,* judgment of 24 September 1992, Series A, No. 235C, para. 45; *De Wilde, Ooms and Versyp* v. *Belgium,* judgment of 18 June 1971, Series A, No. 12, para. 73.
[78] However, in its recent decision in *Chahal* v. *UK,* the majority of the Commission formed the view that it was not necessary for it to consider the complaint under article 5(4), as the question of the adequacy of the remedies available was more appropriately dealt with under article 13 (see below) and the question as to the speediness of the proceedings under article 5(4) was resolved by its finding that the duration of the detention of the applicant violated article 5(1)(f) (Application No. 22414/93, at paras. 124–9). In his partially dissenting opinion, Trechsel took issue with this conclusion on two grounds: (i) the decision on the duration of the detention did not deal with the adequacy of *habeas corpus* proceedings, in particular as the need for article 5(4) control was 'particularly acute' whenever problems arose under article 5(1); and (ii) that this conclusion was not in conformity with the case law of the European Court of Human Rights (Application No. 22414/93, at p. 33); in relation to point (ii) Trechsel particularly referred to the Court's decision in *Bouamar* v. *Belgium* (judgment of 29 February 1988, Series A, No. 129), in which a violation of both article 5(1) and 5(4) was found.

case[79] the Commission held that judicial proceedings under article 5(4) must include a review of the substantive grounds of the detention.[80] The European Court reverted to the theme in *Chahal*.[81] The issue arose in a particularly acute form in that case since the applicant had been accused of very serious crimes of terrorism (though no conviction had been upheld), such that the government alleged that it was not possible to disclose to him fully the confidential information obtained by the UK authorities. They noted that he had been given access to an advisory panel, under the chairmanship of a very senior judge, to review the merits of his case; and that he had pursued judicial review as far as the House of Lords. This, the European Court of Human Rights held, was not sufficient. It acknowledged that the use of confidential material may be unavoidable where national security is at stake; but according to the Court this did not mean that national authorities can be free of effective judicial control where national security is an issue. The Court considered that there are techniques that can be employed which accommodate legitimate security concerns about the nature and sources of intelligence information and yet accord the individual a substantial measure of procedural justice. The UK procedures did not match the standard required by the Convention. Accordingly, there was a breach of article 5(4). Interestingly, the Court did not, however, find it necessary to award compensation for this breach, even though article 5(5) provides for an enforceable right to compensation for everyone who has been a victim of arrest or detention in contravention of any of the provisions of article 5. The European Committee for the Prevention of Torture has made a special point of visiting immigration detention centres, as indicated in paragraph 28 of the *Amnur* judgment.

The International Covenant on Civil and Political Rights

The provisions of the ICCPR concerning detention are more explicit than those of the European Convention on Human Rights. Articles 9(1) and (4) of the ICCPR provide:

1. Everyone has the right to liberty and security of person. No one shall be subjected to arbitrary arrest or detention. No one shall be deprived of his liberty except on such grounds and in accordance with such procedure as are established by law.
   . . .

---

[79] *Caprino* v. *UK*, Application No. 6871/75, 22 *Decisions and Reports*, p. 5.
[80] Article 5(4) only relates to remedies available during the detention and does not, therefore, cover possible actions for false imprisonment which may be brought after the detention has ceased.   [81] *Chahal* judgment, paras. 124–33, especially para. 131.

4. Anyone who is deprived of his liberty by arrest or detention shall be entitled to take proceedings before a court, in order that that court may decide without delay on the lawfulness of his detention and order his release if the detention is not lawful.

Like the European Convention on Human Rights, article 9(5) of the ICCPR also provides an enforceable right to compensation where a person has been the victim of unlawful arrest or detention.

The Covenant also expressly imposes positive obligations on states in article 10(1) to the effect that '[a]ll persons deprived of their liberty shall be treated with humanity and with respect for the inherent dignity of the human person'. This is generally seen as providing for a duty on the contracting state to provide detention conditions which are humane and which secure respect for the dignity of the detained. This can be contrasted with article 7 of the ICCPR or article 3 of the European Convention on Human Rights which only oblige states to refrain from subjecting a person to inhuman or degrading treatment. This positive obligation exists irrespective of the material resources of the contracting state in question.[82]

The UN Human Rights Committee in its *General Comment 8/16* (personal liberty) stressed that article 9(4), 'the right to control by a court of the legality of the detention, applies to all persons deprived of their liberty by arrest or detention'.[83] This is in addition to a contracting state's obligation to provide an effective remedy under article 2(3) (the ICCPR equivalent to article 13 of the European Convention on Human Rights).

Also, if so-called preventive detention is used for reasons of public security, it must be controlled by these same provisions, that is, it must not be arbitrary, and must be based on grounds and procedures established by law (article 10(1)), information on the reasons must be given (article 10(2)) and court control of the detention must be available (article 10(4)) as well as compensation in case of a breach (article 10(5)).[84]

The Committee in its *General Comment 9/16* states that ultimate responsibility for the observance of the principle of humane treatment of detainees rests with the state in respect of all institutions where persons are lawfully held against their will, including detention camps, hospitals

---

[82] Human Rights Committee, *General Comment 9/16* (article 10) in *General Comments*, CCPR/C/21/Rev.1 of 19 May 1989, pp. 8–9.

[83] Human Rights Committee, *General Comment 8/16* (article 9), *ibid.*, pp. 7–8, para. 1.

[84] *Ibid.*, para. 4; a violation of article 9(4) was found in relation to the case of *Hammel* v. *Madagascar*, Complaint No. 155/1983 at para. 20. In that case a French national was arrested and held in incommunicado detention for three days and then expelled. As he was not afforded the opportunity to challenge the expulsion order *prior* to his expulsion, a violation was found.

etc.[85] This was reiterated in the recent Comments of the Human Rights Committee on the fourth UK Periodic Report[86] where the Committee stressed:

The Committee is concerned that the practice of the State party in contracting out to the private commercial sector core State activities which involve the use of force and the detention of persons weakens the protection of rights under the Covenant. The Committee stresses that the State remains responsible in all circumstances for adherence to all articles of the Covenant.[87]

It will also be recalled that the Committee expressed its concern about the treatment of illegal immigrants, asylum seekers and those ordered to be deported and the use of detention and the duration of such detention of persons ordered to be deported.[88]

The right to family life

The European Convention on Human Rights

Article 8 of the European Convention on Human Rights provides:

1. Everyone has a right to respect for his private and family life, his home and his correspondence.
2. There shall be no interference by a public authority with the exercise of this right except such as is in accordance with the law and is necessary in a democratic society in the interests of national security, public safety or the economic well-being of the country, for the prevention of disorder or crime, for the protection of health and morals, or for the protection of the rights and freedoms of others.

Article 8(1) protects the '*famille naturelle*' and does not make a distinction between a 'legitimate family' and 'illegitimate family' in respect of its definition of 'family life'.[89] This includes the right of spouses[90] and children to be given the opportunity to live together, even if a family life 'has not yet been fully established'.[91] Family life as such includes cohabitation by those concerned.[92] The Court even went so far as to state that:

In the Court's opinion 'family life', within the meaning of Article 8, includes at least the ties between near relatives, for instance those between grandparents and

---

[85] *General Comment 9/16*, para. 1.   [86] 27 July 1995, UN Doc. CCPR/C/79/Add.55.
[87] *Ibid.*, para. 16.   [88] *Ibid.*, para. 15.
[89] European Court of Human Rights in *Marckx v. Belgium*, Series A, No. 31 at para. 31.
[90] That is, relationships arising from a lawful and genuine marriage.
[91] European Court of Human Rights in its judgment of *Abdulaziz v. UK*, Series A, No. 94 at para. 62.
[92] See also article 12 (right to found a family). It appeared to the Court in *Abdulaziz* that it was 'scarcely conceivable that the right to found a family should not encompass the right to live together' (para. 62).

grandchildren, since such relatives may play a considerable part in family life. 'Respect' for family life so understood implies an obligation for the State to act in a manner calculated to allow these ties to develop normally.[93]

On the other hand:

Relationships between adults, a mother and her 33 year old son in the present case, would not necessarily acquire the protection of Article 8 of the Convention without evidence of further elements of dependency, involving more than the normal, emotional ties.[94]

However, the Court in *Abdulaziz* established that:

The duty imposed by Article 8 cannot be considered as extending to a general obligation on the part of a Contracting State to respect the choice by married couples of the country of their matrimonial residence and to accept the non-national spouses for settlement in that country. In the present case, the applicants have not shown that there were obstacles to establishing family life in their own or their husbands' home countries or that there were special reasons why that could not be expected of them.[95]

Whether or not there has been an interference will thus depend on whether it is reasonable to expect people to conduct their family life elsewhere. In *Gül v. Switzerland*,[96] the Court found that there was no interference when a Kurdish child was refused permission to join his sister and parents in Switzerland. The father was an asylum seeker who had not pursued his asylum appeal some years previously because he and his wife had been granted humanitarian leave to remain in Switzerland on account of the wife's life-threatening condition. Although the younger child was still in residential foster care near her parents in Switzerland, and the Swiss authorities had not sought to argue that the mother's condition had improved sufficiently for the parents to return to Turkey, the Court nevertheless found that it was reasonable to expect them to do so and that there was thus no interference under article 8(1).

Even if an interference with family life under article 8(1) has occurred, this interference may be justified on the grounds set out under article 8(2). To be so justified the interference has to be in accordance with law; it must pursue one of the 'legitimate aims' listed in article 8(2) and it must be necessary in a democratic society.

In *Chahal*, the Commission found a violation of article 8 on the ground that the interference with the applicant's right to family life was disproportionate and therefore not necessary in a democratic society. The appli-

---

[93] *Marckx* judgment, para. 45.
[94] Commission in Application No. 10375/83, *S. and S. v. UK*, 40 *Decisions and Reports*, p. 196 at p. 198.   [95] *Ibid.*, para. 68.
[96] *Gül v. Switzerland*, Application No. 23218/94, Case No. 53/1995/559/645, judgment of 19 February 1996, *Reports of Judgments and Decisions*, 1996–I; 22 EHRR, 1996, p. 93.

cant in that case had been resident in the UK for nineteen-and-a-half years and his wife for nineteen years; they had two teenage children, both born and brought up in the UK. On that basis the Commission concluded that deportation of the applicant 'would almost certainly lead to a permanent break up of the family'.[97] The Court, however, found it unnecessary to deal with the issue.[98] In the case of *Nasri* v. *France*,[99] the Court ruled that a deaf mute's medical condition made his family connections particularly important to him and that his deportation for serious criminal offences could not be justified.[100]

The International Covenant on Civil and Political Rights

The right to protection from interference of family life is set out in article 17 of the ICCPR which states:

1. No one shall be subjected to arbitrary or unlawful interference with his privacy, family, home or correspondence, nor to unlawful attacks on his honour and reputation.
2. Everyone has the right to the protection of the law against such interferences or attacks.

In interpreting this right the Human Rights Committee has established that the term 'family' has to be given 'a broad interpretation to include all those comprising the family as understood in the society of the State party concerned'.[101] The Committee has held: '[T]he exclusion of a person from a country where close members of his family are living can amount to an interference within the meaning of Article 17(1). In principle article 17(1) applies also when one of the spouses is an alien.'[102]

However, where the members of a family had been separated for seventeen years, the Committee held that there was no family life and the contracting state was under no obligation to take positive steps to facilitate the re-establishment of family life.[103]

The Covenant, in article 23(1), also contains a right of the family to enjoy protection 'by society and the State'.[104] In the case of *Aumeeruddy-Cziffra* v. *Mauritius*,[105] the UN Human Rights Committee held that a

[97] *Chahal*, Commission report adopted 27 June 1995.
[98] *Chahal* judgment, para. 139.   [99] *Nasri* v. *France*, Series A, No. 324.
[100] The Court chose not to consider the question of whether his expulsion would be in breach of article 3.
[101] Human Rights Committee, *General Comment 16/32* (article 17), CCPR/C/21/Rev.1, 19 May 1989, pp. 19–21, para. 5.
[102] *Aumeeruddy-Cziffra* v. *Mauritius*, Communication No. 35/1978, para. 9.2(b).
[103] *A. S.* v. *Canada (Polish Canadian Case)*, Communication No. 68/1980.
[104] Article 23(1) reads: 'The family is the natural and fundamental group unit of society and is entitled to protection by society and the State.'
[105] Communication No. 35/1978.

policy which restricted the access of foreign spouses of Mauritian women to Mauritius but did not restrict the access of foreign spouses of Mauritian men was in breach of article 2(1) in conjunction with article 23(1).[106] It reasoned that there had been discrimination in the way in which the protection of article 23(1) was afforded to a family depending upon whether the Mauritian partner was a man or a woman.[107]

The UN Convention on the Rights of the Child

The special protection of the parent–child relationship recognised by the European Convention on Human Rights jurisprudence has been reinforced by the UN Convention on the Rights of the Child.[108] Under this Convention special protection is provided for refugee children. Article 22 of the Convention provides:

1. States Parties shall take appropriate measures to ensure that a child *who is seeking refugee status* or who is considered a refugee in accordance with applicable international or domestic law and procedures shall, whether unaccompanied or accompanied by his or her parents or by any other person, receive appropriate protection and humanitarian assistance in the enjoyment of applicable rights set forth in the present Convention and *in other international human rights or humanitarian instruments* to which the said States are Parties.
2. ... In cases where no parents or other members of the family can be found, the child shall be accorded the same protection as any other child permanently or temporarily deprived of his or her family environment for any reason, as set forth in the present Convention. (emphasis added)

The protection as required by article 22(2), second sentence, includes 'special protection and assistance provided by the State',[109] provision of 'alternative care',[110] including, for example, 'foster placement'.[111] This protection for the child is *not* dependent on the legal presence of the child within a state party's territory but merely on the fact that it is seeking refugee status or is considered a refugee under *inter alia* the 1951 Geneva Convention.

Furthermore, article 9 provides that:

---

[106] The relevant rules were also held to have been in breach of article 3 (equal rights of men and women) and article 26 (equality before the law and prohibition of discrimination).

[107] See Alfred de Zayas, Jakob Möller and Torkel Opsahl, 'Application of the International Covenant on Civil and Political Rights under the Optional Protocol by the Human Rights Committee' (reprint in 28 *German Yearbook of International Law*, 1985), pp. 9–64.

[108] UN Doc. A/RES/44/25. Adopted and opened for signature by the UN General Assembly (Resolution 44/25) on 20 November 1989 and entered into force on 2 September 1990. As of 4 February 1999 it had been ratified by 191 states (including all UN member states except Somalia and the USA).   [109] *Ibid.*, article 20(1).

[110] *Ibid.*, article 20(2).   [111] *Ibid.*, article 20(3).

. . . a child shall not be separated from his or her parents against their will, except when competent authorities subject to judicial review determine, in accordance with applicable law and procedures, that such separation is *necessary for the best interests of the child.* (emphasis added)

This protection of a child's family is reinforced by article 10 of the Convention which provides that applications by children or their parents to enter or leave a state party for the purpose of family reunification shall be dealt with by the state party in a 'positive, humane and expeditious manner'.

However, unlike the European Convention on Human Rights and the ICCPR, the Convention on the Rights of the Child does not make provision for either inter-state complaints or for the right to individual petition. The compliance with the obligations undertaken by the states party to the Convention is solely monitored by periodic state reports which are considered by the Committee on the Rights of the Child.[112]

The right to effective remedy

The European Convention on Human Rights

Article 13 of the European Convention on Human Rights provides:

Everyone whose rights and freedoms as set forth in this Convention are violated shall have an effective remedy before a national authority notwithstanding that the violation has been committed by persons acting in an official capacity.

In order for article 13 to come into play it is not required that a violation of a right under the Convention has been found: it is sufficient that the applicant has an 'arguable claim' that such a violation has occurred.[113] Furthermore, article 13 does not require access to a court but merely to a 'national authority', as long as that authority is 'sufficiently independent' of the decision-maker.[114] In the case of *Uppal* v. *UK*,[115] the Commission held that recourse to an adjudicator and the Immigration Appeal Tribunal constituted an effective remedy under article 13, as they are 'empowered under the Immigration Act 1971 to review and reverse the Home Secretary's decision'.[116] However, article 13 does not apply where the violation of the applicant's rights has been committed by way of legislation,[117] nor where the

---

[112] Such reports have to be submitted to the Committee in five-yearly intervals: article 44(1).   [113] *Silver* v. *UK*, Series A, No. 61, para. 113.
[114] *Ibid.*, para. 116.   [115] Application No. 8244/78, 17 *Decisions and Reports*, p. 149.
[116] *Ibid.*, p. 157.
[117] Commission in *Young, James and Webster* v. *UK*, Series B, No. 39, pp. 48–9.

violation has been committed by a court of law.[118] Furthermore, article
13 does not create an obligation for a contracting state to incorporate the
European Convention on Human Rights into national law. Where the
Convention has not been incorporated, however, there is a presumption
that no effective remedy is available where the violation has been committed by secondary legislation.[119]

On a number of occasions a question has arisen whether an application
for judicial review constitutes an effective remedy under article 13. In the
judgments of the Court in *Soering* v. *UK*,[120] *Vilvarajah* v. *UK*[121] and *D.* v.
UK[122] the Court found that judicial review proceedings constituted an
effective remedy. The decision in *Soering* is more easily comprehended
than that in *Vilvarajah*, as there was no evaluation of evidence in the
former case. In *Soering* the applicant and the Home Secretary were not in
dispute as to the treatment that the applicant would face if returned to
Virginia: their dispute concerned the reasonableness of the decision to
return him in circumstances known to exist. In the case of *Vilvarajah* on
the other hand the dispute between the parties was one of fact: the applicants complained that they were likely to be maltreated if returned to Sri
Lanka, whereas the Home Secretary did not accept that contention. In
their partly dissenting opinion in that case, judges Walsh and Russo
quoted passages by Lord Brightman and the Lord Chancellor, Lord
Hailsham, in the case of *Chief Constable of North Wales Police* v. *Evans*[123] to
the effect that judicial review was concerned not with the decision but
with the decision-making procedure. On that basis they both concluded:

[A] national system which it is claimed provides an effective remedy for a breach
of the Convention and which excludes the competence to make a decision on the
merits cannot meet the requirements of Article 13.[124]

In *Chahal* the Commission and the Court took the view that nothing in
the case of *Vilvarajah* required them to find that judicial review constituted an effective remedy in the case now before them.[125] The Court in
Chahal stated that in *Vilvarajah* they had accepted that a UK court would
have jurisdiction to quash a decision to send a fugitive to a country if it
had accepted that there was a serious risk of inhuman and degrading
treatment, on the ground that the decision was one that no reasonable

---

[118] The original Convention, article 6 (right to a fair trial), does not provide for a right of
appeal (unlike article 14(5) of the ICCPR). See European Court of Human Rights judgment in *Delcourt* v. *Belgium*, Series A, No. 11, para. 25. Such a right has only been introduced by Protocol No. 7.   [119] *Silver* judgment, para. 118.
[120] *Soering* judgment, paras. 116–24.   [121] *Vilvarajah* judgment, paras. 123–4.
[122] *D.* v. *UK* judgment, paras. 69–73.   [123] [1982] 1 WLR 115.
[124] *Vilvarajah* judgment, para. 3.
[125] *Chahal*, Commission decision, paras. 149–51, Court judgment, paras. 140–55.

Home Secretary could take. In contrast, in *Chahal* neither the courts nor the advisory panel could review the Home Secretary's decision to deport Chahal to India with reference solely to the risk of ill-treatment. On the contrary, the courts and panel had to be satisfied, in that particular case, that the Home Secretary had properly balanced the risk to Chahal against the danger to national security. The Court concluded therefore that neither judicial review nor the advisory panel constituted an effective remedy; and it found that there had been a breach of article 13 of the Convention.

In the authors' view, that passage in the judgment in *Chahal* is unconvincing. The Home Secretary and the courts did not take the view that there was a risk of ill-treatment in India, counter-balanced by the danger to national security at home. They took the view that, while Chahal would face prosecution, he would not face persecution. As in *Vilvarajah*, the decision could have been set aside in judicial review proceedings on the ground that it was one that no reasonable Home Secretary could take. There was then the added consideration that Chahal constituted a security risk. The decision that he constituted such a risk was also one that could be quashed in judicial review proceedings as one that no reasonable Home Secretary could take. There is therefore no sound basis for the European Court to distinguish *Chahal* from *Vilvarajah*. Nor can one reconcile with *Vilvarajah* the Court's statement in *Chahal* that 'the notion of an effective remedy under Article 13 requires independent scrutiny of the claim that there exist substantial grounds for fearing a real risk of treatment contrary to Article 3'.[126]

Such independent scrutiny is not available by judicial review, and the soundness of the Court's judgment in *Vilvarajah* must now be questioned. The Court in its judgment in *D. v. UK*, delivered six months after its statement in *Chahal*, still remained of the view that theoretical availability of judicial review constituted an effective remedy in cases where there was a real risk of a breach of article 3. In *Vilvarajah*, the Court had decided that the judicial review mechanism would ensure that any decision with consequences for a person's life or safety would be subjected to the 'most anxious scrutiny'. In *D. v. UK*, the national court had expressly recognised and accepted the consequences that the destitution which awaited him on expulsion would have on the dying applicant and on his already brief life expectancy. It nevertheless refused to grant the necessary leave to enable the judicial review proceedings to take place and so to enable the courts to examine the reasonableness of the decision to expel. The European Court nonetheless still held that the notional availability of

---

[126] *Chahal* judgment, para. 151.

judicial review constituted an effective remedy in the case of *D. v. UK* where, unlike *Vilvarajah*, it had found a substantive violation of article 3.

The International Covenant on Civil and Political Rights

The equivalent ICCPR provision to article 13 of the European Convention on Human Rights is article 2(3), which states:

Each State Party to the present Covenant undertakes:

a) To ensure that any person whose rights or freedoms as herein recognised are violated shall have an effective remedy, notwithstanding that the violation has been committed by persons acting in an official capacity;

b) To ensure that any person claiming such a remedy shall have his right thereto determined by competent judicial, administrative or legislative authorities, or by any other competent authority provided for by the legal system of the State, and to develop the possibilities of judicial remedy;

c) To ensure that the competent authorities shall enforce such remedies when granted.

The UN Human Rights Committee has, however, taken a different approach to the notion of effective remedy. The Committee's recent *Comments* on the fourth Periodic Report made by the UK[127] stated that:

The Committee notes that the legal system of the United Kingdom does not ensure fully that an effective remedy is provided for all violations of the rights contained in the Covenant. The Committee is concerned by the extent to which implementation of the Covenant is impeded by the combined effects of the non-incorporation of the Covenant into domestic law, the failure to accede to the first Optional Protocol and the absence of a constitutional Bill of Rights.

. . . The Committee also notes with concern that adequate legal representation is not available for asylum-seekers effectively to challenge administrative decisions.[128]

In *Hammel v. Madagascar*, where the applicant was not given the opportunity to challenge his expulsion order, the Committee, in its analysis under article 13 of the ICCPR,[129] found that there was no compelling reason of national security to deprive him of that remedy. Therefore, 'an alien must be given full facilities for pursuing his remedy against expulsion so that this right will in all circumstances be an effective one'.[130]

---

[127] UN Doc. CCPR/C/79/Add.55, 27 July 1995.

[128] *Ibid.*, paras. 9 and 15 (last sentence).   [129] See p. 82 above.

[130] Communication No. 155/1983 at para. 19.2; see also Human Rights Committee, *General Comment No. 15/27.*

Conclusion

International instruments and mechanisms for the protection of fundamental human rights of aliens now constitute a substantial body of international legislation. The development of that legislation by international courts and tribunals, both in cases in which the individual has direct access and in those in which there is no such access, impose substantial restraints on the liberty of states to take actions in respect of aliens: action which not long ago was regarded as the most untrammelled of the sovereign prerogatives of states. Those administering aliens law and those concerned with the protection of individuals must now keep abreast of this substantial body of new law: a body of law which regulates to a substantial degree the procedures connected with entry, refusal, stay, expulsion and detention.

While the ebb and flow of the refugee definition will continue to be of critical importance and merit analysis accordingly, the asylum seeker and refugee must also be positioned within a human rights framework which extends beyond the Geneva Convention. In many circumstances this framework has more to offer in terms of human rights protection.

Bibliography

Davidson, Scott, 'The Civil and Political Rights Protected in the Inter-American Human Rights System' in *The Inter-American System of Human Rights* (ed. David J. Harris and Stephen Livingstone, Clarendon Press, Oxford, 1998)

Mole, Nuala, 'Immigration and Freedom of Movement', in *The International Covenant on Civil and Political Rights and United Kingdom Law* (ed. David J. Harris and Sarah Joseph, Clarendon Press, Oxford, 1995)

Nowak, Manfred, *UNO-Pakt über bürgerliche und politische Rechte und Fakultativprotokoll – CCPR Kommentar* (N. P. Engel Verlag, Kehl, 1989)

UN Human Rights Committee, *General Comments*, CCPR/C/21/Rev.1 of 19 May 1989

General Comment No. 20(44) (article 7), CCPR/C/21/Rev.1/Add.3

General Comment 15 No. (27) (The Position of Aliens under the Covenant) of 22 July 1986, CCPR/C/21/Rev.1/Add.5

General Comment No. 24(52) on issues relating to reservations made upon ratification or accession to the Covenant or the Optional Protocols thereto, or in relation to declarations under article 41 of the Covenant, 11 November 1994, CCPR/C/21/Rev.1/Add.6

de Zayas, Alfred, Jakob Möller and Torkel Opsahl, 'Application of the International Covenant on Civil and Political Rights under the Optional Protocol by the Human Rights Committee' (reprint in 28 *German Yearbook of International Law*, 1985), pp. 9–64

5   Rethinking the refugee concept

Patricia Tuitt[1]

In addressing the question 'Who is a refugee?' this chapter is concerned with the controlling notion of the refugee as one who is displaced in the primary physical sense. It is not preoccupied with the distinction between cross-border and internal displacement, that is between legal and other social constructions of the refugee, rather with the unifying theme which conditions the 'who' of all refugees, that is that the refugee is bounded by the spatial activity of movement.

In an era in which so few victims of internal conflict, natural disaster or severe economic decline are able to secure asylum[2] and with the growing recognition that asylum itself favours particular disenfranchised groups[3] – in short with the increased awareness that many are 'displaced' from mainstream refugee discourses – it is worth pausing to reflect upon how and why such a problematic concept as displacement has come to acquire such prominence in marking out victims of human rights abuses. Problematic, because it presents all such abuses as having an endemic mobilising force. Problematic, because it views 'space' wherein the activity of movement is located as infinitely present.

My argument is that the concept of displacement was not arrived at by chance, nor is it merely a 'practical condition precedent . . . allowing physical access of the international community to the unprotected person' and thus 'beyond the refugee identity', as prevailing commentary would

[1] I would like to thank Audrey Kobayashi for her contribution to the formulation of the ideas contained in this piece and Mark Fenwick for his comments on an earlier draft of this chapter and his help in the preparation of the manuscript.
[2] 'The majority of these populations languish in camps or survive illegally without any hope of a permanent place of settlement or eventual return home. Those that do repatriate frequently return to unstable situations where their physical safety is in doubt and where their economic prospects are poor.' Gil Loescher, *Beyond Charity: International Cooperation and the Global Refugee Crisis* (Oxford University Press, 1993), p. 4.
[3] 'Refugees who are persistent and innovative (and who are overwhelmingly male) dominate the spontaneous arrivals in Canada. In camps women and children predominate.' Howard Adelman, 'Refuge or Asylum: A Philosophical Perspective', 1 *Journal of Refugee Studies*, 1988, p. 9. The same is true of all Western receiving states.

suggest.[4] The general category of the refugee, evolving from the specific name or description 'refugee' originated with the advent of modernity. Having been applied to sporadic groups whose defining moment came about as a result of their exile, it has been inappropriately decontextualised to encompass more than a historically specific process or moment. By privileging these historical moments, a general concept of displacement emerged which has both legitimated and sustained a specific type of humanitarian assistance. In other words, by reifying certain historically contingent moments of exile, the concept of displacement has been applied in a particular way, to a broad range of phenomena.

This chapter focuses upon the movement of peoples in search of refuge from political and religious persecution, in order to argue that displacement is a highly contingent and eclectic concept, which paradoxically was, and to a large extent still is, urged as a unified category. Its organising themes of wealth, status, race and gender have been erased. The durability of the refugee concept is dependent upon the continued resonance of this 'image' of displacement.

There are two principal dimensions to this argument which this chapter attempts to address. The first is that the refugee – a concept embodying displacement, whether viewed as a legal or sociological concept – is conceived of as a *moving entity*. Of course, this kind of understanding captures a certain truth but it tends to obscure how space in its 'physical' and 'mental' form is organised between race, class and gender among other factors.[5] The second is that this dominant conception is situated within a particular reading of the history of the movement of peoples which fails to analyse the particular *as particular*. In Kaplan's terms, this 'works to remove it [that is, the history] from politically or historically specific instances in order to generate aesthetic categories and ahistorical values'.[6]

The implications of my argument should not be obscured: displacement as a defining category of human rights subjects now has a somewhat dubious status. The refugee as a workable and meaningful concept thus has an uncertain future. The imperative behind the argument exists in the undeniable fact that there are fewer and fewer spaces of meaningful refugee movement available, even within the borders of a state. Moreover,

---

[4] Andrew Shacknove, 'Who is a Refugee?', 95 *Ethics*, 1985, p. 274. See also James C. Hathaway, *The Law of Refugee Status* (Butterworths, Toronto, 1991).

[5] The distinction denotes not simply a geographical site but the way in which relations are mediated, and cultural practices played out, to produce different possibilities in relation to the physical site. This is particularly so as between men and women.

[6] Caren Kaplan, *Questions of Travel: Postmodern Discourses of Displacement* (Duke University Press, New York, 1996), p. 28. In this chapter, I use the term 'aesthetic' to highlight the abstract and imagined nature of the category of the refugee.

the forces of modern refugee phenomena often confound the very spatial activity of movement, particularly that of the vulnerable: the young, the old, and the sick.

The refugee as a moving entity

That the refugee is principally conceived of as a moving entity is reflected in the language of refugee discourse which deeply mirrors this perception: flows, movements, tides of refugees form part of the inescapable jargon of refugee discourse, a discourse which purports to articulate something central, not peripheral, to refugeehood. The 'escape from violence' is thus constructed as the primary goal of displacement.[7] Significantly, this constructs movement as a function of a broader quest for safety.

The refugee definition, it is said, has an 'ordinary, natural common sense, even literal' meaning 'signifying someone in flight'.[8] She is 'driven'[9] from her home. Refugee presupposes an 'exodus'. She is a victim of causes – war, famine, drought etc. – which have an endemic mobilising force, that is where 'flight' constitutes 'the only way to escape danger to life or extensive restrictions on human rights'.[10]

These representations of the spatial activity of movement in the discourse belong, as Goodwin-Gill states, to a 'broader, looser'[11] perspective on who the refugee is. The refugee in international law, that overarching aesthetic category, demands even greater spatial mobility on the part of the putative refugee – she must cross international borders. This 'essential quality'[12] characterises the legal refugee above all other social constructions, and is a 'quality' evident in all legal definitions of refugee from the earliest derived in the years following the First World War.

The 1951 Geneva Convention Relating to the Status of Refugees begins with the requirement that the refugee be 'outside his country of nationality' or domicile.[13] Article 1(2) of the Organisation of African Unity (OAU) Convention Governing the Specific Aspects of Refugee Problems in Africa sees the legal refugee as being 'compelled to leave his place of habitual res-

---

[7] The ideology against which refugee movement is based is aptly demonstrated in Aristide Zolberg, Astri Suhrke and Sergio Aguayo, *Escape from Violence: Conflict and the Refugee Crisis in the Developing World* (Oxford University Press, 1989).
[8] Guy S. Goodwin-Gill, *The Refugee in International Law* (2nd edn, Oxford University Press, 1996), p. 3.   [9] *Oxford English Dictionary*, (1993).
[10] Goodwin-Gill, *The Refugee in International Law*, p. 4.
[11] *Ibid.*, p. 3.
[12] Sir John Hope Simpson, *The Refugee Problem – Report of a Survey* (Institute of International Affairs, Oxford University Press, 1938), p. 1.
[13] 189 UNTS 137 (the Geneva Convention), article 1A(2).

idence in order to seek refuge in another place outside his country of origin or nationality'.[14] Likewise the definition adopted in the 1984 Cartagena Declaration on Refugees requires that refugees 'flee' their country.[15] The more restricted sense of spatial activity demanded by the law attests to the fundamentally controlling function of contemporary migration norms. Thus, according to this understanding, persons who have not crossed international borders, the internally displaced, are not refugees.

Since then the term 'refugee' has taken on a wider meaning. It is now said to be a socio-political construct, a term which has many official and non-official usages.[16] Displacement *per se* rather than cross-border displacement has, since the early 1970s, become the pivotal point around which institutional aid and protection are organised. However, this welcome shift in focus has come alongside a paradigm shift in the organising framework of displacement. The world is constantly being confronted, not with liberating scenes of 'escape from violence', but with refugees separated from the wider population in camps – displaced within the places of refuge – more often in the poorer nations of the developing world.[17] In seeking out these baser places of refuge women and young girls often substitute one form of persecution for another and suffer extreme sexual violence.[18] Whether man, woman or child, the supposed escape from violence is often from one state beset by refugee-producing phenomena to another. Displacement has lost its principal rationale.

This crisis is, in large measure, located in the presentation of 'space' as 'fixed, undialectical, immobile'.[19] As stated above, it is portrayed as an

[14] 1001 UNTS 46, article 1(2).
[15] 1984 Cartagena Declaration on Refugees, para. III.3. See Eduardo Arboleda, 'The Cartagena Declaration of 1984 and its Similarities to the 1969 OAU Convention – A Comparative Perspective', 7 *International Journal of Refugee Law*, 1995, Special Issue, pp. 87–102.
[16] Zolberg, *Escape from Violence*, p. 3. See also generally chapter 3 of this volume.
[17] Loescher, *Beyond Charity*, estimated that at that time one in ten of the population of Malawi were refugees from Mozambique (p. 8). As recently observed: 'With over 6.1 million refugees, scarcely any state in Africa is currently spared from the after effects of a refugee crisis, for the African state is either the source of the refugees or the host . . . in all the hot spots in Africa, the double problem of refugees and the internally displaced abounds.' Ahmednasir M. Abdullahi, 'The Refugee Crisis in Africa as a Crisis of the Institution of State', 6 *International Journal of Refugee Law*, 1994, pp. 562–80.
[18] See, for example, Truong Thi Dieu De, 'Women Refugees in the Netherlands: A Caseworker's Approach', in *Refugees: The Trauma of Exile: The Humanitarian Role of the Red Cross and Red Crescent* (ed. Diana Miserez, League of Red Cross and Red Crescent Societies and Martinus Nijhoff, Dordrecht, 1988), p. 287. The author examines the case of women refugees raped by pirates whilst fleeing in search of asylum. This is a common threat that women face. See also Thomas Spijkerboer, *Women and Refugee Status: Beyond the Public/Private Distinction* (Emancipation Council, The Hague, 1994).
[19] Michel Foucault, 'Questions on Geography', in *Power/Knowledge: Selected Interviews and Other Writings 1972–77* (ed. Colin Gordon, Harvester Press, Brighton, 1980).

infinite presence, rather than being prone to expand or contract with politics, history, economics and, in the refugee context, the containment policies mainly of Western states. Also masked within the discourse is the fact that space is socially constructed in different ways for different groups or individuals. Thus, women are less able to conquer space to enable movement towards safety than their male counterparts. Whilst it is not the aim of this chapter to question the 'flows' or 'tides' of refugees, the incidence of which can be proved at least in specific cases, it does aim first to interrogate the 'universalisation' of the discourse of refugee movement in the light of the numbers of people denied the liberating effects of travel, and, secondly, to locate the future prospect of displacement if 'escape from violence' no longer represents the lived experiences of the displaced.

The history of asylum and the social production of space

As stated earlier, the dominant conception of the refugee as a moving entity is founded upon the movement of peoples particularly from the seventeenth century at least until the end of the Second World War. Indeed, it is this historical record which, according to Hathaway's account of the development of refugee definitions, was drawn upon to define the refugee variously in 'juridical, social and individualistic' terms.[20] Kaplan reminds us that 'exile' has 'played a role in Western cultures of narratives of political formation and cultural identity since the Hellenic era'.[21] The term 'refugee', which was first employed in 1573, emerged through this process of identity formation.[22] The privileging of displacement in the identification of victims of human rights abuses is thus rooted in the history of refugee movement. It is suggested here, however, that it is a history that records a particular exilic preference at certain times towards certain groups. The 'abstract and transhistorical universalisation'[23] of that history fails to analyse *as particular* the incidence of displacement in social history, creating an 'imagined community'[24] of refugees where the spatial assumptions outlined above, in particular the gendered nature of space, are veiled.

This reading of the history of refugee movement attempts to highlight the specificity of class, of wealth, of status, of race and, above all, of gender, in the construction of space and the spatial activity of movement.

---

[20] Hathaway, *The Law of Refugee Status*, pp. 2–6.
[21] Kaplan, *Questions of Travel*, p. 27.   [22] Zolberg, *Escape from Violence*, p. 3.
[23] Edward Soja, *Postmodern Geographies: The Reassertion of Space in Critical Social Theory* (Verso, London, 1989).
[24] In Benedict Anderson's view all communities are imagined. What distinguishes various communities is 'the style in which they are imagined'. See Benedict Anderson, *Imagined Communities* (Verso, London, 1990), p. 15.

According to Atle Grahl-Madsen, refugee movements have been recorded 'as far back as the history of mankind'.[25] Peter Rose dates the emergence of a concept of asylum to the writings of Euripides, Sophocles and Virgil.[26] The beginnings of modernity saw larger scale refugee movements, notably with the flight of approximately 200,000 Protestants from France after the Edict of Nantes, which allowed minority faiths to be tolerated under Catholic rule, was renounced in 1685. The flight of 30,000 'Englishmen' during the reign of Mary Tudor in 1553–8, as a result of the re-emergence of Roman Catholicism as the established religion, marked this period as an age of religious intolerance.[27]

The historical narrative continues in this vein from the age of religious persecution to the age of political oppression in the eighteenth century with most countries in Europe being forced to admit political dissidents fleeing from Austria, Russia, Prussia and France.[28] From the early twentieth century to the present, minority groups have been targets of oppression. The movement of the Jews and the Armenians – the largest refugee groups in Europe in the early 1900s – was a strong factor motivating the search at that time for a refugee definition.[29]

These refugee movements marked not only key moments in the production of the cultural identity of the refugee, but can also be viewed as part of a larger phenomenon, namely the social production of space, which was described by Foucault as 'a set of relations that delineate sites'.[30] Movement towards exile claims a 'site' which, in the claiming, excludes the claims of others. In the Greek states, asylum was afforded to 'zealous conquerors', to those emerging conquered from wars, and to the politically oppressed.[31] In mediaeval times asylum became closely allied to the public realm of church and state, with asylum and sanctuary being relatively interchangeable concepts, both representing fundamental underpinnings of the common law.[32] The claiming of the public sphere as the primary site of the lived experiences of the exile contributed to the division between the public and private spheres. This

---

[25] Atle Grahl-Madsen, *The Status of Refugees in International Law*, (A. W. Sijthoff, Leyden, 1966), vol. I, p. 9.

[26] Peter Rose, 'Some Thoughts about Refugees and the Descendants of Theseus', 15 *International Migration Review*, 1981, pp. 8–9.

[27] See W. Gunther Plaut, *Asylum: A Moral Dilemma* (Praeger, London, 1995), p. 38.

[28] For an account of these movements see Eduardo Arboleda and Ian Hoy, 'The Convention Definition in the West: Disharmony of Interpretation and Application', 5 *International Journal of Refugee Law*, 1993, pp. 66–90.

[29] See generally Hathaway, *The Law of Refugee Status*, pp. 1–10.

[30] Michel Foucault, 'Of Other Spaces', 16 *Diacritics*, 1986, pp. 22–7, cited in Soja, *Postmodern Geographies*, p. 17. [31] Rose, 'Some Thoughts', pp. 8–9.

[32] William C. Ryan, 'The Historical Case for the Right of Sanctuary', 29 *Journal of Church and State*, 1987, p. 209.

was a division which crucially affects women's access to places of asylum.[33] The 'site of asylum' was claimed by the 'well to do . . . or at least the once well to do'.[34] It was a relatively exclusive site, importing strong power relations,[35] and was rapidly filled during the three centuries before our own during which the exodus of religious and political dissidents became a feature of European history. Indeed, religious persecution soon came to be known as the 'classic' hallmark of the refugee.

Asylum, and by extension refuge, were therefore never abstract or neutral categories, but, as Zolberg notes, are structured around a 'broader universe', where factors other than the pressing need of the putative refugee determine whether a place of asylum is found.[36] The neutral terms in which the history of movements is depicted tend to deny this and instead picture, in relatively unequivocal terms, a movement of persons, to whom the label 'refugee' was soon attached, who were confronted with 'classic' questions of religious or political conscience. So seemingly universal were these concerns and so seemingly comprehensive its victims, that the historical narrative side-steps the fact that these 'classic' refugees, emerging mostly from the ranks of revolutionary and nationalistic movements or established religious organisations, come from a world seldom inhabited by women, for example, whose politics, even today take a very different form from the 'publicly active religious, racial and nationalistic' groupings so common to those that successfully

[33] The public/private dichotomy which has defined and determined women's access to human rights discourse exists as much within the history of spaces of asylum, as refugee scholars have, of late, sought to illustrate. See, for example, Jacqueline R. Castel, 'Rape, Sexual Assault and the Meaning of Persecution', 4 *International Journal of Refugee Law*, 1992, pp. 39–56; Jacqueline Greatbach, 'The Gender Difference: Feminist Critiques of Refugee Discourse', 1 *International Journal of Refugee Law*, 1989, pp. 518–27; Doreen M. Indra, 'Gender: A Key Dimension of the Refugee Experience', *Refuge*, 1987, pp. 3–4. For a general account see Rebecca J. Cook (ed.), *Human Rights of Women: National and International Perspectives* (University of Pennsylvania Press, Philadelphia, 1994).

[34] Michael R. Marrus, *The Unwanted: European Refugees in the Twentieth Century* (Oxford University Press, 1985).

[35] 'Whatever happened when people sought to migrate or resist migration . . . without the guidance or restraint of commonly accepted rules or principles. Those who were strong, took what they wished; those who were weak, accepted what they must.' Tom J. Farer, 'How the International System Copes with Involuntary Migration: Norms, Institutions and State Practice', 17 *Human Rights Quarterly*, 1995, pp. 72–3.

[36] 'For a refugee flow to begin, certain conditions must be met in one or more of the states of destination as well as the state of origin. People cannot leave their place of origin if they have no place to go. And the availability of such a place is in turn largely determined by those who control the places of destination, usually governmental authorities. Extrapolating from these specific historical circumstances to a more general level, we can think of the classic type of refugee as arising from a broader universe than merely the country in which persecution occurs.' Zolberg, *Escape from Violence*, p. 30.

seek and gain asylum.[37] Thus, although it is a gender-neutral history, its neutral register nevertheless speaks of the taking of asylum by men. Asylum as a site claimed by men is characteristically immutable, certainly unshareable, 'irreducible . . . and absolutely not superimposable'.[38] Space, as Michael Keith and Steve Pile argue, is 'an active component of hegemonic power . . . it tells you where you are and it puts you there'.[39] That this is so, is demonstrated by the low number of women asylum seekers in official statistics. Women, after all, are rendered less mobile by structural conditions, cultural patterns and above all by a 'broader universe' which privileges the public sphere over the private sphere in terms of the general recognition of, and thus by extension access to, human rights.[40]

In recent years the absence of women from cross-border flight statistics has been noted, as has the effect of this absence on the development of the refugee concept. This growing recognition cannot however redress the failure to examine refugee movements *as particular*, since much intellectual investment in the general concept of refugee and its refinement had taken place long before the absence of women from the discourse had been noted. Kaplan aptly describes this process as the 'relentless gendering of expatriation as masculine'.[41] Given that an estimated two-thirds of the total victims of human rights abuse are women and young girls,[42] this process clearly calls into question the normative character of displacement, and, relatedly, the implicit claim that human rights abuses have an endemic mobilising force.

The general concept of refugee

The joining of moments of exile into an abstract and seemingly ahistorical category forms the basis of the refugee concept which now exists as a socio-political construct – one which has a 'diffuse meaning in ordinary parlance and a much more precise one in legal and administrative jargon'.[43] It is a concept which, allegedly because of the various 'official

---

[37] Castel, 'Rape, Sexual Assault', p. 40.

[38] Foucault, cited in Soja, *Postmodern Geographies*, p. 17.

[39] Michael Keith and Steve Pile (eds.), *Place and the Politics of Identity* (Routledge, London, 1993), p. 37.

[40] It has been argued that the marginalisation of women in human rights discourse stems from the privileging of so-called 'first generation' civil and political rights. This privileging serves to define the traditional concerns of human rights and humanitarian aid in ways which leave, at the margin of human rights discourse, those to whom the private, rather than the public, sphere, represents the world. For general discussion see Cook, *Human Rights of Women*.   [41] Kaplan, *Questions of Travel*, p. 45.

[42] See generally Castel, 'Rape, Sexual Assault'; and Spijkerboer, *Women and Refugee Status*.

[43] Zolberg, *Escape from Violence*, p. 3.

and non-official' shades of meaning attributed to it, remains elusive. To locate confusion within a proliferation of meanings is merely to disguise the true nature of the refugee paradox: the term refugee remains elusive because it is employed simultaneously to define a category of persons and to describe a group which has defined itself. The universalisation of moments of exile, the failure to identify these moments as particular not general, lies at the heart of contemporary ambivalence over the refugee concept.

It is the seeming power of the seemingly powerless that needs to be squarely confronted and explained within a logical frame of reference. In my view, this frame of reference lies within the history of asylum from which the term refugee emerged roughly around the time of the exodus of the Huguenots from France in the seventeenth century. It emerged to describe a group of people whose defining moment had come about with their exodus from France, who had, by the process of exile (that is, move-ment) defined themselves. Through usage, the term refugee came to be applied to persons in similar circumstances: French aristocrats and polit-ical dissidents in the eighteenth and nineteenth century, Jews, Armenians and other disenfranchised minority groups in the early part of the twenti-eth century.

These diverse groups – albeit united by a shared sense that the political or religious contexts of their lives made it impossible for them to remain in their countries of nationality or domicile – were distinguished by their will and, above all, *by their ability to move*. In short, their designation as 'refugee' comes *ex post facto* their movement. Their refugeehood is not conditioned upon their movement, rather 'refugee' is a category which attaches itself once exile has occurred, all other things being equal. This is so in both historical and contemporary terms and is a truth which applies universally to movements of those we designate as 'refugees' whatever the motivating cause of their movement. No artificial construction – legal or socio-political – can add to or alter this essential truth.

However, formal constructions of refugee which emerged, particularly in the twentieth century – the Geneva Convention being the most far reaching in this context – exist for purposes other than to give official voice to essential truths. Defining categories is a process heavily imbued with ideology. It invests new meaning (not to mention new emotions) into the everyday. Such definitions determine both official and non-official usages. Thus, 'refugee' becomes more than a convenient label attaching itself to those who are empowered by movement. It becomes not simply a label the use of which is contingent upon the circumstances of individuals and the vagaries of life, but a thing which invests meaning, emotion and ideology into the term 'refugee': the refugee as the oppressed, the deserving subject, the symbol of human rights denied or in conflict. 'Refugee' emerged as a fixed rather than a contingent concept. 'Refugee' existed independently of any defining moment of exile. It no longer depends upon the exile of people to give it life, but lives in a space where movement now conditions refugeehood.

The argument can be more simply put: from moving people becoming refugees the refugee becomes a moving people; from movement becoming a facilitator of the people it becomes the people. However, whilst 'people' in the first half of the foregoing sentence exist, the word 'people' in the second half of the sentence does not allude to an existing or historical group. 'People' here (or the refugee) become an ideal and, whilst the ideal functions upon the existence of the real, it is no less of an ideal. The refugee as an ideal derives from the real Huguenot classification which functioned as a name – a label – no more, but the ideal is always more than the real: a greater investment of the imagination is made. The Huguenot, who is the 'true' refugee, disappears into the annals of history and yet the ideal remains. So now we talk in legal parlance of a refugee 'who is outside his country of nationality', or 'is compelled to leave his place of nationality or habitual residence',[44] or is more generally displaced. History seems to suggest that we do so because groups sporadically from the seventeenth century onwards sought asylum in other countries from religious or political persecution. In short, the end result of an 'immense accumulation of reflexive experiences which synthesize fiction and reality into a vast symbolism'.[45]

This may seem a rather ponderous way of saying that the relationship between asylum and the ideal refugee is a tenuous one and the interdependence of exile or movement (displacement) and the refugee is a challengeable concept, but I believe the detail to be justified. The ability to control spaces is a condition of people and nations, particularly those nations and those people of the nations whose hegemonic reign has so stifled similar opportunities for others. It is a condition neither central nor essential to refugeehood. Rather, controlling spaces, in the sense of the ability to achieve exile, is far from being a privilege which many who require protection can claim, although most would unhesitatingly claim to deserve the protection available to refugees. The world is conceptualised in terms of space, and refugees, like others, occupy that space and have greater or lesser control over it. However, to determine the meaning of refugeehood according to spatial concepts, as we presently do, is to render refugees unique occupiers and controllers of space which accords

---

[44] 1951 Convention, article 1.A(2); OAU Refugee Convention, article 1(2).
[45] Dean MacCannell, *The Tourist: A New Theory of the Leisure Class* (Schocken Books, New York, 1976), p. 23.

ill with the reality of the everyday existence of the majority – women and children.[46]

Conclusion

I have sought to argue that the concept of refugee is one traditionally determined by notions of space, in particular the spatial activity of movement. Movement is her signifier, yet territorial boundaries, cultural perceptions, age and disability all conspire to curtail movement in spatial terms and constantly to withhold the 'official' designation 'refugee' from those most deserving of it. Massey identified the crux of the matter when she argued:

[M]obility, and control over mobility, both reflects and reinforces power. It is not simply a question of unequal distribution, that some people have more than others, and that some have more control than others, it is that the mobility and control of some groups can actively weaken other people. Differential mobility can weaken the leverage of the already weak.[47]

The spatial construction of the refugee is meaningless to those to whom refugeehood is an ever present reality. It is at once the primary indicator of what a refugee must be to reach official cognisance and the most telling example of what the refugee is not.

In saying this, I do not obviously intend to claim that movements of women and children, for example, do not occur, for to do so would be to fly in the face of well-documented evidence to the contrary. Rather, I would argue that such movements occurring within those groups traditionally marginalised outside the category 'refugee' (and of late a growing number of victims of human rights abuses in general) are qualitatively extremely poor, when judged against the aim of immediate protection, temporary asylum and a durable solution, thus making modern-day refugee movements relatively meaningless. I have already alluded to the growing level of research detailing the fact that women refugees, the largest number of the world's refugees, gain less access to state determination procedures in Western states compared to men. Refugee women and children more often gain 'protection' in refugee camps. As recent evidence suggests, camps are often subject to disease-ridden conditions, where food and medical supplies are scarce.[48]

Whilst movement within strictly confined geographical limitations can

[46] See Spijkerboer, *Women and Refugee Status*, p. 10.
[47] Doreen Massey, 'A Global Sense of Place', in *Space, Place and Gender* (ed. Doreen Massey, University of Minnesota Press, Minneapolis, 1994), p. 150.
[48] See, for instance, David Keen, *Refugees: Rationing the Right to Life, The Crisis in Emergency Relief* (Zed Books, London, 1992).

and does take place, it hardly exists to achieve the aim that refugee movement in the historical sense of the concept implied – not merely protection, but a minimum level of social and economic well-being. The
structural inequalities which render spatial concepts like asylum relatively
meaningless to the majority have come to the fore in recent times of mass
civil and political unrest across regional boundaries. Yet, such concepts
remain strong and compelling ideological frameworks for refugees,
refugee-producing and refugee-receiving states.

Bibliography

Abdullahi, Ahmednasir M., 'The Refugee Crisis in Africa as a Crisis of the
    Institution of State', 6 *International Journal of Refugee Law*, 1994, pp.
    562–80
Adelman, Howard, 'Refuge or Asylum: A Philosophical Perspective', 1 *Journal of
    Refugee Studies*, 1988, p. 9
Anderson, Benedict, *Imagined Communities: Reflection on the Origin and Spread of
    Nationalism* (Verso, London, 1990)
Arboleda, Eduardo, 'The Cartagena Declaration of 1984 and its Similarities to
    the 1969 OAU Convention – A Comparative Perspective', 7 *International
    Journal of Refugee Law*, 1995, Special Issue, pp. 87–102
Arboleda, Eduardo and Ian Hoy, 'The Convention Definition in the West:
    Disharmony of Interpretation and Application', 5 *International Journal of
    Refugee Law*, 1993, pp. 66–90
Castel, Jacqueline R., 'Rape, Sexual Assault and the Meaning of Persecution', 4
    International Journal of Refugee Law, 1989, pp. 39–56
Cook, Rebecca J. (ed.), *Human Rights of Women: National and International
    Perspectives* (University of Pennsylvania Press, Philadelphia, 1994)
Farer, Tom J., 'How the International System Copes with Involuntary Migration:
    Norms, Institutions and State Practice', 17 *Human Rights Quarterly*, 1995,
    pp. 72–100
Foucault, Michel, 'Of Other Spaces', 16 *Diacritics*, 1986, pp. 22–7
    'Questions of Geography', in *Power/Knowledge: Selected Interviews and other
    Writings 1972–77* (ed. Colin Gordon, Harvester Press, Brighton, 1980)
Greatbach, Jacqueline, 'The Gender Difference: Feminist Critiques of Refugee
    Discourse', 1 *International Journal of Refugee Law*, 1989, pp. 518–27
Indra, Doreen M., 'Gender: A Key Dimension of the Refugee Experience', 6
    Refuge, 1987, pp. 3–4
Kaplan, Caren, *Questions of Travel: Postmodern Discourses of Displacement* (Duke
    University Press, New York, 1996)
Keith, Michael and Steve Pile (eds.), *Place and the Politics of Identity* (Routledge,
    London, 1993)
Loescher, Gil, *Beyond Charity: International Cooperation and the Global Refugee
    Crisis* (Oxford University Press, 1993)
MacCannell, Dean, *The Tourist: A New Theory of the Leisure Class* (Schocken
    Books, New York, 1976)

Marrus, Michael R., *The Unwanted: European Refugees in the Twentieth Century* (Oxford University Press, 1985)

Massey, Doreen, 'A Global Sense of Place' in *Space, Place and Gender* (ed. Doreen Massey, University of Minnesota Press, Minneapolis, 1994)

Plaut, W. Gunther, *Asylum: A Moral Dilemma* (Praeger, London, 1995)

Rose, Peter I., 'Some Thoughts about Refugee and the Descendants of Theseus', 15 *International Migration Review*, 1981, pp. 8–15

Ryan, William C., 'The Historical Case for a Right of Sanctuary', 19 *Journal of Church and State*, 1987, p. 209

Shacknove, Andrew, 'Who is a Refugee?', 95 *Ethics*, 1985, p. 274

Simpson, Sir John Hope, *The Refugee Problem – Report of a Survey* (Institute of International Affairs, Oxford University Press, 1938)

Soja, Edward, *Postmodern Geographies: The Reassertion of Space in Critical Social Theory* (Verso, London, 1989)

Spijkerboer, Thomas, *Women and Refugee Status: Beyond the Public/Private Distinction* (Emancipation Council, The Hague, 1994)

Thi Dieu De, Truong, 'Women Refugees in the Netherlands: A Caseworker's Approach', in *Refugees: The Trauma of Exile: The Humanitarian Role of the Red Cross and Red Crescent* (ed. Diana Miserez, League of Red Cross and Red Crescent Societies and Martinus Nijhoff, Dordrecht, 1988), p. 287

Zolberg, Aristide, Astri Suhrke and Sergio Aguayo, *Escape from Violence: Conflict and the Refugee Crisis in the Developing World* (Oxford University Press, 1989)

6 Taking the 'political' out of asylum: the legal containment of refugees' political activism

Prakash Shah

Introduction

In January 1996 the case of Dr Al-Masari received a great deal of media coverage. A Saudi Arabian intellectual, he had been imprisoned and tortured in Saudi Arabia and fled via Yemen to the United Kingdom,[1] from where he continued his fax campaign against the Saudi government's corruption. When told by the Home Office that his application for refugee status had been rejected on the basis that Dominica was prepared to grant him asylum, he responded in disbelief at the decision of the then Conservative government. He declared: 'Freedom of speech used to be among the most valued of all traditions and rights but this has now evaporated – and is no doubt the first of many evaporations.'[2] The press concentrated attention on what appeared to be the real reason for Al-Masari's proposed removal, the *Independent* maintaining: 'The decision to expel Mr Al-Masari was taken after the Saudis threatened British firms with the loss of billions of pounds of business in arms contracts.'[3]

The Al-Masari case is illustrative of a new thinking on the status of refugees. While the New World Order takes shape, several new political alignments become more apparent. This is manifest especially in the relations between North and South, where processes of peace are not leading to its actual realisation. There also emerges a new knowledge about the refugee: the refugee has become the political 'other'.

This account begins with a survey of the movements which have given a political content to the laws of asylum. The preoccupations of the East–West divide no longer exist and groups which organise and cam-

---

[1] The Home Office rejected his initial claim for asylum, alleging that he could be sent to Yemen. This decision was overturned by an adjudicator.
[2] Mohammed al-Masari, 'Why are They Moving Heaven and Earth to Send Me into Exile?', *Independent*, 5 January 1996.
[3] Colin Brown, Patrick Cockburn, Steve Crawshaw and Phil Davison, 'Downing Street Meeting Sealed Dissident's Fate', *Independent*, 5 January 1996.

paign against regimes favoured by the West are targeted for repression. Methods have included surveillance, the banning of publications and arrests on political criteria. These actions are increasingly carried out across European states and in consultation with, or at the instigation of, the regimes against which exiles are campaigning. Further, the very concept of asylum is threatened. Asylum laws are remoulded to incorporate conditions warning against political agitation. Where political agitation does occur, one finds an increasing willingness by states to criminalise refugees and use whatever means are at their disposal to remove them into the hands of their persecutors. In the UK, which is the focus of this chapter, 'national security' and 'terrorism' are the vehicles through which asylum may be compromised.[4]

Historical dimensions

The 1905 Aliens Act in the UK marked a definite break with the nineteenth century, of which period it has been claimed that 'asylum was safeguarded . . . precisely because the British despised foreigners'.[5] The new Act brought with it an elaborate system of controls on immigration. It marked the culmination of the problematisation of the alien presence and reflected the insecurity in British society of the subversion of 'the nation, the race, the constitution, etc.'.[6] Operating this Act provided the Home Office with a mass of data and experience.[7] Monitoring and secret registration of aliens was the first step in the mass arrest and detention of those considered to be enemy aliens. During the First and Second World Wars aliens, including refugees, were rounded up, interned and deported.[8]

In the post-1945 atmosphere of the apparently global bipolarity of ideology, refugee laws throughout the West were geared toward the recep-

---

[4] This chapter does not deal with the 'de-politicisation' of asylum claims by women. For analysis and comment on that issue, see, for example, Nancy Kelly, 'Gender-Related Persecution: Assessing the Asylum Claims of Women', 26 *Cornell International Law Journal*, 1993, p. 625; Emily Love, 'Equality in Political Asylum Law: For a Gender-Based Persecution', 17 *Harvard Women's Law Journal*, 1994, p. 133. See also chapter 5 of this volume.

[5] David Cesarani, 'An Alien Concept? The Continuity of Anti-Alienism in British Society Before 1940', 11 *Immigrants and Minorities*, 1992, 3, p. 27. See, in detail, Bernard Porter, *The Refugee Question in Mid-Victorian Politics* (Cambridge University Press, 1979); Dallal Stevens, 'The Case of UK Asylum Law and Policy: Lessons from History?' in *Current Issues of UK Asylum Law and Policy* (ed. Frances Nicholson and Patrick Twomey, Ashgate Publishing, Aldershot, UK, 1998). For a brief account of the general movement of exiles, see Aristide Zolberg, Astri Suhrke and Sergio Aguayo, *Escape from Violence: Conflict and the Refugee Crisis in the Developing World* (Oxford University Press, 1989), pp. 10–11.

[6] Cesarani, 'An Alien Concept?', p. 32.   [7] *Ibid.*

[8] *Ibid.*, pp. 34–7 and 44–6.

tion of exiles from the Communist world.[9] In the United States political considerations were made an explicit component of refugee admission policies[10] and Western European states also eased the entry of exiles from the Eastern bloc.[11] In the UK only a trickle of refugees from the Eastern bloc seems to have occurred as travel was quite difficult. During the Hungarian uprising in 1956 France and the UK announced their intention to take an unlimited number of refugees. Upwards of 20,000 Hungarians found asylum in the UK within a few days, the highest of any European country.[12] The exiles of the 1960s found ready welcome and individuals were granted asylum almost automatically.[13] On the other hand, the immigration laws could equally be put to political use for the removal of unwanted persons. One example from this period concerns the case of Dr Soblen, who had been accused of spying for the Eastern bloc in the USA and sought to escape to Israel with which the USA then had no extradition treaty. He found himself being forcibly removed on a flight to the UK where an application for *habeas corpus* against his proposed onward removal to the USA was dismissed by the Court of Appeal[14] despite the Home Office's attempt to circumvent the extradition procedures.[15]

The bias toward easy admission for nationals of Eastern bloc states began to be compromised by the beginning of the 1980s as applicants for

[9] James C. Hathaway, 'A Reconsideration of the Underlying Premise of Refugee Law', 31 *Harvard International Law Journal*, 1989, 1, pp. 148–51.

[10] See Gil Loescher and John A. Scanlan, *Calculated Kindness: Refugees and America's Half-Open Door* (The Free Press, New York and Collier Macmillan, London, 1986); and Peter H. Koehn, *Refugees from Revolution* (Westview Press, Boulder, CO,1991), pp. 207–13.

[11] Zolberg, Suhrke and Aguayo, *Escape from Violence*, pp. 26–7. For figures of movements from eastern to western Europe between 1950 and 1992, see Heinz Fassmann and Rainer Munz, 'European East–West Migration, 1945–1992', in *Cambridge Survey of World Migration* (ed. Robin Cohen, Cambridge University Press, 1995), p. 473.

[12] Loescher and Scanlan, *Calculated Kindness*, p. 52, put the figure at 21,100 for the UK and 38,121 for the USA. Paul Tabori, *The Anatomy of Exile* (Harrap & Co., London, 1972), p. 339, puts the figure higher at about 30,000. He also notes that, had the UK government not been so generous, 'there would have been something of a revolution, for there was a tidal wave of sympathy and compassion for the men, women and children who were stumbling across the minefields and barbed wire into Austria'.

[13] Tabori, *Anatomy of Exile*, p. 340. Sheila Patterson, 'The Poles: An Exile Community in Britain', in *Between Two Cultures: Migrants and Minorities in Britain* (ed. James L. Watson, Basil Blackwell, Oxford, 1978), p. 216 notes the 'small but significant contingents of active political exiles from Communist Poland'. See also Ann Dummett and Andrew Nicol, *Subjects, Citizens, Aliens and Others: Nationality and Immigration Law* (Weidenfeld and Nicolson, London, 1990), p. 188.

[14] *R. v. Secretary of State for Home Affairs, ex parte Soblen* [1962] 3 All ER 373.

[15] See on the *Soblen* case and more generally, Paul O'Higgins, 'Disguised Extradition: The *Soblen* Case', 27 *Modern Law Review*,1964, p. 522, who speaks of 'many examples of such abuse of the powers of deportation in British practice, both as regards surrender by the United Kingdom as well as surrender to the United Kingdom'.

asylum from those countries were refused in larger numbers. In particular, in response to the increase in the number of Polish exiles, applications
from Poland were scrutinised closely.[16] The case of a Romanian citizen
then raised the whole issue of whether a person who had violated the
restrictive exit laws could found a claim under the 1951 Geneva
Convention Relating to the Status of Refugees.[17] The Minister of State in
the Home Office stated: 'We simply cannot proceed on the assumption
that anybody who comes to this country from Eastern Europe has the
right to asylum here just because if he were returned to his own country
he might suffer penalties. If we followed that policy we would give a contingent right of asylum to every citizen from every country behind the
iron curtain.'[18]

In the post-Cold War atmosphere much talk of a New World Order has
prevailed. New alignments are being forged and the main security considerations now lie in the regions south[19] and east of the European Union
(EU). Laws are being remoulded in reaction to the new priorities. The
exilic bias of refugee law has been transformed into the promotion of containment which is disguised in the terminology of 'repatriation' and 'root
causes'.[20] However, European states are also experiencing a crisis of
liberal political ideology. Thus, Lord Mustill in the House of Lords says of
asylum and extradition laws: 'These laws were conceived at a time when
political struggles could be painted in clear primary colours largely inappropriate today; and the so-called "political exception" which forms part
of these laws . . . was a product of Western European and North American
liberal democratic ideals which no longer give a full account of political
struggles in the modern world.'[21] Thus the framework is elaborated,

---

[16] Vaughan Bevan, *The Development of British Immigration Law* (Croom Helm, London,
1986), p. 216.   [17] 189 UNTS 137.
[18] David Waddington, HC Hansard, vol. 40, cols. 459–60, 31 March 1983. The Home
Secretary similarly declared that: 'If . . . every person who came from an Eastern
European country was automatically to be accepted as a political refugee that would be a
serious matter that would affect all of our immigration policy': *Race and Immigration: The
Runnymede Trust Bulletin*, No. 155, May 1983, pp. 1–3. See also the statement by Lord
Elton for the government in the House of Lords, HL Hansard, vol. 440, col. 1543, 29
March 1983.
[19] Witness the 'Euro-Med' conference of November 1995, Victor Smart, 'A Union Anxious
to Anchor Southern Neighbours', *European*, 23–29 August 1995.
[20] T. Alexander Aleinikoff, 'State-Centred Refugee Law: From Resettlement to
Containment', 14 *Michigan Journal of International Law*, 1992, p. 134.
[21] *T. v. Secretary of State for the Home Department* [1996] 2 All ER 865 at p. 867J–868A. It is
interesting to compare this *dictum* with Hepple's comment on the *Dutscke* case, which
involved a German student whose permission to remain in the UK was refused on
national security grounds: 'It is an ailing foreign revolutionary student whose case has
done most to bring into debate the liberal constitutional values upon which recent
administrative law developments have been staked.' B. A. Hepple, 'Aliens and
Administrative Practice: The Dutscke Case', 34 *Modern Law Review*, 1971, p. 501.

creating a space, a twilight domain, where the ideals of liberal democracy, including its forms of justice, may not prevail. In fact, the rehearsals of the twentieth century now provide the backdrop for even more sophisticated mechanisms of control.

Patterns of domination

The opening up of internal European borders has been a triumph for security forces in the EU states despite some teething problems and national jealousies. Co-ordination between European states introduces a new dimension in the policing of refugees. This co-ordination has enabled the pooling of intelligence among the various agencies involved in internal and external surveillance. Technology provides centralised information on 'undesirable aliens' in the European and Schengen Information Systems.[22] The most significant example of a co-ordinated European approach came during the Gulf War of 1991. The UK authorities rounded up ninety-one Iraqis and Palestinians under the national security provisions in the immigration laws (see below) in January 1991. Another thirty-five detentions followed under the royal prerogative. As a result of a Trevi meeting of European Community (EC) security ministers[23] on 22 January 1991, a large security operation against Arabs was launched across the EC. Raids, searches, deportations and internments were carried out in Greece, Italy, Germany and France.[24]

Security forces are recruiting informants from among refugees or asylum seekers themselves. Threats and intimidation are used where enticement through promises of quick recognition of refugee status have not yielded information on fellow activists. This information has even been directed back to the state of origin. In the UK, Kurds have been the subject of intimidation recently as Special Branch officers have mounted surveillance, conducted house searches, seized possessions, made threats and offered bribes for informers and *agents provocateurs*. Passports, UK

---

[22] On the Schengen Information System, see Pieter Boeles, 'Data Exchange, Privacy and Legal Protection Especially Regarding Aliens', in *Free Movement of Persons in Europe* (ed. Henry G. Schermers *et al.*, Martinus Nijhoff, Dordrecht, 1993), pp. 52–7.
[23] European Community interior ministers established the Trevi Group (on *terrorisme, radicalisme, extrémisme, violence internationale*) in June 1976 as the main forum for inter-governmental co-operation on internal security questions within the EC. With the entry into force of the Maastricht Treaty on European Union in November 1993, the Group was superseded by the K4 Committee, which takes its name from article K4 of Title VI of the Treaty governing co-operation on justice and home affairs issues.
[24] Stephen Dorril, *The Silent Conspiracy: Inside the Intelligence Services in the 1990s* (Mandarin Paperbacks, London, 1994), pp. 116–17.

nationality or rapid family reunion have been promised in return for co-operation with Special Branch.[25]

Another component is the level of co-ordination between governments and security forces in European states and states of origin of refugees. In the wake of the Al-Masari incident it was noted that 'Algerians, Bahrainis, Egyptians, and Tunisians are at the top of the list of activists whom the British government, arms dealers and industrialists, in general would like to see vanish from the London scene; their governments have put strong pressure on Britain to silence these . . . operators.'[26] One may add, among others, Palestinians, Kurds and Sikhs. One result of such interventions may be the eventual inclusion of extraterritorial provisions in Britain's anti-terrorist legislation.[27]

The Algerian government is provided with economic support and help with repression by either deportation or physical extermination of Algerians by the French government in exchange for the co-operation of its secret services in the surveillance of Muslims in France.[28] Meanwhile, France has intervened in the UK, Germany and the USA to obtain reassurances that Algerian activists would not be welcome there.[29] The level of repression in France itself has reached huge proportions. In 1994 mass identity checks were carried out between 5 and 16 August in which 30,000 people were stopped and searched. Five Islamic publications were prohibited and twenty-five Arabs were interned in army barracks, twenty of whom were deported. The then interior minister Charles Pasqua reasoned thus: 'If you don't go fishing, you'll never catch any fish.'[30] The

[25] Defend the Kurds Campaign, 26 April 1995. See the account in *Statewatch*, May–June 1991, and *Statewatch*, November–December 1994, on the activities of the Dutch security force (BVD). Dorril, *The Silent Conspiracy*, p. 114 notes: 'A section of twelve special branch officers keeps permanent watch on Iranians, Iraqis, Palestinians and Libyans, relying heavily on contacts with MI5 and political exiles living in the United Kingdom.' Even library records have been searched to trace the ideological interests of students. Meanwhile the Foreign Office in the UK urged university staff to tip off security services about students from North Korea, Iran, Iraq and Libya: Institute of Race Relations, *IRR European Race Audit*, Bulletin No. 11.

[26] Tim Llewellyn, 'A Taint on Britain's Honour', *Independent*, 5 January 1996. Egypt and the Palestinian National Authority were represented at an EU seminar on Islamic fundamentalism held in Rome in March 1996: *Statewatch*, March–April 1996.

[27] *Statewatch*, January–February 1997.

[28] Michel Wievorka, 'France Faced with Terrorism', 14 *Terrorism*, 1991, p. 167.

[29] Germany has banned a leading Islamic Salvation Front (FIS) spokesman from engaging in political activity, including making political statements. The UK indicated in September 1994 that a leading FIS spokesman would not be issued with a visa if he wanted to speak at the Royal Institute of International Affairs: *IRR European Race Audit*, Bulletin No. 11, December 1994. Germany has concluded a readmission agreement with Algeria to ensure the return of Algerian nationals most of whom are rejected asylum seekers. In return Germany has agreed to provide financial assistance to Algeria: *Migration News Sheet*, June 1995.

[30] *IRR European Race Audit*, Bulletin No. 11, December 1994.

huge rate of arrests in France continued in 1995 and has spread to Germany, Britain, Sweden and Belgium.[31] Two Algerian activists in the Armed Islamic Group (GIA) who were operating from the UK were held under the Prevention of Terrorism Act in 1995.[32] The Turkish government has similarly intervened in European capitals so that repressive measures may be taken against active Kurdish groups. The Kurdistan Workers' Party (PKK) and Dev-Sol (Revolutionary Left) have been banned in France and Germany and it has been claimed that Britain has become a magnet for these groups.[33] The most publicised case of repression in the UK has been that of Kani Yilmaz, the European spokesperson for the PKK, who had been granted refugee status in Germany. He had been invited to London for a meeting but found himself arrested by twelve policemen, detained at Belmarsh maximum security prison, pending deportation to Germany on national security grounds.[34] This event came after Special Branch and the National Criminal Intelligence Service reported through the press that Kurdish groups were 'behind a rising tide of terrorism and other crime' and that they were 'involved in extortion and the transfer of illicit proceeds'. Yilmaz's case was subject to extradition proceedings which were requested by Germany and the extradition has been allowed by the High Court on the basis that Yilmaz's political activities were directed against Turkey and not Germany, the requesting state.[35] He has since been extradited to Germany for trial under German anti-terrorist law and therefore fell outside the defence of 'political offence'.[36]

---

[31] See *Statewatch*, November–December 1994; *Statewatch*, November–December 1995; *Africa Research Bulletin*, 11897A–C, 1–30 June 1995; *Africa Research Bulletin*, 11997C–11998A, 1–30 September 1995; *Africa Research Bulletin*, 12031A, 1–31 October 1995; and *Africa Research Bulletin*, 12066A–12067A, 1–30 November 1995.

[32] One had his application for asylum refused and both are awaiting an extradition request by France: *Africa Research Bulletin*, 12067A, 1–30 November 1995; Hill Taylor Dickinson, 'UK Told to Stop Sheltering Terror', Sunday Telegraph, 5 November 1995. More recently, in May 1998, over 80 people suspected of supporting extremist Islamic groups were questioned by police in five European countries as a preventive measure in advance of the World Cup: Philippe Broussard and Pascal Ceaux, 'Mondial: opération préventive anti-islamistes', *Le Monde*, 27 May 1998.

[33] *IRR European Race Audit*, Bulletin No. 11, December 1994; *Statewatch*, November–December 1994.   [34] *Statewatch*, November–December 1994.

[35] Judgment of 4 July 1996. Defend the Kurds Campaign, press release, 8 July 1996; Sheri Lazier, 'Kani Yilmaz Appeal Hearing: Summary of Observations', 20 May 1996 (on file with author). See also *Statewatch*, May–June 1996.   [36] *Statewatch*, July–August 1997.

The legal options

Good behaviour clauses

Article 15 of the Geneva Convention states: 'As regards non-political and non-profit-making associations and trade unions the Contracting States shall accord to refugees lawfully staying in their territory the most favourable treatment according to nationals of a foreign country, in the same circumstances.' Interestingly, the *travaux préparatoires* of the Geneva Convention reveal that the Danish representative had wanted to move an amendment to what eventually became article 15 which would 'reserve the right to restrict or prohibit political activity on the part of the refugees'. The US representative warned that, were this to be done, it could be interpreted as forbidding refugees even to express political opinions, and would certainly deny them access to an area of human activity in which they should at least have as much right to engage as any other aliens.[37] Nevertheless, the situation as it stands silences the refugee politically.

Engaging in political activity in the state of asylum before the application for asylum has been made, or is pending, is now fraught with danger. The availability of refugee status is made dependent on what may be described as good behaviour clauses. These are an attempt to guarantee that the asylum seeker will engage in the minimum of political activity while on the territory of the state of refuge. Engagement in protests and demonstrations, if used to found an asylum claim, are therefore liable to be discounted, as these activities are prone to be viewed as 'self-serving'.[38]

This principle had already been approved by the judiciary in the UK in two cases. In *Mendis*,[39] the applicant had been involved in activities critical of the Sri Lankan government. He claimed that the articles he had written and photographs taken of him during demonstrations would invite persecution. The Sri Lankan High Commissioner had written an unsolicited letter to the Minister of State in the Home Office that Mr Mendis was not wanted for 'any offence criminal or otherwise'.[40] The adjudicator who heard the first appeal, taking that letter into account, saw Sri Lanka as 'inherently a democracy where the rule of law applies'.[41] A

[37] Paul Weis, *The Refugee Convention 1951: The Travaux Préparatoires Analysed*, (Cambridge University Press, 1995), p. 124.
[38] In Sweden, a good behaviour clause is to be applied to non-Convention refugees in order to deny them residence permits: *Statewatch*, May–June 1995.
[39] *Mendis* v. *Immigration Appeal Tribunal and the Secretary of State for the Home Department* [1989] *Immigration Appeals Reports* 6.   [40] *Ibid.*, p. 9.
[41] *Ibid.*, p. 10. Before the Court of Appeal, the arguments that the letter only confirmed that there was no request for extradition, and that the adjudicator had confused persecution and prosecution, were not accepted.

question which arose was whether by raising his voice in the UK and not in Sri Lanka, he could claim protection. Two of the Court of Appeal judges thought that the Convention did not guarantee worldwide freedom of speech while recognising that, in Sri Lanka, Mendis would not have the freedom to speak his mind about the regime.[42] The standard would have to be stricter since, otherwise, it was feared that whoever was prepared to invite persecution would be entitled to refugee status.[43]

In *Ex parte 'B'*,[44] the High Court had before it an application from an Iranian monarchist who had had minimal political involvement until he arrived in the UK. In the UK he had engaged in the organisation of a monarchist group and also distributed literature and attended demonstrations. He had been photographed at these demonstrations. It was claimed by the Home Office and accepted by the court (and by the adjudicator and the tribunal before it) that these were 'part of a calculated policy to enhance his asylum claim'.[45] So while accepting that the applicant 'had engaged in sufficient overt political activity to create such risk as would ordinarily attract refugee status'[46] the court sought to impose a test of 'reasonableness' as to the type of political activity which would count towards an asylum claim. What constitutes reasonableness was to be left to case-by-case development.[47]

In the UK, consideration of asylum claims by the Home Office is now made subject to more detailed immigration rules, the development of which has no doubt been influenced by judicial decisions discussed here. They provide that such consideration may involve taking into account activities which are deemed to be inconsistent with previous beliefs and behaviour and calculated to create or substantially enhance the claim.[48] It remains to be seen whether claims made by refugees who have been politically active in the UK, and who thus apply as refugees *sur place*, will be subject to the 'fast-track' system extended by the Asylum and Immigration Act 1996.[49]

---

[42] *Ibid.*, p. 18, *per* Neill LJ and at p. 22 *per* Balcombe LJ. Staughton LJ preferred to leave the issue open since there may be persons with such strong political convictions who will inevitably speak out against the regime in the country of origin and would inevitably suffer persecution in consequence. *Ibid.*, p. 22–3.

[43] *Ibid.*, p. 22, *per* Balcombe LJ.

[44] *R. v. Immigration Appeal Tribunal, ex parte 'B'* [1989] *Immigration Appeals Reports* 166.

[45] *Ibid.*, p. 169.   [46] *Ibid.*, p. 170.   [47] *Ibid.*, p. 172.

[48] HC 395 (1993–4), para. 341(iv).

[49] In particular, the new Schedule 2, paras. 5(4)(a) and (b) to the Asylum and Immigration Appeals Act 1993, inserted by the 1996 Act, section 1, may be relevant here.

National security expulsions

The Geneva Convention provides that no refugee who is lawfully in the territory of the state in question may be expelled save on grounds of national security or public order[50] and rights of due process should be accorded except where compelling reasons of national security otherwise require.[51] The Convention also leaves open an exception to the principle of *non-refoulement*[52] in cases where there are reasonable grounds for regarding a refugee as a danger to the security of the country in which he is.[53] In the UK a special provision is provided under immigration law for those liable to deportation or removal on national security grounds.[54] In contrast to other immigration cases, no right of appeal exists. A person served with such an order may appear before a panel of three advisers who report to the Secretary of State. The individual has no right to legal representation, nor any right to know the case against him, and there is no information provided as to the conclusions reached by the panel of the 'three wise men'. Judicial review is available as a remedy but it has been said of this that 'as soon as national security is mentioned, the courts quake'. [55]

The principles which govern such national security concerns were raised in the 1970s in immigration cases[56] and were to be applied with increasing frequency to refugees over the next two decades. N. S. H., a stateless Palestinian with a student visa, was granted a re-entry visa by the UK in order that he could see his sick mother in Lebanon. He was refused leave to enter upon return to the UK.[57] Despite the appearance that the

---

[50] Article 32(1).   [51] Article 32(2).   [52] Article 33(1).   [53] Article 33(2).
[54] Immigration Act 1971, sections 13(5), 14(3) and 15(3) and Asylum and Immigration Appeals Act 1993, Schedule 2, para. 6. The power under the 1971 Act is wider than that provided for in the 1993 Act. Under the 1971 Act deportation or removal is allowed on the basis of the relations between the UK and any other country or for other reasons of a political nature; whereas under the 1993 Act an appeal is only excluded on national security grounds, reflecting the exceptions in articles 32 and 33 of the Geneva Convention. Asylum seekers who are deemed by the state to fall outside the Convention, but who may be allowed to remain for other humanitarian reasons would still be subject to the wider exception in the Immigration Act 1971.
[55] Ian A. Macdonald and Nicholas J. Blake, *Immigration Law and Practice in the United Kingdom* (4th edn, Butterworths, London, 1995), p. 501. See *ibid.*, pp. 499–502 for details on the national security procedure. Sweden also seems to have adopted similar procedures in its anti-terrorist law: *Statewatch*, September–October 1995. For a survey of US law on the matter, see Mary Scott Miller, 'Aliens' Right to Seek Asylum: The Attorney General's Power to Exclude "Security Threats" and the Role of the Courts', 22 *Vanderbilt Journal of Transnational Law*, 1989, pp. 187–215.
[56] Hepple, 'Aliens and Administrative Practice'; *R. v. Secretary of State for the Home Department, ex parte Hosenball* [1977] 3 All ER 452.
[57] *N. S. H. v. Secretary of State for the Home Department* [1988] *Immigration Appeals Reports* 389.

Home Office had acted irregularly,[58] the plea of national security meant that the allegation that he 'had advocated the use of violence in Western Europe' went unexamined.[59]

The issue arose again during the hostilities with Iraq.[60] Distant relatives of people connected with terrorism and members of clubs and societies deemed 'suspect' were among those included for internment. The ninety-one arrests were made on outdated information and were, in fact, reversed by the panel of 'three wise men'. It did become evident through the procedures that some of the information against the detainees had been provided by the Israeli security service Mossad which was thought to be 'getting its own back against moderate Palestinians'.[61] Challenges to the detention orders prior to those hearings produced the expected reactions from judges. Simon Brown J, who feared 'internment by the back door', gave leave to apply for judicial review in one case, 'B.', but he did not follow through his convictions, finding the next day in Cheblak's case, that he could not go behind the national security allegations.[62] The Court of Appeal agreed, urging instead that those aggrieved should pursue the 'three wise men' route.[63]

The national security provision was also applied in the case of Chahal, a Sikh activist, who claimed asylum upon being served with a deportation order on national security grounds.[64] He found it impossible to contest the charge that he 'had close links with Sikh terrorists in the Punjab', that 'he has been involved in planning and directing of terrorist attacks in India, the UK and elsewhere', and further charges of 'supplying funds and equipment to terrorists'.[65] Lord Justice Staughton admitted that 'we have massive evidence as to whether Chahal's life or freedom would be threatened' in India.[66] On the other hand, he could see no ground for doubting the letter of assurance from the Indian High Commissioner that Chahal would enjoy the same legal protection as any other Indian citizen and had no reason to fear any kind of mistreatment at the hands of the Indian authorities.[67] So the Secretary of State was not irrational in relying

---

[58] See concerns raised by Dillon LJ, *ibid.*, p. 392 and Neill LJ at p. 396.

[59] *Ibid.*, p. 397.   [60] See *Statewatch*, March–April 1991.

[61] Dorril, *The Silent Conspiracy*, p. 121. Interestingly, the Court of Appeal emphasised the need to protect sources by not revealing their identity: Lord Donaldson MR in *R. v. Secretary of State for the Home Department, ex parte Cheblak* [1991] 2 All ER 319 at pp. 331–2.

[62] Dorril, *The Silent Conspiracy*, p. 119. The application in B's case was also rejected at the hearing by Mann J, *Independent*, 29 January 1991; Alex J. Carroll, 'The Gulf Crisis and the Ghost of Liversidge v. Anderson', 5 *Immigration and Nationality Law and Practice*, 1991, 3, p. 74.

[63] *R. v. Secretary of State for the Home Department, ex parte Cheblak* [1991] 2 All ER 319.

[64] *R. v. Secretary of State for the Home Department, ex parte Chahal* [1995] 1 All ER 658, Court of Appeal.   [65] *Ibid.*, p. 663D–H.   [66] *Ibid.*, p. 667F–G.

[67] *Ibid.*, pp. 668J–669C.

on the High Commissioner's assurance nor in thinking that India had a constitution which guaranteed freedom of religious belief and an independent judiciary, and that Chahal would only come to harm if he were convicted of a crime by due process and in accordance with the law. If charged he would only be subject to prosecution for alleged criminal activities, and not for his political beliefs or expressions.[68] The relegation of Chahal's alleged activities to mere criminal actions which were not political, and therefore not deserving of protection, represents a consistent theme in asylum cases.[69] Chahal remained in detention for six years[70] until the European Court of Human Rights found that his deportation would amount to inhuman and degrading treatment or torture.[71] The ruling of the Court of Human Rights has now forced the UK government to consider enacting further legislation providing for greater rights of due process within the national security procedure by the constitution of a Special Immigration Appeals Commission.[72] Meanwhile, the process of criminalisation, of turning political dissent into criminal activity deserving of repression, has been transplanted to other cases where charges of terrorism have been made.

Political and non-political offences

Since the early 1970s European states have been concerned to limit the spread of violent political resistance within the boundaries of Europe. Domestic anti-terrorism laws have been enacted, and there has been a concern to reduce the barriers to the transfer of individuals between states. In the UK the Prevention of Terrorism (Temporary Provisions) Act 1989 allows for exclusion of individuals from the UK 'where the Secretary of State is satisfied that a person is, has been or will be upon entering Great Britain or Northern Ireland, concerned in the commis-

---

[68] Exactly such an allegation by the Home Office was dismissed by the Immigration Appeal Tribunal in *Charanjit Singh v. Secretary of State for the Home Department* (13375) 5 March 1996, 3 *Immigration Law Practitioners' Association Case Digest*,1996, 3.

[69] See, for example, *R. v. Secretary of State for the Home Department, ex parte Baljit Singh* [1994] *Immigration Appeals Reports* 42.

[70] For the last domestic challenge to Chahal's detention, see *R. v. Secretary of State for the Home Department, ex parte Chahal* [1996] *Immigration Appeals Reports* 205. Domestic proceedings are, at the time of writing, taking place in an attempt to claim damages for unlawful detention.

[71] *Chahal v. UK, Reports of Judgments and Decisions*, 1996–V; 23 EHRR, 1997, p. 413. See also chapter 4 of this volume.

[72] See Prakash Shah, 'Post-Chahal: The Special Immigration Appeals Commission', 12 *Immigration and Nationality Law and Practice*, 1998, 2, p. 67. For an analysis of the Canadian model which appears to have inspired the drafters, see Brian Gorlick, 'The Exclusion of "Security Risks" as a Form of Immigration Control: Law and Practice in Canada', 5 *Immigration and Nationality Law and Practice*, 1991, pp. 76 and 109 (Part II).

sion, preparation or instigation of acts of terrorism'. Enacted for the repression of Irish nationalism, it has also been used to detain Kurds and Algerians.[73] Decisions under the Act are subject to review under a procedure which is as emasculated as that applicable to national security expulsions. It should not go unremarked that 'terrorism' under the 1989 Act is defined as 'the use of violence for political ends', in contrast to other spheres such as extradition and asylum, where 'terrorism' is regarded increasingly as going beyond the 'political'. Lord Lloyd, one-time chair of the 'three wise men' panel, has now proposed the extension of existing anti-terrorist legislation to prevent certain groups organising by proscribing their activities.[74]

Extradition laws have been changed to limit the defence that the transfer of an individual is being sought for a 'political offence', an exception that has applied when a general power to extradite was first introduced in the Extradition Act 1870. The European Convention on the Suppression of Terrorism 1977[75] is 'essentially based on the conviction that there is no reason to maintain the political offence exception for serious forms of political violence between the member states of the Council of Europe. It is assumed that political violence can never be justified in democratic societies and that these societies therefore have every interest in co-operating with each other in order better to suppress that violence.'[76] The interpretation of the notion of political offence has depended, in any case, on political realities.[77] However, the problem which states face in using the 1977 Convention has been that it applies only to states parties thereto and extradition is a much more cumbersome procedure than deportation.[78] To avoid these problems EU states have now reached agreement in

---

[73] In January 1995 a group of Kurds and a British friend were detained at a British port for up to five hours and interrogated by Special Branch: Defend the Kurds Campaign, *Defend the Kurds: Defend Human and Civil Rights in Britain and Europe*, 26 April 1995. In Germany anti-terrorist legislation has also been used against Kurds and the extradition request against Kani Yilmaz (see above) was made after proceedings had begun in Germany under article 129a of the German Penal Code, a specifically anti-terrorist law.

[74] *Statewatch*, January–February 1997. Meanwhile, the Prevention of Terrorism (Additional Powers) Act 1996 gives the police extreme new powers of stop and search, and entry and seizure.

[75] ETS 90. For the UK implementation provisions, see Michael Forde, *The Law of Extradition in the United Kingdom* (Round Hall Press, Ilford, Essex, 1995), pp. 154–61.

[76] Bert Swart, 'Refusal of Extradition and the United Nations Model Treaty on Extradition', 23 *Netherlands Yearbook of International Law*, 1992, p. 186.

[77] See David Freestone, 'Legal Responses to Terrorism: Towards European Co-operation?', in *Terrorism: A Challenge to the State* (ed. Juliet Lodge, Martin Robertson, Oxford, 1981), pp. 210–11 for a summary of judgments of British courts regarding this defence. See also the survey of case law made by Lord Mustill in *T. v. Secretary of State for the Home Department* [1996] 2 All ER 865 at pp. 878–84.

[78] Freestone, 'Legal Responses to Terrorism', p. 205.

the Convention on Extradition Between Member States[79] to eliminate the notion of a political offence *inter se*.[80]

It is interesting to note that in 1992, while the *Chahal* proceedings were underway, the UK signed an extradition agreement with India.[81] One of the principal aims of the treaty was to take 'concrete steps to combat terrorism'.[82] It has been suggested that '[t]he unexpressed reason for this treaty may be the Indian government's desire to be able to prevent members of the Sikh community in the UK allegedly planning an independent state within the borders of India'.[83] As with the 1977 Convention those offences which have been the subject of international agreements related to the suppression of terrorism do not permit the defence of political offence.[84] In a unique provision, the treaty also excludes 'any other offence related to terrorism which at the time of the request is, under the law of the requested party, not to be regarded as an offence of a political character'.[85] It remains to be seen how judges will react to the insertion of 'terrorism' within an international treaty, a notion which has defied definition by the international community so far.[86]

The issue of terrorism arose again in the case of *T*.[87] which provided an opportunity for the UK government to have its application of article 1F(b) of the Geneva Convention tested.[88] That article provides for the denial of Convention refugee status if 'there are serious reasons for considering that . . . he has committed a serious non-political crime outside the country of refuge prior to his admission to that country as a refugee'. T., an Algerian and a member of the Islamic Salvation Front (FIS),[89] had

---

[79] Convention Drawn up on the Basis of Article K.3 of the Treaty on European Union, Relating to Extradition Between the Member States of the European Union, 27 September 1996, OJ, 1996, C313/12.

[80] *Statewatch*, September–October 1996.   [81] Cm 2095.

[82] Geoff Gilbert, 'Extradition', 42 *International and Comparative Law Quarterly*, 2, 1993, p. 442 at p. 444. For the Indian implementation provisions, see 20 *Commonwealth Law Bulletin*, 1994, 4, pp. 1168–9.   [83] Gilbert, 'Extradition', p. 444n.

[84] Article 6.   [85] Article 5(2)(o).

[86] The League of Nations had attempted to arrive at a definition as long ago as 1937 in the draft Convention for the Prevention and Punishment of Terrorism which provided in article 1.2 '"acts of terrorism" means criminal acts directed against a State and intended or calculated to create a state of terror in the minds of particular persons, or a group of persons or the general public'.

[87] *T. v. Secretary of State for the Home Department* [1996] 2 All ER 865.

[88] The issue arose before the Immigration Appeal Tribunal in a Sikh case, *Gurpreet Singh v. Immigration Officer, Gravesend* (10866), 22 April 1994; 1 *Immigration and Nationality Law and Practice Case Digest*, 1994, 1.

[89] Membership of the FIS would seem to preclude an Algerian from having an asylum claim considered at all by the French Office for the Protection of Refugees and Stateless Persons (OFPRA). Visas are impossible to obtain, except at exorbitant unofficial prices. Since 1991 only between 1 and 4 per cent of Algerians who have requested asylum have received it. See Amnesty International Section Française and France Terre d'Asile, *Droit d'asile en France: état des lieux* (1997).

been involved in the planning of a bomb attack at an airport in Algiers and a raid on an army barracks. The House of Lords took the opportunity to draw parallels between the political offence exception in extradition law and the non-political offence exclusion in asylum law.[90] It was noted that there had been a move toward the depoliticisation of crimes given the attempts of states internationally to limit protection to terrorists. In a Eurocentric interpretation it was found that the 'assumption that political action should be equated with the activities permitted to rival groups seeking power under a parliamentary system of government such as exists in Europe and North America, and under other systems based on the same model'[91] could not protect a member of FIS, 'a political organisation which was thwarted in an attempt to become the government of Algeria by democratic means'.[92] T.'s presence was 'an affront and a danger'[93] placing him beyond the political and, therefore, he was not protected against the state which claimed the monopoly of violence. Thus, without resort to complicated extradition procedures, the UK will find it is able to deny asylum and to remove individuals brought within the exclusion.

Conclusion

As for Dr Al-Masari, he was allowed to remain in the UK after a successful appeal to the chief adjudicator who found that Dominica could not afford him safety,[94] although controversy surrounded him again after the bombing in Dhahran, Saudi Arabia of a military barracks in June 1996.[95] In response, the so-called G8 group of countries have now also reached an accord for the containment of political activism by denying asylum to those who are labelled as terrorists.[96]

Edward Said has said of the terms 'fundamentalism' and 'terrorism' that they 'derive from the concerns and intellectual factories in

---

[90] The Secretary of State had contested other aspects of T.'s asylum claim in the UK, but by the Court of Appeal stage he accepted that he had a valid claim for asylum save for the exclusion clause in article 1F(b). The matter reached the House of Lords, T. having lost at all the prior appeal stages.   [91] [1996] 2 All ER 865 at p. 869J.

[92] *Ibid.*, p. 899F–G.   [93] *Ibid.*, p. 867H–J.

[94] *Mohammed A. S. Masari* v. *Immigration Officer Gatwick and Secretary of State for the Home Department*, Appeal No. HX 75955/94, 5 March 1996.

[95] Roula Khalaf, 'Explosive Mix of Youthful Anger Stalks Saudi Arabia', *Financial Times*, 27 June 1996. Further harassment has been suffered by a group of British Bangladeshi poets who have inspired the interest of Special Branch: Ross Slater, 'Special Branch Targets Poets', *Asian Times*, 1 August 1996.

[96] *Statewatch*, September–October 1996. The G8 (Group of Eight) countries are Canada, France, Germany, Japan, Italy, Russia, the UK and the USA.

metropolitan centres like London and Washington'. He writes: 'They are fearful images that lack discriminate contents or definition, but they signify moral power and approval for whoever uses them, moral defensiveness and criminalisation for whomever they designate.'[97] Thus we find that in the area of regulation concerning refugees a new type of political criminality is evolving, the function of which is to control political expression by refugees and with this to control access to asylum. A whole battery of national security provisions, anti-terrorist laws and extradition laws are deployed with a view to suppressing any dissent from outside 'legitimate' political channels. The question that arises is the extent to which the 'political' dimension of asylum remains relevant and whether it can survive the manoeuvres of Western governments to suppress it.

Bibliography

Aleinikoff, Alexander T., 'State-Centred Refugee Law: From Resettlement to Containment', 14 *Michigan Journal of International Law*, 1992, pp. 120–38

Carroll, Alex J., 'The Gulf Crisis and the Ghost of *Liversidge* v. *Anderson*', 5 *Immigration and Nationality Law and Practice*, 1991, 3, pp. 72–6

Cesarani, David, 'An Alien Concept? The Continuity of Anti-Alienism in British Society Before 1940', 11 *Immigrants and Minorities*, 1992, 3, pp. 25–52

Criss, Nur Bilge, 'The Nature of PKK Terrorism in Turkey', 18 *Studies in Conflict and Terrorism*, 1995, pp. 17–37

den Boer, Monica and Neil Walker, 'European Policing After 1992', 31 *Journal of Common Market Studies*, 1993, 1, pp. 3–28

Dorril, Stephen, *The Silent Conspiracy: Inside the Intelligence Services in the 1990s* (Mandarin Paperbacks, London, 1994)

Forde, Michael, *The Law of Extradition in the United Kingdom* (Round Hall Press, Ilford, Essex, 1995)

Freestone, David, 'Legal Responses to Terrorism: Towards European Co-operation?', in *Terrorism: A Challenge to the State* (ed. Juliet Lodge, Martin Robertson, Oxford, 1981), pp. 195–224

Gilbert, Geoff, 'Extradition', 42 *International and Comparative Law Quarterly*, 1993, 2, pp. 442–8

Guy de Fontgalland, S., *Sri Lankans in Exile* (Ceylon Refugees and Repatriates Organisation, Madras, India, 1986)

Koehn, Peter H., *Refugees from Revolution* (Westview Press, Boulder, CO, 1991)

Lodge, Juliet, 'The European Community and Terrorism: Establishing the Principle of "Extradite or Try"', in *Terrorism: A Challenge to the State* (ed. Juliet Lodge, Martin Robertson, Oxford, 1981), pp. 164–94

Miller, Mary Scott, 'Aliens' Right to Seek Asylum: The Attorney General's Power to Exclude "Security Threats" and the Role of the Courts', 22 *Vanderbilt Journal of Transnational Law*, 1989, pp. 187–215

[97] Edward Said, *Culture and Imperialism* (Chatto and Windus, London, 1993), p. 375.

Porter, Bernard, *The Refugee Question in Mid-Victorian Politics* (Cambridge University Press, 1979)

Swart, Bert, 'Refusal of Extradition and the United Nations Model Treaty on Extradition', 23 *Netherlands Yearbook of International Law*, 1992, pp. 175–222

Tabori, Paul, *The Anatomy of Exile* (Harrap & Co., London, 1972)

Wievorka, Michel, 'France Faced with Terrorism', 14 *Terrorism*, 1991, pp. 157–70

7 Refugee definitions in the countries of the Commonwealth of Independent States

Claire Messina

This chapter outlines the population movements which have taken place within the twelve countries of the Commonwealth of Independent States (CIS) following the break-up of the Soviet Union in late 1991. It sets out the different categories of people affected by these movements and describes the conceptualisation efforts set in motion by the CIS Conference on Refugees and Migrants held in May 1996.[1] During the conference process, a number of definitions were coined which go well beyond the traditional refugee definition, thus revealing the limitations of the 1951 Geneva Convention Relating to the Status of Refugees[2] in the particular context of the CIS.[3]

The collapse of the Soviet Union resulted in population displacements of an unprecedented scale and complexity. The magnitude of the flows, estimated at around 9 million people, makes them the most important migratory movements taking place in the region since the Second World War. Their complexity is a result of a unique intermingling of pre-existing internal flows turned international (repatriation, labour migration); of new flows, whose typology is well known to the international community (refugee flows, flows of internally displaced persons, illegal migration, ecological migration, return of demobilised troops); and of new flows on which little or no international experience exists (return of formerly deported peoples).

These multifarious population movements are posing extraordinary challenges to the CIS countries not only as concerns the management of

---

[1] See United Nations High Commissioner for Refugees (UNHCR), International Organisation for Migration (IOM) and Organisation for Security and Co-operation in Europe (OSCE), CIS Conference on Refugees and Migrants, Geneva, 30–31 May 1996; and UNHCR, 'The CIS Conference on Refugees and Migrants', 2 *European Series*, 1996, 1 and 2. The final report of the Conference, including the Programme of Action, is given in Doc. CISCONF/1996/6 of 4 July 1996.   [2] 189 UNTS 137.
[3] As of 4 February 1999 the Convention had been ratified by only seven of the twelve CIS states: Armenia (6 July 1993), Azerbaijan (12 February 1993), Kazakstan (15 January 1999), Kyrgyzstan (8 October 1996), the Russian Federation (2 February 1993), Tajikistan (7 December 1993) and Turkmenistan (2 March 1998). It has not been signed or ratified by Belarus, Georgia, Moldova, Ukraine or Uzbekistan.

flows, but also – and more fundamentally – as concerns the development of appropriate concepts and regimes. This chapter focuses specifically on the conceptualisation efforts under way in the CIS countries, and most notably at the regional level, to devise displacement categories which adequately fit the profiles of the population groups concerned. This is preceded by an overview of the population movements that have taken place in the CIS countries in recent years, the length of which is justified by the dearth of information presently available on the subject. The categorisation exercise under way in the CIS countries is of interest beyond the region in so far as it illustrates quite vividly, both the inadequacy of some internationally accepted definitions in a context of complex displacement, and the urgent need for new concepts tailored to the blurred profiles of today's refugees.

Population displacement in the countries of the CIS

Massive and diverse population movements are not a novelty for the CIS region. Throughout history, and particularly during the Soviet era, migration significantly reshaped the ethnic composition of the Russian empire and later the Union of Soviet Socialist Republics (USSR). Some of these movements were voluntary, featuring labour migrants in search of better work opportunities; others were coerced, like the mass deportations of political opponents, rich peasants (*kulaki* in Russian) and 'untrustworthy' ethnic minorities. Sometimes they were scrupulously planned by central government, sometimes chaotic and unmanaged; sometimes they were driven by individuals' social, economic or personal motivations, and at others by the state's totalitarian concerns. The result of these movements was an intricate mixing of populations and ethnicities, which has survived the demise of the USSR and today constitutes the human legacy of the Soviet Union. [4]

The unfurling, in the newly independent states of the CIS, of ethnic tensions, internal strife and armed conflicts, the worsening of the social and economic situation, the degradation of the environment, the emergence of a movement towards return to historical homelands, have all provided strong challenges to the social and ethnic fabric inherited from the Soviet era. Shortly after 1991, migratory flows dramatically increased throughout the region, leading to a chaotic and painful unmixing of populations.

The types of movements taking place in the region and the categories of

[4] For a review of migratory patterns in the former Soviet Union, see Claire Messina, 'From Migrants to Refugees: Russian, Soviet and Post-Soviet Migration', 6 *International Journal of Refugee Law*, 1994, 4, pp. 620–35.

persons involved therein are multifarious: refugees and asylum seekers, internally displaced persons (IDPs), 'involuntarily relocating persons', repatriants, returning persons belonging to formerly deported peoples, ecological migrants, labour migrants and illegal migrants. In addition, since the opening of the borders, significant numbers of migrants have left the region, either temporarily or for good, to return to their home-lands (most notably Germans and Jews, but also Greeks and Koreans) or in search of better work opportunities.[5] In this chapter, I will limit myself to movements taking place within the CIS region, thus excluding these latter categories of migrants.

Refugees

The refugees present on post-Soviet territory mostly originate from CIS countries and are fleeing armed conflicts. The total number of such refugees can be estimated at around 870,000.[6] The first refugee flow was reported in February 1988 (hence, still in the Soviet era), and followed a pogrom against ethnic Armenians in Sumgait, Azerbaijan. As a consequence, some 500,000 people were displaced within the country, most of whom were Armenians fleeing to Armenia and Azeris fleeing to Azerbaijan.[7] The pogrom of January 1990 against ethnic Armenians in Baku (which was led by Azeri refugees from Armenia and Nagorno Karabakh) resulted in another wave of displacement of ethnic Armenians towards Armenia, ethnic Azeris to Azerbaijan, and of both to the Russian Federation.[8] In fact, although they were called 'refugees' by the Soviet authorities, these people were technically IDPs, given that they moved within the territory of the USSR. After 1991, however, their legal status changed radically, since for a long time neither Armenia nor Azerbaijan adopted a citizenship law. The displaced therefore found themselves stateless and hence became refugees according to international standards.

The single event that has generated the greatest number of refugees and internally displaced persons in the region has been the armed conflict between Armenia and Azerbaijan over the Nagorno Karabakh enclave. As a whole, the conflict has resulted in 218,950 refugees on the Armenian side and 185,000 on the Azerbaijani side, with many additional thou-

---

[5] See L. Shevtsova, 'Post-Soviet Emigration Today and Tomorrow', 26 *International Migration Review*, 1992, pp. 241–57.
[6] All the data cited in this chapter are taken from IOM Technical Co-operation Centre for Europe and Central Asia, *1996 CIS Migration Report* (IOM, Geneva, 1997).
[7] See M. Jacobs, 'USSR Faces Mounting Refugee Problem', *RFE/RL Report on the USSR*, 21 September 1990, pp. 14–18.   [8] *Ibid.*

sands having fled to the Russian Federation, Ukraine and other CIS countries. Additional numbers of refugees have resulted from the other armed conflicts in recent years. In 1992, Ukraine received more than 60,000 people fleeing armed conflict in Trans-Dniestria (Moldova). As a result of the Abkhazian conflict within Georgia, scores of refugees found shelter in the Russian Federation, Ukraine and other CIS countries; small numbers of people also left South Ossetia for the Russian Federation. The civil war that wrecked Tajikistan in 1992 and 1993 forced some 60,000 refugees to flee to Afghanistan and another 195,883 to neighbouring Central Asian countries, the Russian Federation and other CIS countries. By the end of 1996, 41,047 of the refugees living in Afghanistan and 11,343 of those living in CIS countries had returned to their former places of residence. Finally, the conflict in Chechnya resulted in several thousand refugees fleeing to Ukraine, Kazakstan, Belarus and other CIS countries.

Moreover, the CIS countries host around 47,000 refugees and asylum seekers originating from Africa, southwest Asia and the Middle East. These persons are mostly located in countries close to the western border, such as the Russian Federation, Ukraine and Belarus, although some Central Asian countries report their presence in growing numbers. The Russian Federation alone hosts 30,479 asylum seekers from non-CIS countries, Ukraine 1,105 and Belarus 4,000. Most often, these people only transit through the region in their journey towards western Europe, where they plan to ask for asylum, and do not intend to settle in the CIS countries. Nonetheless, many file asylum applications while waiting to move westwards, or once they have been rejected by their intended country of destination.[9] This population generally uses the same channels, routes and networks as illegal migrants and is therefore very difficult to distinguish from the latter.

Internally displaced persons

Internally displaced persons were first witnessed in the region in conjunction with the conflict over Nagorno Karabakh. The Armenian government records 72,000 IDPs, while in Azerbaijan their number is as high as 549,030. In Georgia, the hostilities between the government and South Ossetian separatists resulted in 10,897 IDPs, and the war in Abkhazia displaced an additional 261,052 people. The 1992 conflict in Trans-

[9] See also Lawyers' Committee for Human Rights, *Commitments Without Compliance: Refugees in the Russian Federation* (Lawyers' Committee for Human Rights, New York, May 1996).

Dniestria led to 51,289 displaced, most of whom returned home after the cessation of the hostilities. In Tajikistan, by the end of 1996, 680,853 of the 697,653 IDPs had returned home. The largest IDP flow of recent years originates from Chechnya, with at least 148,542 persons displaced within the Russian Federation. Overall, the number of IDPs in the CIS countries can be estimated at around 1,100,000 persons as at September 1997.

Involuntarily relocating persons

The category of 'involuntarily relocating persons' (IRPs) was coined within the context of the CIS Conference to define persons compelled to relocate to the country of their citizenship owing to armed conflict. These are mainly Russians, Ukrainians and Belarusians who have fled from Tajikistan or the Caucasus to the Russian Federation, Ukraine and Belarus respectively. The total number of IRPs is difficult to estimate, due to lack of clarity regarding their citizenship status and their motives for leaving, as well as to political manipulation of the statistics.

Repatriants

With 4,207,000 persons, repatriants (defined as persons returning voluntarily to the country of their citizenship or origin for the purpose of permanent residence) constitute by far the largest migrant group within the CIS region. This type of movement, which is motivated by economic, social or personal reasons, is not new to the region, as Russians, Ukrainians and Belarusians have been steadily returning to their eponymous republics since the late 1970s. In the late 1980s this return trend accelerated notably, owing to the deterioration of the socio-economic situation and the sharp worsening of the immigrants' once privileged social status in the non-Slavic republics. The establishment of state borders between the former Soviet republics in late 1991 contributed to this trend, as the Slavic immigrants became anxious about their ability to move freely across the region.

The greatest numbers of repatriants originate from Central Asia, where large Slavic communities had settled in the Soviet era, and from the Caucasus, where living conditions have become unbearable due to continuous warfare. In the latter case, though, it is almost impossible to distinguish repatriants from 'involuntarily relocating persons', as this would entail ascertaining whether people left because of a direct threat to their life or because of worsening living standards. The bulk of the repatriants (some 2,361,700 persons) are Russians and have resettled in the Russian

Federation; an additional 1,400,000 have resettled in Ukraine, and 210,000 in Belarus.

Since the late 1980s, the repatriation trend has involved other ethnic groups as well, particularly in Central Asia. The most notable flow is taking place in Kazakstan, where the government is encouraging ethnic Kazaks from neighbouring countries to settle in the country, with a view to offsetting the ethnic balance, heavily tipped in favour of Russian-speakers. Between 1991 and 1996, 154,941 ethnic Kazaks returned to Kazakstan from the Russian Federation, Uzbekistan, Mongolia and Iran. Similar trends are evident in Uzbekistan and Moldova.

Formerly deported peoples

The return movement of persons belonging to formerly deported peoples is a peculiar feature of the post-Soviet setting. In the 1940s, eight entire peoples were deported from their historical homelands, allegedly for political crimes, and were resettled in the Siberian and Central Asian steppes. Three of them – the Crimean Tatars, the Meskhetians and the Volga Germans – had since then been prevented from returning. However, in the late 1980s, in the context of slackening political control, a return trend began and relatively large numbers of formerly deported peoples started returning to their historical homelands.

Between 1989 and 1996, 183,400 Crimean Tatars returned to the Crimea and 244,241 of them are currently residing there (including those who came back spontaneously in earlier years). As a result of a provision in the German constitution permitting the return to Germany of ethnic Germans,[10] the Volga Germans were allowed to emigrate to Germany. Since 1992, 850,000 of them have done so, while only a few thousand have chosen to move back to their historical homeland in the Russian Federation. As for Meskhetians, in the summer of 1989, 60,000 of those who had settled in the Fergana Valley (between Uzbekistan and Kyrgyzstan) fell prey to communal violence and were forced to resettle, mainly in the Russian Federation and Azerbaijan.

Ecological migrants

Severe environmental degradation – another dire legacy of the Soviet regime – forced some 739,000 ecological migrants to move. The bulk of the displaced originate from the Chernobyl area (which cuts across Belarus, the Russian Federation and Ukraine), the Aral Sea basin

---

[10] Basic Law of the Federal Republic of Germany, article 116.

(between Uzbekistan and Kazakstan) and the area surrounding the former nuclear test site of Semipalatinsk in Kazakstan, as well as some regions of Kyrgyzstan.

Labour migrants

The deterioration of the socio-economic situation and the dramatic drop in living standards in all of the CIS countries since their independence has led to high rates of emigration for work purposes. Since strong social, economic and cultural links still remain among the former Soviet republics, the flows are predominantly confined within the boundaries of the region. Labour migration reached dramatic proportions in countries that have been wrecked by armed conflicts, such as Armenia, Georgia and Tajikistan. In the short term, emigration to other CIS countries may prove beneficial to these countries, as it reduces pressure on the labour market and thus serves as a sort of safety valve. In the long term, however, this phenomenon will be detrimental to them, as it deprives them of much needed skilled labour, which is essential for rebuilding the local economies.

Transit migrants

The slackening of border controls following the demise of the USSR effectively opened up the region to migrants from African, Asian and Middle Eastern countries, who enter the region both legally[11] and illegally, and transit through it on their journey towards Western Europe. As already mentioned, a small proportion of these persons may be genuine asylum seekers. These migrants generally avail themselves of the services of professional traffickers, who are usually linked to criminal networks also involved in arms and drug smuggling. The number of illegal migrants present in the CIS countries at any given moment is significant, as they are either waiting to be taken across the border, or they have been unable to reach their intended destination, or else they have been caught and sent back. As the CIS countries lack the resources to return these migrants to their countries of origin, they remain stranded within the region.

Although illegal migrants in transit can be found throughout the region, they tend to concentrate in westernmost countries such as Belarus, Moldova, the Russian Federation and Ukraine, which have rapidly become major hubs for migrant trafficking. Between 500,000 and

---

[11] CIS visas can easily be obtained for a small sum of money. However, even those who have entered the region legally find themselves in an illegal situation when their visas expire.

1,000,000 illegal migrants (particularly Afghans, Iranians and Iraqi Kurds) are estimated by the Russian government to be living in the Russian Federation alone.[12] The Central Asian and Caucasian countries are increasingly reporting the passage of illegal migrants through their territory, thus testifying to the fact that these regions have become major transit areas.

Another type of illegal migrant found in the CIS countries (and especially in the Russian Federation, Ukraine and Belarus) are former Soviet scholarship holders and former migrant workers from developing countries. When the USSR broke apart, these people had already been living in the country for some time; being unable or unwilling to return home, they overstayed and became illegal. Contrary to 'new' migrants, these workers and former students are more rooted in their host country, know the language, may have a job and even a family there.

The unfurling of these multifarious population movements has had a conspicuous impact on the already difficult social and economic situation of the CIS countries. Outflows have led to a brain-drain and have disrupted the local economy, while inflows have strained the social infrastructure (particularly in the education and health sectors) and distorted the housing and labour markets. Relations between migrants, the local population and the authorities at community level have become increasingly tense. Thus, these flows have aggravated the precarious socio-economic situation of the CIS countries, contributing to their overall instability.

All in all, the CIS countries have proved unable to cope with the problems engendered by these movements. The concepts and regimes inherited from the Soviet period proved both inadequate and insufficient, given that the nature and scale of the flows had radically changed. New policies and legislation had to be devised without any institutional experience or trained personnel. The CIS countries also lacked appropriate and efficient structures to manage the flows of migrants and refugees, which in turn aggravated displacement-related problems.

CIS attempts to conceptualise these flows

In attempting to conceptualise these unprecedented population movements, the CIS authorities had to work on a *tabula rasa*. Worse still, they had to confront a politically loaded heritage. To them, the word 'refugee'

---

[12] IOM Technical Co-operation Centre for Europe and Central Asia, *1996 CIS Migration Report* (IOM, Geneva, 1997), p. 87.

(*bezhenets*) evoked comrades from Chile or Somalia who had fled persecution in their home country and taken refuge in the USSR; but persecution was always of one type – that of right-wing dictatorships – and the
refugees all had the same political credo – they were staunch communists.
On the other hand, a word apparently as neutral as 'resettler' (*pereselenets*)
had been used in the 1930s and 1940s to indicate political deportees, and
evoked cattle wagons, snowy plains and certain death.

The basic problem faced by the CIS authorities in their categorisation
exercise was – and to a large extent still is – insufficient knowledge of the
various types of movements taking place in their own countries. This is
compounded by a nebulous understanding of international concepts and
standards relating to refugees and migrants, as well as by scarce attention
to definitions and, more generally, to precision in legal terminology. In
addition, CIS officials tend to oscillate between two extremes: either
lumping several groups of displaced persons into one single category,[13] or
devising separate legal categories for each and every group.[14] As a result,
CIS policies and legislation have all too often proved to be unclear in
object and imprecise in scope, making use – sometimes in the same text –
of divergent definitions of the same population groups, or otherwise mis-
using internationally accepted definitions.

If one excepts these 'cultural' difficulties, the greatest obstacle to the
coining of accurate and precise definitions of the displaced has been the
lack of clarity concerning their citizenship status. In effect, the citizenship
of hundreds of thousands of former Soviet citizens is yet to be defined. In
the case of refugees and migrants, it is particularly difficult to ascertain
whether they possess a citizenship, and if so which one. In cases where
they are stateless, the problem lies in ascertaining whether they would
have the right to acquire a citizenship, and if so which one.

These difficulties stem from the fact that even the most generous citizenship laws which were adopted shortly after independence did not take
into account the migratory flows, and granted automatic citizenship only
to permanent residents. Persons who moved to a country after 1991 are
therefore not automatically covered, and must apply for citizenship. The
displaced are not always aware of the administrative steps required to
obtain citizenship, which are often lengthy or complicated. As a result,

---

[13] The Russian law on 'forced migrants', for instance, encompasses persons who would otherwise be considered as refugees, IDPs, or 'involuntarily relocating persons'. See Law of
the Russian Federation No. 4530–1, issued on 9 February 1993, article 1.

[14] In the course of the preparatory process leading to the CIS Conference, some delegations
from CIS countries suggested that returnees, resettlers, repatriates or repatriates should
constitute separate categories, while others insisted on the concept of 'mountain
refugees' (from mountainous regions), whose profile and needs were allegedly very
different from those of 'valley refugees' (from the plains).

many refugees and displaced people do not have any citizenship, even though they would have the opportunity to obtain one. This widespread uncertainty over the citizenship status of the displaced makes it difficult to devise distinct categories befitting them.

The categorisation exercise as part of the CIS Conference

Aware of the magnitude and complexity of the population movements taking place on their territory and concerned about their capacity to address them effectively, the CIS countries attempted to attract international attention to these problems by sponsoring Resolution 49/173 of 23 December 1994 in the UN General Assembly, which called upon the UN High Commissioner for Refugees to 'promote and develop a preparatory process, leading to the convening, not later than 1996, of a regional conference to address the problems of refugees, displaced persons, other forms of involuntary displacement and returnees in the countries of the Commonwealth of Independent States and relevant neighbouring States'.[15] The vagueness of the language used in the resolution to define the various categories of displacement is worth noting, as it is indicative of the state of confusion that reigned within the international community, most particularly among the concerned states, as to the exact scope and nature of the problems under discussion.

The Conference, which was held in Geneva on 30 and 31 May 1996 under the joint auspices of UNHCR, International Organisation for Migration (IOM) and the Office for Democratic Institutions and Human Rights of the OSCE, was the result of a prolonged preparatory process. A first Meeting of Experts, held in Geneva in May 1995, formally launched the process by identifying issues of concern and the methodology to address them. Two rounds of sub-regional meetings were then held, where existing problems and possible solutions were identified and discussed. On the basis of these discussions, a draft Declaration of Principles and a draft Programme of Action were prepared by the Conference secretariat, and were subsequently merged into a unified Programme of Action, which was submitted to and approved by the Conference in May 1996.[16]

The objectives of the CIS Conference process were three-fold: (i) to provide a reliable forum for the countries of the region to discuss population displacement problems in a humanitarian and non-political setting; (ii) to review the population movements taking place in the region, clar-

[15] UN Doc. A/RES/49/173 of 24 February 1995.
[16] The Programme of Action is included in the final report of the Conference (Doc. CISCONF/1996/6 of 4 July 1996).

ifying the categories of concern; and (iii) to devise an integrated strategy for the region, by elaborating a Programme of Action.

The clarification of the categories of the displaced constituted the starting point and the underlying theme of the whole Conference process, as well as its main immediate achievement. In the course of the preparatory process, participants thoroughly analysed the various flows taking place in the region, identifying the types of movements of concern (some, like labour migration, were excluded) and scrupulously classifying them. In doing so, they helped depoliticise some of the categories used in the region, which had become sources of tension between CIS countries. Once the categories were clear, participants collectively assessed which ones could be dealt with within the framework of existing international standards, and which ones could not. In the first case, concepts used in the CIS region were standardised and put into line with relevant international instruments, while in the second case existing concepts were clarified and harmonised, and new categories were devised.

The consensus reached on the categories of displaced and on the terminology to be used to define them was enshrined in Annex 2 of the Programme of Action of the Conference, which undoubtedly constitutes the most innovative part of the document. The annex is divided into two parts: Part A contains three categories for which reference is made to 'a universal definition and widely accepted concepts'; while Part B contains five definitions 'applying to situations in CIS countries' which 'have been developed by these countries', 'for the specific purposes of this Conference process'. Participants thus decided to draw a clear line between existing internationally accepted definitions, which were taken on without modification, and new definitions, which were meant to cover situations specific to the CIS context only.[17] An opportunity was thus missed to develop existing international concepts in light of the new realities of displacement in the CIS region.

The definitions contained in Part A include that of 'refugees' (*bezhentsy*), which coincides with article 1.A(2) of the Geneva Convention, that of 'internally displaced persons' (*litsa, peremeshchennye vnutri strany*), which makes reference to a working definition used by the Representative of the UN Secretary-General on Internally Displaced Persons in a 1995 report,[18] and that of 'illegal migrants' (*nezakonnye*

[17] The abundance of *caveats* in the introductory *chapeau* to Part B testifies to the importance attributed by participating states (specifically Western ones) to limiting the applicability of the definitions contained therein to the CIS context alone.
[18] UN Doc. E/CN.4/1995/50 of 2 February 1995. See especially paras. 116–27, where IDPs are defined as 'persons who have been forced to flee their homes suddenly or unexpectedly in large numbers, as a result of armed conflict, internal strife, systematic violations of human rights or natural or man-made disasters; and who are within the territory of their own country'. See also chapter 8 of this volume.

migranty), which is based on the Programme of Action of the International Conference on Population and Development.[19]

In Part B, the category of 'persons in refugee-like situations' (*litsa, nakhodyashchiesya v situatsii, skhodnoy s situatsiey bezhentsev*) comprises 'persons who fled their country of citizenship or, if they are stateless, the country of their permanent residence, as a consequence of armed conflicts because their lives, safety or freedom were threatened. These persons are in need of international protection but may not all be covered by the 1951 Convention and its 1967 Protocol.'[20] This category was coined on the basis of the broad refugee definitions set out in the 1969 Convention of the Organisation of African Unity (OAU) Governing the Specific Aspects of Refugee Problems in Africa[21] and the 1984 Cartagena Declaration on Refugees[22] which encompass persons displaced outside their own country by armed conflicts. During the drafting process, a suggestion to merge this category with that of 'refugees' was vetoed by some European delegations, who feared that such an extended refugee definition might be used as a precedent in the European context. UNHCR did not challenge this stance.[23]

By far the most contentious category was that of 'involuntarily relocating persons' (IRPs, *nedobrovol'no pereselyayushchiesya litsa*), encompassing 'persons who are forced to relocate to the country of their citizenship as a result of circumstances endangering their lives, such as armed conflict, internal disorder, inter-ethnic conflict or systematic violations of human rights and who are in need of assistance to resettle in their countries of citizenship'. This definition was coined to match the term 'forced migrant' (*vynuzhdennyi pereselenets*) found in Russian legislation.[24] In effect, during the preparatory process the Russian delegation had repeatedly requested that the category of 'forced migrants' be discussed within the context of the Conference. Such a request stemmed not only from the delegation's wish to ensure that an international document such as the Programme of Action should reflect their national legislation, but also to ensure international recognition of the problems relating to this group of migrants, for which international funding was being sought.

In the course of the drafting process, however, a number of CIS

[19] UN Doc. A/CONFERENCE.171/13 of 18 October 1994. See especially para. 10.15 where 'undocumented or irregular migrants' are defined as 'persons who do not fulfil the requirements established by the country of destination to enter, stay or exercise an economic activity'.
[20] A footnote states: 'In some CIS countries, these persons are referred to in national legislation as "refugees".'   [21] 1001 UNTS 46.
[22] For a more detailed discussion of these broader definitions, see chapter 3 of this volume.
[23] See also chapters 8 and 10 of this volume.
[24] Indeed, a footnote states: 'In the Russian Federation, such persons are included in the category "forced migrants", which may also include "internally displaced persons".'

countries, supported by the Baltic states, voiced strong concern at including the category of 'forced migrants' in the Programme of Action. In effect,
the Russian authorities tend to categorise all ethnic Russians moving from
the CIS and Baltic states to the Russian Federation as 'forced migrants',
regardless of whether they were actually compelled to leave. The misuse of
this category goes hand in hand, in the Russian discourse, with accusations
of 'gross violations of human rights' or 'Islamic fundamentalism' against
the countries of origin of these migrants. In fact, it has long been clear (and
it has even been unofficially acknowledged by some Russian officials) that
such an intentional misuse amounts to laying the blame for the huge immigration flows into Russia and the problems connected therewith on the
CIS and the Baltic states. Ultimately, the Russian authorities are seeking
to obtain financial compensations from these countries, or at least international recognition of the latter's political responsibility for this phenomenon. Predictably enough, the CIS and Baltic authorities categorically
reject the Russian stance, pointing out that Russian-speakers leave of their
own free will and without being compelled to do so.

As a result of this long-standing, sensitive controversy, the CIS and the
Baltic states resolutely vetoed the use of the term 'forced migrant' in the
context of the CIS Conference, thus offering a rare show of unity against
their former 'big brother'. A compromise was reached by devising two
separate categories, covering respectively persons who were compelled to
leave ('IRPs'), and persons who left voluntarily ('repatriants' or *repatri-
anty*). The latter are defined as 'persons who, for economic, social or personal reasons, have voluntarily resettled in the country of their citizenship
or origin for the purpose of permanent residence'. It should be stressed,
however, that since the original problem consisted principally of the political misuse of the term 'forced migrants' rather than in the term itself, the
new definition will hardly allay any of the existing tensions, unless
the Russian authorities change their behaviour. This was well noted by
the Baltic states, who at the Conference attached reservations to Annex 2,
stressing the non-universal and non-binding character of the definitions
contained therein.[25]

Annex 2 furthermore comprises two definitions referring to movements which are specific to CIS countries: 'formerly deported peoples'
(*ranee deportirovannye narody*), defined as 'peoples who were deported
from their historic homeland during the Soviet period'; and 'ecological
migrants' (*ekologicheskie migranty*), defined as 'persons who are obliged to
leave their place of permanent residence and who move within their
country or across its borders, due to severe environmental degradation or

[25] See Doc. CISCONF/1996/6 of 4 July 1996, pp. 8–9.

ecological disasters'. While they lack precision, these definitions still constitute an initial and much needed attempt at categorising the peculiar movements taking place in the region.

Conclusion

Although it is regrettable that neither the CIS countries nor the international community displayed greater courage, the elaborate terminological review conducted within the framework of the CIS Conference still constituted a first, albeit timid, step towards categorising the population movements taking place in the region. Moreover, the process was instrumental in forging a common language among the CIS countries, which in turn will greatly facilitate regional dialogue on migration and displacement matters in the years to come.

To become meaningful, though, the definitions contained in the Programme of Action will have to be transferred into the national practice of the CIS countries. For this to happen, an immense effort aimed at harmonising the existing terminology would be required in the legislative field, the population registration systems and other related areas. Given the lack of human and financial resources of the CIS countries, it is doubtful, however, that a systematic effort in this direction will be undertaken in the near future.

Bibliography

Human Rights Watch/Helsinki, *Refugees and Internally Displaced Persons in Armenia, Azerbaijan, Georgia, the Russian Federation and Tajikistan*, vol. 8, No. 7(D), May 1996

IOM, *1996 CIS Migration Report* (Geneva, 1997)

Deported Peoples of the Former Soviet Union: The Case of the Meskhetians (Geneva, 1998)

Profile and Migration Intentions of Crimean Tatars Living in Uzbekistan (Geneva, 1998)

Messina, Claire, 'From Migrants to Refugees. Russian, Soviet and Post-Soviet Migration', 6 *International Journal of Refugee Law*, 1994, 4, pp. 620–35

Mukomel, Vladimir and Emil Pain (eds.), *Bezhentsy i Vynuzhdennye Pereselentsy v Gosudarstvakh SNG* (Refugees and Forced Migrants in the CIS Countries) (Centre for Ethnopolitical and Regional Research, Moscow, 1995)

Parliamentary Assembly of the Council of Europe, *Report on Refugees, Asylum-Seekers and Displaced Persons in the CIS* (1997)

Tishkov, Valeri, *Migratsii i Novye Diaspory v Postsovetskikh Gosudarstvakh* (Migrations and New Diasporas in the Post-Soviet States) (Institute of Ethnology and Anthropology of the Russian Academy of Sciences, Moscow, 1996)

United Nations Economic Commission for Europe and United Nations Population Fund (UNECE and UNFPA), *International Migration in Central and Eastern Europe and the Commonwealth of Independent States* (Economic Studies No. 8, United Nations, New York, Geneva, 1996)

UNHCR, IOM and OSCE, 'The CIS Conference on Refugees and Migrants', 2 *European Series*, 1996, 1 and 2, UNHCR, Geneva

Vitkovskaya, Galina, *Vynuzhdennaya Migratsiya: Problemy i Perspektivy* (Forced Migration: Problems and Perspectives) (Institute for Economic Forecasting and RAND, Moscow, 1993)

(ed.), *Migratsiya Russkoyazychnogo Naseleniya iz Tsentral'noy Azii: Prichiny, Posledstviya, Perspektivy* (Migration of the Russian-Speaking Population from Central Asia: Causes, Consequences, Perspectives) (Carnegie Moscow Center, Moscow, 1996)

Zaionchkovskaya, Zhanna (ed.), *Byvshii SSSR: Vnutrennaya Migratsiya* (The Former USSR: Internal Migration) (Institute of Employment Studies and RAND, Moscow, 1992)

Zaionchkovskaya, Zhanna and Jeremy Azrael (eds.), *Migratsionnye Protsessy Posle Raspada SSSR* (Migration Processes after the Collapse of the USSR) (5 vols., Institute for Economic Forecasting and RAND, Moscow, 1992–4)

Part 2

The developing role of the UNHCR

8 The role of UNHCR in the development of international refugee law

Volker Türk[1]

Introduction

The total number of persons of concern to the Office of the United Nations High Commissioner for Refugees (UNHCR) rose from 17 million in 1991 to over 22 million at the end of 1997. This includes approximately 12.1 million refugees, 3.5 million returnees, and 4.4 million internally displaced.[2] What all have in common, whether they have crossed an international border or not, is that they have been forced to flee, as a result of persecution, massive human rights violations, generalised violence, armed conflicts, civil strife or other circumstances which have seriously disturbed public order, threatening their lives, safety or freedom.

While some regions have applied a refined treaty-based refugee definition to include all victims of conflict and upheaval, others have not. Instead, they rely on national laws or discretionary *ad hoc* arrangements, such as temporary protection in situations of large-scale influx. An internationally non-binding approach contributes to the flexibility of states, but places individuals in an extremely vulnerable position and denies them their rights under international treaty law.

The international community recognises that these categories of persons are in need of international protection. Otherwise it would not extend specific protection and assistance functions to UNHCR. At the same time, however, the universal protection regime in the form of treaty law – if only by the failure to apply existing international law – does not necessarily mirror the responsibilities of UNHCR and the recognised protection needs of some of these categories.[3]

---

[1] The views expressed are the personal views of the author, and are not necessarily shared by the United Nations or by UNHCR.
[2] See UNHCR, *Refugees and Others of Concern to UNHCR: 1997 Statistical Overview* (Geneva, 1998).
[3] There are, in particular, obvious inadequacies in a situation where refugees who meet regional definitions, but who are outside the relevant regions, are considered to be of international concern and receive international protection and assistance on a mandatory basis from UNHCR and the international community, yet on a discretionary, *ad hoc* basis from individual states outside these regions (see UN Doc. EC/1992/SCP/CRP.5, para. 1).

154 The developing role of the UNHCR

This constitutes the background to the ongoing discussions concerning the current ambiguities in the international protection regime for refugees and other persons of concern to UNHCR. These questions are related to the process of international law-making and the roles of international institutions in this area – notably UNHCR, which has the most comprehensive international mandate concerning refugees and displaced persons.

UNHCR's mandate, including its personal scope of competence

The legal basis of the UNHCR Statute

The original mandate stems from the General Assembly in the form of Resolution 428 (V) of 14 December 1950, to which the UNHCR Statute was annexed.[4] The UNHCR Statute contains provisions which demonstrate that it is not the only legal basis of UNHCR's operations. Paragraph 9 of the Statute stipulates that the High Commissioner should engage in such additional activities as the General Assembly may determine. Furthermore, the High Commissioner is required to follow policy directives given to her or him by the General Assembly or the Economic and Social Council (ECOSOC), pursuant to paragraph 3 of the Statute. It is the General Assembly, and to some extent ECOSOC, which can amend the mandate, and both bodies have done so ever since its inception. UNHCR therefore has a highly dynamic and fragmented legal basis.

In consequence, the 1950 UNHCR Statute no longer encompasses the entire mandate of UNHCR. Later developments are not reflected, such as subsequent General Assembly and ECOSOC resolutions, organisational practice, implied powers etc. It is therefore necessary to make a distinction between the original 1950 Statute and the *UNHCR Statute in the broad sense*, which constitutes UNHCR's present mandate.

Furthermore, two different sets of General Assembly resolutions relating to UNHCR are adopted yearly: (i) 'omnibus' resolutions referring to UNHCR in general, to its reports and to general developments in the area of forced displacement; and (ii) 'situational' resolutions which are country- or region-specific. An analysis of these resolutions leads to the conclusion that activities, which were originally outside

---

[4] The competence of the UN to deal with refugees is implicitly contained in articles 1, 13, 55 and 60 of the UN Charter. These provisions, in conjunction with articles 7(2) and 22 of the UN Charter, form the constitutional basis of the UNHCR Statute. For a more detailed analysis of UNHCR's mandate see Volker Türk, *Das Flüchtlingshochkommissariat der Vereinten Nationen (UNHCR)* (Duncker & Humblot, Berlin, 1992).

UNHCR's mandate, are later integrated into the omnibus resolution. Arguably, the frequent requirement, or subsequent endorsement, by the General Assembly that UNHCR undertake responsibilities for protecting and assisting specific categories of persons confirms the Office's overall mandate covering such persons. Repeated General Assembly resolutions and the acquiescence by states, therefore, lay down statutory provisions.

UNHCR – and this is unique among the subsidiary organs of the United Nations[5] – is also institutionally linked to international conventions relating to refugees and stateless persons. UNHCR's legal foundation transcends, consequently, the immediate framework of UN law and has also some basis in international refugee and human rights law (directly, for instance, in article 35 of the 1951 Geneva Convention Relating to the Status of Refugees;[6] indirectly, for instance, in articles 22 and 45 of the 1989 Convention on the Rights of the Child[7] or article 11 of the 1961 Convention on the Reduction of Statelessness).[8]

UNHCR's competence *ratione personae*

Demonstrating the underlying broad consensus of the international community to provide UNHCR with specific responsibilities in respect of certain groups of persons, successive General Assembly and ECOSOC resolutions, supported by UNHCR's Executive Committee, have had the effect of extending the High Commissioner's competence to five main categories: (i) refugees and asylum seekers; (ii) stateless persons; (iii) returnees; (iv) the internally displaced; and (v) persons threatened with displacement or otherwise at risk.[9] The latter two categories do not fall under the general competence of the Office. However, there is a selective and limited mandate to provide protection and humanitarian assistance and to seek solutions for these categories under certain conditions.

[5] UNHCR is a subsidiary organ of the General Assembly, according to article 22 of the UN Charter.   [6] 189 UNTS 137.   [7] UN Doc. A/RES/44/25.   [8] 989 UNTS 175.
[9] The activities which UNHCR is required or is authorised to carry out for these categories of persons are set out both in the UNHCR Statute (in particular paras. 1, 8, 9 and 10) and in subsequent General Assembly or ECOSOC resolutions. UNHCR is primarily mandated to provide international protection and humanitarian assistance and to seek permanent solutions for persons within its competence. Mandated activities also include preventive action and participation 'at the invitation of the Secretary-General, in those humanitarian endeavours of the United Nations for which the Office has particular expertise and experience' (General Assembly Resolution 2956, para. 2; see also UNHCR Statute, para. 9). In addition, the institution of 'good offices' and the right to humanitarian initiative remain useful tools for situations outside mandated activities.

Refugees and asylum seekers

Following requests by the General Assembly and endorsement by the international community, UNHCR's competence has been extended generally to all refugees from armed conflict and other 'man-made disasters'[10] who do not otherwise come within the terms of the Geneva Convention and its 1967 Protocol.[11]

The Group of Governmental Experts on International Co-operation to Avert New Flows of Refugees defined man-made disasters in the following terms:

wars, armed conflicts, acts of aggression, alien domination, foreign armed intervention, occupation, colonialism, oppressive segregationist and racially supremacist regimes practising policies of discrimination or persecution, apartheid, violations of human rights and fundamental freedoms, mass forcible expulsions, economic and social factors threatening the physical integrity and survival, structural problems of development; man-made ecological disturbances and severe environmental damages.[12]

The term 'refugee' therefore covers all persons who are outside their country of origin for reasons of feared persecution, armed conflict, generalised violence, foreign aggression or other circumstances which have seriously disturbed public order, and who, as a result, require international protection.[13]

In UNHCR's view, an appropriately liberal interpretation, in the dynamic spirit of international law, of the Geneva Convention criteria would mean that a large number of persons falling within UNHCR's competence could – and indeed should – be considered Convention refugees.[14] For those who are not covered by the Geneva Convention and the 1967 Protocol, arguably, article 35 of the Geneva Convention, which obliges states to co-operate with UNHCR in the exercise of its functions, forms some legal basis for contexts in which a need for international protection exists.

The sub-category of asylum seeker has been employed by the General Assembly in general resolutions relating to UNHCR since 1981. Historically, this concept is closely related to Executive Committee

---

[10] See ECOSOC Resolution 2011 (LXI), endorsed by the General Assembly, which describes them as 'victims of man-made disasters'. More analysis is provided by Guy S. Goodwin-Gill, *The Refugee in International Law* (2nd edn, Oxford University Press, 1996), pp. 8–18.   [11] 606 UNTS 267.
[12] See UN Doc. A/41/324, paras. 30–40, endorsed by General Assembly Resolutions 41/70; 41/124, para. 10; 42/109, para. 9; and 43/117, para. 11.
[13] See UN Doc. A/AC.96/830, paras. 8, 10–11 and 31–2.
[14] See UN Doc. A/AC.96/830, paras. 20–8.

(EXCOM) Conclusion No. 22.[15] The term can refer either to an individual whose refugee status has not yet been determined by the authorities but whose claim to asylum entitles him or her to a certain protective status on the basis that he or she could be a refugee, or to large-scale influxes of mixed groups in a situation where individual refugee status determination is impractical. Clearly, asylum seekers form part of UNHCR's competence *ratione personae*.[16]

Stateless persons

UNHCR has precisely defined responsibilities for refugees who are stateless, pursuant to paragraph 6(A)(II) of the UNHCR Statute and article 1(A)(2) of the Geneva Convention, both of which specifically refer to stateless persons who meet the refugee criteria. In addition, in accordance with General Assembly Resolutions 3274 (XXIX) and 31/36, UNHCR has been designated by the General Assembly, pursuant to articles 11 and 20 of the 1961 Convention on the Reduction of Statelessness, as the body to which a person claiming the benefits of this Convention may apply for the examination of her or his claim and for assistance in presenting it to the appropriate authorities. Furthermore, the prevention and reduction of statelessness and the protection of stateless persons are important for the prevention of situations leading to involuntary displacement. In 1995 the Executive Committee adopted a Conclusion[17] to this effect which requested UNHCR actively to promote accession to the international statelessness instruments. UNHCR also provides technical and advisory services pertaining to the preparation and implementation of nationality legislation.[18]

Returnees

Returnees are former refugees who return to their country of origin spontaneously or in an organised fashion, when the circumstances which caused them to flee no longer exist. Executive Committee

[15] EXCOM Conclusion No. 22 (XXXII) on Protection of Asylum Seekers in Situations of Large-Scale Influx; endorsed by General Assembly Resolution 36/125.
[16] Rejected asylum seekers do not, as such, fall under UNHCR's mandate. There is, however, an increasing interest on the part of some countries to involve UNHCR more in the return of persons not in need of international protection: see UN Docs. EC/48/SC/CRP.29; EC/47/SC/CRP.28; and EC/46/SC/CRP.36 and Corr.1.
[17] EXCOM Conclusion No. 78 (XLVI) on the Prevention and Reduction of Statelessness and the Protection of Stateless Persons; endorsed by General Assembly Resolution 50/152, paras. 14–16.
[18] See Carol A. Batchelor, 'UNHCR and Issues Related to Nationality', 14 *Refugee Survey Quarterly*, 1995, pp. 91–112.

Conclusion No. 40, paragraph (1)[19] recognises UNHCR's legitimate concern for the consequences of return. UNHCR's mandate with regard to voluntary repatriation has been refined and extended, from an initial premise that UNHCR's responsibility ended when repatriants crossed the border into their country of origin, to a substantive involvement in securing protection and providing assistance to returnees in the country of origin.[20]

The internally displaced

There is no generally accepted definition of an internally displaced person, although the 1995 Report of the Representative of the Secretary-General on internally displaced persons proposes a working definition which reads as follows:

> persons who have been forced to flee their homes suddenly or unexpectedly in large numbers, as a result of armed conflict, internal strife, systematic violations of human rights or natural or man-made disasters; and who are within the territory of their own country.[21]

UNHCR's operational definition of an internally displaced person refers to someone who, had she or he managed to cross an international boundary, would have fallen within the refugee definition.[22] The first General Assembly resolution dealing with the subject dates back to 1972, referring to the situation in Sudan.[23]

UNHCR has periodically become involved in enhancing protection and providing assistance to internally displaced persons through special operations, undertaken at the request of the Secretary-General or the General Assembly, on a 'good offices' basis.[24] In 1992, the General

---

[19] EXCOM Conclusion No. 40 (XXXVI) on Voluntary Repatriation; endorsed by General Assembly Resolution 40/118, para. 7.

[20] See UNHCR, *UNHCR Handbook on Voluntary Repatriation: International Protection*, (Geneva, 1996), and EXCOM Conclusions on Voluntary Repatriation Nos. 18 (XXXI) and 40 (XXXVI) and General Conclusion No. 74 (XLV) on International Protection. UNHCR's role has been strengthened by the General Framework Agreement for Peace in Bosnia and Herzegovina, which, in Annex 7, designates UNHCR as the lead agency for the organised voluntary return of refugees and displaced persons to and in the former Yugoslavia, and thus sets an important precedent. See also chapters 9 and 10 of this volume.

[21] See UN Doc. E/CN.4/1995/50, para. 116, and chapter 7, pp. 145–9 above.

[22] See UNHCR, *UNHCR's Operational Experience with Internally Displaced Persons* (Geneva, 1994), p. 76.

[23] See General Assembly Resolution 2958 (XXVII); see also General Assembly Resolution 43/116, preamble, para. 6; and General Assembly Resolution 44/136, preamble, para. 7.

[24] For example, in Laos, Viet Nam, Cyprus and Bangladesh. The activities of UNHCR were subsequently endorsed by the General Assembly: see UNHCR, *Operational Experience*, pp. 3–11.

Assembly, for the first time in an omnibus resolution, acknowledged UNHCR activities in favour of internally displaced persons.[25]

In 1993, UNHCR adopted legal and operational criteria for its involvement with the internally displaced, which were endorsed by the General Assembly.[26]

The three mandatory requirements for UNHCR activities in favour of internally displaced persons are: (i) a specific request from the Secretary-General or a competent principal organ of the United Nations; (ii) the consent of the state or other entities concerned; and (iii) the Office's particular expertise and experience.[27] An additional requirement is the availability of adequate resources. UNHCR emphasises that its principal mandate and expertise lie in the area of protection and solutions and that it should consequently be expected to act in pursuit of these basic objectives when it is requested or allowed to assist the internally displaced.

Persons threatened with displacement or otherwise at risk

With regard to this category of persons, UNHCR's involvement has been primarily of a humanitarian or preventive nature and has largely meant exercising a 'good offices' function or a special humanitarian co-ordination responsibility to channel international assistance and provide protection.

In this sense, UNHCR's protection and assistance roles have been extended to local residents, war-affected civilians and besieged populations, especially in circumstances where it was neither feasible nor reasonable to treat them differently from other categories of concern to UNHCR (particularly in the context of voluntary repatriation or special humanitarian co-ordination functions).

UNHCR as a 'promoter' of international law and standards

Legal basis

The General Assembly has not limited its role in the area of progressive development and codification of international law and standards to the

---

[25] See General Assembly Resolution 47/105, para. 14.
[26] See General Assembly Resolution 48/116, paras. 12 and 14; and General Assembly Resolution 49/169, para. 10 'emphasizing that activities on behalf of internally displaced persons must not undermine the institution of asylum', reiterated in General Assembly Resolution 50/152, para. 8. See also EXCOM Conclusion No. 75 (XLV) on Internally Displaced Persons. These operational guidelines were published in UNHCR, *Operational Experience*, Annex 1.   [27] See General Assembly Resolution 48/116.

International Law Commission (ILC), the United Nations Commission on International Trade Law (UNCITRAL) or its Committees, including its Sixth Committee. It has drawn equally on other bodies, including its subsidiary organs.[28]

UNHCR, as a subsidiary organ of the General Assembly, has been entrusted with specific functions in this regard. According to paragraph 8(a) of the UNHCR Statute, the High Commissioner shall provide for the protection of refugees by, *inter alia*, 'promoting the conclusion and ratification of international conventions for the protection of refugees, supervising their application and proposing amendments thereto'. Consequently, UNHCR has a statutory function of 'proposing amendments' to international conventions for the protection of refugees.

In addition, paragraph 8(b) of the UNHCR Statute grants the High Commissioner competence to promote, through special agreements with governments, the execution of any measures calculated to improve the situation of refugees and to reduce the number requiring protection. The General Assembly has thus devolved upon UNHCR parts of its competence concerning the progressive development and codification of international law and standards for the protection of refugees. It is argued here that the General Assembly has, in entrusting UNHCR with these functions, delimited competencies in this specific field from ECOSOC.[29] It is further argued that UNHCR's competence in this respect, due to the evolution of its mandate *ratione personae*, has been extended to all categories of persons of its concern. Thus, UNHCR's standard-setting functions in the area of international law apply *equally* to asylum seekers, stateless persons, returnees and, to a limited extent, to the internally displaced, as well as persons threatened with displacement or otherwise at risk, to the extent that the General Assembly has charged UNHCR with specific protection functions. Since protection functions are a core part of UNHCR's mandate responsibilities, it is submitted here that the standard-setting aspects which form an integral part of these functions expand in the same manner as UNHCR's competence *ratione personae*.

Furthermore, the General Assembly confers an overall supervisory responsibility on UNHCR in respect of international conventions providing for the protection of refugees. This specific responsibility is *directly* linked to article 35 of the Geneva Convention, article 2 of its 1967

[28] See Carl-August Fleischhauer, 'Article 13', in Bruno Simma (ed.), *The Charter of the United Nations: A Commentary* (Oxford University Press, 1995), article 13, paras. 39 and 59–60.
[29] ECOSOC could equally be competent pursuant to articles 55(c), 60, 62(3) and 68 of the UN Charter. Article 66 of the UN Charter further confirms that the General Assembly has the right to issue instructions, as contained in article 60; see Philip Kunig, 'Article 66', in Simma (ed.), *Charter of the United Nations*, article 66, para. 2.

Protocol and article 8 of the OAU Refugee Convention.[30] These treaty provisions, by calling on contracting states to co-operate with UNHCR in the exercise of its functions generally, establish explicit contractual links with the dynamically evolving UNHCR Statute, that is, with the broader legal framework of UNHCR's functions and operations. UNHCR has, for example, specifically understood its control and monitoring functions, to be applicable also in respect of international *ad hoc* arrangements and agreements of a less formal nature, whether in the context of voluntary repatriation operations or special international arrangements in the case of mass influx situations.

Historical overview

The purpose of this overview is to examine, by choosing selected examples, how UNHCR has fulfilled its competence over the years in the development of international law and related standards with regard to the categories of persons of its concern.[31]

The 1967 Protocol Relating to the Status of Refugees

The Geneva Convention covers only those persons who became refugees as a result of events occurring before 1 January 1951. In addition, article 1(B) of the Geneva Convention requires ratifying states to declare whether the scope of applicability is restricted to Europe. One of the first legal challenges UNHCR faced was how to work towards the removal of the temporal and (optional) geographical limitations of the refugee definition of the Geneva Convention. This constituted, in effect, the first gap between UNHCR's broader institutional responsibilities *ratione personae* and formally limited obligations of states, since the refugee definition contained in UNHCR's Statute did not have any limitations and was to be applied broadly to cover all kinds of future refugee situations.

The temporal limitation was not so much an issue during the Hungarian refugee crisis in 1956[32] but started posing problems in the 1960s when new refugee situations arose in Africa which could hardly be related to events occurring before 1 January 1951. This resulted in legal

---

[30] Convention Governing the Specific Aspects of Refugee Problems in Africa, 1001 UNTS 46.

[31] For a more detailed description of the role of UNHCR in the development of international law until 1972, see Louise W. Holborn, *Refugees, a Problem of our Time: The Work of the UNHCR: 1951–1972* (Scarecrow Press, Metuchen, 1975), vol. I, pp. 174–249.

[32] See Félix Schnyder, 'Les aspects juridiques actuels du problème des réfugiés', 1 *Recueil des Cours*, 1965, pp. 364–5.

inadequacies, as the refugees concerned did not fall within the scope of the Geneva Convention refugee definition. It was clearly desirable that equal status should be enjoyed by all refugees covered by the refugee definition of the Geneva Convention, irrespective of the dateline.

UNHCR, therefore, started consultations with the objective of removing the temporal limitation. In recognition of this problem, the General Assembly, in 1963, invited states to treat new refugee problems in accordance with the principles and the spirit of the Geneva Convention.[33] The issue was also taken up by the Executive Committee in 1964 and 1965.[34] The Carnegie Endowment for International Peace, in co-operation with UNHCR, convened a 'Colloquium on Legal Aspects of Refugee Problems with Particular Reference to the 1951 Convention and the Statute of the Office of the United Nations High Commissioner for Refugees' in Bellagio, Italy, from 21 to 28 April 1965. On the basis of a background paper submitted by UNHCR, thirteen independent experts discussed ways and means to adapt the refugee definition of the Geneva Convention to current realities. The participants recommended the adoption of a Protocol which would delete the existing dateline. UNHCR transmitted the report to the Executive Committee and asked states (Executive Committee members as well as states parties to the Geneva Convention) for their views. In 1966 UNHCR submitted to the Executive Committee a paper and a draft text of a Protocol to the Geneva Convention, in the light of the responses received from governments.[35] The Executive Committee recommended that the draft Protocol be submitted to the General Assembly after consideration by ECOSOC in order to authorise the Secretary-General to open the Protocol for accession by states.[36]

ECOSOC approved[37] and the General Assembly[38] took note of the draft Protocol, thus paving the way for the Secretary-General to transmit the text of the Protocol to states for accession, in order to extend the personal scope of the Geneva Convention.[39]

It is interesting to note that the Protocol was not, as is usually the case, drafted and adopted in the course of a Conference of Plenipotentiaries, and that UNHCR was instrumental in the process of its codification.

[33] See General Assembly Resolution 1959 (XVIII), para. 2(b). Recommendation E of the Final Act of the 1951 UN Conference of Plenipotentiaries on the Status of Refugees and Stateless Persons had the same purpose.   [34] See UN Doc. A/AC.96/270.
[35] See UN Doc. A/AC.96/346.
[36] See UN Doc. A/6311/Rev.1/Add.1, Part two, para. 38.
[37] See ECOSOC resolution 1186 (XLI).
[38] See General Assembly Resolution 2198 (XXI).
[39] For a more detailed account, see Paul Weis, 'The 1967 Protocol Relating to the Status of Refugees and Some Questions of the Law of Treaties', 23 *British Yearbook of International Law*, 1967, pp. 39–70.

The 1967 UN Declaration on Territorial Asylum and subsequent developments

The elaboration of a declaration on asylum had been under consideration by various UN organs for a considerable number of years. This may also be due to the fact that the Geneva Convention did not explicitly address the issue of asylum.[40] The topic was, for instance, part of the ILC's work agenda but in view of other priorities was not further developed by the ILC.[41]

The Human Rights Commission was also seized of this question as early as in 1947,[42] but efforts to codify the right to asylum in international human rights treaties failed. The Human Rights Commission, however, worked on a Declaration on Territorial Asylum which was later transferred to the Third and Sixth Committees of the General Assembly.[43] The General Assembly finally adopted the Declaration unanimously on 14 December 1967.[44]

In this case, UNHCR did not initiate or develop this particular area of refugee protection but tried to influence the debate by sharing its views and observations.[45] Several governments felt that the adoption of a declaration on the subject would facilitate UNHCR's work.[46] There was also a feeling among the sponsors of the Declaration that its adoption should not bring to an end the work of the United Nations in codifying the rules and principles relating to the institution of asylum.[47]

Soon after the adoption of the Declaration, efforts were undertaken to draft a Convention on Territorial Asylum. Again, the Carnegie Endowment for International Peace, in co-operation with UNHCR, convened a 'Colloquium on Territorial Asylum and the Protection of Refugees in International Law' in Bellagio in April 1971. It was agreed

---

[40] See, however, articles 31–33 of the 1951 Convention and Recommendation D of the Final Act of the 1951 UN Conference of Plenipotentiaries on the Status of Refugees and Stateless Persons.
[41] See General Assembly Resolution 1400 (XIV), in which the General Assembly requested the International Law Commission to undertake the codification of the principles and rules of international law relating to the right of asylum. The right of asylum was considered by the ILC at its first session in 1949, in connection with the draft Declaration on the Rights and Duties of States. [42] See UN Doc. E/600, para. 48.
[43] For a more elaborate description of the drafting history of the Declaration, see *UN Juridical Yearbook*, (1967), pp. 234–50; Paul Weis, 'The United Nations Declaration on Territorial Asylum', 7 *Canadian Yearbook of International Law*, 1969, pp. 92–149.
[44] See General Assembly Resolution 2312 (XXII). See also Paul Weis, 'The Present State of International Law on Territorial Asylum', 31 *Annuaire suisse de droit international*, 1975, pp. 71–96.
[45] See UN Docs. E/2085/Add. 1; E/CN.4/781 Add. 1 and 2; E/CN.4/785; and E/CN.4/796; and Weis, 'Declaration on Territorial Asylum', pp. 98–99, 101 and 103.
[46] See *UN Juridical Yearbook* (1967), p. 238. [47] See *ibid.*, 1967, p. 247.

that a set of articles should be prepared, without prejudice to the question of what form the instrument should take. The Colloquium appointed a Special Drafting Committee which included UNHCR.[48] At the end of the discussions there was agreement that the draft instrument should be in the form of a draft Convention. A Working Group to elaborate the Convention was established subsequently and met in Geneva in January 1972. Its deliberations resulted in the 'Bellagio Draft', which UNHCR submitted to the Executive Committee and, through ECOSOC, to the General Assembly. UNHCR was asked to engage in further consultations with governments on this subject. Finally, the General Assembly decided in 1974 to establish a Group of Experts on the draft Convention, composed of twenty-seven government representatives, to be convened not later than May 1975 for a maximum of ten working days, to review the text of the draft Convention. The costs of convening the Group of Experts were, upon request by the General Assembly, borne by UNHCR.[49]

In 1975 the General Assembly took note of the view of the Executive Committee that a Conference of Plenipotentiaries on territorial asylum should be convened and requested the Secretary-General, in consultation with UNHCR, to convene such a Conference from 10 January to 4 February 1977 to consider and adopt a Convention on Territorial Asylum.[50] The Conference failed to carry out its mandate within the allocated time and recommended that the General Assembly consider the question of convening a further session of the Conference *sine die*. The Conference was never resumed.[51]

The Executive Committee

In 1975 the Executive Committee decided to establish a Sub-Committee of the Whole on International Protection, which was supposed to study in

[48] See Paul Weis, 'The Draft Convention on Territorial Asylum of the Carnegie Endowment for International Peace', *AWR-Bulletin*, 1973, pp. 94–101.
[49] See General Assembly Resolution 3272 (XXIX). The Working Group met in Geneva from 28 April to 9 May 1975.
[50] See General Assembly Resolution 3456 (XXX). Again the costs for holding the conference were borne by UNHCR (upon request by the General Assembly). It was held in Geneva. A Drafting Committee and a Committee of the Whole were established to facilitate consultations.
[51] On the draft Convention, see Paul Weis, 'The Draft United Nations Convention on Territorial Asylum', 50 *British Yearbook of International Law*, 1979, pp. 151–71. Weis noted that a Convention on Territorial Asylum undoubtedly raised political problems since most governments had a particular situation in mind when thinking of asylum. He thought it unlikely that a convention would be concluded in the near future and considered that it would be easier to focus on the development of law at the regional level (*ibid.*, pp. 169–70).

more detail certain aspects of the protection of refugees, the results of which are usually adopted as conclusions by the Executive Committee.[52] Although the Executive Committee has only an advisory function, upon UNHCR's request, concerning UNHCR's protection responsibilities,[53] the annual conclusions on international protection have an important standard-setting effect. They document consensus of the international community on a specific protection matter and are usually worked out in close co-operation with UNHCR.[54]

The Executive Committee is the only specialised forum which exists at the global level for the development of international standards relating to refugees and other persons of concern to UNHCR.

Development of further measures to ensure international protection to all who need it

The gap between institutional responsibilities entrusted to UNHCR by the international community and the often limited obligations formally accepted by states (or accepted only on a discretionary basis) has been a recurring issue for UNHCR. This 'gap' discussion is also related to the issue of differing interpretations of the international refugee instruments, as well as the general problem of undefined areas of the international legal framework for the protection of refugees (for example, responsibility-sharing).

In 1994 UNHCR's *Note on International Protection* was dedicated to this issue. The Note stated that 'significant numbers of people who are in need of international protection are outside the effective scope of the principal international instruments for the protection of refugees'.[55] UNHCR concluded in this Note that international or regional declarations embodying guiding principles of international protection and reaffirming states' commitment to ensuring protection to all who require it would be useful additional tools. Discussions in 1994 and 1995 led to

---

[52] See EXCOM Conclusion No. 1. In 1995 the Executive Committee was restructured, leading to the abolition of its Sub-Committees and the establishment of a Standing Committee which would meet four times throughout the year, including on protection matters.

[53] As for the mandate of the Executive Committee, see General Assembly Resolution 1166 (XII) and ECOSOC Resolution 672 (XXV). If a protection conclusion is, however, endorsed by the General Assembly, it is binding for UNHCR. See, for example, General Assembly Resolutions 40/118, para. 7; 41/124, preamble and para. 7; 42/109, paras. 5–6; 43/117, paras. 2–3; 43/117, para. 8; 44/137, paras. 2, 5 and 8–9.

[54] See Jerzy Sztucki, 'The Conclusions on the International Protection of Refugees Adopted by the Executive Committee of the UNHCR Programme', 1 *International Journal of Refugee Law*, 1989, pp. 285–318.

[55] See UN Doc. A/AC.96/830, para. 68.

the Executive Committee 'encouraging UNHCR to engage in consultations and discussions concerning measures to ensure international protection to all who need it; and reiterating its support for UNHCR's role in exploring the development of guiding principles to this end, consistent with fundamental protection principles reflected in international instruments, and calling on UNHCR to organise informal consultations on this subject.'[56]

UNHCR organised a first informal meeting in Geneva on 2–3 May 1996, bringing together six academic and eleven government experts for an initial exchange of views to identify possible areas concerning the provision of international protection to all who need it. There was extensive discussion on the development of temporary protection and agreement that temporary protection required an adequate legal basis, either as a complement to, or as a component of, the Geneva Convention.

There was consensus that further consultations were in the interests of states. Four follow-up meetings have been organised since then. The issues of temporary protection, the application of UNHCR's supervisory responsibility, detention, capacity-building, preventive action in respect of the internally displaced and stateless persons as well as international responsibility-sharing were discussed in more detail in the course of these consultations, with a view to reaching some form of common agreement on the aforementioned subjects in order to strengthen the current protection framework.[57] In October 1997 the Executive Committee reiterated its support for UNHCR's role in this area and called upon UNHCR to continue this process.[58]

Regional developments

The 1966 Bangkok Principles Concerning Treatment of Refugees In 1964 the Asian-African Legal Consultative Committee started its work on refugee issues, in close co-operation with UNHCR. In August 1966 the Committee adopted the Bangkok Principles which are still the only regional instrument, though non-binding, on refugee matters.[59]

The 1969 OAU Convention On 12 September 1969 the Convention Governing the Specific Aspects of Refugee Problems in Africa, the

---

[56] Endorsed by General Assembly Resolution 50/152.
[57] See UN Docs. EC/48/SC/CRP.32; EC/47/SC/CRP.27; and EC/46/SC/CRP.34.
[58] See EXCOM Conclusion No. 81 (XLVIII), 1997, on International Protection.
[59] See Eberhard Jahn, 'The Work of the Asian-African Legal Consultative Committee on the Legal Status of Refugees', 27 *Zeitschrift für ausländisches öffentliches Recht und Völkerrecht*, 1967, pp. 122–38.

regional complement to the Geneva Convention, was adopted under the aegis of the Organisation of African Unity (OAU).[60] Initiatives leading to the adoption of this Convention date back to July 1964, when the Council of Ministers of the OAU invited the Commission on African Refugees to draft a Convention covering all aspects of the problem of refugees in Africa.

In 1965 the Assembly of Heads of State and Government of the OAU requested the Administrative Secretary-General of the OAU, in collaboration with UNHCR, to pursue the necessary studies on the problem of refugees in Africa and to present a draft agreement concerning the specific conditions in Africa. In 1967 it was finally decided that the OAU Convention should be a supplement to the Geneva Convention.[61] Weis notes that the emergence of new refugee problems in Africa was the main reason for UNHCR initiating the deletion of the dateline in the refugee definition of the Geneva Convention. The adoption of the 1967 Protocol, he continues, led the OAU to abandon its initial idea of elaborating an independent African Refugee Convention but instead adopt an instrument complementary to the Geneva Convention.[62]

Due to UNHCR's involvement and in view of the OAU Convention's complementary character, no conflict of authority or any other legal incompatibilities have arisen between UNHCR and a regional organisation with regard to the respective instruments.[63]

The 1984 Cartagena Declaration The 1984 Cartagena Declaration on Refugees was adopted at a colloquium which was held in Cartagena on 19–22 November 1984 in co-operation with UNHCR.[64] While not a Convention, the Declaration is generally considered an expression of regional custom which has been implemented in the national legislation of the states concerned. In this case, UNHCR was closely involved in the preparation of the Declaration at the regional level without going through formal procedures within the UN or a regional organisation. While the Organisation of American States (OAS) has regu-

---

[60] See General Assembly Resolution 2594 (XXIV).
[61] See Paul Weis, 'The Convention of the Organisation of African Unity Governing the Specific Aspects of Refugee Problems in Africa', 3 *Human Rights Journal*, 1970, 3, pp. 3–70.   [62] *Ibid.*, p. 7.
[63] See preamble paras. 9–11 of the OAU Convention; and article 30 of the Vienna Convention on the Law of Treaties.
[64] The colloquium was attended by experts and government representatives under the auspices of the Colombian government and sponsored by the University of Cartagena, the Regional Centre for Third World Studies and UNHCR. See also General Assembly Resolution 42/110.

larly endorsed the Cartagena Declaration, the General Assembly has explicitly referred to it only twice.[65]

Council of Europe Traditionally, regional co-operation on asylum and refugee matters in Europe has mainly been co-ordinated by the Council of Europe.[66] Apart from the role of the European Convention on Human Rights for the protection of refugees,[67] the Ad Hoc Committee of Experts on the Legal Aspects of Territorial Asylum, Refugees and Stateless Persons (CAHAR), which was established by the Council of Europe's Committee of Ministers in 1977, has prepared a number of agreements and recommendations regarding asylum and refugee policies in Europe.[68]

The European Committee on Migration as well as the Committee of Experts on Multiple Nationality, both bodies under the Committee of Ministers, are also particularly relevant in the area of the development of law and standard-setting.

Moreover, the Parliamentary Assembly and its Committees on Migration, Refugees and Demography and on Legal Affairs and Human Rights have dealt with asylum and refugee issues. UNHCR co-operates actively with these bodies and has observer status in most of them, thus being able to fulfil its function as the primary intergovernmental institution responsible for the development of international refugee law and related standards, including at the regional level.

European Union Since 1991 co-operation in asylum matters within the European Communities/European Union has expanded to include the harmonisation of substantive and procedural aspects of immigration, asylum and visa policies.[69] The work programme of the EU under the 'third pillar' of the Treaty on European Union regarding asylum matters has covered a wide range of issues, resulting in the approval of several instruments (Joint Positions, resolutions and conclusions). Though not themselves legally binding, these texts provide impor-

[65] Concerning the OAS, see AG/RES 103 (XXI-0/91) of 7 June 1991; regarding the General Assembly, see General Assembly Resolution 42/110, preamble; and General Assembly Resolution 48/116, preamble.
[66] See Henn-Jüri Uibopuu, 'The Protection of Refugees Within the Council of Europe', 13 *Thesaurus Acroasium*, 1987, pp. 619–50. See also UNHCR, *Briefing Handbook, UNHCR and its Partners in Europe* (Geneva, 1994), pp. 45–63.
[67] See chapter 4 of this volume.
[68] See, for example, Richard Plender, *Basic Documents on International Migration Law* (2nd edn, Martinus Nijhoff, The Hague, 1997), Part IV.
[69] As for the history of EC involvement with refugees, see Gil Loescher, 'The European Community and Refugees', 65 *International Affairs*, 1989, 4, pp. 616–36. See also Part 4 of this volume.

tant evidence of state practice which influences the making and implementation of asylum legislation of EU member states, and indeed of
neighbouring states. However, they have also demonstrated a 'downward'
pull, codifying the 'lowest common denominator' in some areas.[70]
UNHCR does not play any formal role in these harmonisation efforts
but has engaged in an informal dialogue with the relevant EU institutions
and the EU member states as regards matters pertaining to asylum and
refugees.[71] It remains to be seen whether this informal dialogue will
become more formalised due to a Declaration to the Final Act of the
Treaty of Amsterdam, which states that consultations shall be established
with UNHCR and other relevant international organisations on matters
relating to asylum policy. The question also arises as to what happens if
the results of the harmonisation efforts are at variance with UNHCR
interpretations or standards. Since UNHCR is not formally part of the
harmonisation process, one could ask whether its authority as the main
international institution responsible for the development of international
refugee law and protection standards might not be undermined.[72]

An important recent development is, for example, the EU Joint Position
of 4 March 1996 on the harmonised application of the refugee
definition.[73] While the text contains a number of positive elements, it
excludes as valid grounds for granting refugee status, persecution by non-
state agents who have no links with the state and whose activities the state
is unable to control. In the specific context of armed conflicts and civil war,
persecutory acts perpetrated by non-state agents, which the state is unable
to control, may be considered as 'persecution', but only where the perpetrators control part of the state territory. The restrictive interpretation in
the Joint Position would exclude those escaping countries or areas where

[70] See, e.g., Danièle Joly, 'The Porous Dam: European Harmonization on Asylum in the
Nineties', 6 *International Journal of Refugee Law*, 1994, pp. 159–93. Within a period of five
years after the entry into force of the Treaty of Amsterdam, the progressive establishment
of an area of freedom, security and justice will result in the 'communitarisation' of asylum
and immigration policies and in legally binding instruments in this area (see articles 73i
and 73k of the Amsterdam Treaty and also pp. 333–4 of this volume).

[71] See the *UNHCR Briefing Handbook*, pp. 3 and 32. This dialogue offers UNHCR the possibility of exchanging views on relevant texts of the harmonisation process. UNHCR has
often made its views public once the text was adopted by the Council of Ministers for
Justice and Home Affairs.

[72] Arguably, this would be the case when positions adopted at the regional level detract from
recognised protection principles or standards, the application of which UNHCR is mandated to supervise.

[73] Another example, in connection with the Amsterdam Treaty, is the adoption of the
Protocol to the Treaty Establishing the European Community on asylum for nationals of
EU member states. With regard to this Protocol, UNHCR expressed its reservations concerning limitations on the right to seek asylum, since the Protocol allows EU member
states to use their discretion when accepting asylum applications from EU citizens: see
the UNHCR press release on restricted access to asylum in Europe of 20 June 1997.

there is a general breakdown of governmental authority, but where the persecuting agent is not necessarily a *de facto* authority or in control of the territory, and the state is unable to provide protection from persecution.

UNHCR's position on the other hand, based on an interpretation of article 1 of the Geneva Convention and an analysis of the relevant jurisprudence, is that persecution that does not involve direct or indirect state complicity is nonetheless persecution within the meaning of the Geneva Convention. The essential element for the granting of refugee status is the absence of effective national protection, irrespective of the reasons for it.[74]

This EU Joint Position may widen the 'gap' in international protection between persons considered as refugees by UNHCR, and those persons in respect of whom states accept explicit refugee protection responsibility. It would be interesting to examine in detail whether or not this departure from accepted standards, at variance with UNHCR's position, infringes article 1 in relation to article 35 of the Geneva Convention.

Concept of temporary protection In the context of the Comprehensive Response to the Humanitarian Crisis in the Former Yugoslavia, the High Commissioner formally requested states in 1992 to extend temporary protection to persons fleeing the fighting and human rights violations in the former Yugoslavia. UNHCR developed the concept of temporary protection as part of a comprehensive regional approach to mass forced displacements, where persecution may be one of a number of reasons compelling people to flee. UNHCR has pursued an informal and regular dialogue with states on the implementation of temporary protection, with the objective of elaborating on the nature of the protection required and standards applicable.[75] UNHCR not only initiated this concept but has also developed it further.

CIS Conference UNHCR, in co-operation with the International Organisation for Migration (IOM) and the Organisation for Security and Co-operation in Europe (OSCE), convened a Regional Conference to address the problems of forced displacement in the countries of the CIS and relevant neighbouring states in Geneva from 30 to 31 May 1996, pursuant to a specific request from the General Assembly.[76]

---

[74] UNHCR's position was made public in a press release dated 24 November 1995.
[75] See the various UNHCR papers for the informal meetings of government experts on this subject entitled *UNHCR Background Notes* (23 March 1993, 23 March 1994, 20 April 1995); see also UN Doc. A/AC.96/830, paras. 45–51. UNHCR advances the conceptual debate of temporary protection within the informal consultations on the provision of international protection to all who need it: see UN Doc. EC/47/SC/CRP.27, paras. 4–5.
[76] See General Assembly Resolutions 48/113, 49/173 and 50/151; UNHCR, 'The CIS Conference on Refugees and Migrants', 2 *European Series*, 1996, 1 and 2; UN Doc. CISCONF/1996/6 of 4 July 1996; and chapter 7 of this volume.

The Programme of Action agreed at the Conference, which contains a Declaration of Principles, is less relevant in this connection, since the legally non-binding document merely restates already existing standards and is geared more towards an operational plan of action and the implementation of standards than the development of international law in a specific regional context.[77] The document refers, however, to new categories of people, such as repatriants, involuntarily relocating persons, formerly deported peoples or ecological migrants. Their standing in international law needs further analysis.

Other international instruments and areas of law

The Hague Agreement Relating to Refugee Seamen[78] In 1950, UNHCR's predecessor, the International Refugee Organisation, alerted the International Labour Organisation (ILO) to the problem of refugee seamen and asked the ILO to explore measures to overcome their difficulties. The ILO, in turn, decided in 1951 to bring the matter to the attention of UNHCR. Intensive co-operation between both organisations led to the Netherlands convening a conference of eight western European maritime nations, which led to the adoption of the Hague Agreement in 1957. ILO and UNHCR had observer status at the conference.[79]

Specific provisions in international instruments In addition, UNHCR has promoted the inclusion of provisions favourable to refugees and other persons of concern in general international instruments and in national legislation.[80] A most recent example is, for instance, article 6 of the new Hague Convention of 19 October 1996 on Jurisdiction, Applicable Law, Recognition, Enforcement and Co-operation in Respect of Parental Responsibility and Measures for the Protection of Children.[81]

International human rights law and international humanitarian law For various reasons, international refugee law was separated from international human rights law and its developments. This may partly be due to the fact that states had no interest in regulating in detail international

---

[77] UNHCR has, however, not been involved in the drafting of any CIS instruments relating to refugees or other persons of concern to UNHCR, such as the CIS Agreement on Aid to Refugees and Forced Migrants of 24 September 1993: see Plender, *Basic Documents*, p. 882.   [78] 506 UNTS 125.
[79] See Paul Weis, 'The Hague Agreement Relating to Refugee Seamen', 7 *International and Comparative Law Quarterly*, 1958, pp. 334–48.
[80] For a detailed account of the role of UNHCR in initiating a variety of international instruments, including on statelessness, see Holborn, *Refugees*, pp. 202–49.
[81] 35 ILM, 1996, p. 1391. UNHCR participated as an observer in the three-year negotiations concerning this Convention.

obligations which would apply to the sensitive issues of entry and admission, an area still well guarded by the concept of state sovereignty. From states' perspectives, a discretionary 'humanitarian' approach is preferable to a binding human rights-oriented framework of norms in this respect.[82]

This situation has changed to some extent, and considerable efforts are under way to integrate the two bodies of law. Paragraph 23 of the 1993 Vienna Human Rights Declaration,[83] in fact, acknowledges this by dealing extensively with refugees. It reaffirms the basic protection principles and recognises the importance of a comprehensive approach by the international community. UNHCR co-operates extensively with the UN human rights programme, as well as regional human rights institutions, in the area of standard-setting.[84]

Similar co-operation is extended in the area of international humanitarian law, in particular concerning the consolidation of standards regarding internally displaced persons.[85]

Customary international law UNHCR's role in developing customary international law in relation to international refugee protection is mainly of a promotional nature, since it is essentially states which create rules of general application. UNHCR is, therefore, not as such an actor contributing to the creation of norms of customary law but rather an 'agent of consolidation and codification of norms', not least because of its promotional and supervisory responsibilities. Insofar as conclusions adopted by the Executive Committee or, for instance, the 1967 Declaration on Territorial Asylum form part of the law-making process of customary law, UNHCR's involvement in the formulation of these instruments has been described above. The same applies to the Cartagena Declaration, which is generally considered to have contributed to the development and acceptance of regional customary law in the Latin American context.[86] As regards the principle of *non-refoulement*, UNHCR has come to the widely shared conclusion that this cardinal principle of refugee protection has indeed acquired the status of a norm of customary international law.[87]

---

[82] See James Hathaway, 'Reconceiving Refugee Law as Human Rights Protection' in *Problems and Prospects of Refugee Law* (ed. Vera Gowlland-Debbas and Klaus Samson, Graduate Institute of International Studies, Geneva, 1992), p. 10.

[83] See UN Doc. A/CONF.157/23, 12 July 1993.

[84] See, e.g., UNHCR, 'The European Convention on Human Rights and the Protection of Refugees, Asylum-Seekers and Displaced Persons', 2 *European Series*, 1996, 3.

[85] See UN Doc. E/CN.4/1996/52/Add. 2; see also Jean-Philippe Lavoyer, 'Refugees and Internally Displaced Persons', *International Review of the Red Cross*, 1995, pp. 162–91.

[86] See UN Doc. A/AC.96/830, para. 42.

[87] See UN Docs. EC/47/SC/CRP.26, para. 13; and A/AC.96/713, para. 3. UNHCR and its Executive Committee have even argued that the principle of *non-refoulement* is progres-

Conclusion

No one denies that the progressive development of international law is essential for friendly and peaceful relations among states. Yet, in the area of forced displacement, the disparities between the responsibilities of UNHCR and the often limited, legally formalised, obligations of states illustrate the need for increased efforts by the international community to define and regulate international co-operation in this area. Clearly, *ad hoc* and discretionary approaches to refugee issues foster unilateralism in international relations, which is not desirable. A multilateral framework and dialogue, based on consensus, is predictable and foreseeable and allows – at least to some extent – for a system of responsibility-sharing. The insufficient development of such a framework constitutes a major gap in the international protection regime. It is certainly useful to examine in more detail the current development of international standards and fora in this field.[88]

To consolidate all these developments, the process of international law-making in the area of forced displacement becomes crucial. This brief overview has shown that UNHCR is not only legally competent and responsible for developing and codifying progressively international law and standards in the area of forced displacement but has also assumed this responsibility from the outset. While stressing the usefulness of regional approaches, there is a need to integrate these efforts holistically at the international level. In the interests of refugee protection globally, it is therefore essential that UNHCR remains the vehicle for this multilateral dialogue.

Bibliography

Batchelor, Carol A., 'UNHCR and Issues Related to Nationality', 14 *Refugee Survey Quarterly*, 1995, pp. 91–112

Gowlland-Debbas, Vera, and Klaus Samson (eds.), *Problems and Prospects of Refugee Law* (Graduate Institute of International Studies, Geneva, 1992)

Holborn, Louise W., *Refugees, a Problem of our Time: The Work of the UNHCR: 1951–1972* (Scarecrow Press, Metuchen, 1975)

sively acquiring the character of *jus cogens*: see EXCOM Conclusion No. 25, para. (b); and UN Docs. A/AC.96/694, para. 21; A/AC.96/660, para. 17; A/AC.96/643, para. 15; and A/AC.96/609/Rev.1, para. 5.

[88] For instance, standard-setting at the level of the Human Rights Commission and its Sub-Commission. The International Law Commission is currently studying the question of state succession in respect of nationality matters (see UN Docs. A/CN.4/467 and A/CN.4/474). The International Law Association is looking into the issue of temporary protection and general procedural requirements, and the OSCE mechanisms in the field of conflict prevention and mediation are also relevant in this context.

Jahn, Eberhard, 'The Work of the Asian-African Legal Consultative Committee on the Legal Status of Refugees', 27 *Zeitschrift für ausländisches öffentliches Recht und Völkerrecht*, 1967, pp. 122–38

Joly, Danièle, 'The Porous Dam: European Harmonization on Asylum in the Nineties', 6 *International Journal of Refugee Law*, 1994, pp. 159–93

Lavoyer, Jean-Philippe, 'Refugees and Internally Displaced Persons', *International Review of the Red Cross*, 1995, 305, pp. 162–91

Loescher, Gil, 'The European Community and Refugees', 65 *International Affairs*, 1989, 4, pp. 616–36

Schnyder, Félix, 'Les aspects juridiques actuels du problème des réfugiés', 1 *Recueil des Cours*, 1965, pp. 339–450

Simma, Bruno (ed.), *The Charter of the United Nations: A Commentary* (Oxford University Press, 1995)

Sztucki, Jerzy, 'The Conclusions on the International Protection of Refugees Adopted by the Executive Committee of the UNHCR Programme', 1 *International Journal of Refugee Law*, 1989, pp. 285–318

Türk, Volker, *Das Flüchtlingshochkommissariat der Vereinten Nationen (UNHCR)* (Duncker & Humblot, Berlin, 1992)

UNHCR, *Briefing Handbook, UNHCR and Its Partners in Europe* (Geneva, 1994)

'The European Convention on Human Rights and the Protection of Refugees, Asylum-Seekers and Displaced Persons', 2 *European Series*, 1996, 3

UNHCR by Numbers 1997 (Geneva, 1997)

UNHCR Handbook on Voluntary Repatriation: International Protection (Geneva, 1996)

UNHCR's Operational Experience with Internally Displaced Persons (Geneva, 1994)

Uibopuu, Henn-Jüri, 'The Protection of Refugees Within the Council of Europe', 13 *Thesaurus Acroasium*, 1987, pp. 619–50

Weis, Paul, 'The 1967 Protocol Relating to the Status of Refugees and Some Questions of the Law of Treaties', 23 *British Yearbook of International Law*, 1967, pp. 39–70

'The Convention of the Organisation of African Unity Governing the Specific Aspects of Refugee Problems in Africa', 3 *Human Rights Journal*, 1970, 3, pp. 3–70

'The Draft Convention on Territorial Asylum of the Carnegie Endowment for International Peace', *AWR-Bulletin*, 1973, pp. 94–101

'The Draft United Nations Convention on Territorial Asylum', 50 *British Yearbook of International Law*, 1979, 4, pp. 151–71

'The Hague Agreement Relating to Refugee Seamen', 7 *International and Comparative Law Quarterly*, 1958, pp. 334–48

'The Present State of International Law on Territorial Asylum', 31 *Annuaire suisse de droit international*, 1975, pp. 71–96

'The United Nations Declaration on Territorial Asylum', 7 *Canadian Yearbook of International Law*, 1969, 4, pp. 92–149

9   UNHCR as leader in humanitarian assistance: a triumph of politics over law?

S. Alex Cunliffe and Michael Pugh[1]

The international response to the dissolution of Yugoslavia raised the profile of the United Nations High Commissioner for Refugees (UNHCR). On 25 October 1991, the then UN Secretary-General, Javier Pérez de Cuéllar, wrote to UNHCR requesting that it co-ordinate humanitarian action in the region. Although this letter did not formally designate UNHCR as the 'lead agency' for the UN's humanitarian response to the deteriorating situation in Yugoslavia, de Cuéllar's successor as Secretary-General, Boutros Boutros-Ghali, subsequently referred to such a status in his report on the situation in May 1992.[2] There has been a paucity of academic literature on the subject of UNHCR as humanitarian 'lead agency' – though Thomas Weiss and Amir Pasić have praised UNHCR's 'reinvention' during the conflicts arising from Yugoslavia's dissolution.[3] This chapter redresses the balance and, in contrast to Weiss and Pasić, indicates that UNHCR's experience reveals both the difficulties associated with the concept of 'lead' agency and the inappropriateness of UNHCR in such a role. UNHCR's 'reinvention' repre-

---

[1] Some of the themes explored in this chapter emanate from S. Alex Cunliffe and Michael Pugh, 'The Politicisation of the UNHCR in the former Yugoslavia', 10 *Journal of Refugee Studies*, 1997, 2, pp. 134–53; and Michael Pugh and S. Alex Cunliffe, 'The Lead Agency Concept in Humanitarian Assistance: The Case of the UNHCR', 28 *Security Dialogue*, 1997, 1, pp. 17–30. Acknowledgment is made to Oxford University Press and Sage Publications for permission to include this material.

[2] Secretary-General's Report, S/23900, 12 May 1992, para. 16.

[3] Thomas G. Weiss and Amir Pasić, 'Reinventing UNHCR: Enterprising Humanitarians in the Former Yugoslavia, 1991–1995', 3 *Global Governance*, 1997, 1, pp. 41–57. James Ingram (former Executive Director of the World Food Programme, WFP), provides an insider's view of the agency rivalries which have bedevilled the UN's institutional co-ordination in James Ingram, 'The Future Architecture for International Humanitarian Assistance', in *Humanitarianism Across Borders: Sustaining Civilians in Times of War* (ed. Thomas G. Weiss and Larry Minear, Lynne Rienner, Boulder, CO, 1993), pp. 181–3. A team led by Minear emphasised UNHCR's role but without specific analysis of the ramifications of its extended mandate in the former Yugoslavia: Larry Minear *et al.*, *Humanitarian Action in the Former Yugoslavia: The UN's Role 1991–1993* (Occasional Paper No. 18, Thomas J. Watson Jr Institute for International Affairs, Brown University, Providence, RI, and Refugee Policy Group, 1994). This report is also somewhat vague about the process by which UNHCR was designated 'lead agency': see *ibid.*, p. 26.

sented a triumph of politics over law, implying a capitulation to expediency rather than adherence to legal protection. In attempting to protect nationals in the midst of ethnic cleansing, UNHCR was faced with moral and political dilemmas that tended to be solved by diverging from its strict legal mandate. The promotion of repatriation, during and after the wars, partly in response to financial and institutional pressures from donor governments, became particularly problematic. UNHCR's requirement for a secure environment, originally to be provided by the United Nations Protection Force in the former Yugoslavia (UNPROFOR), and then by the Implementation Force (IFOR) led by the North Atlantic Treaty Organisation (NATO), and its successor, the Stabilisation Force (SFOR), also presented a challenge which revealed tensions in military and humanitarian relief policies and demonstrated the need to address the operational relationships between international military forces and humanitarian agencies.

In addressing these issues this chapter advances the argument that UNHCR's experience of implementing a humanitarian co-ordination mandate in the former Yugoslavia suggests the inappropriateness of particular agencies to lead, both in the holistic management of humanitarian assistance and in the co-ordination of military and civilian elements. The chapter explains how the 'lead agency' concept came about as an answer to the problem of co-ordinating the UN's humanitarian missions, and which also became, in the former Yugoslavia at least, a substitute for effective international political management of the crisis. At the outset of the crisis, UNHCR was able to take a *de facto* lead in Croatia with the agreement of the protagonists. However, in a number of respects the responsibility became increasingly controversial as the situation evolved, and the effect may ultimately have been to weaken rather than strengthen the UN's ability to respond to humanitarian emergencies and UNHCR's primary purpose to protect refugees. As Guy Goodwin-Gill argues in chapter 11 of this volume, it is highly questionable whether UNHCR should be engaged in humanitarian co-ordination functions at all, given its statutory responsibility as an independent, non-political actor representing the interests of refugees and people in flight. In the case of the former Yugoslavia, the lead agency concept involved UNHCR in a whole range of activities, including human rights protection, economic development for repatriation, and the protection and security of people displaced and threatened with displacement – activities that extended UNHCR's international role and stretched its capabilities. In particular, the UN Secretary-General had requested that UNHCR direct its efforts towards those persons who had been displaced, but as the conflicts intensified and ethnic cleansing was carried out in Bosnia-Herzegovina, UNHCR's remit began to incorporate those people threatened with displacement but who had not yet left their homes. This reflected the extent to which UNHCR was susceptible to politicisation, already compromised as a consequence of its close association with the militarisation of humanitarian aid and having to operate in the context of international sanctions imposed on the protagonists.

Evolution of the lead agency concept as the answer to co-ordination

To a large extent, the evolution of lead agency status has been a function of operational and structural improvisation. The evolution of the concept has been developed in response to the problems encountered in field operations and to the various pressures for structural reform within the UN. It has thus reflected the political and operational stresses arising from humanitarian interventions, rather than reflecting legal or normative standards. The UN's responses to complex and conflict-related humanitarian emergencies have been the subject of penetrating critiques, highlighting particularly the problems of co-ordination.[4] The lead agency designation has, in effect, been an attempt to answer the problem of co-ordinating humanitarian missions in the field, with the UN Children's Fund (UNICEF), for example, taking a *de facto* lead in the Sudan and Cambodia; the World Food Programme (WFP) in Angola; UNHCR in Cyprus (where the UN Peacekeeping Force in Cyprus (UNFICYP) lacked humanitarian capabilities), in southern Sudan and the Horn of Africa.

Until after the Gulf Crisis in 1991, the main mechanisms for co-ordinating UN emergency assistance at the strategic level were the Disaster Relief Organisation (UNDRO), founded in 1971, and the Resident Representative in recipient states of the United Nations Development Programme (UNDP). Much criticism was directed at UNDRO. It had survived censure by a Joint Inspection Unit report in 1980, but its limited operational capacity was subsequently exposed in complex emergencies, notably in dealing with the exodus of people as a consequence of the Gulf Crisis.

UN planning for humanitarian action in the Gulf Crisis gave UNDRO a co-ordinating role in dealing with an anticipated exodus of several hundred thousand people fleeing Iraq and Kuwait. UNDP

---

[4] See, for example, Stephen Green, *International Disaster Relief: Toward a Responsive System* (McGraw-Hill and Council on Foreign Relations, New York, 1977); Barbara E. Harrell-Bond, *Imposing Aid: Emergency Assistance to Refugees* (Oxford University Press, 1986); Randolph C. Kent, *Anatomy of Disaster Relief: The International Network in Action* (Pinter, London, 1987); and Graham Hancock, *Lords of Poverty* (Macmillan, London, 1989).

Representatives were defined as humanitarian co-ordinators at country level, but the nature of their expertise as development programmers did not automatically equip them for emergency relief tasks, and much depended on the personality and energies of individuals.[5] An innovative feature of the planning for the Gulf Crisis was the assignment of specific fields of responsibility to particular UN agencies according to their expertise.[6] However, the system came under severe strain because no one had foreseen the displacement of people to, and the exodus from, northern Iraq which took place between mid-1989 and 1991. UNHCR came under pressure from the USA to deal with the humanitarian needs of Kurds in a zone in northern Iraq which in effect was created and guaranteed by the coalition's military power.[7] This role may have been politically uncomfortable for UNHCR, but it was certainly effective.

Alternatives to lead agency designation

The Gulf Crisis increased pressure on the UN to review the co-ordination of relief.[8] In Resolution 46/182 of 19 December 1991 the General Assembly called for a new 'high-level official (emergency relief co-ordinator)' with direct access to the Secretary-General; 'a secretariat based on a strengthened Office of the United Nations Disaster Relief Co-ordinator; and the consolidation of existing offices that deal with complex emergencies', such as UNDRO. The official would also act as the chair of a new Inter-Agency Standing Committee which would include UN agencies, the International Committee of the Red Cross (ICRC) and relevant non-governmental organisations (NGOs).

In some quarters it was anticipated that the new post would amount to a high-level co-ordinator or 'trouble-shooter' on the model of the former UN High Commissioner for Refugees, Prince Saddrudin Aga Khan, who had been appointed by the Secretary-General to set up a relief system in Afghanistan, and who had later negotiated a Memorandum of Understanding with Iraq for the disposition of UN humanitarian guards in the Kurdish safe haven.[9] However, the emergency relief and humani-

---

[5] Subsequently, DHA pressed for the country-level humanitarian co-ordinator to be open to candidates from outside UNDP. In Somalia a UNICEF official replaced the UNDP resident as co-ordinator, and the humanitarian co-ordinator in Rwanda was a DHA officer.

[6] UN Office at Geneva, 'Regional Humanitarian Plan of Action Relating to the Crisis Between Iraq and Kuwait', Final Version, 11 January 1991.

[7] See David Rieff, *Slaughterhouse: Bosnia and the Failure of the West* (Vintage Books, London, 1995), p. 199.

[8] Interview with Stephen Green, DHA, New York, 9 March 1995.

[9] Interview by Michael Pugh with Irene Khan, Senior Executive Assistant to the High Commissioner, UNHCR, Geneva, 31 May 1995; and off-the-record discussion at the

tarian co-ordinator was not equipped with the power to 'direct' agencies and institutions which could 'hide behind the undeniable authority of their legislative bodies'.[10] In effect the post became a new agency, a new bureaucracy, accorded secretariat status as the Department of Humanitarian Affairs (DHA), alongside the Department of Political Affairs and the Department of Peacekeeping Operations.[11] The DHA was instrumental in improving information management, but lacked the authority to impose co-ordination and suffered from competition between UN agencies.[12] It was abolished and the function of emergency relief co-ordination was absorbed at the start of 1998 into the new Office for the Co-ordination of Humanitarian Affairs (OCHA). This latest twist in the long-standing attempt to improve the UN's emergency response capacity was an integral part of the reform package, designed to save money and cut posts, that was presented to the General Assembly by Boutros-Ghali's successor, Kofi Annan, in April 1997.[13] Several states, including the USA, had frowned on the way the DHA had become a new layer of bureaucracy in the UN system.[14] The original intention was, in fact, to make the UNHCR responsible for co-ordination but this idea became the target of UN bureaucratic politics.[15] However, in spite of the birth of OCHA, led by Sergio Vieira de Mello, former Assistant High Commissioner for Refugees, UN specialised agencies can still be designated as lead agencies

Foreign and Commonwealth Office, London, 12 June 1995. See also Jürgen Dedring, 'Humanitarian Co-ordination', in *After Rwanda: The Co-ordination of United Nations Humanitarian Assistance* (ed. Jim Whitman and David Pocock, Macmillan, Basingstoke, 1996).

[10] Dedring, 'Humanitarian Co-ordination', p. 39. This contrasts with the job specification for the Disaster Relief Co-ordinator, as given in General Assembly Resolution 2816 XXVI of 14 December 1971, who was expected 'to mobilise, *direct* and co-ordinate the relief activities of the various organisations of the United Nations system'.

[11] Ingram, 'The Future Architecture', pp. 176–7.

[12] *Ibid.*, p. 181. See also Neill Wright, 'The Hidden Costs of Better Co-ordination', in *After Rwanda*, p. 53, for an example of DHA co-ordination in the field – the UN Rwanda Emergency Operation (UNREO). See also Report of 24th Meeting of the Sub-Committee of the Whole on International Protection, 18–19 May 1994, UNHCR, Geneva, EC/SCP/89, 29 September 1994, para. 33.

[13] UN Secretary-General, *Renewing the United Nations: A Programme for Reform* (UN Press and Information Office, New York, 1997), paras. 186–93; ECOSOC Doc. E/1997–98, 'Special Economic, Humanitarian and Disaster Relief Assistance: Review of the Capacity of the United Nations System for Humanitarian Assistance', Report of the Secretary-General, 10 July 1997.

[14] Comments by Melinda L. Kimble (USA), 'Economic and Social Council Discusses Post-Conflict Humanitarian Aid', Press Release, 17 July 1997, UN Information Service, ECOSOC/5728, Geneva, 18 July 1997.

[15] Thomas G. Weiss, 'Humanitarian Shell Games: Whither UN Reform?', 29 *Security Dialogue*, 1998, 1, pp. 9–23; Michael Pugh, 'The Withering of Humanitarian Reform: A Rejoinder', 29 *Security Dialogue*, 1998, 2, pp. 157–61.

in humanitarian emergencies. Indeed the formula is likely to survive because OCHA, like DHA before it, will not have a significant field presence and is intended to be a small unit, albeit with a powerful standing in New York through its responsibility for chairing the cabinet-style Executive Committee for Humanitarian Affairs.

However, the crisis in Yugoslavia deepened while the lessons of the Gulf Crisis were being absorbed and before the necessary re-organisation to create DHA and implement Resolution 46/182 was up and running. The UN Secretariat had to rely on existing capabilities. This largely explains why, in spite of the complexities of the political and military situation in the former Yugoslavia, a specialised agency, whose primary concern is not the co-ordination of humanitarian intervention but the protection of refugees, was chosen to lead the humanitarian response.

The choice of UNHCR

Whilst it is unnecessary here to present a detailed account of the UN's involvement in the former Yugoslavia, it is important to understand the immediate context in which the UN Secretary-General designated UNHCR as the lead agency.[16] The resort to reliance on UNHCR as the situation unfolded then becomes clear.

First, constitutionally, UNHCR's operations in Croatia fell both within its mandatory role in dealing with refugees and its case-specific role in dealing with displaced persons.[17] UNHCR had been able to act with greater flexibility in Africa since 1969, when the Organisation of African Unity had expanded the definition of refugees to encompass those fleeing general warfare and disorder, as well as those escaping persecution.[18] Moreover, General Assembly resolutions have referred to specific groups of displaced persons which fell outside the restricted definition of refugee.[19] Prince Sadruddin Aga Khan had also made use of the growing demand for UNHCR's services to expand UNHCR's work,[20] and custo-

---

[16] For useful surveys of the conflict itself, see Susan L. Woodward, *Balkan Tragedy: Chaos and Dissolution after the Cold War* (Brookings Institution, Washington DC, 1995); A. Betts Fetherston, Oliver Ramsbotham and Tom Woodhouse, 'UNPROFOR: Some Observations', 1 *International Peacekeeping*, 1994, pp. 179–203; and James Gow, *Triumph of the Lack of Will: International Diplomacy and the Yugoslav War* (C. Hurst and Co., London, 1997).   [17] See also chapters 8 and 10 of this volume.
[18] OAU Convention Governing the Specific Aspects of Refugee Problems in Africa 1969, 1001 UNTS 46, article 1(2).
[19] For further details see chapter 8, pp. 158–9 above.
[20] Lawyers' Committee for Human Rights, *The UNHCR at 40: Refugee Protection at the Crossroads* (Lawyers' Committee for Human Rights, New York, 1991), pp. 32–3; and B. G. Ramcharan, *Humanitarian Good Offices in International Law* (Martinus Nijhoff, Dordrecht, 1983), p. 94.

mary practice has been for UNHCR to protect displaced persons if their situation is linked to, and analogous with, that of a potential or existing refugee problem, and provided the Secretary-General or competent principal organs of the UN make a request with the consent of the concerned state.[21]

Second, the humanitarian emergency in Yugoslavia was identified in similar terms to the Gulf Crisis, as a problem of dealing with refugees and displaced persons. However, the circumstances in Yugoslavia, where a war was still in progress, were quite different to the strategic conditions in northern Iraq. Population movements intensified after Croatia's declaration of independence on 25 June 1991 and by the autumn of 1991 about 500,000 refugees required assistance. The government of what was then still the Socialist Federal Republic of Yugoslavia formally asked UNHCR for help in dealing with the problem, and an approach was made to the UN Secretary-General. After discussions between Pérez de Cuéllar and the High Commissioner for Refugees, the formal request for UNHCR assistance was made in the letter of 25 October 1991 which referred to UNHCR as having a preventive impact on the situation in other parts of Yugoslavia.

UNHCR seemed the most appropriate agency, given its unrivalled experience in assisting refugees since its formation in 1951. This is not to say that the agency has been free of criticism or that its reputation since 1951 has been entirely free of blemish. For example, it has been claimed that UNHCR has failed to represent the interests of refugees from Viet Nam, Haiti and Cambodia and has been indirectly responsible for the negligent treatment of asylum seekers in southern Africa, El Salvador and Cambodia.[22] Nevertheless, it was the only humanitarian agency with anything like the bureaucratic infrastructure and field capacity to cope with a huge movement of people. In the early 1950s UNHCR's budget of US$300,000 was designed to address the needs of 1 million refugees. By 1997 the High Commissioner estimated that there were in excess of 20 million refugees and others of concern to UNHCR.[23] It had also made its mark in co-ordinating relief for the Kurds from June 1991 to

---

[21] This was lately reiterated by General Assembly Resolution 48/116, 20 December 1993, which also added at para. 20 the proviso 'and taking into account the complementarities of the mandates and expertise of other relevant organisations, to provide humanitarian assistance and protection to persons displaced within their own country'.

[22] See, for example, Gil Loescher, *Beyond Charity: International Cooperation and the Global Refugee Crisis* (Oxford University Press, 1993), p. 146; Barbara Harrell-Bond, 'Repatriation: Under What Conditions is It the Most Desirable Solution for Refugees? An Agenda for Research', 32 *African Studies Review*, 1989, pp. 41–68.

[23] UNHCR RefWorld, *UNHCR Statistics 1997 – Refugees and Others of Concern to the UNHCR, 1996* (5th edn, UNHCR RefWorld, Geneva, 1998, CD-ROM).

August/September 1992 after which the problem was deemed to be an internal one and UNICEF took over.

Thirdly, in comparison with other aid organisations, UNHCR had also established some representation in the Yugoslavia. UNHCR was acting in support of the ICRC in the area and was already handling routine refugee issues from its long-standing offices in Belgrade and in the surrounding states. Although there were still only nineteen international staff members on duty in the former Yugoslavia at the end of 1991, the number expanded so that by the end of 1993, UNHCR's potential had been mobilised and it had at least twenty-nine offices and almost 700 international and local staff operating within a budgetary request in excess of US$295 million.[24] In the summer of 1991, UNHCR also appointed a Special Envoy, José-Maria Mendiluce, who established an office in Sarajevo before Bosnia-Herzegovina existed as a separate entity. The Sarajevo office was perceived at the time as a way of emphasising UNHCR's impartiality and avoiding Croat suspicion of the Belgrade office. Indeed UNHCR personnel from that office were not allowed to travel directly to Zagreb.

UNHCR carved out its role quite independently of the establishment of the UNPROFOR peacekeeping mission in 1992. Indeed, the force was not finally authorised for deployment until 21 February 1992 when a cease-fire and other conditions had supposedly been met and a peace of sorts could be kept. The UN was mandated to stabilise, demilitarise and provide law and order in each designated protected area, whilst also assisting the voluntary return of displaced persons and refugees.[25] By the end of March 1992, when UNPROFOR was in place, UNHCR had already been undertaking its humanitarian role for six months and had established a presence in Bosnia, although it had been unable to secure the voluntary return of refugees and had to cope with non-Serbs forced out of the protected areas.

The trials of UNHCR in the former Yugoslavia were to parallel those of UNPROFOR I and II with the added complication of being part of a militarised aid operation. UNHCR's independence was compromised and its lack of experience or mechanisms for dealing with conflict and ethnic cleansing threatened to overwhelm it. Instead of coping with refugees as a fall-out from conflict, UNHCR would have to deal with a situation where the creation of displaced people was a primary object of the participants to the conflict.

---

[24] Minear et al., *Humanitarian Action in the Former Yugoslavia.*
[25] Security Council Resolution 743, 21 February 1992.

Politicisation

The UN Secretary-General's decision to appoint UNHCR to the lead agency role may have been logical but it compounded UNHCR's difficulties in adopting new and potentially controversial areas of responsibility. Above all, it increased the risk of politicisation. UNHCR's primary role is treaty-based and legal rather than political. It was founded to protect and assist the world's refugees according to the international laws of asylum, statelessness and refugee status. It was designed to be an independent, non-political actor within the administrative and financial framework of the United Nations. Article 2 of the Statute of UNHCR declares: 'The work of the High Commissioner shall be of an entirely non-political character; it shall be humanitarian and social and shall relate, as a rule, to groups and categories of refugees.'[26] Several general factors have conspired to increase the fragility of this ideal, including changes in UNHCR policy.

For example, the UN High Commissioner for Refugees, Sadako Ogata, had even expanded the operational concept of protection to include the expectation that UNHCR officers in the field would not only observe human rights violations but report on them and seek remedial action from appropriate authorities. Yet, given that reporting violations is itself likely to be regarded as a political act in errant states, this risks contradicting her own statement that UNHCR should not investigate human rights abuses since its humanitarian role 'should be broadly non-judgemental'.[27] In sum, the emphasis on comprehensive responses to crises, meant that UNHCR was drawn more deeply into intricate political processes, which included close interaction with other external participants such as third party mediators.[28]

Donor pressures

UNHCR has been criticised for reacting to the preferences of the donor governments of the industrialised world in the formation of policy towards Third World refugees.[29] Such preferences include a desire to

---

[26] UNHCR, *Statute of the United Nations High Commissioner for Refugees*, HCR/INF/Rev.3, United Nations, General Assembly Resolution, 428 (V), 14 December 1950.

[27] Address by Sadako Ogata, 51st Session of the UN Commission on Human Rights, 7 February 1995.

[28] UNHCR, *The State of the World's Refugees: The Challenge of Protection* (Penguin Books, Harmondsworth, 1993), pp. 28–9.

[29] See, for example, Harrell-Bond, 'Repatriation', pp. 41–68; and S. Alex Cunliffe, 'Vietnamese Boat People in Hong Kong: Policies and Prescriptions', 4 *Pacific Review*, 1991, 3, pp. 272–7.

limit the numbers of refugees seeking asylum and a reluctance to implement comprehensive resettlement programmes as a durable solution for large-scale refugee movements. Official UNHCR statistics indicate a rapid increase in the number of asylum applicants in the late 1980s and early 1990s. The number of applicants to industrialised countries rose from less than 102,000 in 1983 to over 839,000 in 1993, a more than eightfold increase within one decade. Several western European governments have tightened their asylum laws by introducing stringent determination procedures, visa restrictions and fines for carriers bringing in those with inadequate travel documents.[30] Moreover, in 1990, Germany, France and the Benelux countries signed the Schengen Convention which contained provisions to prevent multiple asylum requests.[31]

Criticisms that UNHCR has been developing contemporary refugee policy in line with the wishes of the developed world is not really surprising. UNHCR is well aware that the industrialised countries are becoming increasingly uneasy about the growing number of asylum seekers.[32] Of the funds needed by UNHCR to finance its Annual Programmes, 99 per cent come from *voluntary* contributions made by member states of UNHCR's Executive Committee. As the number of refugee movements has increased by at least 50 per cent over recent decades, the gap between assessed needs and likely resources has assumed crisis proportions. By October 1989, there was a shortfall of over US$100 million between the funds which donors actually provided and the budget they had approved a year earlier. The financial crisis led to a situation whereby voluntary contributions from donor governments were based upon what was available rather than on an assessment of refugee needs.[33] Given UNHCR's financial dependence upon voluntary contributions from industrialised

---

[30] John Carvel, 'EU Moves to Tighten Frontiers', *Guardian*, 14 February 1995. For an insight into increasing donor intransigence towards resettlement programmes, see Lawyers' Committee for Human Rights, *The UNHCR at 40*.

[31] For more information on European developments see Part 4 of this volume.

[32] UNHCR, *The State of the World's Refugees*, 1993, p. 38; and Loescher, *Beyond Charity*, p. 138.

[33] Historically, the major donors have included the USA, western European states, Japan, Canada and Australia. During the 1980s, a number of donors, including the USA, became increasingly unwilling to provide support. The strain upon UNHCR can be seen in the fact that, during the same period, the number of refugees under UNHCR protection rose by 50 per cent. UNHCR cut spending by US$70 million during the year but a deficit of US$40 million remained. The resultant financial crisis led to a change in the nature of the budget and established a political environment whereby voluntary contributions from donor governments would be based upon what was available rather than on an assessment of refugee needs. For an insight into the effects of budgetary crises within UNHCR, see Nicholas Morris, 'Refugees: Facing Crisis in the 1990s – A Personal View from Within the UNHCR', 2 *International Journal of Refugee Law*, 1990, Special Issue, pp. 38–58. For an analysis of UNHCR's budgetary allocations, see the annual reports of the US Committee for Refugees, *The World Refugee Survey* (Washington DC).

nations, the High Commissioner may frequently be placed in the invidious position of attempting to solicit funds from donors for refugee programmes which they may find politically sensitive.

It is against this political background that the outbreak of war in the former Yugoslavia should be viewed. This conflict has created the largest European flow of refugees since the Second World War. By July 1993, barely twenty months after the Secretary-General's request for UNHCR to adopt the role of 'lead agency' in the region, the total number of people seeking sanctuary in Croatia, Serbia, Montenegro, Slovenia and Macedonia totalled over 1,200,000. In addition, at least 600,000 more had sought refuge outside the immediately affected region. UNHCR was pragmatic about the prospects of Western governments offering resettlement and political asylum:

Today, the opportunities for permanent integration in receiving countries are limited. It seems very unlikely that people who have fled en masse to a neighbouring country will in future be offered large-scale resettlement elsewhere.[34]

In addition, Western governments have preferred to offer 'temporary protection' from violent conflict. This usually takes the form of 'humanitarian status' or 'temporary protected status' and falls short of full refugee status. These impermanent classifications allow asylum seekers to remain temporarily at the discretion of the authorities until it is deemed safe for them to return home. UNHCR made two appeals to Western governments to provide such contingency places. Under the first programme from October 1992 to July 1995, 31,870 people were given temporary refuge, the most accommodating states being the USA (which took 5,812 refugees), Denmark (5,954), Sweden (3,970) and Germany (3,117). The UK government agreed to participate in the programme in October 1992 but, by simultaneously imposing the need to obtain a visa on all those travelling from the former Yugoslavia before they arrived in the UK, successful applications were limited (1,723).[35] UNHCR's second appeal to the UK and other Western governments to provide refuge for those fleeing the conflict included 5,000 Bosnian Muslims who had fled their homes for the 'safe havens' of Srebrenica and Zepa. However, of the 11,000 people from the former Yugoslavia who applied for asylum in the UK after the outbreak of the conflict, 2,000 applications had been processed by July 1995 and only 25 people had been granted full refugee status.[36]

In the 1990s UNHCR increasingly emphasised 'country of origin solutions' to eradicate the causes of refugee flight, thus shifting the focus to

[34] UNHCR, The State of the World's Refugees, 1993, p. 40.
[35] Alan Travis and Ian Black, 'Britain Asked to Let in More Bosnians', Guardian, 31 July 1995.   [36] Alan Travis, 'UK Less Than Generous', Guardian, 8 August 1995.

displacement within borders. It presumes that there is a 'right to remain' and a 'right to protection' and that addressing the causes of flight is not only of domestic concern but a concern also of other states.[37] The request by the UN Secretary-General for UNHCR to bear more responsibility and leadership within the conflict in the former Yugoslavia must also be viewed in the context of the pressure to prevent people crossing international boundaries. In theory, a co-ordinated approach would lead to a more efficient and cost-effective utilisation of resources. In reality, a well-orchestrated and common effort was slow to materialise. In the early years of UNHCR's involvement, it interpreted its role as lead agency in terms of maintaining a direct operational control across a wide range of sectors, rather than delegating certain responsibilities to agencies with the established expertise. As the number of displaced persons and people at risk escalated to over 4 million in 1993, UNHCR's ability to maintain direct responsibility became more difficult logistically. Thus, UNHCR delegated early medical evacuations to actors such as the International Organisation for Migration (IOM), the primary activities of which were limited in 1992 to the transport of 1,000 refugees to Switzerland. In addition, the World Health Organisation (WHO), UNICEF and WFP also assumed a relatively limited role throughout the initial phases of the conflict. Indeed, WHO did not become functional in the Serbian-controlled areas until the middle of 1993. To a certain extent, these early, operational difficulties were recognised by the UN Secretary-General in 1992 when he established the DHA to bring more co-ordination to the UN's humanitarian activities. However, DHA could not assert itself *post facto* and was primarily concerned with raising funds for UN operations.

Humanitarian action as a substitute for political resolve

One can go further and argue that in the former Yugoslavia the dangers of politicisation were amply demonstrated by UNHCR's role as a substitute for international diplomacy and political resolve. As several commentators, including the High Commissioner herself, remarked: 'The political problem should not be given the façade of being dealt with through humanitarian assistance.'[38] UNHCR was pushed into a vacuum where

---

[37] UNHCR, *The State of the World's Refugees*, 1993, pp. 9–10. See also chapter 10 of this volume.
[38] Sadako Ogata, 'Concluding Remarks', *Conflict and Humanitarian Action* (Report of a Conference at Princeton University, 22–23 October 1993), p. 49. See also Rosalyn Higgins, 'The New United Nations and the Former Yugoslavia', 69 *International Affairs*, 1993, 3, pp. 465–83; and Alain Destexhe, 'Foreword' in *Populations in Danger 1995: A Médecins sans Frontières Report* (ed. Jean François, MSF, London, 1995), pp. 13–15.

there was no overall UN strategy, and humanitarianism became a substitute for a coherent international political response, from the pressure within the European Union by the German Foreign Ministry for recognition of Croatia's independence to the disputes over management of airstrikes by NATO.

Co-ordination or control

A major problem was lack of clarification about the concept of lead agency co-ordination, as acknowledged in UNHCR itself.[39] UNHCR had a wide latitude to interpret the role to embrace a whole range of activities, including protection and security, on behalf of people displaced and threatened with displacement throughout the region. The lead role concept was not defined and there were no clear guidelines outlining the responsibilities within this function. In fact UNHCR interpreted its role as having:

prime responsibility for logistics/transport, food monitoring, domestic needs, shelter, community services, health, emergency transition activities in agriculture and income generation, protection/legal assistance, and assistance to other agencies in sectors under their responsibility.[40]

In practice the burden of such a wide range of responsibilities was alleviated because other UN agencies took on specialist roles. WFP assumed responsibility for food aid and the mobilisation and delivery of food. A UNHCR seed distribution programme in 1993–4 was handed over to the Food and Agriculture Organisation. WHO became responsible for the health sector including rehabilitation of health services and provision of medical equipment and supplies. UNICEF had responsibility for the survival and development needs of women and children. Even so, UNHCR's responsibilities under the rubric of 'protection' were extremely broad.

For example, acting on a UNHCR proposal and operating under UNHCR, an International Management Group Infrastructure for Bosnia and Herzegovina (IMG–IBH) was formally established by donor governments in November 1994 to address the infrastructure needs of Bosnia-Herzegovina and bridge the gap between emergency relief and reconstruction in anticipation of refugees' return.[41] In short there is some substance to the criticism that, although a holistic approach may be desirable, UNHCR was spreading its capacities too thinly.

---

[39] Steven Wolfson and Neill Wright, *A UNHCR Handbook for the Military on Humanitarian Operations* (UNHCR, Geneva, 1994), p. 24.
[40] UNHCR Office of the Special Envoy for the Former Yugoslavia, External Relations Unit, *Information Notes on the Former Yugoslavia*, No. 1/95, January 1995.
[41] Statement by Sadako Ogata to the Humanitarian Issues Working Group of the International Conference on the Former Yugoslavia, Geneva, 18 March 1994.

In addition, and as already argued, the lead agency concept primarily concerned operational and field co-ordination. Although the Secretary-General's Special Representative was the overall co-ordinator of UN activities in the former Yugoslavia, UNHCR, in its capacity as lead agency, was expected not only to act independently in refugee assistance and operate jointly with others (such as a medical evacuation programme with the ICRC), but also to co-ordinate a variety of relationships with the other UN agencies, UNPROFOR, the European Community Humanitarian Office (ECHO), NATO and the military and political representatives of the belligerents. This has involved, for example, UNHCR opening a liaison office in NATO headquarters in Brussels.

Nevertheless the exact meaning of the term 'co-ordination' is not clear either in this context or, it would appear, in UN operational circles. As the liaison officer for the UN's Rwanda Emergency Operation (UNREO), Anita Menghetti, commented in regard to Rwanda: 'The C-word throws everyone into a tizzy. There is the perception in the agency world that if you are being co-ordinated you are being controlled.'[42] Co-ordination has not been defined in any detailed fashion within the UN secretariat. It would appear to reject any implication of subjection over participants, but it inevitably implies an exercise of authority and leadership in order to create an environment, which promotes an integrated operation and avoids unnecessary duplication. Whether the OCHA in New York and Geneva, and the UNDP Resident Co-ordinator in the field, will be any more competent than the DHA/Humanitarian Co-ordinator system is a moot point.

In regard to the protection of internally displaced people, the humanitarian agencies involved argued that existing *co-operation* needed 'reinforcing and structuring without losing the benefits of a flexibility which would allow for allocation of responsibility in accordance with the specific characteristics of any given situation'.[43] In fact, NGOs do work closely with UNHCR through a Partnership in Action Programme which drew up the Oslo Declaration in June 1994. This declaration 'recommends' that NGOs 'should recognise the co-ordinating responsibility of UNHCR as the lead agency in refugee emergencies, and UNHCR should ensure that it has the capacity to undertake this co-ordination effectively'.[44] Nevertheless, many of the diverse bodies involved are likely

---

[42] Cited in International Federation of Red Cross and Red Crescent Societies, *World Disasters Report: Under the Volcanoes. Special Focus on the Rwandan Refugee Crisis* (IFRC, Geneva, 1994), p. 21.

[43] 24th Meeting of the Sub-Committee of the Whole on International Protection, UNHCR, 18–19 May 1994, EC/SCP/89, para. 33.

[44] Partnership in Action, *Oslo Declaration and Plan of Action* (UNHCR and International Council of Voluntary Agencies, June 1994), p. 17. They also agreed to advocate a broader

to guard their freedom of action, often to maintain a distance from the perceived partiality in the field of UN agencies. The most that could be agreed in Oslo was to flesh out co-operation, to establish consultation mechanisms, dialogue and information sharing, the establishment of repatriation committees in countries of origin, regular NGO involvement in policy formulation and joint advocacy of refugee rights. In any event, there is a risk, recognised in UNHCR, that co-ordination could become a substitute for protection, rather than the former being the means to achieve the latter.[45]

Of course, neither the problems of politicisation nor of establishing and defining an appropriate role would have been so crucial had the situation on the ground not become increasingly fraught during 1992 and 1993 as the fighting spread to Bosnia-Herzegovina and the protagonists sought to consolidate territorial gains.

UNHCR and ethnic cleansing

The number of internally displaced people and potential refugees threatened to overwhelm UNHCR's capacity. Between March and July 1992, atrocities in prison camps and a Serbian campaign of ethnic cleansing expanded the number of refugees seeking to escape the conflict. Along with the ICRC, UNHCR had to pull out of Sarajevo temporarily after an ICRC member was killed on 18 May 1992. In June UNHCR began an airlift operation to Sarajevo, staffed by serving airforce officers from France, Germany, the UK and the USA. However, by the middle of 1992, UNHCR reported the existence of 1,300,000 Bosnian refugees. By the autumn, estimates of 20,000 rapes of Bosnian Muslims by Serbs were made public and the UN estimated that the numbers in need of urgent assistance in the region was in excess of 4 million people. It was ethnic cleansing in particular which confronted UNHCR with a fundamental challenge to its extended mandate.

UNHCR lacks a general mandate for dealing with internally displaced persons.[46] Its activity is generally limited to providing assistance to people who cross international boundaries and seek political asylum. True, in requesting UNHCR to direct its efforts towards displaced people within the disintegrating Yugoslavia the Secretary-General had not broken new ground: the precedent had already been established in Africa and was to

refugee definition and a flexible definition of internally displaced persons which should not be restricted by existing mandates of concerned UN agencies and/or NGOs, and should be based on practical and empirical analysis of the root causes of displacement.
[45] Interview with Khan, UNHCR, Geneva.
[46] See also chapter 8, pp. 158–9 above.

be continued in Azerbaijan, Tajikistan, Georgia and Sri Lanka. However, Pérez de Cuéllar's initial invitation to deal with displaced persons in Croatia was to plunge the organisation into an unfamiliar political environment. By early 1992 UNHCR was working for the first time in the midst of war, and it was no more prepared for the atrocities and ethnic cleansing than the rest of the international community.

The policy of ethnic cleansing, especially in Bosnia-Herzegovina, placed UNHCR in a difficult position. Although historically UNHCR's *modus operandi* was to assist people who had been forced to flee intolerable circumstances, the UN's universal condemnation of ethnic cleansing pointed to a policy of keeping people in their homes. However, as the conflict intensified and ethnic cleansing crystallised in areas of Bosnia-Herzegovina, UNHCR's remit began to incorporate those people threatened with displacement but who had not yet left their homes.[47] UNHCR then found itself in the 'ironic and awkward position of trying to save lives by helping people become refugees'.[48] UNHCR had to reconcile the dilemma of facilitating people's departure from life-threatening circumstances, whilst not being accused of complicity in ethnic cleansing. Ogata encapsulated the problem thus:

In the context of a conflict which has as its very objective the displacement of people, we find ourselves confronted with a major dilemma. To what extent do we persuade people to remain where they are, when that could well jeopardise their lives and liberties? On the other hand, if we help them to move do we not become an accomplice to 'ethnic cleansing'?[49]

At the same time, governments could use their opposition to ethnic cleansing to limit resettlement programmes.[50] In July 1992, UNHCR responded to the predicament with a significant departure from its traditional policy of assisting refugees and displaced persons, by engaging in 'preventive protection'. An internal working group recommended that, whilst the right to asylum remains intact 'at least on a temporary basis and until a solution can be found', UNHCR should also strengthen protection in order to prevent refugee flows. By 1994 this had been amended

---

[47] See UN Doc. S/24333, 21 July 1992; Security Council Resolution 762, 30 June 1992 based on UN Doc. S/24188, 26 June 1992; and Security Council Resolution 769, 7 August 1992 based on UN Doc. S/24353, 27 July 1992.
[48] José-Maria Mendiluce, Special Envoy of the High Commissioner in the former Yugoslavia, cited in Minear *et al.*, *Humanitarian Action in the Former Yugoslavia*, p. 18.
[49] Sadako Ogata, 'Refugees: A Humanitarian Strategy', statement at the Royal Institute for International Relations, Brussels, 25 November 1992.
[50] Resistance to resettlement as a durable solution to refugee movements has been expressed by a number of donor governments, and has been evident in Washington's policy towards Cuban asylum seekers in 1994 and the general decline in the resettlement of Vietnamese refugees based in Hong Kong. See S. Alex Cunliffe, 'The Refugee Crises: A Study of the UNHCR', 43 *Political Studies*, 1995, pp. 278–90.

to a strategy of temporary protection, including admission to safety, respect for basic human rights, protection against *refoulement*, and facilitating safe return when conditions permitted.[51]

Whilst in some contexts it may be regarded as laudable that attempts were being made to prevent refugee flows at source, such a policy does raise a number of questions. First, is such a policy practical in an environment where ethnic cleansing places lives at risk? Secondly, is UNHCR an appropriate independent organisation to judge and implement decisions on the relative safety of people whose lives are at risk in their own homes? To a large extent, confidence in the ability of UNHCR to judge the safety of people whose lives are threatened depends upon the availability of UNHCR staff and resources to co-ordinate adequate protection. In the absence of sufficient personnel and resources to ensure protection, a policy of preventive protection is open to criticism.

Even though UNHCR had 738 staff members in the former Yugoslavia at the peak of its involvement in 1995,[52] there were only approximately twenty-five UNHCR officers with protection responsibilities when they were needed most, at the end of 1993. This latter figure hardly represented a presence sufficient to protect people in their homes so as to justify refusing to move people to safety. Without additional resources, UNHCR's policy of preventive protection left UNHCR open to the charge of bowing to the preferences of donor governments rather than representing refugee interests. By first attempting to inhibit large-scale refugee movements, and then to give protection on a temporary basis, UNHCR personnel avoided becoming accessories to ethnic cleansing and chose the lesser of two evils. However, the policy appears to have meshed with the reluctance of many donor governments to participate in resettlement programmes for refugees.

Relations with the military

Further political complications arose from UNHCR's intervention while conflicts were still underway in the former Yugoslavia, and because of the need for close relations with international military forces in situations where consent for the international presence was usually fragile and humanitarian aid was targeted by the protagonists. As noted above, UNHCR and UNPROFOR began on separate tracks, but the former's role as lead agency and the continual expansion of the latter's mandate

---

[51] UNHCR Executive Committee, Conclusion on International Protection, No. 74 (XLV) 1994, para. (r).
[52] UNHCR, *Refugees at a Glance: The Monthly Digest of UNHCR Activities* (Geneva, February 1995).

brought the humanitarian and military arms together. On 29 June 1992 the Security Council expanded UNPROFOR's mandate to open Sarajevo airport for UNHCR airlifts (Resolution 764), and on 13 August, Chapter VII of the UN Charter was invoked, calling on states to take 'all measures necessary' to secure humanitarian aid deliveries (Resolution 770). On 14 September 1992, the Security Council expanded UNPROFOR's responsibilities that would allow it to provide protective support to UNHCR-organised convoys (Resolution 776). UN directives expanded its role to include: organising patrols to protect homes; immigration and customs functions at the borders of UN protected areas (UNPAs); and interviewing individuals who had been forced to flee their homes.[53] In April and May 1993, the Security Council attempted to expand UNPROFOR's role further by adding Sarajevo, Srebrenica, Tuzla, Zepa, Gorazde and Bihac to the list of 'safe areas'. UNPROFOR's mandate was also strengthened with additional observers to monitor humanitarian assistance in those areas. By June 1993, the configuration of military and civilian personnel within UNPROFOR was 22,749 and 1,879 respectively. Since UNPROFOR operations in Bosnia were deployed on a humanitarian support mission, such a military predominance may well have been in need of a more comprehensive training programme in humanitarian skills and law.[54]

The structural challenge which this created was summarised by UNHCR as follows:

The co-ordination of humanitarian efforts with political and military actions in refugee-producing conflicts is not without its difficulties. It blurs traditionally distinct roles and, if mismanaged, could compromise the strictly neutral character of humanitarian aid, which is the best guarantee of access to people in need.[55]

Assessing the civilian–military relationship in July 1994, Ogata highlighted the benefits of the military facilitation of the delivery of assistance, including the securing of Sarajevo airport and airdrops to inaccessible areas.[56] The military role has been well documented by the Minear team: escorting convoys, deterring pillage, facing down violence, removing physical obstacles and providing heavy lift, including airlift.[57] However, Ogata also noted that negotiation, not force, had been used to obtain humanitarian access and that negotiations and consent were critical for

---

[53] See Fetherston, Ramsbotham and Woodhouse, 'UNPROFOR: Some Observations', p. 183.   [54] This prospect is discussed in *ibid.*, pp. 196–7.
[55] UNHCR, *The State of the World's Refugees*, 1993, p. 78.
[56] Sadako Ogata, 'Role of Humanitarian Action in Peacekeeping Operations', keynote address at 24th Annual Vienna Seminar, 5 July 1994.
[57] Minear *et al.*, *Humanitarian Action in the Former Yugoslavia*, pp. 83–5.

ensuring 'humanitarian space'.[58] She also acknowledged that the use of air-strikes had increased the risk to the lives of humanitarian staff and by implication endangered the perceived impartiality and neutrality of humanitarian organisations associated with the operation. 'In these circumstances', she said, 'humanitarian organizations may need to distance themselves from the UN military operations.'[59]

The military operations of UNPROFOR did not always work in tandem with the humanitarian goals of UNHCR. From the beginning of operations in Sarajevo, Mendiluce resisted the militarisation of aid, for, as Ogata acknowledged, political and humanitarian objectives are not necessarily coincidental.[60] Indeed, on a significant number of occasions UNHCR's humanitarian activities were apparently compromised by being associated with the UN's military actions.

In Croatia, for example, UNPROFOR personnel were responsible for controlling and policing the UNPAs. Their primary concern was to fulfil the agreement with the Croatian authorities and maintain order in the UNPAs and adjacent areas ('the pink zones'). In order to accomplish this, military personnel were anxious to restrict movement in and out of the UNPAs. However, UNHCR had only limited direct representation in the UNPAs, and UNPROFOR personnel were frequently unfamiliar with international humanitarian law or interpreted their role in ways which did not automatically accord with human rights protection. As a result, it is apparent that movement restrictions were imposed upon asylum seekers or displaced people seeking repatriation to their homes. In October 1992, the Special Rapporteur of the Commission on Human Rights, Tadeusz Mazowiecki, reported that there were 700,000 refugees in Croatia and declared:

UNPROFOR, which controls much of the border between Bosnia and Herzegovina and Croatia, is being forced to limit their entry into the [UNPAs]. Many displaced Muslims have been turned away at the border and some of those persons who have already crossed it, including those of military age, are being sent back both by UNPROFOR and the Croatian authorities. It is extremely regrettable that UNPROFOR has been forced to violate the principle of *non-refoulement*.[61]

In April 1994, to prevent UNPROFOR and NATO intervening in the siege of Gorazde, Bosnian Serb authorities arrested and detained UNHCR staff in Serb-controlled areas. As Wolfson and Wright observed: 'Allowing humanitarian objectives to become linked to military or politi-

---

[58] Ogata, 'Role of Humanitarian Action in Peacekeeping Operations'.   [59] *Ibid.*
[60] Sadako Ogata, 'Humanitarianism in the Midst of Armed Conflict', address at Brookings Institution, Washington DC, 12 May 1994; and Rieff, *Slaughterhouse*, p. 205.
[61] Cited in Minear *et al.*, *Humanitarian Action in the Former Yugoslavia*, pp. 92–3.

cal events can cause paralysis in mission, where extraneous issues are allowed to cloud the primary principle of *humanity*.'[62] This issue of association with the politics of international military intervention became more acute as military doctrine for 'peace support operations' in NATO's member states placed traditional peacekeeping on a spectrum that included coercion and enforcement.[63] The robustness of IFOR and SFOR, compared to UNPROFOR, improved physical access to certain areas and facilitated the creation of a security space. However, because these NATO-led forces were coercively implementing the Dayton Agreement, and had adopted combat-oriented doctrines, their overriding concern was to protect themselves. More important from the agency and NGO point of view, the 'militarisation of peacekeeping' was bound to affect perceptions of impartiality and to associate aid and relief with military imposition. In the Peace Agreement, IFOR was authorised to assist in the movement of organisations in the accomplishment of humanitarian missions, and explicitly to assist UNHCR, and to prevent interference with the movement of civilian populations.[64] Distancing humanitarian action from military action, to maintain local perceptions of impartiality and independence was thus one of the fundamental problems confronting agencies such as UNHCR after, as well as during, the conflict.

Impartiality, neutrality and independence was under threat in a second sense. Western military forces have institutionalised their involvement in relief and peace-building activities. The Dayton Agreement specified in Annex 1A that IFOR could fulfil supporting tasks 'within the limits of its assigned principal tasks and available resources, and on request'. Subsequent implementation reviews authorised IFOR to assist with wider reconstruction tasks, and the British Army, for example, became a significant channel for distributing UK government aid, with some 600 projects concerned with potable water, sanitation and refuse collection, power supplies, primary health care, education and income generation. However, this involved conditionality and economic leverage that seem likely to contribute to the erosion of classical humanitarian principles. IFOR and SFOR in Bosnia were quite open about the political purpose of their humanitarian operations. Among the advantages that were claimed

---

[62] Wolfson and Wright, *A UNHCR Handbook for the Military on Humanitarian Operations*, p. 30.
[63] UK Joint Warfare Publication 3–01, 'Peace Support Operations', 2nd Study Draft, September 1997; and Michael Pugh, 'The Politics of New Peacekeeping Doctrine', in *European Approaches to Crisis Management* (ed. Knud Jørgensen, Kluwer Law International, The Hague, 1997).
[64] Dayton Peace Agreement, Annex 1A, Agreement on the Military Aspects of the Peace Settlement, 1995, article VI, para. 3.

were that it gave the military commander a 'carrot' to complement his 'stick' to ensure compliance with Dayton. Municipalities in Bosnia were denied economic incentives if they failed to give up suspected war criminals and accept returnees from minority ethnic groups.[65] UNHCR thus became part of a manipulative system designed to achieve 'peace-building with people'.

Peace-building with people

Article VII of the General Framework Agreement at Dayton in late 1995 maintained that the protection of refugees and displaced persons was 'of vital importance in achieving a lasting peace'. Repatriation was to achieve the multi-ethnic peace that the Agreement had singularly failed to do. UNHCR was assigned, by Annex 7 of the Agreement, to take the leading role in repatriating anything up to 2.1 million people who had the right to return to their homes in safety and reclaim their property (or receive compensation). However, the rate of repatriation was well below forecasts. In 1996 the repatriation of 870,000 refugees and displaced persons had been planned by UNHCR, but only 252,000 actually returned. The forecast of 200,000 for 1997 had to be halved, and many refugees returning from abroad simply became internally displaced, settling in areas where they were part of the ethnic majority rather than forming minorities in their place of origin. The sheer numbers involved, the difficulty in establishing property rights and the need to repair homes have ensured a slow rate of return. But above all, the intimidation of returnees was rife throughout the war-torn areas. UNHCR could not guarantee their safety, and nor could IFOR/SFOR. In Stolac, south of Mostar, for example, the return of Muslim and Serb families was initially violently resisted by the local Croats. Elsewhere, UNHCR buses were stoned and their passengers abused while IFOR troops stood idly by.[66]

Moreover, UNHCR was conducting a programme that was in part driven by the interests of asylum states that were keen to see Bosnian exiles returned. As Sophie Albert argues, there were loopholes in the implementation of 'voluntary' repatriation of Bosnians to their 'homes of origin'. No alternative to repatriation, such as permanent asylum, was on offer and if the 'home of origin' was unsafe, Bosnians could be sent back

---

[65] Overseas Development Agency and Ministry of Defence, 'Initiatives in Bosnia', MND/SW, Report on Activities April 1996–September 1996, unclassified document, 1997; Michael Pugh, 'Military Intervention and Humanitarian Action: Trends and Issues', 22 *Disasters*, 1998, pp. 309–17; and in the same issue, Joanna Macrae, 'The Death of Humanitarianism: An Anatomy of the Attack', 22 *Disasters*, 1998, pp. 339–51.

[66] Carl Hallergård, 'Bosnia and Herzegovina: Problems and Progress in the Return Process', 1 *Forced Migration Review*, 1998, pp. 21–4.

to the relative safety of an ethnic majority area without asylum states contravening the *non-refoulement* principle.[67] UNHCR complied with this by scrupulously avoiding coercion or confrontation with locals. 'Peace-building with people' reinforced ethnic divisions and implicated UNHCR in a programme that afforded protection to asylum states from the continuing presence of Bosnian exiles by giving them little option but to become displaced persons in the region.

Sanctions

UNHCR's humanitarian role was also hampered by the Security Council's imposition of economic sanctions on the Federal Republic of Yugoslavia (Serbia and Montenegro). In May 1992, the Security Council demanded an end to the war and to ethnic cleansing and passed Resolution 757 forbidding trade with the Federal Republic of Yugoslavia. These sanctions were also reaffirmed by Resolution 820 in April 1993. Foodstuffs, medical supplies and 'other essential humanitarian supplies' were to be exempted on a case-by-case basis and UNPROFOR, naval forces in the Adriatic and monitors on the Danube were charged with the responsibility of policing the sanctions.

Whatever the political intention, an inevitable outcome was to delay aid programmes for refugees in these areas. Thus, every item in UN aid convoys for refugees in Serbia and Montenegro was in theory subject to scrutiny. This added to costs as well as response times. In early 1993, UNHCR paid financial penalties of US$30,000 per day in demurrage costs, whilst a truck convoy carrying 4,000 tonnes of food to Sarajevo was scrutinised at the border between Austria and Hungary.

The imposition of sanctions created similar problems for health workers. UNHCR, WHO and ICRC all complained of the detrimental, time-consuming problems in acquiring drug imports and medical equipment on the basis of a case-by-case review. In one instance, before a scanner for detecting cancer in children could be sent to the Federal Republic of Yugoslavia, separate applications had to be submitted to the Sanctions Committee for each component part. Indeed, by late 1993, Judith Kumin, UNHCR's Chief of Mission in Belgrade felt sufficiently frustrated to comment that 'trying to implement a humanitarian program in a sanctions environment represents a fundamental contradiction'.[68]

---

[67] Sophie Albert, 'The Return of Refugees to Bosnia and Herzegovina: Peace-Building with People', 4 *International Peacekeeping*, 1997, 3, pp. 1–23.

[68] Cited in Larry Minear and Thomas G. Weiss, *Mercy Under Fire: War and the Global Humanitarian Community* (Westview Press, Boulder, CO, 1995), p. 69. See also International Institute for Strategic Studies (IISS), *Military Support for Humanitarian Aid*

Conclusion

The experiences of UNHCR in the complex violence within the former Yugoslavia has raised several questions of a conceptual and operational character which have not yet been addressed in the UN. First, the concept of the lead agency and the nature of its mandate requires clarification. Irrespective of how well the lead agency performs, as James Ingram points out, two main problems arise. On the one hand, the concept is in conflict with the idea of co-ordinators who are supposed to be independent of agency battles. On the other hand, the concept assumes the willingness of autonomous agencies with conflicting mandates to be subordinate to one of their number.[69] UNHCR's rapidly expanding operational responsibilities, which drew it into running an air operations cell in Geneva, reporting on human rights abuse and deploying military advisers in Zaire, have exposed it to accusations of 'imperialism'.[70] The experiences of UNHCR in the former Yugoslavia have illustrated the ambiguous nature of the lead agency's operational and co-ordinating responsibilities. Whilst some commentators have questioned the utility of a lead agency *per se*, it would seem that the need remains for an overall co-ordinating body in conflicts as bitter and multidimensional as the war in the former Yugoslavia. In operations which demand humanitarian, political and multinational military responses, the international community requires a structured organisational framework and the co-ordination of priorities. OCHA's ability to define the UN's humanitarian response without compromising the particular mandates of agencies such as UNHCR has not, at the time of writing, been tested.

Secondly, whilst the need for a lead agency to co-ordinate UN operations has considerable rationale, extension of this role to UNHCR in the former Yugoslavia confronted UNHCR with problems of politicisation. As has already been noted, the Commission's experience and expertise in providing assistance to refugees who have crossed international boundaries does not automatically translate into being able to co-ordinate UN humanitarian operations in an environment which also demands a military response by the international community. UN operations in the conflict within the former Yugoslavia have highlighted the difficulties of humanitarian–military operations in general. In particular, they have placed a focus upon the role and utility of UNHCR as a lead organisation

---

Operations (Strategic Comments, IISS, London, 22 February 1995); and Thomas G. Weiss, 'Military–Civilian Humanitarianism: The "Age of Innocence" is Over', 2 *International Peacekeeping*, 1995, 2, pp. 157–4.
[69] Ingram, 'The Future Architecture', p. 182.
[70] Interview with Khan, UNHCR, Geneva.

to co-ordinate humanitarian operations whilst representing the interests of refugees and people threatened with displacement in the context of a military conflict. As Ogata noted:

The fundamental issue in the former-Yugoslavia . . . is the following: how long and how far can a humanitarian institution go in assisting and, to some extent, saving the victims, without damaging its image, credibility and principles and the self-respect of its staff in the face of manipulation, blackmail, abuse, humiliation and murder?[71]

However, this complaint begs the question: to what extent was UNHCR itself a willing victim of a triumph of politics over law? As Goodwin-Gill argues in chapter 11 of this volume, the 'humanitarian' role of UNHCR is misplaced, and this is a problem partly of UNHCR's own making. Absorbing critical responsibility for dealing with complex humanitarian emergencies has detracted from UNHCR's legally mandated 'protection' role. Nowhere was this more apparent than in the former Yugoslavia.

Thirdly, UNHCR's policies towards refugee movements in southeast Asia and Africa have led to accusations of responding to the financial and institutional pressures imposed by donor governments rather than representing the interests of refugees, of poor supervision of the private relief organisations which it has funded, and of failure to employ local expertise.[72] UNHCR's policy of preventive protection as a response to ethnic cleansing was similarly controversial. Of course, UNHCR does not operate in a political vacuum. Personnel must be aware of the reticence of many industrialised states to implement comprehensive resettlement programmes for refugees. Nevertheless, if UNHCR is to counter criticisms that it is primarily the agent of donor governments which control UNHCR's budget, it must concentrate on its protection responsibilities to refugees and proselytise the three durable solutions for refugees enshrined within its historical mandate, that is, resettlement, assimilation or voluntary repatriation.

Finally, UNHCR could be more explicit and forthright in its responsibility for facilitating claims for political asylum. Whilst recognising UNHCR's discomfort in being unfairly perceived as an accessory to ethnic cleansing, the priority for legal protection over the politics of humanitarian action must remain. UNHCR is not necessarily the most appropriate organisation to determine and implement decisions on the relative safety of people whose lives may be at risk in their own homes. In

---

[71] Sadako Ogata, 'Opening Address', Conference on Conflict and Humanitarian Action, Princeton, NJ, 22–23 October 1993, p. 7.
[72] Kofi N. Awoonor, 'The Concerns of Recipient Nations', in *A Framework for Survival: Health, Human Rights, and Humanitarian Assistance in Conflicts and Disasters* (ed. Kevin M. Cahill, Basic Books and Council on Foreign Relations, New York, 1993), pp. 75–6.

the absence of a comprehensive increase in personnel and resources with an experience in providing protection, UNHCR should not attempt to limit the numbers of people fleeing life-threatening situations and seeking political asylum, or to be involved in social engineering of the kind promoted by the Dayton Agreement.

Bibliography

Albert, Sophie, 'The Return of Refugees to Bosnia and Herzegovina: Peace-Building with People', 4 *International Peacekeeping*, 1997, 3, pp. 1–23

Cunliffe, S. Alex, 'The Refugee Crises: A Study of the UNHCR', 43 *Political Studies*, 1995, pp. 278–90

Cunliffe, S. Alex and Michael Pugh, 'The Politicization of the UNHCR in the Former Yugoslavia', 10 *Journal of Refugee Studies*, 1997, 2, pp. 134–53

Higgins, Rosalyn, 'The New United Nations and Former Yugoslavia', 69 *International Affairs*, 1993, 3, pp. 465–83

Loescher, Gil, *Beyond Charity: International Cooperation and the Global Refugee Crisis* (Oxford University Press, 1993)

Minear, Larry, Jeffrey Clark, Roberta Cohen, Dennis Gallagher, Iain Guest and Thomas G. Weiss, *Humanitarian Action in the Former Yugoslavia: The UN's Role 1991–1993* (Occasional Paper No. 18, Thomas J. Watson Jr Institute for International Affairs, Brown University, Providence, RI, 1994)

Minear, Larry and Thomas G. Weiss, *Mercy Under Fire: War and the Global Humanitarian Community* (Westview, Boulder, CO, 1995)

Morris, Nicholas, 'Protection Dilemmas and UNHCR's Response: A Personal View from Within UNHCR', 9 *International Journal of Refugee Law*, 1997, pp. 492–7

Pugh, Michael, 'Military Intervention and Humanitarian Action: Trends and Issues', 22 *Disasters*, 1998, pp. 309–17

'The Withering of UN Humanitarian Reform: A Rejoinder', 29 *Security Dialogue*, 1998, 2, pp. 157–61

Pugh, Michael and S. Alex Cunliffe, 'The Lead Agency Concept in Humanitarian Assistance: The Case of the UNHCR', 28 *Security Dialogue*, 1997, 1, pp. 17–30

UNHCR RefWorld, *UNHCR Statistics 1997 – Refugees and Others of Concern to the UNHCR, 1996* (5th edn, UNHCR RefWorld, Geneva, 1998, CD-ROM)

Weiss, Thomas G. and Larry Minear (eds.), *Humanitarianism Across Borders: Sustaining Civilians in Times of War* (Lynne Rienner, Boulder, CO, 1993)

Weiss, Thomas G. and Amir Pasić, 'Reinventing UNHCR: Enterprising Humanitarians in the Former Yugoslavia, 1991–1995', 3 *Global Governance*, 1997, 1, pp. 41–57

Whitman, Jim and David Pocock, *After Rwanda: The Co-ordination of United Nations Humanitarian Assistance* (Macmillan, Basingstoke, 1996)

Wolfson, Steven and Neill Wright, *A UNHCR Handbook for the Military on Humanitarian Operations* (UNHCR, Geneva, 1994)

10 In-country protection: out of bounds for UNHCR?

Erin D. Mooney[1]

The responses of the United Nations High Commissioner for Refugees (UNHCR) to displacement crises this decade have manifested an approach to protection which many observers perceive as a change that is both disconcerting and dramatic. The international refugee regime is criticised for having become 'intensely solution-oriented when confronted with impending refugee crises, so much so that a new paradigm is emerging' that seemingly is contrary to traditional approaches to the problem of displacement.[2] Instead of heeding the calls to reverse this trend, however, UNHCR has embraced and institutionalised it, unabashedly continuing to use terms virtually identical to those with which it was forewarned, and thereby suggesting that it is a welcome development. A 'search for solutions' has indeed ushered in a 'new paradigm': 'Whereas the older paradigm can be described as reactive, exile-oriented and refugee-specific, the one which has started to emerge over the past few years can be characterized as proactive, homeland-oriented and holistic.'[3]

Central to this approach, with its emphasis on root causes, responsibility of the country of origin and certain categories of persons other than refugees, is the notion of in-country protection. In the refugee context,

[1] The author is grateful to Patricia Hyndman, Maria Stavropoulou, Jeff Crisp and Marc Weller for their valuable comments on earlier drafts of this chapter or the paper on which it was based, both of which were written with the support of the Social Sciences and Humanities Research Council of Canada. The views expressed in this chapter are those of the author alone.
[2] Bill Frelick, 'Preventing Refugee Flows: Protection or Peril?', *World Refugee Survey 1993* (US Committee for Refugees, Washington DC, 1993), pp. 5–14. See also James C. Hathaway, 'New Directions to Avoid Hard Problems: The Distortion of the Palliative Role of Refugee Protection', 8 *Journal of Refugee Studies*, 1995, pp. 288–94; Andrew Shacknove, 'From Asylum to Containment', 5 *International Journal of Refugee Law*, 1993, pp. 516–33; B. S. Chimni, 'The Meaning of Words and the Role of UNHCR in Voluntary Repatriation', 5 *International Journal of Refugee Law*, 1993, pp. 442–60; Mikhael Barutciski, 'The Reinforcement of Non-Admission Policies and the Subversion of UNHCR: Displacement and Internal Assistance in Bosnia-Herzegovina (1992–94)', 8 *International Journal of Refugee Law*, 1996, pp. 49–110.
[3] UNHCR, *The State of the World's Refugees: In Search of Solutions* (Oxford University Press, 1995), p. 43.

international protection signifies, at a minimum, ensuring respect for the fundamental rights and freedoms that the refugee is unable to secure from the country of origin.[4] Whether the provision of international protection to displaced persons still within, or returning to, their country of origin is a task lying outside of the mandate, interests and expertise of UNHCR is a question that tends to elicit two very divergent answers.

The critics of UNHCR's current approach form a highly cohesive group bonded by three arguments in common. First, UNHCR's broadened conceptualisation of protection to cover countries of origin, populations other than refugees and the root causes of displacement is considered contradictory to the organisation's mandate. A corollary of this concern explains the increased attention paid to in-country protection in terms of the interests of asylum states in curbing refugee influxes. Finally, critics claim that UNHCR has proven incapable of providing protection in countries of origin. In other words, UNHCR's current approach is censured for being inconsistent with UNHCR's mandate, induced by the ulterior motives of asylum states, and ineffective in practice.

This chapter calls into question the validity of the three counts on which UNHCR's current approach is indicted. To begin, the enlargement of UNHCR's area of competence will be shown to be constitutive of UNHCR's evolving legal mandate.[5] Evidence that the current approach has developed gradually over the course of UNHCR's history serves to counter what essentially is a conspiracy theory that explains it strictly in terms of the recent strategic imperative of states to reduce refugee inflows. To be sure, states are likely to support UNHCR's engagement in in-country protection for precisely this reason, but pre-existing, more meritorious motivations prompted and continue to justify this involvement.

In practice it is true that, notwithstanding UNHCR's good intentions, in-country protection efforts have had mixed results. While it will be conceded that the critics are largely correct that the cases of Croatia and Bosnia-Herzegovina evidence the limitations and resulting dangers of UNHCR's efforts of in-country protection, elsewhere in the former Yugoslavia there exist examples pointing to its positive potential. Moreover, if practical experience is to provide the basis on which to accept, reject or, as will be argued is necessary, refine UNHCR's current approach, then surely the scope of analysis must extend beyond a single case. Ideally, all of the recent attempts to provide in-country protection in situations of

---

[4] Convention Relating to the Status of Refugees 1951, 189 UNTS 137, preamble. See also Guy S. Goodwin-Gill, 'The Language of Protection', 1 *International Journal of Refugee Law*, 1989, pp. 6–18.   [5] See also chapter 8 of this volume.

displacement should be surveyed. In light of the length of this chapter and the focus of its author's research to date, however, any references to other cases will be limited to the former Soviet Union, with special emphasis on the Caucasus region, where the problem of displacement is particularly acute.[6] Though this sampling of displacement situations is still small and region-specific, it is nonetheless sufficient to reveal reasons in support of UNHCR's sustained interest and involvement in in-country protection.

Mandate

While it is true that the UNHCR Statute[7] does not explicitly prescribe all of the activities in which UNHCR currently engages, it does not automatically follow that those which are not prescribed are inconsistent with it. The search for solutions which guides UNHCR's present approach is inherent in its initial mandate. From the outset, UNHCR has been directed by article 1 of its Statute to seek 'permanent solutions for the problem of refugees'. In addition to prescribing for UNHCR the palliative role of providing protection and assistance to refugees, the UNHCR Statute provides, in article 9, that UNHCR 'shall engage in such additional activities . . . as the General Assembly may determine'. Successive General Assembly resolutions provide the legal basis for UNHCR's present approach to protection.[8]

Over the course of UNHCR's history, resolutions of the General Assembly have extended its competence *ratione personae* beyond refugees and asylum seekers to cover four other groups: stateless persons; repatriating refugees; internally displaced persons; and war-affected populations. UNHCR no longer refers strictly to refugees, but also to 'persons of concern to UNHCR'. Apart from refugees, internally displaced persons form the largest of such groups of concern.[9] Though the UNHCR Statute does not explicitly invest UNHCR with any competence for persons displaced within their country, the effect of various case-specific

---

[6] Even prior to the conflict in Chechnya, beginning in December 1994, over 1,500,000 people were displaced in the Caucasus, as a result of the three secessionist armed conflicts ravaging the region. These concern the attempted secession of Nagorno-Karabakh from Azerbaijan; and of both Abkhazia and South Ossetia from Georgia. UNHCR, 'Conflict in the Caucasus', *Information Bulletin*, July 1994, p. 6.

[7] Statute of the Office of the United Nations High Commissioner for Refugees, Annex to General Assembly Resolution 428 (V) of 14 December 1950.

[8] See chapter 8 of this volume.

[9] As of 31 December 1996, UNHCR's concern extended to 4,853,712 internally displaced persons of whom 1,532,695 UNHCR actually assisted. UNHCR, *Refugees and Others of Concern to UNHCR: 1996 Statistical Overview*, 1997, Table 1, p. 11. Notably, this figure represents only a fraction of the global population of internally displaced persons, currently estimated at some 30 million.

and omnibus General Assembly resolutions over the past twenty-five years has conferred upon UNHCR a selective and limited mandate to undertake action on their behalf. On the basis of a request from the Secretary-General or a competent principal organ of the United Nations and with the consent of the state concerned, UNHCR is authorised to provide humanitarian assistance and protection to internally displaced persons in situations calling for its 'particular expertise' and 'especially where such efforts could contribute to the prevention or solution of refugee problems'.[10]

UNHCR has identified, on the basis of its own criteria for involvement, four such situations.[11] Most obvious are the three possible situations when internally displaced and refugee populations are intermingled to such an extent that it would be impractical as well as inhumane to distinguish between them when providing protection and assistance. First, UNHCR's involvement on behalf of internally displaced persons traditionally occurred only in the cases when they were present in, or returning to, areas of actual or potential refugee repatriation. Secondly, in the reverse scenario, refugees may seek asylum in countries already containing persons internally displaced by the same regional conflict, who share a need for international assistance and protection. Thirdly, when internal displacement and refugee flows are common in cause, there may be operational or humanitarian advantages to addressing the plight of both categories of displaced persons by a single operation as part of a comprehensive strategy. Fourthly, UNHCR may become involved in a country of origin with a view to preventing, or at least mitigating, a refugee crisis. In this regard, it is important to bear in mind that a situation of internal displacement may be instantly transformed into a refugee crisis as a result of state partition, such as occurred in the former Yugoslavia and the former Soviet Union.

At the same time as UNHCR has increased its involvement with persons of concern in countries of origin, it has also enlarged the scope of its activities on their behalf, beyond merely providing assistance, to include addressing their protection needs as well. This expansion in UNHCR's competence is validated by General Assembly resolutions directing UNHCR to undertake preventive measures,[12] and recognising

---

[10] General Assembly Resolution 48/116 (1993), para. 12.

[11] UNHCR actually delineates three situations of possible involvement, subsuming the first two scenarios into one category. UNHCR, 'UNHCR's Role with Internally Displaced Persons', Inter-Office Memorandum No. 33/93, 28 April 1993; *Note on International Protection*, UN Doc. A/AC.96/815, 1993, para. 46.

[12] General Assembly Resolution 46/106 (1991), preamble and para. 9; reaffirmed in General Assembly Resolution 47/105 (1992), preamble and para. 13; and General Assembly Resolution 48/116 (1993), preamble and para. 11.

that it has 'a legitimate concern for the consequences of return'.[13] Strategies towards these ends primarily concentrate on emphasising the responsibilities of countries of origin, strengthening national capacities for protection, promoting respect for international human rights and monitoring compliance with these standards.

Unlike the United Nations human rights bodies which have long recognised the nexus between displacement and human rights violations,[14] UNHCR played it down until recently for fear of jeopardising the consent of host governments on which its refugee work relies. The argument espoused in an attempt to justify this passive stance made an appeal to the statutory provision prescribing that UNHCR's work shall be 'of an entirely non-political character . . . [and] shall be humanitarian and social'.[15] Yet, human rights work, insofar as it is concerned with ensuring the well-being of and respect for individuals, is fundamentally humanitarian in nature.[16] As such, it is compatible with UNHCR's statutory mandate. The fact that the General Assembly resolutions supporting UNHCR's undertaking of in-country protection all the while reaffirm the 'purely humanitarian and non-political character of the Office' further attests to the lack of any conflict with its mandate.

Moreover, UNHCR arguably has not only a mandate but a duty, under the UN Charter, to incorporate protection into its activities in countries of origin. It seems inconsistent with the purposes delineated in the UN Charter, among which are 'to promote and encourage respect for human rights', that a UN agency, and especially one having a protection mandate, should limit its activities, whether in countries of asylum or of origin, to the delivery of humanitarian assistance. This logic similarly would confer a certain duty to address human rights concerns upon even those agencies, such as the UN Children's Fund (UNICEF), the UN Development Programme (UNDP) and the World Food Programme (WFP), which are also typically involved in situations of displacement but

---

[13] General Assembly Resolution 40/118, para. 7, endorsing UNHCR's Executive Committee Conclusion No. 40.

[14] The UN Commission on Human Rights, the General Assembly and the Sub-Commission for the Prevention of Discrimination and Protection of Minorities have been examining this linkage since 1980. Moreover, the UN Secretary-General has been entrusted with a mandate precisely on the issue of human rights and mass exoduses.

[15] UNHCR Statute, para. 2.

[16] For a most helpful clarification of the confusion surrounding the characterisation of mandates, see Claire Palley, 'Legal Issues Arising from Conflicts Between UN Humanitarian and Political Mandates – A Survey', in *The Problem of Refugees in the Light of Contemporary International Law Issues* (ed. Vera Gowlland-Debbas, Martinus Nijhoff, The Hague, 1995), pp. 150–1. Moreover, while the work of UNHCR is also required to be non-political, protection work, by its very nature, is inherently political. See chapter 11 of this volume.

which lack an explicit protection mandate. Involvement of the field staff of UNHCR and other UN humanitarian agencies in human rights protection is not to deny that the protection of human rights falls principally within the mandate and expertise of the UN human rights mechanisms; nor to discount the need to strengthen their operational capacity. However, it is in recognition of the reality that a UN human rights field presence is lacking in most displacement situations and, even in the exceptional cases where it does exist, is sorely inadequate relative to the protection problems needing to be addressed.

For instance, the human rights mission in the former Yugoslavia as well as that more recently established in Abkhazia, Georgia, were both delayed – by several years – in their establishment and, even then, severely short-staffed.[17] The magnitude and severity of abuses in both of these cases, as in many others, demanded that other UN agencies in the field, foremost among which was UNHCR, contribute to efforts to promote and protect human rights. In these cases and, all the more so, in those where the UN does not have a human rights field presence, the importance of UNHCR and other UN agencies assuming their role, under the UN Charter, in in-country protection becomes paramount.

The enlargement of UNHCR's competence beyond its statutory mandate to cover other areas of operation, categories of beneficiaries and activity therefore is not such a dramatic change after all. Its historical roots run deep, from the very purposes of the UN itself through to successive resolutions of the General Assembly urging or endorsing UNHCR activities exceeding its initial mandate. UNHCR's present approach is merely the culmination of a decades-long process of evolution of its intentionally dynamic mandate.[18] There therefore exists, as UNHCR explains, 'a somewhat greater degree of continuity in UNHCR's activities than is implied by the notion of an "old" and "new" approach',[19] at least insofar as it relates to protection. It is this essential emphasis to UNHCR's work that in recent years has arguably dwindled in favour of assistance.[20]

---

[17] In 1993, in the midst of the armed conflict in Bosnia-Herzegovina, the UN human rights mission to the former Yugoslavia numbered nine human rights officers, charged with covering the *whole of the region*. The only UN human rights field mission in the Caucasus is found in Abkhazia, Georgia, where it was established in December 1996, over three years after most of the displacement occurred, and it consists solely of one person, supported by an OSCE counterpart stationed in the capital.

[18] Guy S. Goodwin-Gill, 'New Mandate? What New Mandate?' 88 *Refugees*, 1992, pp. 38–40.   [19] UNHCR, *State of the World's Refugees*, 1995, p. 52.

[20] See chapters 9 and 11 of this volume.

Motivations

Many critics of UNHCR's enlarged mandate tend to explain its genesis strictly in terms of the interests of asylum states in reducing refugee influxes. However, other strategic interests of states may predominate, as in the Great Lakes.[21] Held up as evidence of the supposed asylum state conspiracy of containment are recent increases in UNHCR's budget which has more than doubled in the years immediately after the end of the Cold War.[22] In light of the fact that refugee-receiving states constitute UNHCR's primary sources of funding,[23] their increased generosity for UNHCR's operations in countries of origin precisely at a time when they are keen to reduce refugee inflows cannot be considered mere coincidence. The correlation can be carried too far, however, to suggest that UNHCR's increased involvement in countries of origin was 'purposefully engineered by affluent Western States primarily for their convenience'.[24]

As mentioned above, the enlargement of UNHCR's mandate to include in-country operations originated in a period when the strategic interests of states lay in precisely the reverse strategy, of promoting protection through asylum. Moreover, the increased financial support of UNHCR must be in large part a function of the enhanced international profile and credibility that the organisation gained, particularly as a result of its response to the humanitarian crisis in Iraq after the Gulf War. To be sure, the interests of asylum states have strengthened UNHCR's capacity for undertaking in-country operations but, at the same time, other, more meritorious, motivations prompted and continue to justify this broadened scope of activity.

Consider, for instance, the discrepancies in state support for UNHCR's in-country operations in the former Yugoslavia and in the Caucasus. In the former Yugoslavia, it is undeniable that strong donor interest in containing the displacement crisis within the region furnished UNHCR with the financial resources necessary to undertake its largest in-country operation to date.[25] At the time of the conflict in Croatia, in November 1991, UNHCR received a mandate from the UN Secretary-General to bring relief to needy internally displaced persons affected by the conflict in the hope that this would have 'a welcome preventive impact in helping to avoid the further displacement of population, as well as contributing to the creation of conditions that would ultimately permit refu-

---

[21] See chapter 11 of this volume.
[22] UNHCR expenditure rose from US$544 million in 1990 to US$1,307 million in 1993. UNHCR, *State of the World's Refugees*, 1995, p. 255, Table 15.
[23] 'How UNHCR is Funded', 102 *Refugees*, 1995, pp. 8–9.
[24] Barutciski, 'Reinforcement of Non-Admission', p. 59, see also pp. 51–3.
[25] See also chapter 9 of this volume.

gees and displaced persons to return to their places of origin'.[26] With the expansion of the conflict southward into Bosnia-Herzegovina, where displacement was already underway, UNHCR's strategy of so-called 'preventive protection' aimed to obviate the need for other threatened persons to flee from their homes.[27] In the Former Yugoslav Republic of Macedonia, UNHCR's involvement was designed to help pre-empt a threatened displacement crisis. Although the proximity of Yugoslavia to many of UNHCR's principal donors may indeed explain the generosity with which European states funded the operation,[28] it does not account for the fact that the far-off states of Japan and the USA are the single largest contributors.[29] Nor does the theory hold in the Caucasus. Despite the proximity of this region to western European states fearful of mass influxes and the threats posed by displacement crises to regional security, UNHCR's in-country operations there suffer from a chronic *lack* of funds.[30] To argue that donor interest is the determining factor of the current approach fails to explain why, despite the discrepancy in the degrees of financial support for the two operations, UNHCR emphasises in the Caucasus the same strategies of in-country prevention, protection and solutions as it does in the former Yugoslavia.

In both cases, factors other than donor interest in containing the displacement crisis to the region prompted UNHCR to seek to provide in-country protection. First, the high degree of inter-linkage between the various conflicts within each region as well as between their concomitant displacement crises created situations where local countries hosting refugees from a conflict in a nearby country also contained internally displaced populations from a variant of the conflict occurring on their own territory. UNHCR, which was present in the country on account of the refugee influx, tended to assume responsibilities for the internally displaced as well, on the grounds that distinguishing between the similarly needy refugee and internally displaced populations would be inhumane, if not also impossible.

Also relevant is the very nature of the conflicts causing displacement.

---

[26] Letter from the UN Secretary-General to the UN High Commissioner for Refugees, 14 November 1991.

[27] UNHCR, 'A Comprehensive Response to the Humanitarian Crisis in the Former Yugoslavia', UN Doc. HCR/IMFY/1992/2, 24 July 1992, para. 8.

[28] Hathaway, 'New Directions', p. 292.

[29] UNHCR, *Information Notes: Bosnia and Herzegovina, Croatia, the Federal Republic of Yugoslavia, the Former Yugoslav Republic of Macedonia*, No. 10-11/96, October/November 1996, p. 6.

[30] The problem of shortfalls in the UNHCR budget is particularly acute in Georgia. UNHCR, 'Caucasus Update: Georgia, Armenia and Azerbaijan', *Information Bulletin*, July 1994, p. 6.

Disputes over the status of borders, such as those characterising the conflicts in the former Yugoslavia and the Caucasus, inevitably blur the distinction between refugees and internally displaced persons. The dissolution or disintegration of states into separate, self-proclaimed, independent entities complicates the application of the criterion of being outside one's country of origin which is a prerequisite for refugee status and the international protection it affords. The question therefore arose whether a citizen of the former Soviet Union or the Socialist Federal Republic of Yugoslavia (SFRY) who fled from one of its self-proclaimed independent constituent republics to another would be considered as outside of the country of origin. The answers of countries of potential asylum depended upon whether or not they accepted the partition of the federation concerned. For the international community, the question was settled definitively with the recognition of the disintegration of the Soviet Union into fifteen separate states in December 1991 and of the dissolution of the SFRY in April 1992. The very fact that recognition instantly could, and did, transform internally displaced persons into *prima facie* refugees underscores the operational utility of UNHCR's early involvement, well before any debate over the legitimacy of the state partition is settled.

Even when the transformation, through a process of state creation, of internally displaced persons into refugees is unlikely, strong reasons nonetheless exist for UNHCR's involvement in countries of origin. According to international law and practice at present, the secessionist areas within the newly independent states of the former Yugoslavia and the former Soviet Union, for example, are unlikely to receive international recognition as independent states.[31] As a result, persons displaced from these areas to elsewhere in the country or *vice versa* will remain internally displaced persons even though the *de facto* division of the country effectively places them in a refugee-like situation. UNHCR has rightly recognised that such situations call for its expertise.[32] The logic of UNHCR's designation as 'lead agency' for the international humanitarian response in the former Yugoslavia, as well as its predominant role in each of the humanitarian crises in the Caucasus therefore cannot be denied.[33]

---

[31] See Marc Weller, 'The International Response to the Dissolution of the Socialist Federal Republic of Yugoslavia', 86 *American Journal of International Law*, 1992, pp. 569–607; and Rein Müllerson, 'The Continuity and Succession of States, by Reference to the Former USSR and Yugoslavia', 42 *International and Comparative Law Quarterly*, 1992, pp. 463–93.

[32] UNHCR, Executive Committee of the High Commissioner's Programme, *Protection Aspects of UNHCR Activities on Behalf of Internally Displaced Persons*, UN Doc. EC/1994/SCP/87, 17 August 1994, para. 2.

[33] Even those who argue that the lead agency concept is flawed concede that of all the agencies to fulfil this role in the former Yugoslavia UNHCR was the logical choice. See chapter 9 of this volume.

The absence of any one agency with an automatic and exclusive mandate for internally displaced persons and the resulting need for this lacuna in the international institutional framework to continue to be filled by existing agencies provides a further rationale for UNHCR to contribute to efforts of international in-country protection. This is not to suggest that UNHCR should incur responsibility for all internally displaced persons. Instead, in any given situation of internal displacement there should be a division of labour, according to institutional expertise, in meeting the particular needs of the population concerned.[34] The General Assembly has recognised that, taking into account the mandates and expertise of other relevant organisations, UNHCR's particular expertise would seem to warrant its undertaking activities in certain situations of internal displacement.[35] UNHCR's actual engagement would, of course, still be subject to satisfaction of its own criteria, most notably 'a clear link' with its refugee mandate, either in terms of returnees, refugees or the potential of a refugee outflow. The existence of the requisite link among the internally displaced populations of the former Yugoslavia and the Caucasus affirms that UNHCR possesses particular expertise to contribute to efforts attempting to address their plight and that its concern for them is well placed.

Protection in practice

Notwithstanding its legitimacy and good intentions, the extension of UNHCR's concern to returnees and certain internally displaced and war-affected populations cannot of itself ensure the provision of international protection in a country of origin. Invoking the argument of ineffectiveness, opponents of UNHCR's increased involvement in countries of origin focus their criticism almost exclusively on its experimentation in the former Yugoslavia.[36] Indeed, it is undeniable that UNHCR proved incapable, despite its sizeable presence in the area, of providing effective protection against displacement or to internally displaced

---

[34] For an examination of the roles played by various international agencies in addressing the protection and assistance needs of the internally displaced, see Roberta Cohen and Jacques Cuénod (eds.), *Improving Institutional Arrangements for Internally Displaced Persons* (Brookings Institution, Washington DC, Refugee Policy Group Project on Internal Displacement, 1995).

[35] General Assembly Resolution 47/105 (1992), para. 14; General Assembly Resolution 48/116 (1993), para. 12.

[36] See, for example, Bill Frelick, '"Preventive Protection" and the Right to Seek Asylum: A Preliminary Look at Bosnia and Croatia', 4 *International Journal of Refugee Law*, 1992, pp. 439–54; Barutciski, 'Reinforcement of Non-Admission', pp. 49–110; and Shacknove, 'From Asylum to Containment', pp. 416–33.

persons still under threat in Croatia and Bosnia-Herzegovina.[37] Yet, insofar as displacement was not merely a consequence of the hostilities but their conscious aim, it is equally true that the provision of international in-country protection clearly demanded more than a strictly humanitarian response.

Even the humanitarian response, however, was incomplete, on account of the low priority that it gave to protection. Commonly considered at fault is the designation of UNHCR as the lead agency responsible for co-ordinating the entire international assistance operation, since this responsibility seems to have had the effect, considered by some as symptomatic of the lead agency concept, of distracting it from its specialised function of protection.[38] Cited as evidence of the overwhelming extent to which UNHCR focused on assistance over protection is the fact that UNHCR's nearly 700-strong field staff in the former Yugoslavia at the end of 1993 included only twenty-five protection officers, not all of whom were assigned to this role full-time.[39] Belying this statistic, however, is the fact that all UNHCR staff have a protection function[40] and that there were numerous occasions on which courageous UNHCR staff attempted to exercise it.[41] Though these efforts, and similar ones in the Caucasus, would prove powerless to prevent displacement, they nonetheless often exerted a certain, and not insignificant, protective effect in diminishing the severity of means employed towards this end.[42]

Although the displacement toll in the former Yugoslavia points to UNHCR's overall impotence against violent campaigns of deliberate displacement, the fact that the number of persons uprooted was not greater owes to the success of its preventive efforts elsewhere in the region. In the

---

[37] Erin D. Mooney, 'Presence, *ergo* Protection?': UNPROFOR, UNHCR and ICRC in Croatia and Bosnia and Herzegovina', 7 *International Journal of Refugee Law*, 1995, pp. 407–35.   [38] See chapter 9 of this volume.
[39] Larry Minear, Jeffrey Clark, Roberta Cohen, Dennis Gallagher, Iain Guest and Thomas G. Weiss, *Humanitarian Action in the Former Yugoslavia: The UN's Role, 1991–93* (Occasional Paper No. 18, Thomas J. Watson Jr Institute for International Studies, Brown University, Providence, RI, and Refugee Policy Group, 1994), pp. 18, 27 and 114.
[40] As Goodwin-Gill argues on p. 247 of this volume, for UNHCR staff, 'protection is thus not just lawyers' business . . . protection is and ought to be the business of everyone'.
[41] The protection strategies employed were not necessarily sophisticated. They could be as simple as UNHCR staff choosing, on their own initiative, to park a UNHCR vehicle visibly in front of the home of a threatened person. See Mooney, 'Presence, *ergo* Protection?,' p. 423. The degree to which UNHCR staff were encouraged to exercise their protection function in the country of origin reportedly varied considerably, depending upon the person in charge of the overall operation. See David Rieff, *Slaughterhouse: Bosnia and the Failure of the West* (Vintage Books, London, 1995), pp. 212–14.
[42] Mooney, 'Presence *ergo* Protection?'; and Erin D. Mooney, 'Internal Displacement and the Conflict in Abkhazia: International Responses and their Protective Effect', 3 *International Journal on Group Rights*, 1995–6, pp. 197–226.

Former Yugoslav Republic of Macedonia, the presence of UNHCR, along with the UN Preventive Deployment Force (UNPREDEP) and a long-term monitoring mission of the Organisation for Security and Co-operation in Europe (OSCE), has contributed to staving off the threat of a region-wide armed conflict and further displacement crisis. At the same time, UNHCR and UNPREDEP have capitalised on their pre-emptive deployment to develop contingency operational plans to be used in the event of a conflict and displacement crisis erupting, thereby suggesting a serious continued commitment to protection should preventive efforts fail.[43]

In addition to being unprecedented, the preventive, and thus far effective, concerted international effort to stave off conflict and a con-comitant displacement crisis in Macedonia remains exceptional. It is an unfortunate fact that efforts providing early warning of displacement and other humanitarian crises continue to suffer from an absence of corre-sponding early action.[44] In the first few years of the Yugoslav conflicts and the ethnic cleansing characterising them, repeated warnings were issued by UNHCR, among others, that similar forces were at work in the former Soviet Union.[45] In the Caucasus, the international community failed to heed these warnings and, in so doing, lost the opportunity to undertake action that could have prevented or at least attenuated the conflicts and their significant displacing effects. Moreover, even when the eruption of conflict confirmed the predictions, the international commu-nity was equally slow to respond to the resulting humanitarian needs, addressing these in a concerted manner only after most of the displace-ment had occurred. UNHCR's operations in this area therefore focus on providing protection and assistance to persons already uprooted and attempting to ensure that the return which most of them desire occurs in conditions of 'safety and dignity', as called for in agreements to which UNHCR is a party.[46] It is in this capacity that UNHCR has, in accor-dance with Annex 7 of the Dayton Agreement, continued to engage in in-country operations in the former Yugoslavia. Though these efforts also face considerable obstacles, it is arguably in the post-conflict search for

[43] Barutciski, 'Reinforcement of Non-Admission', p. 62.
[44] Where preventive action is attempted, as by the OSCE in Kosovo, it may be impeded by problems of access. At the time of writing, problems of international access to Kosovo persisted, preventing humanitarian efforts to address the large-scale internal displace-ment crisis that did indeed arise along with the refugee outflows in 1998.
[45] See, for example, 'The Former Soviet Union: A Prevention Test Case,' in UNHCR, *The State of the World's Refugees: The Challenge of Protection* (Penguin, London, 1993), p. 123.
[46] In the case of Abkhazia, for example, see the Quadripartite Agreement on voluntary return of refugees and displaced persons, signed on 4 April 1994, UN Doc. S/1994/397 (1994), Annex II.

solutions to displacement crises that UNHCR could most effectively contribute to the in-country protection of displaced persons by facilitating and monitoring their safe return. It could also contribute to international efforts to strengthen national protection capacities so that responsibility for protection can, as it should, revert to and be effectively discharged by the state.

In this latter regard, UNHCR's approach to the problem of displacement in the former Soviet Union, like its experience in the former Yugoslavia, provides proof both of the limits and of the positive potential of its engagement in in-country protection. The recent regional conference on forced migration in the Commonwealth of Independent States,[47] sponsored by UNHCR in collaboration with the OSCE and the International Organisation for Migration (IOM), adopted a Programme of Action for the development, with the assistance of UNHCR and the IOM, of national institutions, legislation and administrative structures not only for addressing the plight of the over 9 million people displaced since the dissolution of the Soviet Union but also the very real threat of further mass population displacements in this region.

While recent experience provides reason for UNHCR's engagement in efforts of in-country protection, it also underlines the need to recognise its limitations in this area. Most notably, when displacement is not merely a consequence of conflict but its conscious aim, UNHCR itself concedes that its efforts to prevent displacement cannot compete against the logic of a war intent on displacing populations.[48] Even so, UNHCR can, through its presence, active monitoring and representations to the local and national authorities, delay the displacement and diminish the severity of the coercive means employed towards that end.

Even in such circumstances when UNHCR may not itself be able to provide direct and effective protection against displacement, it nonetheless can have a profound protective effect by prompting action on the part of international and regional actors in a better position to fulfil this need. UNHCR's in-country operations therefore have an important role to play in monitoring not only the conditions causing displacement but also the response of other international and regional actors to them. Capitalising on its vantage point on the ground, UNHCR can communicate the urgency of situations of insecurity and massive violations of human rights to the international community at large, for the purpose of attempting to prompt it into taking the required protection response. This advocacy role for UNHCR has proven particularly important in instances, as

---

[47] For further details see chapter 7 of this volume.
[48] UNHCR, *Note on International Protection*, UN Doc. A/AC.96/815, 31 August 1993, para. 20.

occurred in both the former Yugoslavia and in the Caucasus, when UNHCR's public pronouncements of the human rights and security conditions on the ground contradicted the assessments made by UN military missions which played down the perilousness of the local population's situation and their urgent need for international protection.[49] Though the success of this tactic in triggering a more effective international response will depend on other actors, UNHCR can, in drawing attention to the failure of international efforts, including its own, to provide protection in the country of origin, serve the equally important purpose of underlining the continued need for outside states to make protection available within their own borders through the provision of asylum.

In this latter regard, the critics are correct to cite the case of Yugoslavia as evidence of the risk that UNHCR's efforts to provide in-country protection may be manipulated by asylum states eager to reduce the demands upon them to provide this protection within their own borders. Even when it became clear that UNHCR and the misleadingly named UN Protection Force (UNPROFOR) were unable to provide displaced and threatened populations within Bosnia-Herzegovina with adequate protection, outside states increasingly limited the opportunities for the uprooted to seek international protection elsewhere. Although western European states were initially generous in their admission of asylum seekers from Croatia, once the conflict and concomitant displacement crisis expanded southward to encompass Bosnia-Herzegovina, these states as well as the neighbouring newly independent states of the former Yugoslavia began severely limiting the availability of protection through asylum.[50]

In attempting to justify their restrictive admissions policies, some western European states contended that providing asylum to threatened populations from the former Yugoslavia amounted to complicity in ethnic cleansing.[51] Adding political force to this indefensible claim was its echoing by the countries of origin. For their own reasons, namely to reinforce the military effort against their common enemy and to consolidate claims to territory, the governments of Croatia and Bosnia-Herzegovina

---

[49] Consider, for example, UNHCR reports countering UNPROFOR's assessment of the security of local populations in the 'safe area' of Gorazde in Bosnia-Herzegovina in April 1994 and compensating for the silence of the UN Observer Mission in Georgia (UNOMIG) after renewed attacks on the Georgian population in the Gali region of Abkhazia in March 1995. See, respectively, Rieff, *Slaughterhouse*, pp. 188–9, and 206–7; and Mooney, 'Internal Displacement and the Conflict in Abkhazia', pp. 222–3.

[50] For an indication of the extent to which neighbouring Yugoslav republics as well as European states restricted the availability of asylum to persons attempting to flee Bosnia-Herzegovina, see Mirjana Morokvasic, 'La guerre et les refugiés dans l'ex-Yougoslavie', 8 *Revue européenne des migrations internationales*, 1992, pp. 5–26; and Mooney, 'Presence *ergo* Protection?', pp. 409–13.   [51] See Frelick, '"Preventive Protection"', p. 443.

were also eager to contain the population of the latter republic.[52] There thus arose a convergence of interests among certain asylum states and the countries of origin to contain the displacement problem to its source. Aside from violating, *inter alia*, the rights to seek asylum, to *non-refoulement* and to freedom of movement, the shared argument that containment served the long-term interests of the threatened populations by preserving their territorial claims was inherently flawed. It ignored the realities on the ground that the lack of effective in-country protection against ethnic cleansing made the consequences of this policy for the populations concerned often nothing short of lethal.

An equally erroneous argument held that to offer Bosnians asylum would undermine their so-called 'right to remain'.[53] In the midst of the conflict, though not specific to it, UNHCR had articulated this right with the laudable aim of focusing attention on the responsibility of local and national authorities to safeguard against the creation of conditions necessitating flight.[54] At the same time, it was designed to remind the international community of its duty to provide protection when the state concerned proved unwilling or unable to provide such protection. On both these counts, UNHCR's championing of the right to remain failed to elicit either the national or international response required to ensure its realisation in Bosnia-Herzegovina: the country of origin proved unable and outside states proved unwilling to provide effective in-country protection of fundamental human rights, which would have obviated the need for the population to flee. In principle, the traditional recourse of receiving protection through asylum remained. From its initial conception, the right to remain has always been accompanied by the qualification and insistence that it in no way negates the right to seek

---

[52] That containment was a policy objective shared by the governments of Bosnia-Herzegovina and Croatia is evident in their Friendship Agreement of July 1992 which provided for the return of all men aged 18 to 60 and all women aged 18 to 55 not having children under the age of 14 who had fled areas deemed 'safe'. According to the realities on the ground, however, no area of war-ravaged Bosnia-Herzegovina could truly be considered safe enough to warrant return. Moreover, the forced return of refugees affected by this policy violated the principle of *non-refoulement*. See Tom Argent, *Croatia's Crucible: Providing Asylum for Refugees from Bosnia and Herzegovina* (US Committee for Refugees, Washington DC, 1992), pp. 14 and 16.

[53] German Federal Chancellor Helmut Kohl explicitly invoked the 'right to remain' when turning away asylum seekers from Bosnia-Herzegovina in late 1993: Hathaway, 'New Directions', p. 293. A newspaper editorial at that time articulated what seemed to be Kohl's underlying argument: 'If we forget the existence of "the right to stay", we will have no title to prevent the enormous and unstoppable exercise of "the right to migrate".' Antonio Garrigues Walker, 'The Right to Stay Where They Are', *International Herald Tribune*, 20 October 1993, p. 4.

[54] 'The Right to Remain: Excerpts from the Statement of the High Commissioner to the Commission on Human Rights', 92 *Refugees*, April 1993, p. 11.

asylum.[55] Indeed, the relevance of these rights to separate stages of displacement discounts the possibility of conflict between them: the right to
remain aims to remove or alleviate the conditions that force people to flee;
whereas the right to seek asylum is meant to provide an escape route for
people who, owing to the persistence of these conditions, can no longer
remain safely in their homes. Invocations of the right to remain that
attempt to gild restrictive asylum policies in human rights rhetoric are
thus inherently flawed. They ignore the complementary rather than competing relationship between the two modes of preventive and palliative
protection. The fact that only a single state espoused the argument that
the right to remain justified a denial of the right to seek asylum suggests
wide recognition among other states of its dubious nature. Whenever
national or international in-country protection proves inadequate, the
right to seek international protection through asylum remains inviolable.

However, displaced persons in need of international protection do not,
or cannot, always seek asylum. In many cases, situations of internal displacement occur for reasons other than efforts on the part of asylum
states to contain potential outward flows of refugees. Several reasons
explain why uprooted persons might become internally displaced persons
rather than refugees, even though this latter identity would be likely to
afford them more international protection and assistance.

In situations of localised internal armed conflict, persons displaced
from the area of hostilities may seek safety elsewhere in the country, especially in areas where they have reason to expect protection. Typifying this
scenario are the displacement crises in the Caucasus where the majority
of persons displaced from areas of hostilities have sought refuge in more
peaceful areas of the country. The containment of these various displacement crises to the country of origin owes more to the ethno-territorial
character of the conflicts than to the imposition of restrictive asylum policies by European states. For UNHCR, however, the lack of a threat of
mass refugee flows towards Europe did not discount the need to engage
in in-country protection. As it has learned in other such cases, including
Croatia, even when there exists a positive relationship between the local
authorities and the population under its *de jure* or *de facto* jurisdiction,
some protection issues are likely to arise.[56]

The distance to borders or topographical obstacles, such as mountains
and rivers, can also be a significant factor impeding flight across borders.
Even the proponents of what essentially may be considered the theory of
a state conspiracy of containment concede in the case of Bosnia-

[55] See, for example, UNHCR, *Note on International Protection*, UN Doc. A/AC.96/799, 25
August 1992, para. 5; and *Note on International Protection*, UN Doc. A/AC.96/815, 31
August 1993, para. 3.   [56] UNHCR, *UNHCR's Operational Experience*, para. 241.

Herzegovina that endangered populations in certain areas of the war-torn republic did not, for these reasons, represent a potential threat of a refugee influx into western Europe.[57] In such cases, the danger that UNHCR's in-country activities would compromise the right to seek asylum accordingly would be negligible. Although the internal restrictions on movement, as imposed by the various belligerent parties in Bosnia-Herzegovina, could not be considered natural impediments to cross-border flight, they nonetheless further demonstrate that asylum states are not necessarily, or solely, responsible for uprooted persons in need of international protection remaining within their country of origin.

To argue that UNHCR has engaged in in-country protection motivated only by the interests of asylum states in containment rests on the mistaken assumption that all internally displaced and threatened persons could, or would prefer to, become refugees.

Defining the boundaries

While in-country protection does indeed often fall within the bounds of UNHCR's mandate and particular expertise, it is equally clear that boundaries need to be defined around this concept in order to safeguard against its abuse. When asylum states view UNHCR's activity in countries of origin within their narrow interests, it may change in meaning, from preventing displacement *strictu sensu* to pre-empting its cross-border character in the form of refugee flows. In this sense, UNHCR's welcome and well-intentioned efforts to contain the *problems* in countries of origin that force people into flight are at risk of being misinterpreted and manipulated to mean confining within the country of origin the *people* attempting to flee these conditions. Recent experience demonstrates that this danger is very real.

Addressing this concern, however, does not require the outright rejection of UNHCR's reorientation but rather its refinement. Indeed, this process has already begun. Insofar as the catch-phrases 'preventive protection' and the 'right to remain' proved susceptible to misuse by asylum states as pretexts for restrictive asylum policies, the terminology of the present approach to protection was the logical starting point for reform.[58] Although UNHCR continues to engage in preventive activities, the infamy gained by the notion of 'preventive protection' after its abject failure in Croatia and Bosnia-Herzegovina has induced the purging of

---

[57] Barutciski, 'The Reinforcement of Non-Admission Policies', pp. 86–7.
[58] Chimni, 'Meaning of Words'.

this expression from UNHCR's lexicon. Expressions of the 'right to remain', meanwhile, continue to appear in institutional usage but in a significantly altered form, with two alternative expressions having been suggested in order to better safeguard against the concept's misuse.[59] The 'right not to be displaced' aims to address the lack of an explicit and general prohibition of displacement in international law and to reinforce the accountability of the authorities responsible.[60] The 'right to remain in safety', meanwhile, expressly elaborates the underlying assumption on which the 'right to remain' always has been based: that merely invoking the right to remain or any relevant provision of human rights law is insufficient to prevent displacement. The determining factor is the actual safety of the threatened individuals.[61] This, in turn, depends upon a commitment by the international community to provide effective protection of human rights in the country of origin when local authorities prove unwilling or unable to discharge this responsibility towards the populations under their jurisdiction.

Accepting the existence of the rights to remain and to return in safety, the question more demanding of attention is how the international community can encourage and ensure the existence of protection that is required for the realisation of these rights. Identifying the situations and strategies best suited to UNHCR's involvement in countries of origin constitutes its principal protection challenge at present.[62] On the basis of UNHCR's experiences in Croatia, Bosnia-Herzegovina and the Caucasus, it may seem a foregone conclusion that all of its recent operations in countries of origin to be covered by such a 'protection audit'[63] will show a deficit. Yet, insofar as even the critics of UNHCR's reorientation concede that there conceivably exist situations in which strategies of in-country international protection may prove not only effective but absolutely essential,[64] the potential for positive evaluations cannot be discounted. Recent, ongoing and future efforts to provide in-country protection therefore need to be considered as experimental, as a process of trial and error that is not yet complete. As an essential qualification, it should be understood, but often is not, that in-built into such experiments to

[59] UNHCR, *State of the World's Refugees*, 1995, pp. 69–70.
[60] Maria Stavropoulou, 'The Right Not to be Displaced', 9 *American University Journal of International Law and Policy*, 1994, pp. 689–749.
[61] Michel Moussalli, 'International Protection: The Road Ahead', 3 *International Journal of Refugee Law*, 1991, p. 611.
[62] Arthur C. Helton, 'UNHCR and Protection in the 90s', 6 *International Journal of Refugee Law*, 1994, pp. 1–5.
[63] Guy S. Goodwin-Gill, Editorial, 8 *International Journal of Refugee Law*, 1996, p. 4.
[64] Frelick, '"Preventive Protection"', p. 453; and Shacknove, 'From Asylum to Containment', p. 527.

provide protection in countries of origin there remains, untrammelled, the right of persons under threat of persecution to seek protection elsewhere in countries of asylum.

In defining the boundaries of its in-country activities, UNHCR therefore faces twin protection challenges. On the one hand, it needs to continue to develop and test strategies for providing international protection in countries of origin in order to determine how it can most effectively contribute to such efforts. At the same time, it must remain accountable to its primary mandate of refugee protection by ensuring that these innovations do not disregard the wisdom of traditional solutions.[65] Accordingly, the increased emphasis on in-country protection should be perceived in the light in which it is intended: as a helpful supplement rather than a harmful substitute to the form of protection found in countries of asylum.

Bibliography

Barutciski, Mikhael, 'The Reinforcement of Non-Admission Policies and the Subversion of UNHCR: Displacement and Internal Assistance in Bosnia-Herzegovina (1992–94)', 8 *International Journal of Refugee Law*, 1996, pp. 49–110

Chimni, B. S., 'The Meaning of Words and the Role of UNHCR in Voluntary Repatriation', 5 *International Journal of Refugee Law*, 1993, pp. 442–60

Frelick, Bill, 'Preventing Refugee Flows: Protection or Peril?', *World Refugee Survey 1993* (US Committee for Refugees, Washington, DC, 1993)

'"Preventive Protection" and the Right to Seek Asylum: A Preliminary Look at Bosnia and Croatia', 4 *International Journal of Refugee Law*, 1992, pp. 439–54

Goodwin-Gill, Guy S., 'New Mandate? What New Mandate?' 88 *Refugees*, January 1992, pp. 38–40

Hathaway, James C., 'New Directions to Avoid Hard Problems: The Distortion of the Palliative Role of Refugee Protection', 8 *Journal of Refugee Studies*, 1995, pp. 288–94

Helton, Arthur C., 'UNHCR and Protection in the 90s', 6 *International Journal of Refugee Law*, 1994 pp. 1–5

Mooney, Erin D., 'Internal Displacement and the Conflict in Abkhazia: International Responses and their Protective Effect', 3 *International Journal on Group Rights*, 1995–6, pp. 197–226

'Presence, *ergo* Protection?: UNPROFOR, UNHCR and ICRC in Croatia and Bosnia and Herzegovina', 7 *International Journal of Refugee Law*, 1995, pp. 407–35

Moussalli, Michel, 'International Protection: The Road Ahead', 3 *International Journal of Refugee Law*, 1991, p. 611

---

[65] See chapter 11 of this volume; and Moussalli, 'International Protection', p. 609.

Rieff, David, *Slaughterhouse: Bosnia and the Failure of the West* (Vintage Books, London, 1995)

Shacknove, Andrew, 'From Asylum to Containment', 5 *International Journal of Refugee Law*, 1993, pp. 516–33

Stavropoulou, Maria, 'The Right Not to be Displaced', 9 *American University Journal of International Law and Policy*, 1994, pp. 689–749

11   Refugee identity and protection's fading prospect

Guy S. Goodwin-Gill[1]

Introduction: the legal, institutional and political premises of the regime of international protection

Nearly fifty years ago, the *ad hoc* committee which prepared the first draft of the 1951 Convention Relating to the Status of Refugees was moved by one human rights aspect in particular, now often forgotten in refugee discourse:[2] the right to recognition as a person before the law, set out in article 6 of the 1948 Universal Declaration of Human Rights.[3] Though it was not mentioned in the preamble as adopted, the drafters at the time were impressed by the fact that the lack of any clear legal status for refugees and stateless persons prejudiced their right to 'lead a normal and self-respecting life'. Their intuitive sense of the refugee's need for identity, and for dignity and integrity, is as relevant today as it ever was. The notion of refugee identity, seen in an uncomplicated, rights-based way, is under threat, not only as a consequence of state policies and state practices, but also, more seriously, because of institutional developments in sources traditionally identified exclusively with refugee protection, such as the Office of the United Nations High Commissioner for Refugees (UNHCR).

Founded in 1951, UNHCR has a unique statutory responsibility – to

---

[1] The author served with the Office of the United Nations High Commissioner for Refugees (UNHCR) in various, mainly legal, posts from 1976 to 1988. Since 1988, his editorship of the *International Journal of Refugee Law*, in the establishment of which UNHCR played an important supportive role, has kept him in touch with the organisation and many individual staff members, although the *International Journal of Refugee Law*, which is owned and published by Oxford University Press, is and always has been entirely independent. The views of the author in the present chapter draw on the sources cited and on his experiences and knowledge, but they are in no way to be identified with UNHCR (unlikely in the circumstances), or with any past or present staff member of that organisation other than himself.

[2] UN Doc. E/AC.32/2, 3 January 1950, *Ad Hoc* Committee on Statelessness and Related Problems, Memorandum by the Secretary-General; Annex; Preliminary Draft Convention, para. 13.

[3] 1948 Universal Declaration of Human Rights, General Assembly Resolution 217 A (III), 10 December 1948.

provide international protection to refugees and, together with governments, to seek permanent solutions to their problems.[4] Its protection
functions, some of which are described in the UNHCR Statute, include
the supervision of international instruments and the promotion of new
ones; also, and despite references in paragraph 2 of the UNHCR Statute
to its working with 'groups and categories of refugees', UNHCR has traditionally played an important role in many jurisdictions in relation to
individual cases. Although initially set up as a temporary institution,
essentially intended to wrap up the refugee problems remaining after the
Second World War and in the late 1940s, UNHCR has acquired quasi-
permanent status, as well as universal support, even among those initially
opposed to the 'politics' of refugee protection.[5]

One hundred and thirty-seven states now also subscribe to the ideal of
international protection in its treaty-based formulation, as represented by
the 1951 Convention and the 1967 Protocol Relating to the Status of
Refugees.[6] By way of these two instruments, states have accepted a range
of fundamental obligations as crucial for protection, as they are for assistance and solutions. Among them are a near universal consensus on the
refugee definition, often regionally enlarged but not restricted, and
acceptance of the fundamental principle of *non-refoulement*, obliging
states, even now non-parties, not to return a refugee to a territory where
his or her life or freedom may be endangered.[7]

In the years since UNHCR's establishment as a subsidiary organ of the
General Assembly, the 'refugee regime' has evolved to meet new challenges, and, like all such regimes, its configuration has mirrored not only
the legal but also a succession of varying political, economic and humanitarian factors, as well as the influence of its most powerful members. The
system of international protection of refugees remains a unique combination, bringing together states, international organisations, non-governmental organisations and the refugees themselves in the pursuit of
common ends. It can be seen, on the one hand, as a partnership between
states and UNHCR; but also, on the other hand, as institutionalised

---

[4] General Assembly Resolution 428 (V), 12 December 1950, Annex, Statute of the Office of
the United Nations High Commissioner for Refugees, para. 1. For a brief history, see Guy
S. Goodwin-Gill, *The Refugee in International Law* (2nd edn, Clarendon Press, Oxford,
1996), pp. 7–18 and 207–20. See also chapters 8 to 10 of this volume.

[5] On the political background, see Guy S. Goodwin-Gill, 'Different Types of Forced
Migration Movements as an International and National Problem', in *The Uprooted: Forced
Migration as an International Problem in the Post-War Era* (ed. Göran Rystad, Lund
University Press, Lund, 1990), p. 15.

[6] Up-to-date details of ratifications and reservations can be found at www.unhcr.ch/ref-
world

[7] Generally on the refugee definition and *non-refoulement*, see Goodwin-Gill, *Refugee*, chapters 1 and 4.

confrontation between national and international interests. States, which provide the territorial dimension to both causes and solutions, have their sovereign interests, and from time to time these will conflict with UNHCR's duties of protection and supervision. In the middle ground of difference, solutions have to be found for refugees, that is, individuals who are not criminals, but who have made the perfectly rational choice to flee an intolerable situation. In a very practical sense also, UNHCR's protection and solution responsibilities take place in a context that is increasingly likely to involve the provision of material assistance, either short- or long-term, the uncertain availability of durable solutions dependent, as always, on the political will of states, weaknesses in the system of ensuring compliance with international obligations, and increasing resource demands.

UNHCR's work is intended, indeed required, to be humanitarian, social and non-political,[8] but it clearly takes place in a political context, frequently characterised by tension between the national and international arms of protection, between sovereignty and international responsibility. This is by no means unhealthy, for it can be, and has been, a positive factor in the progressive development of international refugee law and standards. Indeed, the extent to which the status of the refugee has developed from the beneficiary of a paternalistic system of certification to the claimant of rights is witness in part to this process of interaction.

Much of that progress now seems under threat, however, in a context in which, more than ever before, the political dimensions of population movements are inclining to prevail over the rights, claims, and even the identity of individuals; and in which the supposedly impartial and humanitarian institutional dimension to refugee protection yields increasingly to other state interests.

The political aspects of today's refugee problems signal, in particular, the policy dimensions, and the choices that must be made by governments and international organisations. Those choices include whether to abide by international obligations; whether to follow established principles, or to respond *ad hoc* to situations; whether to promote the development of new international instruments or agencies; whether to refine

---

[8] UNHCR Statute, para. 2. The 'politics' of refugee protection and assistance are clear from the 1949 UN debates. See, for example, GAOR, 4th Session, Third Committee, Summary Records, pp. 104–50; and 4th Session, Plenary, Summary Records, pp. 473–95. The 'non-political' injunction was included in the first draft of the UNHCR Statute, General Assembly Resolution 319 A (IV), 3 December 1949, Annex; see also GAOR, 5th Session, Third Committee, Summary Records, 336th Meeting, 6 December 1950, paras. 7–10, accepting by thirty-six votes to five, with one abstention, Yugoslavia's proposal to add the words 'humanitarian and social' to 'non-political'.

national responses to refugee flows, by changing laws and procedures or introducing obstacles to arrival; whether to go beyond the precedents; whether to support international humanitarian relief; whether to promote solutions, and which ones; and whether to try to deal with causes. Each of these political decisions, of course, takes place within a context in which legal rules – human rights law, refugee law, international humanitarian law – ought to have their impact.

The end of the Cold War has brought a change in attitude, however, that is not necessarily beneficial for refugees at large. It has removed an imperative, in the sense that refugee movements throughout the world can no longer be slotted into Cold War classifications; they are no longer distant reflections of imminent conflicts nearer home, and no longer result from conflicts waged by client and counter-client forces. The 'political' interest in supporting refugee relief as part of an overall strategy to defeat or contain communism has vanished. Instead, we are confronted with refugee movements in all their humanitarian dimensions; and humanitarian need, it seems, may not be enough.[9]

International protection and UNHCR[10]

1991–1997: substituting 'humanitarian action' for the duty to provide international protection

The pursuit of protection objectives necessarily results in a tension between state and individual, and between states and the international agency charged with that responsibility. UNHCR cannot expect always to please all sides, but the art is to stay close to principles, not to throw them overboard in an excess of 'realistic' cohabitation. Transparency and accountability, therefore, are not only about dollars, but also about consistency and conformity to principle. There is no constitutional court or

---

[9] Consider the negative and hostile reaction of the German Minister of the Interior, Manfred Kanther, to the unexceptional statement by the President of Italy regarding the continuing willingness of his country to grant asylum to genuine refugees; see, for example, Ian Traynor and Helena Smith, 'EU Passport-Free Regime Buckles', *Guardian*, 6 January 1998.

[10] In subjecting UNHCR to critical attention, I aim to distinguish between the processes of policy-making and the daily work of protection, assistance and solutions. This is a viable and functional distinction even though there is obviously overlap and movement between both levels. The distinction is important, however, for UNHCR's historically sound reputation for protection continues to be built on the shoulders of those at the front end. Unfortunately, a few minor consultative mechanisms apart, UNHCR's operating circle lacks any forum for effective, serious, critical discourse; in the author's experience, and with some noteworthy exceptions, external criticism and review tend to be met with hurt silence and foreclosure.

review jurisdiction to judge the actions of international agencies as such, nor would this necessarily be a good thing.[11] One reason why the international community chose the particular structure for UNHCR which it did – election of the High Commissioner by the General Assembly on the nomination of the Secretary-General and reporting directly to the General Assembly and the Economic and Social Council (ECOSOC)[12] – was precisely to shield it from the politically charged atmosphere of the United Nations. Though expressly directed to be 'non-political', UNHCR's protection work will always be political, in so far as it opposes agency to government or governments; the organisational context, however, is one in which the agency may be expected to remain accountable to its primary, as it were, constitutional function.[13]

To a certain extent, the development of UNHCR policy can be tracked through the various submissions made each year to the Executive Committee (EXCOM). Besides copious documentation, each session traditionally opens with an address by the High Commissioner, summarising the events and challenges of the previous twelve months, sometimes justifying and rationalising operations *ex post facto*, and laying out future plans and objectives.[14] Where the policy aspects of these statements can be linked to, or find their reflection in, activities and programmes at field level, the appropriate inferences can be drawn.

An examination of these statements in the years 1991 to 1997 reveals a distinct, formal disinclination to characterise UNHCR in terms of its statutory duty to provide international protection, and a preference instead for locating its role in a field to be called 'humanitarian action'.[15]

[11] The UNHCR Statute calls upon the High Commissioner, should problems arise, to 'request the opinion of the advisory committee on refugees if it is created': UNHCR, Statute, para. 1; Goodwin-Gill, *Refugee*, p. 215. The committee in its present form dates from 1958, with its original terms of reference being to advise the High Commissioner, on request, in the exercise of statutory functions, and on the appropriateness of providing international assistance in specific cases. Over the years, it has come to exercise considerable influence on management and on the development of protection and assistance policy, to the extent that it now more closely approximates to the 'executive' function implied by its name.

[12] On a controversial issue of 'succession', see 'United Nations High Commissioner for Refugees: Election or Appointment', 3 *International Journal of Refugee Law*, 1991, pp. 121–4.

[13] EXCOM is not a review body, however, and its responsibilities do not include mandate accountability.

[14] A measure of general policy thinking can also be found today in the biannual, in-house productions, *The State of the World's Refugees* (Penguin, 1993; and Oxford University Press, 1995 and 1997), subtitled respectively 'The Challenge of Protection', 'In Search of Solutions' and 'A Humanitarian Agenda'.

[15] Significantly also, perhaps, *The State of the World's Refugees* (1997) opens with the statement, not that UNHCR is responsible for the international protection of refugees, but for their *welfare* (*ibid.*, p. 2); the word 'legitimate' is also a common substitute in passages requiring legal precision (*ibid.*, pp. 2 and 14).

The timing of the emphasis is important, and the High Commissioner struck a chord among many who, perhaps understandably, saw the limitations inherent in a purely reactive approach to the problems of forcible population displacement.[16] The 'security of people' living within their own boundaries was now to be the guiding principle; comprehensive approaches were needed; relief and human rights protection were to be combined and offered even in situations of conflict; and preventive strategies were to be developed to ensure that flight did not take place.[17] A number of related themes also emerge: an urgent desire to be a part of solutions, and, above all, to be a part of prevention.

In the early 1990s, the call for novel approaches seemed so timely. Strains, it was said, were appearing in the 'orthodox approach to refugee protection', though that was somewhat simplistically represented as a movement from flight to durable solution. 'Asylum', long considered the high point of refugee protection (though rarely defined or placed in context, and often unattainable),[18] was seen to be under threat; hence 'the challenge of solutions', the emphasis on the temporary nature of protection, and the prevention of new crises, 'as humanitarian action increasingly [became] a part of the wider agenda for peace and stability'.[19] The major challenges facing the United Nations in maintaining international peace and security and promoting economic and social development seemed to offer the 'right' conceptual place for UNHCR's humanitarian work. Hence, there was an increased emphasis on an international presence in countries of origin in order to encourage people to remain; and international assistance to the internally displaced, wherever this could have 'a preventive impact'; that is, not just humanitarian relief, but relief with a purpose.

[16] This was not a new perspective, even in 1991. In various papers and publications, Gervase Coles had called attention to what he called the 'exile bias' of the refugee regime; see, for example, Gervase J. L. Coles, 'Approaching the Refugee Problem Today', in *Refugees and International Relations* (ed. Gil Loescher and Laila Monahan, Clarendon Press, Oxford, 1989), p. 373. This in turn can be seen in the historical (i.e., early Cold War) influences on the regime in its early formative stage: Kim Salomon, *Refugees in the Cold War: Toward a New International Refugee Regime in the Early Postwar Era* (Lund University Press, Lund, 1991); and Goodwin-Gill, 'Different Types of Forced Migration', p. 15.

[17] These and subsequent indicators are taken from the opening statements to the Executive Committee in the years 1992–7, published as annexes to the annual report of each session in the UN document series A/AC.96/. See UN Docs. A/AC.96/783 (1991); A/AC.96/804 (1992); A/AC.96/821 (1993); A/AC.96/839 (1994); A/AC.96/860 (1995); A/AC.96/878 (1996); and A/AC.96/895 (1997). Hereafter each statement is identified as 'HCR' followed by the year in question. The latest statements can be consulted on UNHCR's website (www.unhcr.ch), while a more comprehensive collection is available on *RefWorld*, UNHCR's twice yearly CD-ROM produced by the Centre for Documentation and Research (CDR).

[18] Why? Perhaps because states always knew that asylum was relative to context . . .

[19] HCR, 1992.

UNHCR was consequently positioned to try to fill this need, but as if it had no other role, no pre-existing mandate, just a blank slate on which to write out its new purpose. The circumstances were propitious, however, as developments in a variety of contexts reveal.

Former Yugoslavia

In his letter of 14 November 1991, the then UN Secretary-General, Javier Pérez de Cuéllar, invited the High Commissioner to become more closely involved with events in the former Yugoslavia 'to assist in bringing relief to needy internally displaced persons affected by the conflict . . . [which] . . . involvement . . . may also have a welcome preventive impact in helping to avoid the further displacement of population'.[20] It was this operation, in particular, that inspired that notion of humanitarian action which, it was said, could be seen in UNHCR's 'initiatives to provide protection and assistance to displaced populations within countries of origin', where 'pre-emptive assistance' would serve as a tool for preventive protection.[21] Although it was stressed that prevention was not a substitute for asylum, events on the ground suggest that the former Yugoslavia was something of a pilot project, in which UNHCR's strategy was directed away from protection of refugees strictly so-called, to the more idealistic political goal of preventive solutions.

The political and humanitarian failures in the former Yugoslavia provide many lessons and illustrations. Responsibility can hardly be laid exclusively at UNHCR's door,[22] yet its assumption in fact of the lead agency role and its relief activities necessarily involved it, from the start, in the politics of the war.[23] It was hardly surprising, as Bill Frelick has remarked, that its humanitarian mandate was manipulated;[24] UNHCR was not only obliged

---

[20] Copy on file with UNHCR Centre for Documentation and Research, Geneva, and with the author.   [21] See HCR 1992.

[22] See chapters 9 and 10 of this volume; Bill Frelick, '"Preventive Protection" and the Right to Seek Asylum', 4 *International Journal of Refugee Law*, 1992, p. 439; Erin D. Mooney, 'Presence *ergo* Protection? UNPROFOR, UNHCR and ICRC in Former Yugoslavia', 7 *International Journal of Refugee Law*, 1995, p. 436; Mikhael Barutciski, 'The Reinforcement of Non-Admission Policies and the Subversion of UNHCR: Displacement and Internal Assistance in Bosnia-Herzegovina', 8 *International Journal of Refugee Law*, 1996, p. 49; S. Alex Cunliffe and Michael Pugh, 'The Politicization of the UNHCR in the Former Yugoslavia', 10 *Journal of Refugee Studies*, 1997, p. 134; and Michael Pugh and S. Alex Cunliffe, 'The Lead Agency Concept in Humanitarian Assistance: The Case of the UNHCR', 28 *Security Dialogue*, 1997, 1, pp. 17–30.

[23] Given its specific humanitarian and non-political role, as well as its independent responsibility to provide international protection to refugees, the attribution to, or assumption by, UNHCR of a 'lead agency' role is incompatible with its mandate in any situation having serious political content, such as mediation or conflict resolution.

[24] Frelick, 'Preventive Protection', p. 449.

to negotiate away substantial quantities of relief aid as the price for access, but was also caught between the devil and the deep blue sea in the politics and practice of ethnic cleansing and evacuation.[25] When facilitating the transit of persons leaving Bosnia, for example, UNHCR appeared tacitly to endorse 'organised flight' and to be a party to restrictions on spontaneous movement in search of refuge.[26] This was obviously not intended, but it was nonetheless a reasonably foreseeable consequence of the policies of prevention and assistance to populations at risk.

Just eight months or so after UNHCR's engagement in the former Yugoslavia, Commission on Human Rights Special Rapporteur Tadeusz Mazowiecki had already noted the inadequacy of protection (and indeed the helplessness of UN agencies and others).[27] Yet UNHCR nonetheless consolidated its involvement in a massive relief operation in which protection just could not figure (no matter the courage, dedication and selflessness of individual staff members). Here, UNHCR's primary directive was unnecessarily compromised by newly fashionable 'humanitarian action'. The notion of 'pre-emptive assistance as a tool for preventive protection'[28] was ever and always based on false premises; the politics of the situation were quite beyond the influence of any party, and particularly one whose service delivery was dependent on the armed force of a military contingent considered not impartial by at least one, if not all, parties to the regional conflict.[29]

Moreover, UNHCR's response to the Secretary-General's invitation to engage in operations not clearly within its mandate confused established lines of authority. Under paragraph 11 of its Statute, UNHCR reports to the General Assembly through ECOSOC. Realigning operations in the direction of political objectives set by the UN Secretariat necessarily compromised the autonomy of the High Commissioner, whose manner of election by the General Assembly was intended precisely to protect the

---

[25] *Cf.* Mooney, 'Presence *ergo* Protection?', pp. 419–23; and Cunliffe and Pugh, 'Politicization', pp. 145–6.

[26] See chapter 9, pp. 189–91 above; and Cunliffe and Pugh, 'Politicization', p. 144.

[27] Report on the situation of human rights in the territory of the former Yugoslavia, submitted by Tadeusz Mazowiecki, Special Rapporteur of the UN Commission on Human Rights, UN Doc. E/CN.4/1991/S1–9, 28 August 1992, para. 56, cited in Mooney, 'Presence *ergo* Protection?', p. 429. October 1992 found the High Commissioner informing the Executive Committee that: 'Our experience in former Yugoslavia convinces me that international presence is an essential element of prevention. While the precise beneficial impact of presence is difficult to quantify, and while it may not always succeed in preventing forcible displacement, it nevertheless allows for international monitoring of humanitarian treatment and can have a restraining effect': HCR 1992.

[28] HCR 1992.

[29] Cunliffe and Pugh, 'Politicization', p. 137, which states that 'one constant appears to have been a perception by the warring parties that UNHCR was unable to operate in a non-political fashion'.

Office from the politics, if not the political context, of humanitarian crises.[30]

The problems faced by UNHCR were due not only to the complexities of the situation, but also to the fact that the terms of its engagement in the former Yugoslavia were not clearly laid down in advance.[31] Although the situation was quite unlike any in which it had been involved, some see the choice of UNHCR as 'logical', at least so far as it was driven by recognition of the agency's recognised logistical capacity. At the same time, however, its lead agency status 'propelled it into a policy vacuum and detracted from its primary role as a . . . body for protecting and assisting . . . refugees'.[32] This resulted in problems in balancing its lead agency functions with its statutory responsibilities, and in maintaining impartiality in a civilian–military relationship.[33]

The relationship between 'preventive protection' and asylum was never worked out in this strategy, either theoretically or on the ground. The idea that 'international protection reflects the convergence of humanitarian and political interests'[34] leaves little room for principle, and although the rhetoric of protection has resurfaced with some regularity, particularly since 1996,[35] the reality is somewhat different. If effective protection generally requires being there, 'merely being there' is never the sufficient condition for protection; the situation of ongoing conflict ought to have signalled that fact from the start.[36] In seeking to link preventive protection to solutions, or in pursuing the return of refugees as a political end and not a humanitarian ideal, UNHCR unleashed forces having the potential to overwhelm established rules. Unfortunately, developments in the Great Lakes region from July 1994 onwards were to reveal even greater strategic confusion.

Rwanda and the Great Lakes

The precarious situation of armed settlements is hardly unknown to UNHCR. In southern Africa in the late 1970s and early 1980s, UNHCR

[30] On the background, see 'United Nations High Commissioner for Refugees: Election or Appointment', 3 *International Journal of Refugee Law*, 1991, p. 121.
[31] Pugh and Cunliffe, 'The Lead Agency Concept', p. 20.
[32] *Ibid.*, p. 25. Pugh and Cunliffe note that the lead agency concept 'represents a "default" position to fill a co-ordination vacuum', and query whether agencies with 'defined roles as independent, non-political actors in specialist fields' are *ever* appropriate for co-ordination functions.   [33] *Ibid.*, pp. 21–2.   [34] HCR 1995.
[35] See, in particular, HCR 1997; and '1997 Year in Review', *Refugees*, 1997, 109.
[36] As Mooney observes: 'Given that a concern for physical safety is the primary impetus for flight, the protective effects which the High Commissioner attributes to assistance are minimal.' 'Presence *ergo* Protection?', p. 430. UNHCR's 1993 *Note on International Protection*, UN Doc. A/AC.96/815, p. 20, appears to have recognised this reality: cited in Mooney, 'Presence *ergo* Protection?', p. 423.

was under pressure from interested parties to turn a blind eye to guerrillas and freedom fighters among the civilian refugee population; and when those fighters were killed or captured with UNHCR medical and food packs in their kits, the camps in turn became 'legitimate' military targets and many hundreds of civilian deaths resulted. What came out of that experience in 1987, after five years of protracted and often acrimonious debate, was not simple acceptance by the Executive Committee of the paramount need for protection, but recognition that the price for protection was the 'exclusively civilian and humanitarian character' of refugee camps and settlements, for which both states and international organisations have obligations and responsibilities.[37] The Executive Committee urged UNHCR to make every effort to promote conditions ensuring safety, for example, by locating refugees at a reasonable distance from the frontier of their country of origin – a basic principle and policy already accepted by the Organisation of African Unity (OAU) in its 1969 Convention on refugees,[38] in the 1981 African Charter on Human and Peoples' Rights,[39] and repeated by the Executive Committee in Conclusion No. 72 (1993) on the personal security of refugees.[40]

States members of the Executive Committee clearly recognised that protection cannot be assured unless refugee camps retain an exclusively humanitarian and civilian character; and that, subject to the rules of international law and international humanitarian law, a settlement which fails to meet these criteria is likely to be the object of military attack.[41]

---

[37] EXCOM Conclusion No. 48 (1987); for a brief summary and references to sources, see Goodwin-Gill, *Refugee*, pp. 254–5.   [38] 1001 UNTS 46, articles II(6) and III(2).

[39] 21 ILM, 1982, p. 58. Article 23(2) states: 'For the purpose of strengthening peace, solidarity and friendly relations, States parties to the present Charter shall ensure that: (a) any individual enjoying the right of asylum under article 12 of the present Charter shall not engage in subversive activities against his country of origin or any other State party . . . (b) their territories shall not be used as bases for subversive or terrorist activities against the people of any other State party to the present Charter.' See also the 1954 Caracas Convention on Territorial Asylum, article 9; the 1984 Cartagena Declaration, Part III, paras. 6 and 7; and Steven Corliss, 'Asylum State Responsibility for the Hostile Acts of Foreign Exiles', 2 *International Journal of Refugee Law*, 1990, p. 181.

[40] Refugees also are duty-bound to, *inter alia*, 'abstain from any activity likely to detract from the exclusively civilian and humanitarian character' of camps, whilst states should do 'all within their capacity' to maintain this character: EXCOM Conclusion No. 48, para. 4(a); and see the 1951 Geneva Convention, article 2; the OAU Convention, article III; and the African Charter, article 23(2).

[41] Under international humanitarian law, civilians, that is, those not taking a direct part in hostilities, are generally not to be subject to attack: Additional Protocol I to the 1949 Geneva Conventions, articles 49–52; and Additional Protocol II, article 13. However, 'the presence of organized bodies of soldiers amidst the civilian population does not give the soldiers any immunity from an attack directed against them': Richard R. Baxter, 'The Duties of Combatants and the Conduct of Hostilities', in Henry Dunant Institute/UN Educational, Scientific and Cultural Organisation (UNESCO), *International Dimensions of Humanitarian Law* (1988), p. 93 at pp. 114–23 at p. 118). Equally, civilians, though not

The principles are clear and the lesson simple enough; both were forgotten or ignored. Less than a year after EXCOM Conclusion No. 72, UNHCR is found servicing camps in eastern Zaire that failed by a considerable margin to maintain their 'exclusively humanitarian and civilian character'. Indeed, they were used not only for recruitment and training purposes, but also as bases for cross-border raids into Rwanda.[42] The relevant international instruments confirm that the primary responsibility for ensuring the civilian character of camps and settlements and that 'refugees' do not engage in attacks on their country of origin rests with the state of refuge.[43] UNHCR has no police or security personnel,[44] and neither does it have the authority alone to require that refugees be located safely. Its activities are nevertheless constrained by its mandate, and it has no lawful authority at all to be present in military or militarised settlements being used as bases for armed attacks on other states, let alone to provide relief supplies to combatants either directly or indirectly. The fact that a proportion, even a sizeable proportion, of the population is in need of assistance is not sufficient to justify UNHCR's presence, whatever its relevance for agencies *not* founded upon the principle of international protection of refugees. The military character of the settlements was known and understood by October 1994.[45] Once the

footnote 41 (*cont.*)
subject to direct attack, will be at risk when located in a 'military objective', that is, one 'which by [its] nature, location, purpose or use make[s] an effective contribution to military action and whose total or partial destruction, capture or neutralization, in the circumstances ruling at the time, offers a definite military advantage': Additional Protocol I, article 52(2), cited in Baxter, 'The Duties of Combatants', p. 119.

[42] In an interview with John Pomfret in mid-1997, Rwandan Defence Minister Paul Kagame said that he had advised the USA of his government's intention to take military action and that the aims were to 'dismantle the camps' and to 'destroy the structure' of the Hutu army and militia based in and around the camps. He stated further that he and other Rwandan officials had attempted to persuade the UN and Western countries to demilitarise the camps: 'Either You Do Something About the Camps, or You Face the Consequences', *Washington Post*, 9 July 1997. See also Human Rights Watch/Africa and Féderation internationale des ligues des droits de l'homme, 'Democratic Republic of the Congo: What Kabila is Hiding – Civilian Killings and Impunity in Congo', October 1997, pp. 16 and 34–5. For further detail, see Joint Evaluation of Emergency Assistance to Rwanda, *The International Response to Conflict and Genocide: Lessons from the Rwanda Experience* (4 vols., Steering Committee of the Joint Evaluation of Emergency Assistance to Rwanda, Copenhagen, March 1996) (hereinafter 'Rwanda Joint Evaluation'), especially Study 2, 'Early Warning and Conflict Management', p. 58 (on military control of Goma and the nearby separate settlement of Mugunga from August 1994 onwards); and Study 3, 'Humanitarian Aid and its Effects', pp. 96–7 (on food distribution and the role of the military, and the high levels of malnutrition in Mugunga, particularly in female-headed households).

[43] This point was also repeatedly emphasised by the High Commissioner: see, for example, HCR 1994.

[44] In a novel and also controversial move, UNHCR employed Zairean troops in an attempt to improve order in the border camps: for a summary account, see 'Rwanda Joint Evaluation', vol. II, 'Early Warning and Conflict Management', p. 61.   [45] HCR 1994.

initial emergency relief phase was over, some reflection would have confirmed that the separation of military and civilian personnel, which could only have been carried out by or in the country of asylum, was just not going to happen. For UNHCR, which does appear to have recognised the 'inappropriateness' of continued military presence, if not its wider implications, this point had clearly arrived by December 1994, when the UN Secretariat failed to come up with an effective solution to the problem.[46] By then, the status of the settlements was irretrievably compromised and the risks to the security of those who had fled were correspondingly heightened. While practically able to continue providing relief, UNHCR not only had no lawful justification for its presence, but was also quite unable to ensure or contribute to the protection of the inhabitants against the military attacks which duly followed in 1997.

In such situations, a deeper knowledge of law, principle and history will ensure that policies at least have a rational basis other than a general feeling that someone has to do something about all that's wrong in the world. UNHCR's mandate is not to provide food and relief to the needy, but to provide protection. In the face of the international community's unwillingness to take the necessary supportive steps, UNHCR's inability to fulfil its primary responsibility to provide international protection to refugees in accordance with the international law that binds even itself, let alone to promote its declared objective of promoting return, ought to have prompted a decision to withdraw.[47] Such decisions are not to be

[46] Rwanda Joint Evaluation, vol. II, 'Early Warning and Conflict Management', pp. 60–1, 73 and 76.

[47] *Cf.* the following remarks of the former president of Médecins sans frontières, Rony Brauman:

Le grand scandale a consisté à présenter comme une situation humanitaire classique un scénario complètement différent: des camps où les réfugiés étaient sous l'emprise de véritables geôliers, les miliciens hutus. Dans cette prison à ciel ouvert, les ONG [organisations non-gouvernementales] ont fait office de service social. Pour le HCR, tout se résumait à un problème logistique, administratif . . . [L]a pression de l'urgence ne doit pas anéantir toute réflexion sur l'humanitaire et sur les actions à entreprendre. Ensuite, les ONG ne doivent pas confondre leur intérêts propres avec l'intérêt des victimes et s'enferrer dans une logique purement administrative. Parfois, la meilleure forme d'aide consiste à se retirer d'une opération. (*Tribune de Genève*, 23–24 November 1996, p. 7)

See also Stephen Buckley, 'Relief Agencies Defend Response to Refugees', *International Herald Tribune*, 12 November 1996. John Pomfret remarked: 'In some cases, UN officials and other aid workers actually encouraged Hutu radicals to take control of the camps, reasoning that it was easier to rely on a government-in-exile to distribute food and keep order.' Nicholas Morris, on the other hand, argues that UNHCR 'will rarely have the option of stopping' a humanitarian operation: 'Whatever the strength of the arguments in favour, the pressures to continue, particularly acute when humanitarian action is substituting for problem solving, and the unavoidable perception (and, in most cases, the necessary reality) of the abandonment of innocent victims, leave little choice.' Nicholas Morris, 'Protection Dilemmas and UNHCR's Response: A Personal View from Within UNHCR', 9 *International Journal of Refugee Law*, 1997, p. 492 at pp. 496–7.

taken lightly, of course, and they are not made any easier by the continuous inflow of substantial funds for operations in less than ideal conditions; but there are, after all, other agencies capable of meeting human and material needs, and able to do so in complex situations without putting mandate responsibility and constituents at risk.[48] That such issues are not resolved on the basis of established principles, however, speaks even more eloquently to the existence of major organisational weaknesses.

The 'humanitarian agenda' and United Nations reform

UNHCR's 'humanitarian action' agenda found natural room for expansion, at least in theory, during the development of proposals for United Nations reform in 1997. At the invitation of Maurice Strong, Executive Co-ordinator for United Nations reform, UNHCR examined the implications of the High Commissioner assuming the functions of Emergency Relief Co-ordinator (ERC).[49]

Conscious of the risk to its mandate, yet confident of its ability to carry on regardless, UNHCR's proposals seem to have reflected the separate and divisible nature of the British Crown.[50] The High Commissioner would assume the responsibilities of the ERC, but to avoid 'any negative impact on the statutory responsibilities of UNHCR', no fusion of functions would take place. Instead, an Office of the ERC would be established at UNHCR's Geneva headquarters, to be responsible for complex humanitarian emergencies. Perceived as 'folding' ERC and the

---

[48] Some might assume, without more thought, that UNHCR's withdrawal would have led to still greater loss of life. Obviously, this cannot be determined one way or the other, but it is no less possible that withdrawal would have led to the separation in fact of military and refugee elements, with the latter returning to their country of origin and the former retreating further westwards.

[49] See UNHCR, 'Humanitarian Co-ordination: Some Preliminary Reflections', 20 May 1997. This paper was prepared by UNHCR independently, that is, without consultation with or reference to other actors in the humanitarian and human rights domain, such as the UN Children's Fund (UNICEF), the World Health Organisation (WHO), the World Food Programme (WFP), the Department of Humanitarian Affairs (DHA), the UN High Commissioner for Human Rights, other inter-governmental organisations such as the International Organisation for Migration (IOM) and the International Committee of the Red Cross (ICRC), or to any of UNHCR's operational partners in the provision of assistance and protection in the non-governmental field. The status of the document is probably equivalent to that of an internal (that is, within the UN) memorandum. However, none of the copies provided to and on file with the author indicate that it was considered confidential, although publication is unlikely to have been intended. On the background to the creation of the post of Emergency Relief Co-ordinator, see Goodwin-Gill, *Refugee*, pp. 223–5.

[50] The Queen of the United Kingdom is thus not the 'same' as the Queen of Canada, though the separate functions may be united in a single human being.

Department of Humanitarian Affairs activities into UNHCR, this would entail co-ordination of the UN's response to complex humanitarian emergencies, the development of humanitarian policy on specific issues of system-wide concern, and advocacy for humanitarian issues, particularly where they cross agency mandates.[51]

Although these suggestions appeared to satisfy the Executive Co-ordinator for UN reform,[52] they received less than wholehearted endorsement from observers and other participants in the humanitarian field. Much of UNHCR's criticism of existing institutions, particularly the Department of Humanitarian Affairs, seemed equally applicable to its own processes, while many of the key strengths supposedly to be derived from UNHCR's takeover turned out, on closer examination, to be somewhat insubstantial.[53]

Notwithstanding the specificity of its responsibility to provide international protection, UNHCR asserted its own comprehensiveness: 'UNHCR . . . is the only agency whose responsibility is to meet all humanitarian needs of those of its concern, as opposed to responsibilities defined by nature of need, age or gender.'[54] Not surprisingly, this jarred with agencies having, and meeting, responsibilities in the health, child and nutrition areas, and it was either unfortunate or significant that UNHCR neglected to mention that its own primary responsibility is defined by, *inter alia*, reference to flight.[55] While those responsible for

[51] UNHCR, 'Humanitarian Co-ordination', paras. 4, 5 and 8.
[52] In a press conference in Geneva on 4 June 1997, the Executive Co-ordinator referred to 'the *de facto* lead role of UNHCR – 80 per cent of its work was humanitarian with the interface between refugees and others becoming harder to define'. Criticism of UNHCR's protection failings which, in the present writer's view, are in no small way responsible for confusing the interface, was dismissed briefly with a reference to the need to strengthen the protection function. UN Information Service, Geneva, 'Note on Press Briefing on 4 June 1997 by the Executive Co-ordinator for United Nations Reform'.
[53] For example, despite the weaknesses revealed in its own internal review, UNHCR specifically criticised DHA for its lack of competence in policy development, 'constrained by reliance on generalists who have not specific competence in areas that need to be addressed': UNHCR, 'Humanitarian Co-ordination', para. 13. As noted above, the majority of the relevant posts in UNHCR's Centre for Documentation and Research currently assigned to 'policy research' are filled (as are UNHCR posts generally) on the basis of 'rotation' and not specifically by reference to specialisation, experience or proven competence. The law of averages, of course, means that from time to time, but not more frequently, the right person ends up in the right job.   [54] *Ibid.*, para. 20.
[55] The consequential implication that the new ERC/HCR should thereafter chair the Inter-Agency Standing Committee (IASC) instead of ERC alone (*ibid.*, para. 25) also will not have gone down too well; on aspects of UNHCR's record in the IASC, see Sue Lautze, Bruce Jones and Mark Duffield, *Strategic Humanitarian Co-ordination in the Great Lakes Region, 1996–1997: An Independent Assessment* (Policy, Information and Advocacy Division, Office for the Co-ordination of Humanitarian Affairs, United Nations, New York, March 1998), paras. 162–77 at para. 174 (available on ReliefWeb website at http://wwwnotes.reliefweb.int and OCHA-Online http://156.106.192.130/dha_ol/).

drafting UNHCR's original bid were clearly conscious of the political dimension that would come with the ERC, it seems to have been imagined that 'actual responsibility for co-ordinating the humanitarian response' could be separated from any required political mechanism and, though this is not made explicit, presumably left within UNHCR strictly so-called. The lessons of political and operational inseparability, which one might have thought had been hammered home time and again in complex situations such as the former Yugoslavia and the Great Lakes, seemed still to be unlearned.

In the event, another solution was chosen.[56] The Department of Humanitarian Affairs was effectively wound up and replaced by a slimmed-down 'Co-ordinator for Humanitarian Affairs', focusing on three 'core functions'.[57] Many DHA responsibilities were redistributed within the UN system, but the possibility of designated lead agencies to co-ordinate complex emergencies remains.[58]

Management for protection

Management is the art of using human and material resources effectively in the pursuit of achievable objectives. Amongst others, those objectives may be profit or promotion, but in the case of UNHCR, paragraph 1 of its Statute identifies the provision of international protection as *the* principal objective; this has been reaffirmed time and again by EXCOM and the General Assembly. How an organisation distributes authority, and how it provides for accountability, are obvious indicators of its capacity to deliver.

---

[56] 'Renewing the United Nations: A Programme for Reform', UN Doc. A/51/950, 16 July 1997.

[57] These were '(1) policy development and co-ordination functions in support of the Secretary-General, ensuring that all humanitarian issues, including those which fall in gaps of existing mandates of agencies such as protection and assistance for internally displaced persons, are addressed . . . (2) advocacy of humanitarian issues with political organs, notably the Security Council; and (3) co-ordination of humanitarian emergency response, by ensuring that an appropriate response mechanism is established, through IASC consultations, on the ground.' *Ibid.*, para. 186.

[58] *Ibid.*, Action 13 and para. 192. An earlier 25 June 1997/Rev.1 draft of the reform proposals had included two options, one of which anticipated the ERC 'normally' designating UNHCR as lead agency. No such specific mention occurs in the final document, although ironically the individual chosen by the Secretary-General to assume the redefined role of ERC (now renamed Office of the Co-ordinator for Humanitarian Assistance) is the former Assistant High Commissioner for Refugees, Sergio Vieira de Mello, who assumed office on 13 January 1998. It will be interesting to follow inter-agency relations hereafter, including the use made of the lead agency concept and the extent to which it may impact on the mandates of organisations having specifically humanitarian and non-political responsibilities.

Internal organisation

UNHCR's internal organisation has radically altered since the middle of the 1980s, when the Division of International Protection dominated a rigid hierarchy. As UNHCR's operational activities increased, and as an increasing proportion of staff and resources were to be found in the field, substantial decision-making authority was devolved, rightly in the author's view, to regional bureaux and beyond.[59] Unfortunately, however, no steps were taken to ensure that the principles, doctrine and 'culture' of protection were maintained. Responsibility and accountability to mandate fell by the wayside, to the extent that many organisational units today appear institutionally incapable of relating their performance and activities to the mandate of UNHCR as a whole.

Observers both in and outside UNHCR have regretted the sidelining of the Division of International Protection.[60] While there was an evident need for a devolution of authority to enhance effectiveness and response, there was no such obvious need to remove the supervisory or line authority of the Division, or to remove it so completely from operations. Already in the late 1980s serious protection errors were made in the formulation and implementation of policy without reference to principle, but that lesson too has been unlearned. That portion of UNHCR protection work that was rooted in international law, standards and principles, has been eclipsed by so-called pragmatic approaches to refugee problems, in which everything seems to be negotiable.[61]

As 'organisation', UNHCR nevertheless faces formidable challenges. Refugee crises are not generally predictable, as to timing, size, needs or duration. Their nature means that UNHCR must be able to field a pro-

---

[59] The locus of power has since shifted yet again, in ways familiar to students of organisation theory, but which do not address the concerns described below. The power (and the size) of the 'Executive Office' – the 'Seventh Floor', as it is often referred to, in reference to the uppermost level of UNHCR's Geneva Headquarters – has grown correspondingly, with significant consequential enhancements of influence flowing also from the Office's increasing involvement in extra-curricular activities and special operations.

[60] See 'NGO Concerns Regarding the Dilution of UNHCR's Protection Function in the New Organisational Structure of UNHCR', September 1996, discussion paper developed by an NGO working group and distributed at the Executive Committee in October that year. On the other hand, there were also times in UNHCR's past when excessive legalism within the Division of International Protection disabled the organisation's response to new issues, such as human rights. As Senior Legal Research Officer in UNHCR in 1986–7, the author was responsible for developing doctrine in these directions. Two papers ('The Duty to Provide Protection' and 'The Meaning of Protection') were drafted to this end, and discussed in several sessions in early 1987; copies are held in UNHCR's CDR.

[61] Or possibly in management newspeak, 'responsive to [the] external environment', as set out in *Delphi* (see note 62), para. 12, principle 4.

tection and assistance service, almost at a moment's notice, and to meet recruitment, training and procurement requirements, while maintaining an efficient and professional service in relation both to staff and donors. It is hardly surprising that an organisation which must expand and contract in response to conditions largely outside its control should find itself challenged at every level of management. Some of UNHCR's problems are common to other agencies within the UN system, for example with regard generally to recruitment; but others are self-inflicted, such as its attachment to the 'rotation' of staff and to arcane processes of postings and promotions.

In late 1995, UNHCR embarked on a 'far-reaching ambitious programme' of internal reform, which came to be known as the 'Delphi Project'.[62] Premised on a peculiar sense of mission – 'UNHCR is a broad humanitarian organisation, dealing with the search for solutions to population displacement and centred on the protection of refugees'[63] – the final report of the Change Management Group (CMG) inverts the principles, values, objectives and assumptions which might hitherto have been considered central to its mandate.[64] Protection figures no more than two or three times in what is, from a purely management perspective, an otherwise unexceptional analysis of the ways and means to improve policy development, planning and delivery, rectify deficiencies in the use of resources, extend accountability throughout the system, and raise the performance of staff.

It is this 'purely management perspective', however, that distorts the whole. For example, having recognised that 'many important policy deci-

<hr>

[62] *Delphi: The Final Report of the Change Management Group* (UNHCR, Geneva, 1 May 1996) (hereinafter '*Delphi*'). The status of this document is unclear. It was annexed to 'Project Delphi', UN Doc. EC/46/SC/CRP.38, 28 May 1996, when submitted to the EXCOM Standing Committee; however, neither this document nor the later 'Project Delphi: Plan of Action', UN Doc. EC/46/SC/CRP.48, 4 September 1996, is included either on UNHCR's website (http://www.unhcr.ch/refworld) or on the UNHCR/CDR CD-ROM, *RefWorld*. The final report is labelled 'For Internal UNHCR Distribution Only', but it has in fact been widely distributed outside the organisation, to missions in Geneva and elsewhere. To the writer's knowledge, the *Delphi* nomenclature has never been explained; for a concise account of the successes and failures of the Greek original, see Norman Davies, *Europe: A History* (Oxford University Press, 1996), 'Omphalos', pp. 112–13.   [63] *Delphi*, para. 1.

[64] *Ibid.* Para. 12 identifies the first two principles as follows: 'UNHCR is driven primarily by the needs of persons and groups of concern to it' . . . 'UNHCR's efforts are geared toward finding solutions to the problems of refugees and others of concern. This search is informed [*sic*] by protection, solutions being the ultimate objective of protection.' Para. 1 of the UNHCR Statute prescribes that the High Commissioner 'shall assume the function of providing international protection . . . to refugees'. The problem with the reformulation is precisely that it allows for refugee interests to be sacrificed for a political 'ultimate objective' that is not necessarily compatible with 'protection'. *Cf. Delphi*, para. 21, on the 'politicisation of humanitarianism'.

sions appear to be made at bureau or field level in an *ad hoc* manner, without much regard for consistency',[65] the CMG report proposes a response in which neither the Division of International Protection nor the concept of protection has any place.[66] In a report, most of which is fact dedicated to 'Processes – Money and People defined in the Context of Operations', protection is remarkable for its absence or only incidental inclusion.[67] In proposing a 'situational approach' to improve operational response, for example the desirable objectives of management – the best use of resources in the attainment of strategic objectives – yields to the apparently freestanding goal of management for management's sake.[68] Protection or legal staff do not even figure in the illustrative list of the situation manager's support staff.[69]

Given that Delphi is primarily about *internal* management processes, none of these concerns may appear to count for much. 'Accountability', in Delphic terms, is 'a management requirement to be answerable "for something to someone" . . . an individual obligation to perform against an agreed objective.'[70] It is evidently not about UNHCR's accountability to mandate,[71] and there is no *a priori* requirement that protection as an international and therefore an external responsibility should appear in a prescription for internal organisation. As a practical matter, however, repeatedly distancing protection from policy, operations and implementation has contributed to policy weakness, failings on the ground, even unlawful activity.

---

[65] *Delphi*, para. 27.   [66] *Ibid.*, para. 30.
[67] 'The Operations Plan will be derived from the needs of a particular situation. The needs assessment will include provision for all stages of the programme leading to realisation of the exit strategy, that is it will include objectives for protection and life sustaining assistance, but also those relating to the end of an operation . . . for example, objectives to deal with reparation of damage to the environment, capacity building, provision for terminating local staff etc.' *Ibid.*, para. 46.   [68] *Ibid.*, paras. 119–20.   [69] *Ibid.*, para. 120.
[70] *Ibid.*, Glossary, at p. 51. The glossary also defines 'audit' as the '*independent* verification of the systems, procedures and practice of internal controls which may lead to recommendations for corrective action', but it defines 'independent' as 'exercised by someone *internal . . .*' (emphasis added in both cases).
[71] The Change Management Group Report (*Delphi*, para. 12) identified UNHCR's external accountability as lying 'both to the people it protects and assists' – a constituency conveniently lacking either leverage or a loud voice – and its 'state stakeholders, including countries of asylum and donors' – a constituency conveniently ignoring the larger membership of the General Assembly, let alone the 'peoples of the United Nations' (UN Charter, article 1), and the multiple non-governmental organisations through which they both act and speak out. Agency accountability, and the mechanisms by which an agency can or might be held to account for its actions and omissions, is obviously part of the present thesis, but reasons of space mean that in the present chapter it cannot receive the detailed attention it deserves.

Institutional weaknesses reviewed

In January 1997, almost immediately after the forced return of many thousands of Rwandans from Tanzania and not so very long after the attacks on settlements in what was then eastern Zaire, UNHCR submitted a paper to the Executive Committee's Standing Committee, on the lessons learned (to be learned?) from the Burundi and Rwandan emergencies.[72] After recalling the generally favourable conclusions of an evaluation of UNHCR's relief response in 1994 made by the Organisation for Economic Co-operation and Development/Development Assistance Committee (OECD/DAC),[73] which it characterises as 'compelling evidence' in support of the agency's Emergency Response Team (ERT) formula,[74] the paper acknowledges: 'The exodus from Rwanda . . . presented . . . a host of very serious protection problems, yet few of them were addressed in the early stages of the emergency.'[75] In fact, many were never dealt with at all. UNHCR's internal review calls attention to the 'lack of sufficient senior protection staff in the area', and to a resulting failure to give protection considerations 'sufficient priority in the formulation of an overall policy'.[76] Further failings included 'lack of understanding of the social, cultural and political background',[77] inadequate training, and the reluctance of senior staff 'to accept posts in remote and insecure duty stations'.[78]

The independently conducted evaluation commissioned by the Inter-Agency Standing Committee, published in March 1998, noted:

The abuse of humanitarian space and resources is endemic in the Great Lakes region. Protection of vulnerable populations has been effectively abandoned, refugee law has been routinely violated, and humanitarian principles have been made a mockery. The use of humanitarian assistance for political, military and economic purposes is not limited to the governments, armies and militias of the Great Lakes region; political and military actors within the donor and UN communities have likewise abused the role of humanitarian assistance. Those responsible for advocacy of humanitarian principles, and the establishment and maintenance of humanitarian space have not fulfilled their obligations.[79]

---

[72] UNHCR, 'Lessons Learnt from the Burundi and Rwanda Emergencies: Conclusions of an Internal Review Process', UN Doc. EC/47/SC/CRP.11, 2 January 1997. The Standing Committee is part of the revised EXCOM working arrangements; it is a committee of the whole which meets regularly through the year.

[73] 'Rwanda Joint Evaluation'.   [74] UNHCR, 'Lessons Learnt', para. 2.

[75] Ibid., para. 8. The paper attributes many of the problems to 'the support of the international community' for the 'virtual transportation [into Zaire] of a political, social and security structure': ibid. Para. 10 further notes that UNHCR's protection failings 'had already been the subject of criticism in previous emergencies' (emphasis added).

[76] Ibid., para. 8.   [77] Ibid., para. 9.   [78] Ibid., para. 16.

[79] See Lautze et al., 'Strategic Humanitarian Co-ordination in the Great Lakes Region', para. 337; see also para. 107. The system-wide lack of training in humanitarian principles or human rights was also commented on: ibid., para. 116.

UNHCR's internal evaluation, moreover, has its own internal protection failings. In the case of Zaire/Rwanda, it focuses almost entirely on the topical subject of *génocidaires* and exclusion from refugee status, quite failing to note that the militarisation of the settlements and their use as bases for cross-border raids took them outside the (protected) category of 'refugee camps' and removed any lawful justification for UNHCR's continued presence.

In addition, the internal evaluation neglects the very institutional weaknesses responsible for the agency's 'lack of understanding' of the refugees' background. In 1992, UNHCR's Centre for Documentation on Refugees initiated a country of origin information project precisely to fill the knowledge gap. By 1994, it had undertaken significant studies into the background to the crisis in the Great Lakes region,[80] but in late 1995, the emphasis on seeking authoritative and credible information on social, political and cultural issues relating to the causes of flight was downgraded in favour of so-called 'policy research'.[81] So far as one can gather, this retooling has not yet produced anything of significance, particularly in regard to protection.[82] At the time of writing (June 1998), the (now renamed) Centre for Documentation and Research allocates five 'research officers' and one clerk to 'policy', and one 'associate research officer' alone to country of origin work, the latter being responsible for all research on questions submitted by protection officers at UNHCR head-

---

[80] Many studies by independent analysts were published on the UNHCR website and shared with agencies (such as the Centre for Information, Discussion and Exchange on Asylum (CIREA), the European Union's clearing house on refugee-related information), governments and international organisations; others were published in *Refugee Survey Quarterly* (the successor to UNHCR's *Refugee Abstracts*); see, for example, Gérard Prunier, 'La crise rwandaise', 13 *Refugee Survey Quarterly*, 1994, 2 and 3, p. 13 – an issue also reproducing various UN reports on the Rwanda crisis; and Writenet UK, ' Burundi: Descent into Chaos or a Manageable Crisis?' 14 *Refugee Survey Quarterly*, 1995, 1 and 2, p.128. See also chapter 14 of this volume.

[81] Heralded by the High Commissioner as 'a powerful tool both in the planning of policy and in the support of operations', Introductory Statement to the Standing Committee of the Executive Committee of the High Commissioner's Programme, Geneva, 30 January 1996.

[82] There is no 'freedom of information' component in UNHCR's Statute, nor any general culture of information sharing and dissemination. Anecdotal information from various sources indicates that 'policy research' output so far has been a series of non-finalised papers on topics such as 'reintegration: from war to peace', 'standby forces', 'prevention', and several iterations of 'ethnic cleansing'. These may be circulated on a limited internal basis, but they are not otherwise made public or even shared regularly within UNHCR. It is therefore impossible to assess such efforts, to verify sources used and the soundness of judgments, or the extent to which, if at all, they make any contribution to UNHCR's capacity to fulfil its mandate responsibilities. In another, not unrelated cultural context, Nicholas Morris has remarked on UNHCR's too frequent failure 'to provide others with a timely explanation of its reasoning' for the adoption of particular responses to the dilemmas with which it is faced: Morris, 'Protection Dilemmas', p. 497.

quarters or from its offices around the world. The main task of the 'policy research section' in fact appears to be the in-house production of UNHCR's principal promotional exercise, the biannual *The State of the World's Refugees*.[83]

Mandates and structures, principles and responsibility

Where there is law and principle, so there is strength and the capacity to oppose. Where there are merely policies and guidelines, everything, including protection, is negotiable, and that includes refugees.[84] The value of a mandate (which may of course evolve around its core of certainty) is like that of a constitution: it lies in its opposability, the one to state, the other to government, actors. For UNHCR, its Statute, regularly renewed and endorsed by its parent body, the General Assembly, is its source of authority in refugee matters,[85] even as its effectiveness is conditioned by other elements in the regime of international protection.

The idea that UNHCR had no choice but to remain in settlements that failed to meet internationally agreed criteria and were thereby liable to attack may have been due to a variety of elements, and given the place of UNHCR in the *regime*, it is more than likely that several influential factors had their impact. One among them appears to be a new, institutionalised sense of 'negative responsibility', which certainly seems to underlie the organisation's espousal of a generalised humanitarian agenda as the basis for its operations. The doctrine of 'negative responsibility', namely, the idea that we are as much responsible for what we do, as for what we do not do, for deliberately harming others, as for failing to relieve their suffering, however remote, 'loads everyone,' as J. R. Lucas cogently remarks, 'with unbearable burdens and induces unassuageable feelings of guilt'.[86] While

---

[83] 'Why', a senior government official from a country with limited overseas representation asked the author in 1997, 'can we no longer get from UNHCR the information that we need to do a better protection job? Why can we no longer get information on asylum seekers' countries of origin?'

[84] See J.-P. Hocké, 'Dans la foire humanitaire, le Haut-Commissariat pour les réfugiés perd son âme', *Nouveau Quotidien*, 4 December 1995, generally and quoting Olivier Russbach, *L'ONU contre l'ONU*:

En se plaçant en effet dans la perspective de la création du nouveau droit international, on se met automatiquement sous la dépendance des Etats, seuls à pouvoir signer de nouveaux textes . . . En se plaçant en revanche dans la perspective du Droit existant, on est en mesure de demander le respect d'obligations déjà contractées. La première perspective conduit à une démarche politique où les Etats sont acteurs, la seconde conduit à une démarche juridique où les Etats sont débiteurs d'obligations.

[85] Goodwin-Gill, *Refugee*, pp. 214–20.

[86] J. R. Lucas, *Responsibility* (Clarendon Press, Oxford, 1993), pp. 37–9; on the effect of consequentialism in diluting responsibility, see *ibid.*, pp. 45–8.

it may occasionally spur individuals to unprecedented levels of self-sacrifice, it is generally more likely to result in the dissipation of effort and a corresponding diminution of effectiveness.

Transposed to the institutional context, 'negative responsibility' can be seen to have led UNHCR to embrace every humanitarian operation remotely connected to the issue of displacement, in a vain effort to remedy wrongs that do or might give rise to flight. Given the complexity of causes, however, not to mention their political dimensions and the finite resources available, such engagement is doomed to failure. The feeling that UNHCR is somehow responsible for *not* doing something, anything, is ultimately unproductive; indeed, its engagement in the former Yugoslavia during the conflict, and certainly at the Zaire–Rwanda border, can even be said to have dulled 'the sense of real responsibility that leads to effective action'. With UNHCR's presence on the Zaire–Rwanda border, operational though unlawful, the 'general lack of political will' so frequently castigated by the High Commissioner and others,[87] became simply the lack of no one's will in particular; and the rest is history.

There was no statutory justification for anything but the most basic and 'traditional' UNHCR presence in the former Yugoslavia, that is, a presence in countries of refuge in which protection and assistance were sorely needed. The acceptance of the Secretary-General's request in late 1991[88] and its involvement in so-called preventive protection compromised the statutory injunction linking UNHCR's work to the non-political.

Equally, once it became clear in mid-to-late 1994 that the settlements along the Zaire–Rwanda border were and would remain either militarised bases for armed operations or sources of supplies, including recruits, for such activities, UNHCR had no lawful basis upon which to continue its presence. The servicing of combatants and non-combatants contributed

---

[87] HCR 1993; HCR 1994; and, José-Maria Mendiluce, 'War and Disaster in the Former Yugoslavia: The Limits of Humanitarian Action', *World Refugee Survey – 1994* (US Committee for Refugees, Washington, DC, 1994), pp. 10 and 14. In her 1997 statement, the High Commissioner appears to have identified responsibilities for the location and civilian character of camps, and for the prosecution of war criminals, and so forth, as *exclusively* state responsibilities: HCR 1997. Notwithstanding para. (d) of the General Conclusion on International Protection adopted in 1997 (in which the Executive Committee emphasised 'that refugee protection is primarily the responsibility of States, and that UNHCR's mandated role in this regard cannot substitute for effective action, political will, and full co-operation on the part of States'), one part of the thesis of this chapter is that UNHCR's statutory responsibilities impose important legal constraints on its own freedom of action; another is that 'political will' is as much the business of states, as it is of those organisations which states have created to fulfil particular political purposes (in this case, the provision of international protection to refugees).
[88] See pp. 226–8 above.

to, even if it was not directly responsible for, the decision to neutralise those settlements as threats to the security of Rwanda.[89]

At a more general level, the failure to inform policy with principle can be seen in the approach to the voluntary repatriation and return of refugees, at least in some theatres of operations. Though the solutions to refugee problems (voluntary repatriation, integration in the first country of refuge, resettlement in a third state) may be hierarchically organised to indicate a preference for return to the country of origin, decades of experience provide ample reasons against adopting any *a priori* endorsement of one or other response. Action since 1991, however, the year in which UNHCR predicted a decade of repatriation,[90] seems to have been especially oriented to achieving the return of refugees, above all else. Even before the events in eastern Zaire and Tanzania,[91] UNHCR was promoting return in less than appropriate conditions, and in a less than open and transparent process, as several NGOs have found.[92]

[89] A less dramatic example of the institutional problem can be seen in the March 1997 formulation (by the Division of Operational Support) of the 'UNHCR Comprehensive Policy on Urban Refugees'. Widely criticised for contradicting long-established principles of refugee protection, it was withdrawn, revised and reissued in December 1997. See Steve Edminster, 'UNHCR and Urban Refugees', 18 *Refugee Reports*, 1997, 11; the new policy is contained in an internal and field office memorandum, UNHCR/IOM/90/97/FOM/95/97, 12 December 1997.

[90] HCR 1991; HCR 1993.

[91] On the involvement of UNHCR in the forced returns from Tanzania, see Government of the United Republic of Tanzania/UNHCR, 'Message to All Rwandese Refugees in Tanzania', December 1996, 9 *International Journal of Refugee Law*, 1997, p. 328; Amnesty International, 'Great Lakes Region. Still in Need of Protection: Repatriation, *Refoulement* and the Safety of Refugees and the Internally Displaced', AI Index, AFR 02/09/97, International Secretariat, London, 24 January 1997 (noting also at p. 9 its earlier expressed concern that UNHCR did not underline, before the repatriation began, Tanzania's obligation to screen and examine the cases of any Rwandese who did not want to return); Amnesty International, 'Rwanda. Human Rights Overlooked in Mass Repatriation', AI Index, AFR/47/02/97, International Secretariat, London, 4 January 1997, pp. 7–8; Amnesty International, 'International Co-operation in Forcing Rwandese Refugees Back from Tanzania', AI Index, AFR/02/35/96, 6 December 1996; and Human Rights Watch/Africa, 'Tanzania – Government and UNHCR Must Respect International Law', hrw-news@igc.org, 17 December 1996. On the attacks in eastern Zaire, see Human Rights Watch/Africa and Fédération internationale des ligues des droits de l'homme, 'What Kabila is Hiding', pp. 10 and 16.

[92] Human Rights Watch/Asia and Refugees International, 'Bangladesh/Burma. Rohingya Muslims in Bangladesh: The Search for a Lasting Solution', August 1997, pp. 2 and 11–12; Human Rights Watch/Asia, 'Burma/Thailand. No Safety in Burma, No Sanctuary in Thailand', July 1997 (reporting at p. 18 an instance of repatriation in which the presence of UNHCR's local representative 'was unclear, and UNHCR Bangkok did not make public their objection to the repatriation, even though it appeared to fall far short of the relevant standards'); and Human Rights Watch/Asia, 'Burma: The Rohingya Muslims – Ending a Cycle of Violence?' September 1996, pp. 14–21. See also Human Rights Watch/Asia, 'Protection Needed for Karenni Refugees', hrw-news@igc.org, 3 January 1996, noting also the vulnerability to military attack of camps in Thailand close to the border to which UNHCR was not permitted access.

The return of refugees to their homelands has always been seen as the humanitarian ideal, in which the once displaced take up their lives again in a country restored to peace and security. If ever there was one, the repatriation of refugees, involving questions of change, human rights and cessation of status, is by definition a *protection* exercise, requiring facts to be assessed on the basis of rules and principles, and for steps to ensure both respect for individual choice and security of life and liberty on return.[93] Return, however, seems to have become a political end, to be achieved by whatever means are available and regardless of principle. In this scenario, a purely utilitarian approach to protection prevails, in which its value is exclusively linked to its capacity to produce 'utility', that is, the return of refugees to their country of origin.

While UNHCR has a recognised interest in the fate of refugees returning to their country of origin,[94] a potentially serious conflict of interest arises if it should elect both to 'promote' repatriation on one side of the border, while certifying the absence of risk on the other. Monitoring of the human rights situation is clearly called for, but it should not be UNHCR's responsibility. Reviewing the repatriation to Tanzania in December 1996, Amnesty International discerned a failure by UNHCR to include in its public statements information about human rights violations gathered by the United Nations Human Rights Field Operation for Rwanda (UNHRFOR).[95] Ian Martin, on the other hand, recounts an earlier instance in which UNHCR's own report of violations was 'suppressed' by external interests concerned to develop the repatriation momentum.[96] The politics of the process clearly suggest that UNHCR's protection capacity would be strengthened by disassociation from direct information gathering and analysis, but by close association with independent and impartial monitoring.[97]

[93] Goodwin-Gill, *Refugee*, pp. 270–5; see also James C. Hathaway, 'The Meaning of Repatriation', 9 *International Journal of Refugee Law*, 1997, p. 551; Jens Vedsted-Hansen, 'An Analysis of the Requirements for Repatriation', 9 *International Journal of Refugee Law*, 1997, p. 559; Simon Bagshaw, 'Benchmarks or Deutschmarks? Determining the Criteria for the Repatriation of Refugees to Bosnia and Herzegovina', 9 *International Journal of Refugee Law*, 1997, p. 566; and Saul Takahashi, 'The UNHCR Handbook on Voluntary Repatriation: The Emphasis of Return over Protection', 9 *International Journal of Refugee Law*, 1997, p. 593.
[94] EXCOM Conclusions No. 18 (1980) and No. 40 (1985).
[95] Amnesty International, 'Rwanda: Human Rights Overlooked', p. 17.
[96] Ian Martin, *After Genocide: The United Nations Human Rights Field Operation in Rwanda*, (Papers in the Theory and Practice of Human Rights, No. 20, Human Rights Centre, University of Essex, 1998), p. 10.
[97] Martin records that responsibilities were eventually divided functionally between UNHCR and UNHRFOR, with the former concentrating on assurances in regard to voluntary repatriation, and the latter on localised monitoring of the situation of returnees: *ibid.*, pp. 14–15.

Against these critiques it may be argued that UNHCR should be judged 'on the basis of whether, given the specific constraints faced and options available . . . its actions were justified and principled'.[98] The political realities being what they are, UNHCR has only limited capacity to influence outcomes or to ensure that states fulfil their international obligations. It can also be argued that UNHCR today is merely doing what the international community wants; that billion dollar budgets can only be explained as approval of the direction, as a manifestation of donor desire to keep refugees away from their doors. Spending or not spending money in the Great Lakes region is unlikely to have any effect on extracontinental movements, nevertheless, and other strategic interests were clearly at work. The financial dimension carries weight, however. Apart from a small percentage of administrative costs met from the budget of the General Assembly, UNHCR is entirely dependent on voluntary contributions, and even if not earmarked for specific operations, donations frequently come with the baggage of the donors' agenda.[99] A succession of billion-plus dollar budgets may lead not just to 'agency capture',[100] but to an agency's enslavement, significantly undercutting its capacity for independent or objective thought and action. Contributions voluntarily made can just as easily be voluntarily unmade. Recent events put in question UNHCR's capacity to remain faithful to its primary responsibility; it may be that the range of additional activities now expected of it has so compromised the organisation that the only role left is to provide relief at politically negotiated moments, and subject to another agenda. In this sense, UNHCR can be likened to a country deeply in debt, now so dependent on continuing massive financial support, that rule and principle themselves are threatened with structural adjustment.

[98] Morris, 'Protection Dilemmas', p. 493. Morris also makes the point that the expectations often placed on UNHCR by human rights advocates and others 'are incompatible with the realities that the organization must confront', and that 'the practical achievements for which it should be held accountable can only be the best that was possible in the circumstances': *ibid.*, pp. 498–9.

[99] On donors and their frequently unrealistic expectations and demands, see Nicholas Morris, 'Refugees: Facing Crisis in the 1990s: A Personal View from Within UNHCR', 2 *International Journal of Refugee Law*, 1990, Special Issue, p. 38.

[100] UNHCR's budget topped US$1 billion for the first time in 1992. It has since exceeded that mark every year, primarily because of refugee emergencies in the former Yugoslavia, the Great Lakes region of Africa and elsewhere. The overall 1998 budget is US$1,075.4 million, including a target of US$440 million for the 'general programmes', that is, basic, continuing refugee protection and assistance activities planned and approved in advance (which have remained more or less constant over the last ten years). The target for special programmes in 1998 is US$635.4 million; these include refugee emergency operations, voluntary repatriation and assistance to non-refugees, such as internally displaced people. About 95 per cent of UNHCR's budget is funded by fifteen governments. Regularly updated funding information is available on UNHCR's website: http://www.unhcr.ch

Conclusions

Lessons learned

From each of the instances described above, certain inferences may be drawn. For example, either the applicable principles of international law[101] were brought to the attention of and integrated into the UNHCR senior management policy process; or they were not. If they were, then UNHCR's senior management is accountable for such breaches of organisational principle as resulted; or for having contributed to or facilitated such violations of international law as may then have been committed by states (or possibly also by non-state entities). If the applicable principles of international law, such as the non-refugee and therefore internationally unprotected status of armed cross-border settlements, were not in fact brought to the attention of UNHCR senior management, other inferences also are reasonably open: either the Division of International Protection did not have the knowledge or an opinion on the matter, or it did not have the institutional means (that is, effectively, the authority) to ensure that its views were known and heard and, moreover, that the applicable principles of international law sufficiently controlled the design and implementation of such 'Operations Plans' as resulted.

The last-mentioned explanation seems most plausible, in the light of what is known about UNHCR's present internal organisation. That the institutional problems go deeper still, however, seems clear from recent internal and external performance reviews.

Among the most important practical lessons to emerge from the last five or so years, is that UNHCR should wait for a comprehensive plan of action or solution to emerge from the political consensus of states before it engages in country of origin activities in situations of conflict.[102] Of course, this does not and should not mean inaction, but in the face of international, coerced population displacement, UNHCR's statutory responsibility to solutions requires it to inspire, call for and encourage such a process among the membership of the United Nations, making the best use of the resources at its disposal, including other UN agencies and regional, governmental, inter-governmental and non-governmental mechanisms.

Secondly, while relief and protection may have beneficial effects at the individual level, the notion of 'preventive protection' does not work and is

---

[101] 'Applicable principles of international law' is used here simply as a shorthand substitute for the appropriate rules (for example, 'organisational rules' in UNHCR's Statute; or international obligations, such as *non-refoulement*, or others from the field of human rights and refugee law).   [102] *Cf.* Morris, 'Protection Dilemmas', pp. 495–6.

not worth conceptualising in UNHCR doctrine. UNHCR has no legal authority to 'protect' persons within their own country; there is no treaty, no customary international law, and no *locus standi*. So far as UNHCR purports to 'protect' internally displaced persons or even returnees, it must necessarily rely on consensual arrangements outside the rule of law, strictly so called, and therefore negotiable and renegotiable by states at will. The timely identification of an agency generally competent for and on behalf of internally displaced persons (such as the Office of the Co-ordinator for Humanitarian Affairs, or the International Committee of the Red Cross) will likely be one other crucial factor in rescuing UNHCR's mandate.

Thirdly, an 'in-country' presence on behalf of internally displaced persons is potentially incompatible with UNHCR's primary responsibility to provide international protection to refugees, that is, to those who have fled. The relief that may be due in such politicised and conflict-ridden situations should be left to those organisations better able to maintain independence, neutrality and impartiality.

Future prospects

Protection seems to be fading rapidly from the refugee agenda. UNHCR's embrace of 'humanitarian action' and the willing endorsement of this move by many states, has compromised the agency's mandate responsibility: it is no longer identified primarily as a protection agency, but primarily as an assistance provider.[103] The identity of the refugee is at yet greater risk of being lost in 'situations' and the new pragmatism, which view the refugee no longer as a woman, a man or a child in need of protection, but rather as a unit of flight, a unit of displacement, to be contained and thereafter channelled down whatever humanitarian corridor leads to whatever political end.

The ultimate objective of protection may be solutions, but protection is nevertheless intrinsically important, and not just as a means to an end. The relegation of the Division of International Protection to the sidelines is fundamentally incompatible with the High Commissioner's statutory responsibility to provide international protection to refugees. By driving an organisational wedge between principles and operations, the agency has effectively and institutionally disabled itself from fulfilling the one duty which it was established to serve.

---

[103] Some respondents to recent criticism of UNHCR practice have seen a false dichotomy between protection and assistance (the relationship is in fact long-standing: see the UN debates cited at note 8 p. 222 above).

UNHCR's commitment to its reason for being needs reaffirmation, however, not just in public statements, but in actions, organisational structures and the commitment of state partners in the process. Institutionally, the 'line authority' of the Division of International Protection must be re-established in concrete terms. This does not mean returning to the bureaucratic stranglehold of the past, but it may well mean that every regional bureau and every special operational division or unit should have at least a Deputy Director (Protection), reporting not to some policy-oriented executive office, but to a Director of International Protection with the requisite personal authority (say, at the Deputy High Commissioner level), responsible for the consistent application of protection principles in practice, and at every stage of policy development.

Structures alone, of course, are not enough to ensure either that goals will be achieved, or that policies will be premised upon such primary directives. A culture of protection is also required, and, given the level of institutional changes over the past years, more than structural alterations may be required today. Experience again provides some guidelines. Within its fundamental constitutional framework, a measure of flexibility will always be required if the agency is to respond to the political and humanitarian nuances of successive crises. It is as necessary to ensure that the international response is not dominated by the 'dead hand' of the legalist,[104] as it is to maintain consistency and adherence to principle. A culture of protection is thus not just lawyers' business; on the contrary, while it supposes recognition of an international legal context and a commitment to the principles of the UNHCR Statute,[105] protection is and ought to be the business of everyone. In this regard, it is relevant to recruitment, training and career development throughout the organisation.

External mechanisms to ensure accountability are also needed, both in fiscal terms, and in relation to the mandate of international protection. Article 35 of the 1951 Geneva Convention does not go far enough to secure state compliance, while EXCOM itself is not suited either to the overview of state actions, or to determining UNHCR's accountability to

---

[104] *Cf.* Coles, 'Approaching the Refugee Problem Today', p. 399.

[105] Protection lawyers, of course, will require a much deeper knowledge and experience of international law, including refugee law, human rights law, international humanitarian law, the law and practice of international organisations, and the relationship, across legal cultures, of international law and municipal law. They require a sense of the place of UNHCR in the system of the United Nations, and of states in their relations to each other and to international organisations; as a practical matter, protection lawyers also need a capacity for analysis and evaluation that transcends the frequently constraining tendencies of domestic systems.

mandate.[106] An independent mechanism, perhaps founded initially on a regional basis and competent to monitor and evaluate refugee protection in both their legal and institutional perspectives, may be just what is needed to strengthen international law and the processes of United Nations reform.

'To protect' implies either to provide physical shelter, or to use legal authority to secure the rights and freedom of those at risk. Except within limited circumstances outside the scope of this chapter, the first is generally ruled out. The second option, though, has a long history and a firm legal and institutional base. UNHCR thus has *locus standi* to intervene on behalf of refugees outside their country, and a supportive base of treaties and customary international law. To 'provide international protection' thus means, first, to insist on the fulfilment of international obligations; secondly, to use all available mechanisms for the assurance of protection (municipal law; regional and international supervisory mechanisms; and protest); thirdly, to disengage from, and not to engage in, activities incompatible with international protection standards (the forced return of refugees, and the provision of material assistance in unlawful situations or to persons excluded from refugee status); and, fourthly, actively to promote (but not to drive) the political processes that determine solutions.

It may be that the fading prospect of international protection is more an eclipse than perpetual night. One would be a fool to imagine that you can ever 'do' protection without being pragmatic, or that the practical application of principles never calls for compromise. The *art* of protection resides precisely in the ability to be flexible, while remaining close by, and faithful to, the core of fundamental principles.

Bibliography

Barutciski, Mikhael, 'The Reinforcement of Non-Admission Policies and the Subversion of UNHCR: Displacement and Internal Assistance in Bosnia-Herzegovina', 8 *International Journal of Refugee Law*, 1996, p. 49

Coles, Gervase J. L., 'Approaching the Refugee Problem Today', in *Refugees and International Relations* (ed. Gil Loescher and Laila Monahan, Clarendon Press, Oxford, 1989), p. 373

Edminster, Steve, 'UNHCR and Urban Refugees', 18 *Refugee Reports*, 1997, 11

---

[106] In the conclusions that emerged from its 1997 Refugee Theme Campaign, Amnesty International also noted that 'at the international level, there is no co-ordinated scrutiny or monitoring of refugee protection, and considerations other than human rights often drive refugee policies', and suggested that such 'an independent, impartial mechanism be established', Amnesty International, 'Refugees: Human Rights Have No Borders. Conclusions and Recommendations. 1997 Refugee Theme Campaign', AI Index, ACT 34/08/97, International Secretariat, London, March 1997, pp. 10 and 12.

Frelick, Bill, '"Preventive Protection" and the Right to Seek Asylum', 4 *International Journal of Refugee Law*, 1992, p. 439

Goodwin-Gill, Guy S., 'Different Types of Forced Migration Movements as an International and National Problem', in *The Uprooted: Forced Migration as an International Problem in the Post-War Era* (ed. Göran Rystad, Lund University Press, Lund, 1990)

The Refugee in International Law (2nd edn, Clarendon Press, Oxford, 1996)

Joint Evaluation of Emergency Assistance to Rwanda, *The International Response to Conflict and Genocide: Lessons from the Rwanda Experience* (4 vols., Steering Committee of the Joint Evaluation of Emergency Assistance to Rwanda, Copenhagen, 1996)

Lautze, Sue, Bruce Jones and Mark Duffield, *Strategic Humanitarian Co-ordination in the Great Lakes Region, 1996–1997: An Independent Assessment* (Policy, Information and Advocacy Division, Office for the Co-ordination of Humanitarian Affairs, United Nations, New York, March 1998)

Lucas, J. R., *Responsibility* (Clarendon Press, Oxford, 1993)

Martin, Ian, *After Genocide: The United Nations Human Rights Field Operation in Rwanda* (Papers in the Theory and Practice of Human Rights, No. 20, Human Rights Centre, University of Essex, 1998)

Mooney, Erin D., 'Presence *ergo* Protection? UNPROFOR, UNHCR and ICRC in Croatia and Bosnia and Herzegovina', 7 *International Journal of Refugee Law*, 1995, p. 407

Morris, Nicholas, 'Protection Dilemmas and UNHCR's Response: A Personal View from Within UNHCR', 9 *International Journal of Refugee Law*, 1997, p. 492

'Refugees: Facing Crisis in the 1990s: A Personal View from Within UNHCR', 2 *International Journal of Refugee Law*, 1990, Special Issue, p. 38

Prunier, Gérard, 'La crise rwandaise', 13 *Refugee Survey Quarterly*, 1994, 2 and 3, p. 13.

UNHCR, *Delphi: The Final Report of the Change Management Group*, (UNHCR, Geneva, 1 May 1996)

Writenet UK, 'Burundi: Descent into Chaos or a Manageable Crisis?' 14 *Refugee Survey Quarterly*, 1995, 1 and 2, p.128

Part 3

State responses and individual rights

12   The refugee state and state protection

Daniel Warner[1]

Introduction

'The security of individuals is locked into an unbreakable paradox in which it is partly dependent on, and partly threatened by, the state.'[2]

There has been a growing interest in refugees among certain scholars in the international relations community who have not been traditionally interested in refugee matters.[3] Following on from Hannah Arendt's definition of the relationship between refugees and the modern condition,[4] these authors have analysed in some detail how the situation of the refugee is paradigmatic of the modern condition. These authors, as well as those concerned with human rights, focus on the refugee state or refugees as individuals.

On the other hand, there is an enormous and growing literature by international lawyers and practitioners about the problem of the physical protection of refugees, such as Howard Adelman's concerns with early warning and prevention set out in chapter 14 of this volume. While the first group of writers is often critical of the state and eager to question the concept of state sovereignty and its inherent violence in order to protect individuals, the second group argues that states should be more responsible in respecting their international obligations. In general terms, the first group sees the state as a major problem, the second group sees the state as a major solution.

Is there some form of reconciliation between the two positions? In other words, is there some form of reconciliation between concern for individuals and concern for states? This chapter examines both positions in order to assess the possibility of reconciliation. First, it offers an

---

[1] With all due respect to Friedrich Kratochwil and John G. Ruggie, 'A State of the Art on an Art of the State', 40 *International Organization*, 1986, 4, pp. 139–74. I would like to thank Michael Dillon, Guy Goodwin-Gill and Vera Gowlland for comments on earlier drafts of this paper.

[2] Barry Buzan, *People, States and Fear* (2nd edn, Harvester Wheatsheaf, London, 1991), pp. 363–4.   [3] For example, Michael Dillon, Nicholas Xenos and Nevzat Soguk.

[4] Hannah Arendt, 'We Refugees', 31 *Menorah Journal*, January 1943, pp. 69–77.

overview of how the first group sees the refugee as paradigmatic in the sense of a physical representation of the dislocation of the modern condition, while the second group sees the refugee as an atypical, special category of persons. Following on from this analysis, it traces the relationship between an assessment of the parameters of what it means to be a refugee in terms of the state and the need for protection. Within this analysis is the double problem of the general position of the refugee and the relationship between the refugee and the state.

Refugees and the refugee condition

When Hannah Arendt published her short article entitled 'We Refugees' in 1943,[5] she spoke of refugees in a collective sense. In the article, Arendt described the arrival of the refugees from Europe in the following way:

We lost our home, which means the familiarity of daily life. We lost our occupation, which means the confidence that we are of some use in this world. We lost our language, which means the naturalness of reactions, the simplicity of gestures, the unaffected expression of feelings. We left our relatives in the Polish ghettos and our best friends have been killed in concentration camps, and that means the rupture of our private lives.[6]

That rupture, Arendt argued, created a situation of anomie in which eastern European Jews tried in vain to assimilate to different new surroundings: 'Whatever we do, whatever we pretend to be, we reveal nothing but our insane desire to be changed.'[7] That situation of anomie and unfulfilled assimilation is not limited to Jews; Arendt concluded that '[r]efugees driven from country to country represent the vanguard of their peoples'.[8]

The notion of the refugee as representing the vanguard of their peoples or paradigmatic of the modern condition has been taken up in several different contexts suggested in Arendt's article. Giorgio Agamben, for example, spoke of the refugee as paradigmatic in terms of the dissolution of the nation-state and the 'decomposition of traditional political-legal categories'.[9] Agamben's point, taken from a chapter by Arendt in her book on totalitarianism,[10] is that '[i]n the system of nation-states, the supposed sacred and inalienable rights of man become senseless from the moment when it is no longer possible to configure them as rights of citizens of a State'.[11]

Agamben stressed the distinction between rights of man and rights of

---

[5] *Ibid.*   [6] *Ibid.*, p. 69.   [7] *Ibid.*, p. 75.   [8] *Ibid.*, p. 77.
[9] Giorgio Agamben, 'Au-delà des droits de l'homme', *Libération*, 9 June 1993, p. 8 (as translated by the author).
[10] Hannah Arendt, *The Origins of Totalitarianism* (World Publishing, New York, 1951).
[11] Agamben, 'Au-delà des droits de l'homme'.

citizen because he wanted to show that the rights of man separated from citizenship are inconceivable in a world of nation-states. One must be the citizen of somewhere, according to Agamben, to enjoy one's fullest rights. In that sense, the refugee who is stateless can only be in a temporary situation since citizenship is the only legally politically satisfactory condition. It is only within the state as a proper citizen, according to this argument, that full rights may be enjoyed. Statelessness, in other words, denies the full expression of the reconciliation of the rights of man and the rights of citizens expressed in the French revolution.

Agamben's point is that with the decline of the nation-state, the refugee becomes an embarrassing figure for the international system because the refugee breaks the singular identity of man and citizen and puts into crisis 'the original fiction of sovereignty . . . because he destroys the old trinity state–nation–territory'.[12] Although the rights of man separated from citizen may be implied in the 1948 Universal Declaration of Human Rights,[13] and embodied in various interpretations of human rights instruments, Agamben's reminder of the refugee's position in terms of the distinction between rights of man and rights of citizens shows an enormous gap once the assumption of citizenship is questioned. In most countries, he concluded, there are stable denizens who live in a situation of a- or extra-territoriality exemplifying new constructions of person–citizen responsibility.

However, there is no definitive replacement for responsibility beyond the state with its obligations and the assumed citizenship of each person. No other formulation has arisen other than singular identification of citizenship and man in spite of the problematisation of the trinity state–nation–territory. The state–nation–territory trinity includes the necessary primacy of citizenship, and the situation of the refugee outside the bounds of citizenship merely points to the crumbling of the trinity and hence the crumbling of the person–citizen singularity; that is, Arendt's positive vanguard. For both Arendt and Agamben, the situation of the refugee outside traditional formulations is indicative of new, positive forms of identity politics.

The argument of de-territorialisation of the state and the refugee as the forefront or symbol of that de-territorialisation is very appealing in the sense of the vanguard of new forms of relationships outside traditional identity politics.[14] For, in a sense, it shows how the exceptional condition

---

[12] *Ibid.*

[13] General Assembly Resolution 217 A (III) of 10 December 1948, 42 *American Journal of International Law*, 1949, Supplement 127.

[14] An early expression of the problem of de-territorialisation appears in John Herz, 'Rise and Demise of the Territorial State', 9 *World Politics*, 1957, 4, pp. 473–93. A more recent version would be John Gerard Ruggie, 'Territoriality and Beyond', 47 *International Organization*, 1993, 1, pp. 139–74.

of the refugee outside normal state relations and responsibility becomes more and more common because of the dissolution of state authority. The refugee becomes emblematic of the changing political–legal–territorial–spatial relationships that are evolving. The refugee is symbolic of something new in the sense of something that corresponds to changes in technology and mobility. Nonetheless, the traditional state–territory–citizenship relationship still exists in a dysfunctional manner; it has not been replaced in terms of protection or in terms of reconciling the person–citizen schism. Other descriptions of the symbolic nature of the refugee have been taken up in different ways by Liisa Malkki, Nicholas Xenos and Michael Dillon.[15] All these writers examine the implications of the destruction of the state–nation–territory trinity and it is worth reviewing their arguments to position our immediate concern about the state and protection.

Following several recent anthropologists,[16] Malkki is concerned with exile and other forms of territorial displacement in relation to the imaginative construction of homeland and roots. Her primary focus is the relationship between mobility and origins:

There has emerged a new awareness of the global social fact that now, more than perhaps ever before, people are chronically mobile and routinely displaced, and invent homes and homelands in the absence of territorial, national bases – not *in situ*, but through memories of, and claims on, places that they can or will not longer corporeally inhabit.[17]

For Malkki, the social construction of identity can be separated from a physical reality and follows from the de-territorialisation of spatial relations. Refugees in exile can create an image of identity that is divorced from their current situation and from their place of origin.[18] Malkki's focus on de-territorialisation and social constructs of roots and

---

[15] My own thinking on this subject appeared in 'We Are All Refugees', 4 *International Journal of Refugee Law*, 1993, pp. 365–72. In that article, I was concerned with the difference in categorisation between refugees and non-refugees in the sense of their similar dislocations. Here, I am more interested in the problem of protection and the role of the state as it relates to the situation described in that article.

[16] Indeed, Malkki's fellow anthropologists raise the following question as a key one for anthropological inquiry: 'What does it mean, at the end of the twentieth century, to speak ... of a "native land"? What processes rather than essences are involved in present experiences of cultural identity?': Akhil Gupta and James Ferguson, 'Beyond "Culture": Space, Identity, and the Politics of Difference', 7 *Cultural Anthropology*, 1992, 1, p. 9.

[17] Liisa Malkki, 'National Geographic: The Rooting of Peoples and the Territorialization of National Identity Among Scholars and Refugees', 7 *Cultural Anthropology*, 1992, 1, p. 24.

[18] An interesting investigation of this phenomenon is Finn Stepputat, 'Repatriation and the Politics of Space: The Case of the Mayan Diaspora and Return Movement', 7 *Journal of Refugee Studies*, 1994, 2 and 3, pp. 175–85; and Sidra Ezrahi, 'Our Homeland, The Text ... Our Text, the Homeland: Exile and Homecoming in the Modern Jewish Imagination', 31 *Michigan Quarterly Review*, 1992, 4, pp. 463–97.

origins accentuates Agambem's problematisation of the trinity of state–nation–territory and is a helpful step in conceptualisation beyond classical ties between citizens and territorial states. By focusing on imagined communities, Malkki begins to fill in the space created by the de-territorialisation process.

For our immediate concern with the refugee and states, we shift from this anthropological perspective of the social construction of identity beyond territoriality to the direct political concerns of Xenos and Dillon. While Malkki highlights the social identification of refugees, Xenos and Dillon reveal the political construction of refugees. Xenos is specifically focused on 'the political context of the refugee question'.[19] That is, Xenos is most concerned with refugees being used as pawns in struggles between states, as was the case with the Haitian boat people or the Albanians fleeing to Italy in what he refers to as 'strategic human flows'. The basis of these flows, he maintains, is the development of the nation-state in terms of national identity and the social construction of a people within specific territory, the hyphenating of nation-state within borders. The overarching drive for territorial nation-state expels those who either resist or cannot accommodate those pressures. Where Agamben saw the refugee as destroying the trinity of state–nation–territory, Xenos emphasises that it is the pressure to construct that trinity that causes refugee flows. The refugee does not destroy the trinity for Xenos; rather, the refugee is the victim of the pressures to create the unholy alliance of the trinity or to maintain the trinity in the face of technological advancement and mobility.

Beyond Malkki's de-territorialisation of the social construction of identity, Xenos locates two uprootings within the overall pressures of hyphenating nation-state within borders. The first is the necessity to homogenise groups in order to make them fit into a unified national character: '[T]he French revolution gradually supplanted complex, fragmented, sometimes overlapping local identities in favor of a single, undifferentiated national identity.'[20] The creation of a nation or national identity excludes heterogeneous groupings. The second uprooting is the concept of statelessness, similar to Agamben's separation of person and citizen, in which the absence of citizenship excludes the protection of state-guaranteed rights. In this case, the legal drive for state identity forces out or leaves unprotected those who will not or do not qualify as complete citizens. Without citizenship, one is stateless, and hence unprotected. Only citizens can be protected, mere persons cannot. The first uprooting creates cultural refugees, the second creates legal refugees.

[19] Nicholas Xenos, 'Refugees: The Modern Condition', in *Challenging Boundaries: Global Flows, Territorial Identities* (ed. Michael J. Shapiro and Hayward R. Alker, University of Minnesota Press, Minneapolis, 1996), p. 235.   [20] *Ibid.*, pp. 241–2.

For both, these uprootings entail a lack of rights in a specific sense. One who is pushed outside a nation or state cannot call upon a nation or state to allow that person full expression within the system. Rights can only exist when there is a duty or obligation on some body to protect or help express those rights. As a result of the hyphenating process, the first uprooting excludes the possibility of expressing one's own culture in a particular community; the second forbids having the space in that community within which that culture can be expressed. In sum, the exclusion of the refugee or the exceptional status of the refugee results from the entirety of the hyphenating process. Both uprootings cited by Xenos place the refugee outside the confines of the nation-state, within which traditional norms and rules exist and rights are allowed to be expressed.[21]

Dillon's approach is more philosophical, but perhaps more profoundly political in its general thesis.[22] Dillon argues:

> The advent of the stranger in the form of the refugee emphasises . . . that human being is always in the position of articulating this 'we' without the authorisation of any God, Leader, Party, Nation or State. Indeed, [the refugee] is most often in the position of having to do so despite, or against, the authorisations of any God, Leader, Party, Nation or State. It is in this . . . sense that the refugee is a scandal.[23]

The scandal of the refugee that causes Dillon to react is the situation of being outside, of being 'other' and part of 'otherness'. The 'inter' in international relations, according to Dillon, is that which comes between but which is not part of the nation-state. It is that 'inter', on-the-margins scandal that Dillon wishes to problematise.

For the scandal is not the refugee: the scandal is the marginalisation process that places the refugee outside the national and into the grey zone of the 'inter'. Dillon sees the scandal as the centripetal force pulling the outsider within. In this sense, where Xenos sees the stultifying effort at closure in both the nation and state as moves toward exclusion, Dillon wants to highlight the very 'otherness' of the refugee as being outside of the fundamental ontological determination of international politics and

---

[21] See my critique of this position in 'Voluntary Repatriation and the Meaning of Return to Home: A Critique of Liberal Mathematics', 7 *Journal of Refugee Studies*, 1994, 2 and 3, pp. 160–74. There are several layers of pressure here. Not only is there the pressure for homogeneous nation, homogeneous state and the clear relationship between the two, but there is also an assumption that the homogeneous nation-state will exist on a given territory. That is part of my understanding of simplistic liberal mathematics.

[22] Michael Dillon, 'The Scandal of the Refugee: Some Reflections on the "Inter" of International Relations and Continental Thought' (private paper, copy with the author). See also Michael Dillon, 'The Asylum Seeker and the Stranger: An Other Politics, Hospitality and Justice' (paper presented at the International Studies Association Conference, Chicago, 1995).   [23] Dillon, 'The Scandal', p. 5

its inclusionary pressures.[24] Where Xenos sees exclusion within the uprooting of the hyphenating, Dillon wants us to step back to analyse the entire nature of the political within modernity that underscores the hyphenating processes. Dillon looks beyond the trinity to the larger underpinnings of modernity and the drive to enclose or exclude, and he finds emancipation in the problematisation of the ontology of centripetal inclusion.

To show that emancipation through the refugee, Dillon attacks the fundamental ontology of international politics, positively by saying that the refugee 'effects [a] fundamental destruction of the ontological horizons which constitute the . . . heterogeneous into which, as refugees, these people are precipitated'[25] and, negatively by enquiring: 'If . . . the vernacular political architecture of modern international power commonly produces 1:115 forcibly displaced people globally, one is inclined to ask about the foundations upon which that architecture is itself based.'[26] Dillon eloquently states:

> Neither in nor out – while nonetheless, of course, actually bearing the name of some previous identification, and existing in a carefully defined no-where place within the boundaries of some nation or state, so clearly also undeniably present – s/he brings the very 'inter' of International Relations to the foreground in a disturbing and unusual way, insisting that it become the concentrated focus of attention which it deserves to be.[27]

The position of the refugee as 'inter' is similar to that which strives to de-hyphenate state and nation and de-territorialise while at the same time pushing the limits of, if not exploding, what state and nation mean.

Dillon's argument is against modern politics or the politics of modernity that seeks to inhibit, stifle, enclose and exclude. The refugee is thus not to be pitied as someone without physical protection: the refugee is to be celebrated because he or she is on the margins of the political ontology of modernity that Xenos described in the hyphenation and Dillon in the 'inter'. The liberation of the refugee or the celebration of the recognition of the complexity of human heterogeneity is exactly because the refugee is outside the geographic and/or legal constraints of boundaries and home. Not being protected also means not having to conform; it means not being submitted to the centripetal violence of the nation and the state.[28]

---

[24] I have written about the problem of otherness in 'Levinas, Buber and the Concept of Otherness in International Relations: A Reply to David Campbell', 25 *Millennium: Journal of International Studies*, 1996, 1, pp. 111–28.

[25] Dillon, 'The Scandal', p. 13.   [26] *Ibid.*, pp. 13–14.   [27] *Ibid.*, p. 15.

[28] For Dillon's thoughts on the inherent violence of the state, see *The Political Subject of Violence* (ed. David Campbell and Michael Dillon, Manchester University Press, Manchester, 1993).

The refugee, in this sense, represents the alien or the stranger who is outside of the forces of conformity. In sum, the refugee is celebrated by Dillon because he or she is outside the nation, outside the state and outside the forces that strive to hyphenate the two together on a given territory.

How do we treat those outside any of these three pressures to conform? Can those inside accept those outside? Are they forced to be included somewhere? Can they even be celebrated by being left alone? The very distinction between refugees and others prioritises those inside by categorising a certain group as being outsiders, as being exceptions. The very identification and valorisation of citizenship marks those who are stateless and non-citizens. Refugees are not part of the normal political identification: they have their own special taxonomy such as denizens or refugees-in-orbit. For Dillon, '[t]he advent of the refugee – one whose very own ontological horizons have been devastated; one removed from a world – thereby dramatically exposes and radically disrupts the onto-political horizons not only of the hosts in which they arise, but also of the political Modernity as such'.[29] That, for the first group of writers, is something positive.

The refugee condition and the state

Very briefly, and to stay within our particular topic, it is important to understand the specific role of the state in this understanding of the refugee condition. It is not enough to realise that refugees are outside the normal categorisation, or even that there are pressures to conform in some liberal identity politics. No, there is an argument here that is more powerful and more relevant. For, indeed, Dillon is concerned with the very identification of the political with violence. That is, according to Dillon the politics of modernity is inherently bound up with the violence of exclusion. Different forms of statelessness or refugeehood represent one form of this violence. In this sense, not only is the state violent in Weber's sense of the highest legitimiser of violence,[30] but, according to Dillon, the state is violent by its very act of exclusion and/or refugee creation. The centripetal forces of inclusion are violent forces.

The violence of the state is in its very nature an autonomous, subjective body. The violence is included in the very act of defining those who are

---

[29] Dillon, 'The Scandal', pp. 29–30.
[30] Weber, *Economie et société* (Librarie Plon, Paris, 1971), p. 57, in which Weber says: 'We understand the State as a political enterprise of an institutional nature when and as long as its administrative direction claims with success the legitimate monopoly of physical constraint in the application of rules.' (author's translation).

inside and those who are outside. By being a self-defined sovereign body, the state is necessarily exclusive and hence violent. As Tiyanjana Maluwa notes, citing Ibeanu and Ake in the context of refugee flows in southern Africa:

[I]t is argued that there exist forms of structural violence in the State which not only belie the idea of equal protection of citizens, but also form the deep-seated basis of the refugee problem. Thus, the causes of refugee flights lie in indirect forms of violence exerted through channels that are not immediately visible as violence.[31]

Or, to put it another way, Dillon, in another context, refers to Levinas and the idea of 'responsibility for other' and resisting the hyphenating.[32] In this context, Dillon refers to a different form of relationship, one that denies exclusive subjectivity and autonomy. This is not to say that there will be no demarcations or different forms of relationships, but it does indicate the possibility that there can be other forms of relationships or demarcations that will not be violent in an exclusionary manner. This is not necessarily to call for the withering away of the state. Rather, it is to suggest that the modern state has its own particularities, that there may be other types of relationships that are not autonomous or subjective.

The understanding of violence and its relation to the state presented by Dillon is importantly ambiguous and worth exploring in terms of a conciliation of the two positions we are examining. Dillon and Campbell explain that:

Modern politics . . . regards violence as *both* the practice which constructs the refuge of the sovereign community, and the condition from which the citizens of that community must be protected. Indeed, as violence is set against violence, to account for the establishment of a secure, reflexive self or the production of (inter)national political order, it is first espoused then excoriated, legitimised then disavowed, exposed then concealed.[33]

The state–violence relationship is thus one wherein the violence of the state within its borders allows people within the state to be protected *and* at the same time creates the inter-state tensions which cause the violence between states from which people must be protected. In refugee language, the state is at the same time the root cause of refugee flows and the durable solution for refugees in exile. The state by its very nature is violent and causes uprootings of people for which we seek solutions by looking for state responsibility, protection and resettlement. The conclusion of Dillon, therefore, is that it is only by re-examining the very

---

[31] Tiyanjana Maluwa, 'The Refugee Problem and the Quest for Peace and Security in Africa', 7 *International Journal of Refugee Law*, 1995, p. 666.

[32] Dillon and Campbell, *The Political Subject of Violence*, especially the last section.

[33] Campbell and Dillon, 'The Political and the Ethical', in *The Political Subject of Violence*, pp. 161–2.

foundations of the politics of modernity, including statehood, that we can truly get to the root causes of the condition of the refugee and those who are victims of violence, as well as properly understanding repatriation and resettlement.

This first part of this chapter has moved from the symbolic nature of the condition of the refugee through the de-territorialisation of the nation-state and the important political place on the margins refugees occupy. The final discussion of Michael Dillon's work has postulated an ambiguous relationship between the situation of the refugee and the state. Having surveyed this ambiguous relationship, we are now prepared to see how the state is perceived from a different perspective, and why.

Refugees and protection

Whereas the previous discussion dealing with refugees and the refugee condition cited anthropologists, philosophers, political theorists and other members of the social science academic community, discussions of refugee protection as such are dominated by lawyers and practitioners. These people must deal directly with the paradox of the state as the guarantor of protection and the state as a possible cause for disruption. However, the tools available to the lawyer and practitioner are much different than those available to the social science academic, and the objectives of the reflection are very different as well.

Guy Goodwin-Gill begins his recent edition of his classic work on refugees in international law by attempting to taxonomise the refugee:

The refugee in international law occupies a legal space characterized, on the one hand, by the principle of State sovereignty and the related principles of territorial supremacy and self-preservation; and, on the other hand, by competing humanitarian principles deriving from general international law . . . and from treaty.[34]

In both cases, that of obvious state sovereignty and that of general international law and treaty, the state is the primary actor. The difficulty for the lawyers and the practitioners is to locate the refugee in terms of some state or within some regime generated by general international law or treaty that is based on state compliance.

The process of taxonomising is different from the hyphenating process mentioned in the previous section in that it has the ostensible goal of physical protection. While the previous writers sought to celebrate the 'inter' or outsideness of the refugee in opposition to the violence of the centripetal forces, the lawyers and practitioners seek to include the

---

[34] Guy Goodwin-Gill, *The Refugee in International Law* (2nd edn, Clarendon Press, Oxford, 1996), p. v.

refugee within some regime in order to find solutions to a situation of unprotected marginalisation. The lawyer and practitioner look for state responsibility because they see homeless and uprooted people as being in need, not as those who are in the vanguard of destroying the state–nation–territory trinity. For lawyers and practitioners, the drive to categorise is a positive attempt to include in order to protect.

Within Goodwin-Gill's legal analysis of the regime for refugee protection, the refugee is important precisely because the refugee is an exception; the refugee is outside of some overarching framework. Whereas the previous section sought to illustrate the paradigmatic notion of the refugee condition of outsideness and to celebrate the exceptional position of the refugee beyond violent state constraints, lawyers and practitioners seek to put the refugee inside some type of regime to avoid the violence of the inter. For the lawyers and practitioners, refugees are exceptions, it is crucial to repeat, in the sense that there is no obvious entity to protect them. Whereas the previous section has sought to liberate people from the constraints of state domination if not the violence that is inherent to all states by virtue of inclusionary/exclusionary pressures, the legal refugee regime seeks to protect citizens who have fallen outside the borders of traditional state responsibility. As Goodwin-Gill notes:

Refugee law . . . remains an incomplete legal regime of protection, imperfectly covering what ought to be a situation of exception. It goes some way to alleviate the plight of those affected by breaches of human rights standards or by the collapse of an existing social order in the wake of revolution, civil strife, or aggression; but it is incomplete so far as refugees and asylum seekers may still be denied even temporary refuge or temporary protection, safe return to their homes, or compensation.[35]

They are denied, that is, by states which are not fulfilling their obligations. Goodwin-Gill assumes that if all states were fulfilling all their obligations there would be no exceptions and hence no refugees. International lawyers and practitioners assume that the internal basis of the state system is non-violent and that violent outbreaks are exceptions and hence cause exceptions called refugees. In Dillon's terms, international lawyers try to find solutions to the problem of the inter within the nation-state.

Citizens are protected first by their governments because the primary obligation of states is to protect their citizens.[36] Further, governments are supervised by various treaties and organisations overseeing those treaties to make sure that states fulfil their legal obligations to their citizens. These

---

[35] *Ibid.*, p. v.
[36] The question here of a failed state is an intriguing one: if a state fails to protect its citizens, is it still a state? With a legitimate government?

organisations themselves do not protect citizens; they try to guarantee that states do. Refugees are exceptions only in so far as either their citizenship is in question – that is why statelessness is so important and the determination of citizenship crucial – or the responsible government is no longer capable of, or unwilling to offer, proper protection. The role of the United Nations High Commissioner for Refugees (UNHCR) or the International Organisation for Migration (IOM) is not to create new state obligations in the normal function of states, but rather to see that states function in such a way that citizens will be protected. As Arthur Helton has clearly stated: 'UNHCR's protection responsibility, which is entrusted to it by the international community, makes it distinct among traditional organizations . . . In a fundamental sense, protection means to secure the enjoyment of basic human rights and to meet primary humanitarian needs.'[37] Or, as Gervase Coles wrote: 'Recognition of the full scope of the refugee problem . . . [has] ensured logically that the concept of protection should be that of human rights generally within which the principles peculiar to the particular problem of the refugee should find their proper and integrated place.'[38]

In this sense, the protection of refugees is an extension of human rights protection taken in very specific and exceptional situations. The protection function is normal: it is the situation in which the function must operate that is extraordinary. Basic human rights have not changed. The assumption is that if all states respected their obligations to their citizens in terms of human rights there would be no refugees or refugee flows, which are caused by violations, by exceptions to the rules of proper state behaviour. Therefore, norms dealing with refugees are extensions of the normal obligations of states in extraordinary situations: they are not extraordinary rules.

Refugee protection and the state

Specifically, Goodwin-Gill mentions several state roles or obligations in dealing with refugees in order to make explicit this protection function and state obligations: (i) states must respect the principle of *non-refoulement*; (ii) states have protection obligations with regard to admission and treatment after entry; and (iii) most interesting for our discussion: 'Established rules of international law nevertheless permit the conclusion

---

[37] Arthur Helton, Editorial, 6 *International Journal of Refugee Law*, 1994, pp. 1 and 2.
[38] Gervase J. L. Coles, *Solutions to the Problem of Refugees and the Protection of Refugees: A Background Study*, (prepared for the Round Table on Durable Solutions and the Protection of Refugees convened by UNHCR in conjunction with the International Institute of Humanitarian Law, 1989), p. 241.

that States are bound by a general principle not to create refugee outflows and to co-operate with other States in the resolution of such problems as they emerge.'[39]

What does this mean? In terms of our previous discussion, it is obvious that there is a school of thought that believes that states are inherently violent and naturally cause exclusion. Goodwin-Gill recognises this to some extent when he says that: 'even if at a somewhat high level of generality, States now owe to the international community the duty to accord to their nationals a certain standard of treatment in the matter of human rights'.[40] This would indicate that states have not always recognised this obligation.

The problem we are now confronting is the nature of the exceptionalism of the refugee situation. Is the refugee situation exceptional because the refugee is merely outside some state responsibility? Or, and this is what we are implying, is the refugee situation exceptional because of the de-territorialisation of the trinity, the inherent violence of the state, and the incapacity of all states to fulfil their human rights obligations consistently? Without entering into a complicated examination of this situation, it seems that a part of all three is correct. That is, we are witnessing a technological mobility in that certain aspects of state authority and territoriality are certainly changing. In addition, we are also seeing more and more failed states that are unable or unwilling to carry out the very basic duties of government. Finally, we are witnessing states wherein obvious human rights violations are causing refugee flows. This is a somewhat regressive form of Dillon's position, but I am trying to be as reconciliatory as possible between the two groups in order to make a final point.

The final point, and in effect the reconciliation between the two groups, is that the fundamental question of the role of the state and state responsibility for refugee flows and refugee protection is a very crucial question. For, if we see the devolution of state authority and question the role of the state in terms of violence causing outflows or internal displacements, then we should reconsider many of the durable solutions for refugees that are being put forward. James Hathaway has tried to elaborate an ambitious proposal for reorienting the refugee regime.[41] One of the interesting aspects of this proposal is its attempt to move away from state-centric solutions in several situations. In recognising the failures of many states to fulfil their obligations and the limitations of intergovernmental organisations, Hathaway sought to introduce a supranational protective body. Indeed, Hathaway, like other progressive international lawyers, is

[39] Goodwin-Gill, *The Refugee*, p. vi.   [40] *Ibid.*, p. vii.
[41] James Hathaway, 'Reconceiving Refugee Law as Human Rights Protection', 4 *Journal of Refugee Studies*, 1991, 2, pp. 113–31.

frustrated by the state-centric bias of traditional refugee solutions as practitioners in the field are often hindered by the recognition that governments remain the primary actors when in fact the very governments they
have to deal with are often the main causes of the problem.

Is there any alternative? Hathaway's original proposal for a supranational supervisory organisation is unacceptable at this moment in history.
As with many situations in international organisation today, we seem to be
in a grey zone wherein the traditional solutions based on the trinity are
incapable of dealing with complex movements. Indeed, I have used the
writings of Xenos and Dillon to try to force reflection on the inherent limitations of state responses to refugee flows. At the end of a presentation of
my paper on repatriation at Oxford in 1994,[42] I stated to a UNHCR
official that the policy implication of my paper was that, once the refugees
return home, they go through as much a process of habilitation as those
newly arriving in the country. Taking that idea one step further, on the
basis of these observations in terms of repatriation, I would say that the
problem of repatriation or even resettlement needs greater consideration.
If internal violence has been recognised as the cause of refugee flows and
UNHCR has become more attentive to preventive diplomacy in the
country of origin, perhaps it is time to see how the organisation of states
and their bases of authority in hyphenating may also be part of the violence that causes movements. In this sense, organisations such as
UNHCR must be more attentive to those on the margins to recognise the
enormous forces that underlie stability within a country, and the complexity of heterogeneous forms of democracy that de-hyphenate and permit a
responsiveness to 'other' that is beyond legal obligation. Where refugees
resettle or return to is not merely a question of stability. It is not enough to
say that once a refugee returns home the country of origin is now responsible for protection. That responsibility must be more than legal.

It is within a positive sense of responsiveness to 'other' that the cause of
refugee flows can be stemmed and the successful repatriation or resettlement of refugees will occur. What it is within a country that causes violence to some is the same form of politics that denies entry to others.
Dillon's indictment of the politics of modernity and the rigidity of the
autonomous state is recognisable in Goodwin-Gill's sensitivity to the fact
that '[e]stablished rules of international law nevertheless permit the conclusion that States are bound by a general principle not to create refugee
outflows and to co-operate with other States in the resolution of such
problems as they emerge'.[43] In this sense, responsible states are not the
autonomous, subjective selves implied by Xenos and Dillon.

[42] Warner, 'Voluntary Repatriation and the Meaning of Return to Home'.
[43] Goodwin-Gill, *The Refugee*, p. vi.

What does it mean, however, for a state to be responsible? The refugee represents the vanguard in both a positive and negative answer to this question. It is by examining the root causes of refugee flows and the possibilities for return or resettlement that answers may begin to appear. Dillon and the first group of writers push us to reflect on the role of the state and the nature of protection. The legal regime of state responsibility is far too facile an answer. For example, to say that State X is responsible once the refugee returns home is unacceptable. Most states are legally responsible for many aspects of their behaviour including human rights violations and *non-refoulement*: they have signed the 1951 Convention Relating to the Status of Refugees.[44] But very few are responsive in the larger sense of responding to the needs of people, including their own citizens.[45] In this sense, Chaloka Beyani, an international lawyer, recognises that 'a general, or even specific, rendition of State responsibility in the context of forcible flows of populations is unhelpful where the root causes lie in the collapse of normal political processes in given States.'[46] It is thus the reconciliation between responsiveness and legal responsibility that must be examined.

Beyani tries to do this in recognising the importance and limitations of legal responsibility. He agrees that '[t]he theory of State responsibility rests on a simplistic but complex practical proposition. It is that every State must be held responsible for the performance of its international obligations under the rules of international law, whether such rules derive from custom, treaty, or other sources of international law.'[47] However, he then goes on to qualify this by noting that there are limits to using state responsibility: 'Resort to State Responsibility as a means of preventing and resolving the problem of forced displacement of populations is an innovative and challenging prospect . . . However, the international legal enforcement machinery is still developing, as are the rules of State responsibility.'[48]

Beyani's limited optimism about or focus on the prospects for improving legal enforcement, be it through human rights instruments or state responsibility, is a function of his training as an international lawyer. What this chapter suggests is that greater sensitivity to the area between responsiveness and responsibility, some form of reconciliation between the first group of writers and the lawyers and practitioners, will enhance the protection of refugees and the situation of refugeehood. It is only by being

[44] 189 UNTS 137.

[45] For more on the difference between responsibility and responsiveness, see my *An Ethic of Responsibility in International Relations* (Lynne Rienner, Boulder, CO, 1991), pp. 96–100.

[46] Chaloka Beyani, 'State Responsibility for the Prevention and Resolution of Forced Population Displacements in International Law', 7 *International Journal of Refugee Law*, July 1995, Special Issue, p. 130.   [47] *Ibid.*, p. 132.   [48] *Ibid.*, p. 147.

sensitive to both sets of concerns presented that there can be a space created, or a space maintained, such that demarcations are not marginalisations, and that centripetal forces are repelled and the 'inter' collapsed. Looking at only one group of concerns such as individual human rights or state responsibility is necessary but not sufficient for this enterprise. For, finally, those who are unresponsive are also irresponsible and *vice versa*.

Bibliography

Agamben, Giorgio, 'Au-delà des droits de l'homme', *Libération*, 9 June 1993, p. 8
Arendt, Hannah, 'We Refugees', 31 *Menorah Journal*, January 1943, pp. 69–77
Beyani, Chaloka, 'State Responsibility for the Prevention and Resolution of Forced Population Displacements in International Law', 7 *International Journal of Refugee Law*, July 1995, Special Issue, p. 130
Campbell, David and Michael Dillon (eds.), *The Political Subject of Violence* (Manchester University Press, Manchester, 1993)
Dillon, Michael, 'The Scandal of the Refugee: Some Reflections on the "Inter" of International Relations and Continental Thought' (private paper, copy with the author)
    'The Asylum Seeker and the Stranger: An Other Politics, Hospitality and Justice' (paper presented at the International Studies Association Conference, Chicago, 1995)
Ezrahi, Sidra, 'Our Homeland, The Text . . . Our Text, the Homeland: Exile and Homecoming in the Modern Jewish Imagination', 31 *Michigan Quarterly Review*, 4, 1992, pp. 463–97
Goodwin-Gill, Guy, *The Refugee in International Law* (2nd edn, Clarendon Press Oxford, 1996)
Hathaway, James, 'Reconceiving Refugee Law as Human Rights Protection', 4 *Journal of Refugee Studies*, 1991, 2, pp. 113–31
Malkki, Liisa, 'National Geographic: The Rooting of Peoples and the Territorialization of National Identity Among Scholars and Refugees', 7 *Cultural Anthropology*, 1992, 1, p. 24
Ruggie, John Gerard, 'Territoriality and Beyond', 47 *International Organization*, 1993, 1, pp. 139–74
Xenos, Nicholas, 'Refugees: The Modern Condition', in *Challenging Boundaries: Global Flows, Territorial Identities* (ed. Michael J. Shapiro and Hayward R. Alker, University of Minnesota Press, Minneapolis, 1996), p. 235

13 Non-admission policies and the right to protection: refugees' choice versus states' exclusion?

Jens Vedsted-Hansen

Over the last couple of decades, states have developed a variety of practices and corresponding legal concepts which, directly or indirectly, restrict the possibility for refugees to choose their country of asylum, and even undermine any right to seek protection at all. This chapter examines the different presumptions and concepts behind these developments in an effort to find the appropriate balance between a state's sovereign right to admit whom it chooses to its territory and the refugee's right to obtain international protection. It looks at state policies of non-admission and other mechanisms adopted by states to reduce refugees' choices.

In particular, it assesses whether there is a right for refugees to choose their country of asylum either under the 1951 Geneva Convention Relating to the Status of Refugees[1] or under other sources of international law. This analysis relates especially to the 'safe third country' and 'first country of asylum' policies developed primarily in western Europe, as states have sought to control the irregular movement of people across borders. It reveals a wide divergence of views as to the question of refugees' choices when seeking asylum and concludes that the combination of refugee law and general human rights law challenges contemporary trends in Europe, as a result of which the restriction of refugees' choices has failed to secure access to asylum procedures or effective implementation of internationally recognised protection standards.

Non-admission and non-arrival

The preferred solution for an increasing number of states is to prevent refugees and asylum seekers from ever arriving at their borders, thus keeping asylum seekers 'from the procedural door'.[2] *Non-arrival* policies have evolved notwithstanding the general recognition, as a matter of prin-

---

[1] 189 UNTS 137.
[2] Guy S. Goodwin-Gill, *The Refugee in International Law* (2nd edn, Clarendon, Oxford, 1996), p. 333.

269

ciple, of the importance of access to fair and efficient asylum procedures. Such policies are regularly pursued by means of visa requirements, and the enforcement of those requirements by carrier sanctions, as well as by other forms of pre-arrival screening or deterrence. As often observed, this form of non-admission may result in the containment of potential refugees in their countries of origin, or in *refoulement* from highly unsafe countries of first arrival.

Another policy mechanism aims to prevent asylum seekers from moving on once they have arrived in a country which may be expected to protect them, thereby more or less effectively restricting their choice of asylum country. While forming part of the overall scheme of policies of non-admission or *non-entrée*,[3] the introduction of 'safe third country' practices has often been justified by asserting that one, and only one, single state should be responsible for the examination of an asylum application.[4] 'Safe third country' grounds for refusing access to asylum procedures tend, however, to be based on a mere *presumption* that the relevant third country will offer protection to refugees.

In this chapter I classify the different approaches taken by states with regard to the latter form of non-admission. The basis and legitimacy under international law for states' refusal of access to their territory and asylum procedures are discussed; correspondingly, the legal basis and various aspects of a *refugee's right* to choose her or his country of asylum are examined. Resulting from this analysis, the nature of any right of choice emerges, as well as the existence of major exceptions or restrictions to such a right. The changing notion of 'asylum country' appears to be an important legal feature of this process, the possible result of which may contribute to threatening the effectiveness of international refugee protection, along with the adoption of increasingly vaguely defined 'safe third country' practices.

Mechanisms reducing refugees' choices

Domestic policies and practices in Europe concerning 'safe third country' issues might be more adequately described by a scale, or even a system of co-ordinates allowing for the combination of substantive and

---

[3] *Cf.* James C. Hathaway, 'The Emerging Politics of *Non-Entrée*', *Refugees*, 1992, 91, p. 40.

[4] Binding obligations based on this principle have been laid down in article 3 of the Dublin Convention of 15 June 1990 Determining the State Responsible for Examining Applications for Asylum Lodged in One of the Member States of the European Communities (30 ILM, 1991, p. 425), and article 29 of the Schengen Convention of 19 June 1990 on the Implementation of the Schengen Agreement of 14 June 1985 . . . Relating to the Gradual Abolition of Controls at Their Common Borders (30 ILM, 1991, p. 84). For a more detailed analysis of these issues see Part 4 of this volume.

procedural elements of decision-making. For the purpose of this analysis, however, it may suffice to place the mechanisms employed by states in order to reduce or eliminate asylum seekers' choice of country of asylum (or, as it may appear, country of procedure) into three categories, characterised by specific legal tenets. All of the three exclusionary mechanisms mentioned below are based on the *assumption of protection elsewhere*; what distinguishes them is the quality of such protection, the legal basis of the assumption, and the practical effects of the exclusion of individual asylum seekers.

Exclusion from refugee status

Article 1E of the Geneva Convention reads:

This Convention shall not apply to a person who is recognized by the competent authorities of the country in which he has taken residence as having the rights and obligations which are attached to the possession of the nationality of that country.

This provision is the only direct basis under the Convention for limiting the right of refugees to choose their country of asylum. Strictly speaking, it does not even affect the right of actual refugees, in so far as the very essence of the provision is to exclude the persons concerned from Convention refugee status; as a result of this definitional provision they are not, or are no longer, *refugees* under the Convention. Furthermore, the operation of this provision will frequently be based on the ex-refugee's own *previous choice*, as it refers to the person's status in the country in which he has already taken residence. This is why article 1E may adequately be referred to as a *cessation* clause rather than, as is normally the case, an exclusion clause.[5]

In spite of these characteristics, I shall examine further the specific elements of article 1E later in the chapter.[6] This may appear pertinent to the discussion due to the fact that this article is illustrative of the Convention's expectations of refugees' conduct and situation in order to remain within the scope of international protection.

Exclusion from the granting of asylum

More precisely, this refers to refusal of protection in the form of territorial asylum because the refugee concerned has already obtained, or will be entitled to, effective protection elsewhere.

[5] See James C. Hathaway, *The Law of Refugee Status* (Butterworths, Toronto, 1991), pp. 189 and 205; *cf.* UNHCR, *Handbook on Procedures and Criteria for Determining Refugee Status* (Geneva, 1979, re-edited 1992), paras. 144–6.   [6] See pp. 276–7 below.

Exclusion from asylum under this category can be described as a *substantive* decision, referring the refugee to a country of first asylum on the premise that the individual person is in need of international protection, *and* that such protection is actually available in that other country. Hence, this type of decision presupposes a determination on the merits both of the applicant's refugee status, and of the individual circumstances relating to the protection foreseen in the first asylum country. The line of reasoning anticipated under this approach can be demonstrated by quoting section 7(3) of the Danish Aliens Act, which states:

> The issue of a residence permit may be refused if the alien has *already obtained protection* in another country or if, because of a prolonged stay or close relatives living there or other like circumstances, the alien has closer ties with another country where he must be deemed to be *able to obtain protection*. (emphasis added)

Refusal of asylum on these grounds has been a feature of policies adopted by a number of traditional asylum countries for several years. It has also gained some recognition in standards of international law connected to the Geneva Convention, as shown below.[7]

Exclusion from asylum procedures

This *procedural* form of exclusion refers to refusal of access to refugee status determination procedures on grounds of a presumption that protection could be obtained elsewhere. This is of course the cornerstone of recent 'safe third country' practices which are based on the assumption that another state should undertake the examination of the asylum application, and is likely to do so. Under this form of exclusion the state of incidental or preferred arrival neither considers the individual need for protection in substance nor takes the individual asylum seeker's possible choice of asylum country into account. Exclusion from the asylum procedure is often linked to formal *non-admission* to the territory; in practice, however, the removal of the inadmissible asylum seeker often takes place only after a period of physical presence in the country of destination, for instance in waiting zones, detention centres or other locations designed for aliens in an irregular position.[8]

Formal exclusion from procedures can most appropriately be analysed in connection with the substantive decisions mentioned above.[9] In recent European non-admission policies, the formal or procedural form of exclusion has generally taken over from the latter. These two types of

[7] See pp. 279–82 below.
[8] See examples of such practices among the case studies in European Council on Refugees and Exiles, *'Safe Third Countries': Myths and Realities* (ECRE, London, 1995), Appendix B.   [9] See pp. 271–2 above.

'protection elsewhere' clauses will be discussed in more detail in the sections which follow.

State obligations and the individual right to protection

In order to establish the legal basis and limits of the disputed right of refugees to choose their country of asylum, it may be appropriate to set out from the corresponding obligations of states. In other words, what commitments have states made under international law, *vis-à-vis* asylum seekers in general, and, hence, to what degree are states bound to accommodate the preferences of the individual asylum seeker as to which country should offer protection, if and when the refugee status of the individual has been determined?

Even though the concept of *state sovereignty* is being constantly challenged and has been remarkably in decline during the second half of this century, it still prevails as such, in theory as well as in practice. Indeed, controlling the entry and residence of non-citizens in individual states remains among the core features of sovereignty. As has frequently been noted, this was clearly expressed, not only at the drafting of the 1948 Universal Declaration of Human Rights,[10] but also at the time of the adoption of the Geneva Convention. It was confirmed in connection with the 1977 Conference on the Draft Convention on Territorial Asylum which primarily failed due to the preoccupation of states with safeguarding their sovereign right to grant asylum.[11]

Developments in recent years have not rendered the concept of sovereignty obsolete. Resistance similar to that regarding a right to asylum has also occurred in respect of new conventions aiming at the protection of migrant workers and their families; this has led to very vague provisions concerning issues of entry and residence rights, or to a clear failure of signatures and ratifications by states.[12] Perhaps ironically, however, some of the most far-reaching *restrictions of sovereignty* in this context have occurred in the 1990 Dublin and Schengen Conventions. Both instruments oblige states parties in certain circumstances to admit non-citizens

---

[10] 42 *American Journal of International Law*, 1949, Supplement 127.
[11] Hathaway, *The Law of Refugee Status*, pp. 13*ff.*; Goodwin-Gill, *The Refugee in International Law*, pp. 179*ff.*
[12] As remarkable examples, see the 1975 International Labour Organisation (ILO) Convention No. 143 Concerning Migrations in Abusive Conditions and the Promotion of Equality of Opportunity and Treatment of Migrant Workers, and the 1990 UN Convention on the Protection of the Rights of All Migrant Workers and Members of Their Families. The former had only eighteen parties as at 20 January 1999 and entered into force on 19 December 1978. The latter had only ten parties as of 4 February 1999 and requires twenty ratifications to enter into force.

with a view to examining their request for asylum and eventually potentially granting asylum, while simultaneously limiting the right of asylum
seekers to choose their country of asylum and procedure.[13]

Hence, the sovereign right of states to control the entry of non-citizens
cannot be exercised in an unfettered manner. Rather, on the basis of sovereignty, states have undertaken international obligations which increasingly erode their discretionary powers to exclude non-citizens. While the
personal and territorial scope of *non-refoulement* may still be subject to
some debate, it is beyond doubt that this basic principle of human rights
and refugee law does restrict the exercise by states of their sovereign competence to control the entry and residence of aliens.[14]

It is probably at the point of intersection between the two principles
discussed above that we can identify the legal basis for states overriding a
refugee's preference for seeking protection in a particular country. It has
been said that what is left of state sovereignty in the field of asylum is the
possibility of indicating with respect to the individual asylum seeker that
another country is considered more appropriate to provide protection for
that person. The option of referring an asylum seeker to such a 'country
of first asylum' is thus the scope of action left between *state sovereignty* and
the principle of *non-refoulement*.[15] Lengthy discussions have been conducted as to which prerequisites have to be fulfilled for a third country to
be deemed a 'safe country' or an adequate 'country of first asylum'; some
indications of a possible answer will be given on the basis of the following
analysis.[16]

One issue, closely connected to the problem of a state's right to refer an
asylum seeker to another state, is whether the individual asylum seeker
has a right to have the application examined on the merits. Such a right
may be derived from international customary law based on article 14 of
the Universal Declaration of Human Rights, which provides for a right to
seek asylum. A more solid basis for the individual right to have an asylum
application examined, however, can possibly be found in the *non-refoule-*

[13] See, in particular, articles 3(7) and 10(1) of the Dublin Convention, and articles 31(3) and 33(1) of the Schengen Convention.

[14] *Cf.* Hathaway, *The Law of Refugee Status*, pp. 24–7; Goodwin-Gill, *The Refugee in International Law*, pp. 136–7 and 167–71; and UNHCR, *Note on International Protection*, 1994, UN Doc. A/AC.96/830, paras. 30 and 38–40. On extra-territorial effects of the prohibition of torture, see Terje Einarsen, 'The European Convention on Human Rights and the Notion of an Implied Right to *de facto* Asylum', 2 *International Journal of Refugee Law*, 1990, pp. 361–89 at pp. 365–6; Walter Suntinger, 'The Principle of *Non-Refoulement*: Looking Rather to Geneva than to Strasbourg?', 49 *Austrian Journal of Public and International Law*, 1995, pp. 203–25 at pp. 206–8.

[15] Morten Kjærum, 'The Concept of Country of First Asylum', 4 *International Journal of Refugee Law*, 1992, pp. 514–15.

[16] See in particular pp. 279–84 below.

ment provision in article 33 of the Geneva Convention.[17] In addition to relying on an obligation bindingly undertaken by states party to the Convention, this line of reasoning also links the individual right to the state's obligation to protect basic human rights in the exercise of its jurisdiction. If a state is to be sure *not* to violate article 33 by returning an asylum seeker from its border or territory, it will necessarily have to examine whether the person would be at risk of persecution in the event of being returned, as prohibited by article 33. This position is valid for direct return to persecution in the country of origin, as well as indirect return in the form of deportation to a country from which there might be a risk of further deportation to a territory where there is a danger of persecution.[18]

It thus follows that, in order to avoid contravening, or being in danger of contravening, the principle of *non-refoulement*, the state in which the asylum seeker has sought asylum will have to identify whether the individual might be a refugee as defined in article 1 of the Geneva Convention. Only by examining the application can the state ascertain that an eventual decision to return the individual will not result in *refoulement*. By reference to the principle that recognition of refugee status is declaratory, not constitutive, this conclusion can be formulated in the sense that asylum applicants enjoy *presumptive refugee status*. Thus, the declaratory nature of the recognition of refugee status implies that an asylum seeker has the same rights as a refugee unless and until his or her non-refugee status has been established.[19]

The latter assumption needs to be qualified, as far as applicants are concerned whose status is in the process of being determined.[20] In ordinary circumstances where asylum applications are being processed in good faith by the relevant state, the authorities may retain the right to

---

[17] Article 33(1) states:

> No Contracting State shall expel or return ('*refouler*') a refugee in any manner whatsoever to the frontiers of territories where his life or freedom would be threatened on account of his race, religion, nationality, membership of a particular social group or political opinion.

[18] *Cf.* Reinhard Marx, '*Non-Refoulement*, Access to Procedures, and Responsibility for Determining Refugee Claims', 7 *International Journal of Refugee Law*, 1995, p. 393.

[19] *Ibid.*, p. 403; and Kjærum, 'The Concept of Country of First Asylum', p. 515. See also Patricia Hyndman, 'The 1951 Convention and its Implications for Procedural Questions', 6 *International Journal of Refugee Law*, 1994, p. 246; James C. Hathaway and John A. Dent, *Refugee Rights: Report on a Comparative Survey* (York Lanes Press, Toronto, 1995), pp. 7 and 21–2; and UNHCR, *Note on International Protection*, 1993, UN Doc. A/AC.96/815, para. 11.

[20] Thus, the following remarks do not cover instances of extraordinarily *protracted* asylum procedures, be it in individual cases or due to *suspension* of the processing of certain types of cases.

limit the applicants' enjoyment of certain rights according to the Geneva Convention. This seems to follow from the wording of a number of provisions defining such rights, referring to refugees 'lawfully resident', 'lawfully staying', etc. In the circumstances as just described, the still-undeclared refugee will not be fully entitled to all refugee rights immediately. The general obligation to respect the *non-refoulement* principle still persists, however. By its very nature, as well as by the way article 33 is phrased, this particular right is clearly not dependent on a prior formal recognition of the individual's refugee status. As mentioned above, the unconditional compliance with this principle is indispensable in order for states to avoid the risk of violating article 33 by returning a person who, after further examination of the circumstances of the case, might be identified as a refugee.

While the right to have an asylum application examined in substance is beyond doubt, the questions then remain: What is the legal basis of the asylum applicant's right to choose the country of asylum? To what extent are states, in their compliance with the obligations described above, bound to respect the choice of the individual claimant as to where she or he should seek and enjoy asylum? Conversely, to what extent do these state obligations allow for the restriction of an applicant's choice? Further, in setting up such restrictions, can one state relieve itself of its obligations by shifting them to another state?

A right under the Convention to choose the country of asylum?

As mentioned above, article 1E of the Geneva Convention provides for the exclusion from refugee status of persons who have been recognised as having the rights and obligations of a national of the country of their residence. The resident status foreseen in article 1E is often referred to as '*de facto* nationality'. It thus follows that formal naturalisation is not required, but enjoyment of the full scope of basic citizens' rights in the host country must be guaranteed *de facto*.[21]

By its very nature article 1E restricts the right of a refugee to choose the country of asylum, in so far as it simply brings the refugee status, and the protection inherent in such status, to an end in situations where the requisite protection has already been obtained in a country of previous residence. On the other hand, the application of the provision is obviously restricted to a very narrow class of (persons who would otherwise be) refugees. First, this is because article 1E only becomes relevant if the

---

[21] *Cf.* UNHCR, *Handbook*, para. 145; and Hathaway, *The Law of Refugee Status*, p. 212.

asylum seeker has already taken *residence* in another country.[22] Secondly, the applicability is restricted by the narrow criteria which must be fulfilled before the article can be invoked by a second host state as the basis for refusing asylum on the grounds that the applicant is no longer a refugee.

Beyond the requirement that the individual has taken residence in another country, it also has to be established that this entails basic *entitlements* similar to those deriving from nationality of that country. By definition, the latter prerequisite must be considered 'qualitatively distinct from even long-term residence in a state'.[23] The most essential further protection, compared to mere actual residence in a state, is the right to (re-)enter and the unconditional protection against expulsion or deportation from the previous country of asylum.[24] There seems to be general agreement on the minimum condition that such rights as are granted to '*de facto* nationals' must be at least on the same level as those protected under the Geneva Convention, in order to bring article 1E into operation.[25] Yet there would be persuasive legal reasons in favour of requiring an even higher level of protection, in particular as far as expulsion and extradition are concerned.

Article 1E is not the only provision of the Geneva Convention which may have some bearing on the right of asylum applicants to choose their country of asylum or, as is more and more frequently the issue at stake, their country of asylum procedure. Most importantly, it has been suggested that article 31[26] might be interpreted so as to imply that states have a right to refuse asylum to an applicant not arriving *directly* from the country of origin. Rather, if this provision is seen as pertinent to the question of 'direct flight', it indicates that the asylum seeker has to arrive directly from a territory where she or he was at risk of persecution *or*, at least, not guaranteed sufficient protection.[27]

---

[22] Exactly for this reason the provision can be more adequately described as a *cessation* clause than as an exclusion clause, in spite of its wording; see p. 271 above.

[23] Hathaway, *The Law of Refugee Status*, pp. 212–13.

[24] *Cf.* UNHCR, *Handbook*, para. 145; Hathaway, *The Law of Refugee Status*, p. 213; and Goodwin-Gill, *The Refugee in International Law*, pp. 94–5.

[25] *Cf.* Atle Grahl-Madsen, *The Status of Refugees in International Law* (A. W. Sijthoff, Leyden, 1966), vol. I, p. 270.

[26] Article 31(1) states:

The Contracting States shall not impose penalties, on account of their illegal entry or presence, on refugees who, coming directly from a territory where their life or freedom was threatened in the sense of article 1, enter or are present in their territory without authorization, provided they present themselves without delay to the authorities and show good cause for their illegal entry or presence.

[27] *Cf.* Kjærum, 'The Concept of Country of First Asylum', p. 515; and Goodwin-Gill, *The Refugee in International Law*, pp. 90 and 152. See also UNHCR, *Background Note on the Safe Country Concept and Refugee Status*, submitted to the Sub-Committee of the Whole

In my view, however, article 31 cannot adequately be construed so as to settle the country of first asylum issue as such, or the corresponding question of the applicant's right to choose his or her asylum country. The provision does refer to refugees 'coming directly from a territory where their life or freedom was threatened in the sense of article 1', but it is very specific about the legal context to which this 'direct arrival' requirement applies. That is, it refers to the scope of protection against *penalisation* for illegal entry or presence.[28] It would be conceivable for a state to punish an asylum seeker for illegal entry, and nonetheless undertake a commitment to protect that person as a refugee in accordance with the rest of the Convention scheme. While article 31 does not *per se* establish any requirement of 'direct arrival' or 'direct flight', the circumstances resulting in non-culpability for illegal entry may, of course, provide some evidence as to whether *adequate protection* could have been obtained elsewhere. Such requirements should, however, preferably be decided on another and more precise legal basis.

Article 33 of the Geneva Convention clearly provides a more appropriate basis for solving the problem of individual choice, as this article circumscribes states' possibilities to return refugees and asylum seekers to another country. The wide personal scope of the *non-refoulement* principle, which includes asylum applicants as well as recognised refugees, follows from the legal reasoning described above.[29] The questions relating to the territorial scope of article 33 have been settled by way of general recognition that the *non-refoulement* principle applies not only in the actual territory of states, but also at their borders, as well as beyond their borders.[30]

A third question is probably more important in the context of the present discussion. To what extent does the provision on *non-refoulement* imply 'direct flight' so as to limit the prohibition of deportation to *direct*

footnote 27 (*cont.*)
on International Protection, 26 July 1991, recognising with reference to article 31(1) that the 'safe country of asylum' concept has 'some basis in the phraseology of the Convention, where the Convention requires direct arrival from territories where life/freedom is threatened before a particular provision can apply': UN Doc. EC/SCP/68, para. 12. A slightly different approach was taken by UNHCR in its *Note on International Protec*tion, 1990, which states: 'Not only is this ["country of first asylum"] principle not a consideration necessarily to be taken into account under the definition, it is in itself too ill-defined while concepts such as "safe country" or "transit country" lack satisfactory definition.': UN Doc. A/AC.96/750, para. 18.

[28] *Cf.* Rosemary Byrne and Andrew Shacknove, 'The Safe Country Notion in European Asylum Law', 9 *Harvard Human Rights Journal*, 1996, pp. 185–288 at 189–90.

[29] See pp. 274–6 above.

[30] See Guy S. Goodwin-Gill, 'The Haitian *Refoulement* Case: A Comment', 6 *International Journal of Refugee Law*, 1994, pp. 103*ff*; and Marx, '*Non-Refoulement*, Access to Procedures', pp. 390*ff*.

return to the refugee's country of origin (and original risk of persecution), and thus allow for return to any other country? The wording suggests a broad interpretation of article 33, including *any* 'frontiers of territories where his life or freedom would be threatened'. Furthermore, the 1967 UN Declaration on Territorial Asylum[31] confirms this understanding of a wide application of the *non-refoulement* principle, article 3(1) of the Declaration reading as follows:

No person . . . shall be subjected to measures such as *rejection at the frontier* or, if he has already entered the territory in which he seeks asylum, expulsion or compulsory return to *any State* where he may be subjected to persecution. (emphasis added)

Even when applying such a broad interpretation of article 33 – in terms of its personal, territorial and functional scope, as referred to above – the crucial issue as regards the right of states to restrict asylum applicants' choice of country of asylum remains unsolved. Is protection against *refoulement* all that is needed to permit the state of arrival to return an asylum applicant to another country? Taking into account the content and structure of the Geneva Convention, as well as the declaratory nature of the determination of refugee status, it must follow that, in order to be considered an adequate country of first asylum, the relevant state has to provide refugee protection of a *quality*, and at a *level*, in conformity with the protection scheme laid down in the Convention. This conclusion is perhaps too brief, and qualifications may be needed as to some of the specific elements of protection. Essentially it can be concluded, however, that respect for the *non-refoulement* principle is a necessary, but not of itself a sufficient, criterion to establish a state as a genuine country of first asylum.

International standards for protection in the 'country of asylum'

While the Geneva Convention does not stipulate 'direct flight' nor a corresponding 'safe third country' criterion as such, it still has to be acknowledged that it gives neither explicit nor implicit support to any refugee right to choose the country of asylum. Given this *vacuum* in the Convention, let us now turn to the alternative sources of international law which might provide some basis for determining countries of first asylum, thus implicitly permitting the restriction of a refugee right to choose her or his country of asylum. In the same way as 'safe third country' policies are being increasingly implemented, so too the substance and impact of

---

[31] General Assembly Resolution 2312 (XXII).

such legal standards has become still more relevant. As will appear from the analysis which follows, the standards also establish significant constraints on state practice.

Against the background of the discussion above, problems relating to the 'country of first asylum' issue can be identified at three levels. These concern first, the *quality* of refugee protection required from such a state; secondly, whether some *personal relationship* between the asylum applicant and the country in question has to be established, and to what degree (which may in itself be relevant, if not decisive, to the problems of access and quality of protection); and, thirdly, what *procedure* should be adhered to in cases where the 'first asylum' issue is raised by the state of arrival. More specifically, with respect to the latter problem, can the transfer of asylum applicants be conducted on the basis of *general* inter-state arrangements? If so, what are the requirements to be met by such bilateral or multi-lateral agreements? Alternatively, does international law require a *specific* agreement to readmit the individual asylum applicant or refugee prior to such return?

Already in 1979, the UNHCR Executive Committee (EXCOM) adopted Conclusion No. 15 in which some general principles for the identification of a 'country of first asylum' were set out. In elaborating common criteria identifying the country responsible for examining an asylum application, EXCOM recommended that the following principles be observed:

(i) The criteria should make it possible to identify in a positive manner the country which is responsible for examining an asylum request and to whose authorities the asylum-seeker should have the possibility of addressing himself;

(ii) The criteria should be of such a character as to avoid possible disagreement between States as to which of them should be responsible for examining an asylum request and should take into account the *duration and nature of any sojourn* of the asylum-seeker in other countries;

(iii) The *intentions* of the asylum-seeker as regards the country in which he *wishes to request asylum* should as far as possible be taken into account;

(iv) Regard should be had to the concept that asylum should not be refused solely on the ground that it could be sought from another State. Where, however, it appears that a person, before requesting asylum, already has a *connexion or close links with another State*, he may if it appears fair and reasonable be called upon first to request asylum from that State;

(v) The establishment of criteria should be accompanied by arrangements for regular consultation between concerned Governments for dealing with cases for which no solution has been found and for consultation with the Office of the United Nations High Commissioner for Refugees as appropriate;

(vi) Agreements providing for the return by States of persons who have entered their territory from another contracting State in an unlawful manner should be applied in respect of asylum-seekers with due regard to their special situation.[32]

Having been granted asylum, even in accordance with these criteria, does not, however, render the refugee absolutely incapable of discarding the *quality of protection* offered in the 'first asylum' country on grounds of inadequate protection. Essential guidance for such cases was also given by EXCOM in the Conclusion:

Where a refugee who has already been granted asylum in one country requests asylum in another country on the ground that he has *compelling reasons* for leaving his present asylum country due to *fear of persecution* or because his *physical safety or freedom* are endangered, the authorities of the second country should give favourable consideration to his asylum request. [33]

The problems relating to asylum applicants and refugees moving unlawfully or irregularly to another state from a country where they have *already* been granted asylum or protection, have been elaborated upon in later Conclusions. The general trend is, on the one hand, to put stronger emphasis on the problem of *irregular movements* while, on the other hand, simultaneously specifying the circumstances in which such irregular movement may nonetheless be considered *justifiable*. In 1985 EXCOM noted 'with concern the growing phenomenon of refugees and asylum seekers who, having found protection in one country, move in an irregular manner to another country and expressed the hope that the problem this represents can be mitigated through the adoption of global solutions in a spirit of international co-operation and burden-sharing'.[34] The following year the Committee recognised that 'the search for durable solutions includes the need to address the causes of movements of refugees and asylum seekers from countries of origin and the causes of onward movements from countries of first asylum'.[35]

Again in 1987 and 1988 EXCOM noted 'with concern the growing phenomenon of refugees and asylum seekers who, having found protection in one country, move in an irregular manner to another country'.[36] Finally, in 1989 it adopted a separate Conclusion (No. 58) on the problem, still referring to persons having already found protection. The 'growing concern' was explained to result from the 'destabilizing effect which irregular movements of this kind have on structured international efforts to provide appropriate solutions for refugees'. Concerted action

[32] UNHCR EXCOM Conclusion No. 15 (XXX) (Refugees without an Asylum Country), 1979, section (h) (emphasis added).   [33] *Ibid.*, section (k) (emphasis added).
[34] EXCOM Conclusion No. 36 (XXXVI) (General), 1985, section (j).
[35] EXCOM Conclusion No. 41 (XXXVII) (General), 1986, section (e).
[36] EXCOM Conclusions No. 46 (XXXVIII) (General), 1987, section (i), and No. 50 (XXXIX) (General), 1988, section (n).

by governments and UNHCR in different areas was recommended and, not least importantly, the implications of having found protection in another country were pointed out as follows:

e) Refugees and asylum-seekers, who have found protection in a particular country, *should normally not move* from that country in an irregular manner in order to find durable solutions elsewhere but should take advantage of durable solutions available in that country through action taken by governments and UNHCR as recommended . . .

f) Where refugees and asylum-seekers nevertheless move in an irregular manner from a country where they have already found protection, they may be returned to that country if
  i) they are protected there against *refoulement* and
  ii) they are permitted to remain there and to be treated *in accordance with recognized basic human standards* until a *durable solution* is found for them. Where such return is envisaged, UNHCR may be requested to assist in arrangements for the readmission and reception of the persons concerned;

g) It is recognized that there may be *exceptional cases* in which a refugee or asylum-seeker may justifiably claim that he has *reason to fear persecution or that his physical safety or freedom are endangered* in a country where he previously found protection. Such cases should be given favourable consideration by the authorities of the State where he requests asylum.[37]

Much can be said about the non-mandatory legal nature of EXCOM Conclusions. This does not, however, make them totally irrelevant as sources of international refugee law, given the regulatory intent and the normative content embodied in a number of the provisions.[38] Conclusion No. 15 contains regulatory elements, which look 'like miniature draft codes of conduct'.[39] In particular, it has to be noted that paragraph (k), while recommending in vague terms that states 'should give favourable consideration to his asylum request', actually implies certain *minimum standards* of refugee protection. These standards have been further elaborated and specified in Conclusion No. 58 paragraphs (e)–(g), as just quoted.

What most decisively attributes legal impact to such 'soft law' provisions is the fact that they are backed up by the full scheme of congruent standards of general human rights law. While the rationale of a specific

---

[37] EXCOM Conclusion No. 58 (XL) (The Problem of Refugees and Asylum-Seekers who Move in an Irregular Manner from a Country in Which They Had Already Found Protection), 1989 (emphasis added). This Conclusion was recalled by EXCOM in Conclusion No. 65 (XLII) (General Conclusion on International Protection), 1991, section (o); Conclusion No. 65 was itself recalled in Conclusion No. 68 (XLIII), 1992, section (g) referring to access to effective and expeditious status determination procedures and to the discouragement of 'clear and intentional misuse of these procedures'.

[38] *Cf.* Jerzy Sztucki, 'The Conclusions on the International Protection of Refugees Adopted by the Executive Committee of the UNHCR Programme', 1 *International Journal of Refugee Law*, 1989, pp. 295*ff.*   [39] *Ibid.*, p. 301.

refugee rights regime, against the background of prevailing human rights standards, may in itself be debatable,[40] it is beyond doubt that general human rights commitments of states also apply to the situation of refugees and asylum seekers. This is intrinsic to the question of what conditions in a country of 'first asylum' may permit a second state of arrival to return asylum applicants to that country. Again, protection against *refoulement*, and access to proper procedures, will be preconditions *sine qua non*, but are clearly not sufficient to achieve an adequate quality of refugee protection.

As regards the procedure to be followed in this context, the state considered as the country of 'first asylum' must clearly consent to the readmission of the asylum seeker prior to deportation, in order to secure compliance with these requirements. Various viewpoints have been advanced as to whether such prior consent should be explicit or implicit.[41] UNHCR has taken the position that, in the absence of agreements determining responsibility for examining asylum requests, the explicit or at least implicit prior consent to readmit the applicant should be provided, and that, as an absolute minimum, the authorities of the state to which the asylum seeker is being returned should be explicitly informed that the asylum claim has not been examined as to substance.[42] It may be difficult to draw a general conclusion as to whether the consent needs to be explicit in each individual deportation case. This could well depend on the circumstances and general practices established between the states involved. For instance, if an adequate international agreement exists, the explicit *ad hoc* consent to readmission may become less relevant.

Against this background, the European Community Immigration Ministers' 1992 London Resolution sets out remarkably low requirements for establishing whether a country is a 'host third country'.[43] By phrasing the requirements primarily in negative terms – such as the *absence* of threats to life or freedom within the meaning of article 33 of the

[40] See Hathaway and Dent, *Refugee Rights*, in particular chapter 3.
[41] Marx, '*Non-refoulement*, Access to Procedures', pp. 395–7; Goodwin-Gill, *The Refugee in International Law*, pp. 339 and 343; ECRE, '*Safe Third Countries*', pp. 11–12; and UNHCR, 'An Overview of Protection Issues in Western Europe: Legislative Trends and Positions Taken by UNHCR', 1 *European Series*, 1995, 3, pp. 18–20.
[42] UNHCR, 'An Overview of Protection Issues in Western Europe', p. 20.
[43] EC Immigration Ministers' Resolution of 30 November–1 December 1992 on a Harmonised Approach to Questions Concerning Host Third Countries (SN 4823/92), para. 2. For critical comments, see Roel Fernhout and Herman Meijers, 'Asylum', in *A New Immigration Law for Europe? The 1992 London and 1993 Copenhagen Rules on Immigration* (ed. Pieter Boeles *et al.*, Dutch Centre for Immigrants, Utrecht, 1993), pp. 17–18; Byrne and Shacknove, 'The Safe Country Notion in European Asylum Law', pp. 200–4 and 211–12; and Goodwin-Gill, *The Refugee in International Law*, pp. 334 and 338. For further details, see also chapter 17 of this volume.

Geneva Convention, and the *absence* of exposure to torture or inhuman or degrading treatment – the resolution apparently fails to take account of the broader positive protection standards under international law, including some of those previously recognised by states on the UNHCR Executive Committee. On the other hand, the drafters of the resolution may have been aware of this when referring to 'fundamental requirements', and could thus be seen as taking no explicit stand against the broader principles of refugee protection.

Regardless of how 'safe third countries' are to be defined, the fundamental problem remains that the criterion of 'safety' is often established by the operation of a firm, and practically non-rebuttable, *presumption* that a given country should provide adequate protection. However, this is not inherent in the concept as such, and the rationale of 'safe third country' policies may well be maintained if the presumption is open to challenge. Even the otherwise restrictive 'third country' provisions introduced by Germany in 1993 are interpreted in a manner allowing for the procurement of evidence to negate the 'normative ascertainment' of safety under exceptional circumstances.[44] Hence, presumptions concerning the safety of a 'first country of asylum' generally have to be *rebuttable*, unless they are substituted by concrete evidence that the individual concerned has already gained protection which is still accessible and effective in that state.[45]

Various approaches to the question of refugees' choice

Legal theory dealing with the issue and with contemporary state practice has demonstrated important, if not actually extreme, variations in the analytical approach to the question of a right of choice for refugees and asylum seekers. Back in 1978 Göran Melander explained that western European states' line of reasoning on the 'direct flight' requirement, which has parallels with 'third country' practices, implied that asylum seekers ought to *come directly* from their country of origin to the country of asylum, in order to avoid return to a 'country of first asylum'. He wrote:

---

[44] See Reinhard Marx and Katharina Lumpp, 'The German Constitutional Court's Decision of 14 May 1996 on the Concept of "Safe Third Countries" – A Basis for Burden-Sharing in Europe?', 8 *International Journal of Refugee Law*, 1996, pp. 419–39; and Gregor Noll, 'Non-Admission and Return of Protection Seekers in Germany', 9 *International Journal of Refugee Law*, 1997, pp. 415–52 at pp. 424–32 and 445–7.

[45] As recognised by EXCOM in Conclusion No. 58, sections (f) and (g), and to the same effect in Conclusion No. 15, sections (h)(iv) and (k). *Cf.* UNHCR, *Note on International Protection*, 1993, UN Doc. A/AC.96/815, paras. 21–2; and UNHCR, 'An Overview of Protection Issues in Western Europe', p. 19.

It is considered that an asylum seeker should ask for asylum in the state he first enters after his flight from a country in which he has a well-founded fear of persecution. He has no right to choose his country of asylum. The movement of refugees should be controlled – with the self-evident exception of applicants coming directly from a country of persecution.[46]

While this last exception may be less self-evident in the 1990s, and the consequences of controlling refugees' and asylum seekers' movements are not the same as in the 1970s either, the underlying rationale seems at least partly similar:

Western European States mostly consider that an asylum seeker/refugee has no right to choose his country of asylum and residence. To prevent movement of refugees almost all states have prescribed further criteria for being admitted to a recognition procedure and to be granted asylum or a residence permit. These provisions have in common that there must be some links or connections between the asylum state and the asylum seeker. Or to put it another way: the country with which the applicant has the strongest links or connections should normally be responsible for him. Unfortunately, States have not agreed on any criteria to determine and balance the links or connections. As a consequence the situation of refugees in orbit is created . . . The situation has not arisen because of a negative attitude towards refugees in Western Europe, but as each State considers itself to be the country of asylum *par préférence* it is believed that there will be a mass influx of refugees, unless preventive steps are taken.[47]

As a theoretical basis for criticism of recent state practice designed to limit the right of refugees and asylum seekers to choose the country of asylum, James Hathaway has articulated the principled viewpoint that such a *right of choice* does exist in international law. In a section entitled 'Choice of the Country of Asylum' of his book *The Law of Refugee Status*, he states:

There is no requirement in the Convention that a refugee seek protection in the country nearest her home, or even in the first state to which she flees. Nor is it requisite that a claimant travel directly from her country of first asylum to the state in which she intends to seek durable protection. The universal scope of post-Protocol refugee law effectively allows most refugees to choose for themselves the country in which they will claim refugee status.[48]

Accordingly, Hathaway characterises 'third country' schemes such as the Dublin Convention as being inconsistent with the spirit of the Geneva Convention, since they reflect a weakening of the commitment to the refugee's right to decide for herself or himself the most effective means of securing safety from persecution.[49] This seems to suggest, however, that

---

[46] Göran Melander, *Refugees in Orbit* (International University Exchange Fund, Geneva, 1978), p. 2.   [47] *Ibid.*, p. 25 and p. 107, respectively.
[48] Hathaway, *The Law of Refugee Status*, p. 46.   [49] *Ibid.*, p. 47.

the critical remarks must be understood within a *protective* framework. Thus, effective access to protection is the guiding criterion of the right of choice, just as the quoted statement refers to the problem of the recognition of refugee status under the Convention.

Dealing with the same European schemes, Hélène Lambert has, as recently as 1995, advanced the opposite principle that there is *no choice* at all left with the individual refugee. No modification to this principle is being proposed, yet she does not develop any specific legal basis of the position taken:

> A refugee is expected to seek asylum in the first country he arrives [in] after fleeing, provided that country is safe from persecution and from *refoulement*. A refugee who, before arriving in the target country, has stayed in a 'first country of asylum' or 'safe third country' may be returned, as a rule, to that country. This principle is applied by almost all countries which have acceded to the 1951 Convention . . . As a matter of principle, a refugee cannot choose his country of asylum. Accordingly, a refugee who could have sought and be [*sic*] granted asylum in another country should be returned to that country. The principle is to be decided by the state in which the refugee arrives.[50]

So far, theory is not exactly unequivocal on the issue of a right of choice for asylum seekers and refugees. At first appearance, it might seem that the one position tends to be absolutist in its defence of such a right, while the latter position which denies any right or ignores the legal problem of choice might be characterised as rather simplistic. The disagreement is modified by the protective framework and refugee status-related context of the former position. However, the problem cannot yet be considered exhausted in legal theory. It deserves further analysis and this chapter is meant to be a contribution to that end.

Concluding remarks: choice versus protection

A decision by a state to refuse to grant asylum to a person, who is either *recognised* as a refugee or whose asylum application is not examined on its merits as a result of *non-admission* to that state, implies the denial of that person's right to choose his or her country of actual or potential asylum. In the context of discussing the concept of 'safe third country' or 'country of first asylum' it is therefore relevant to analyse the very question of the existence of any *right to choose* one's country of asylum or, at the procedural level, the country of examination of the asylum application. To the extent that such a right does exist, the discussion of alternative countries of asylum can be brought to an end relatively soon. A right to choose on

[50] Hélène Lambert, *Seeking Asylum: Comparative Law and Practice in Selected European Countries* (Martinus Nijhoff, Dordrecht, 1995), pp. 91 and 98, respectively.

the part of the refugee or the asylum seeker presumes a constraint on, or even the denial of, the right of states to refuse asylum or examination of the application, respectively, on 'safe third country' grounds.

Even if the Geneva Convention contains no explicit and little implicit restriction on refugees' right to choose their country of asylum, the problem cannot be isolated from the context of sovereign state control over immigration issues. In short, there is neither a strict 'direct flight' requirement, nor any legally protected right of individual choice. Yet the totality of international law pertinent to the issue, including especially human rights standards and refugee protection principles, results in a relatively limited scope of action for states intending to restrict refugees' choice. Against this background, recent developments in European 'safe third country' policies are noteworthy and, indeed, debatable.

Rather than giving a definite answer to the question of refugees' right to choose their country of asylum, it might possibly be concluded that the question has been inadequately put. There has been considerable controversy over the issue, with regard to the existing legal norms as well as *de lege ferenda*.[51] Thus, it seems relevant to pay analytical attention to the legal framing of the problems discussed above. The combined focus on refugee law and standards of human rights law represents a considerable challenge to contemporary developments in the European refugee protection system. As indicated, these issues are increasingly relevant in the evolving system of 'one state responsibility' for examining asylum applications. This becomes particularly clear when 'safe third country' practices are taken together with the parallel and more general policies of non-arrival and non-admission to the territory and asylum procedures of the European Union and associated states.

Bibliography

Byrne, Rosemary and Andrew Shacknove, 'The Safe Country Notion in European Asylum Law', 9 *Harvard Human Rights Journal*, 1996, pp. 185–228.

Einarsen, Terje, 'The European Convention on Human Rights and the Notion of an Implied Right to *de facto* Asylum', 2 *International Journal of Refugee Law*, 1990, pp. 361–89

European Council on Refugees and Exiles, *'Safe Third Countries': Myths and Realities* (ECRE, London, 1995)

Fernhout, Roel and Herman Meijers, 'Asylum', in *A New Immigration Law for Europe? The 1992 London and 1993 Copenhagen Rules on Immigration* (ed. Pieter Boeles *et al.*, Dutch Centre for Immigrants, Utrecht, 1993)

---

[51] See Kay Hailbronner, 'The Concept of "Safe Country" and Expeditious Asylum Procedures: A Western European Perspective', 5 *International Journal of Refugee Law*, 1993, pp. 58 and 61*ff.*

Goodwin-Gill, Guy S., 'The Haitian *Refoulement* Case: A Comment', 6 *International Journal of Refugee Law*, 1994, pp. 103–9

Hailbronner, Kay, 'The Concept of "Safe Country" and Expeditious Asylum Procedures: A Western European Perspective', 5 *International Journal of Refugee Law*, 1993, pp. 31–65

Hathaway, James C., 'The Emerging Politics of *Non-Entrée*', *Refugees*, 1992, 91, p. 40

Hathaway, James C. and John A. Dent, *Refugee Rights: Report on a Comparative Survey* (York Lanes Press, Toronto, 1995)

Hyndman, Patricia, 'The 1951 Convention and Its Implications for Procedural Questions', 6 *International Journal of Refugee Law*, 1994, pp. 245–52

Kjærum, Morten, 'The Concept of Country of First Asylum', 4 *International Journal of Refugee Law*, 1992, pp. 514–30

Lambert, Hélène, *Seeking Asylum. Comparative Law and Practice in Selected European Countries* (Martinus Nijhoff, Dordrecht, 1995)

Marx, Reinhard, '*Non-Refoulement*, Access to Procedures, and Responsibility for Determining Refugee Claims', 7 *International Journal of Refugee Law*, 1995, pp. 383–406

Marx, Reinhard and Katharina Lumpp, 'The German Constitutional Court's Decision of 14 May 1996 on the Concept of "Safe Third Countries" – A Basis for Burden-Sharing in Europe?', 8 *International Journal of Refugee Law*, 1996, pp. 419–39

Melander, Göran, *Refugees in Orbit* (International University Exchange Fund, Geneva, 1978)

Noll, Gregor, 'Non-Admission and Return of Protection Seekers in Germany', 9 *International Journal of Refugee Law*, 1997, pp. 415–52

Raoul Wallenberg Institute of Human Rights and Humanitarian Law, *Responsibility for Examining an Asylum Request* (Report No. 1, Lund, 1986)

Suntinger, Walter, 'The Principle of *Non-Refoulement*: Looking Rather to Geneva than to Strasbourg?', 49 *Austrian Journal of Public and International Law*, 1995, pp. 203–25

Sztucki, Jerzy, 'The Conclusions on the International Protection of Refugees Adopted by the Executive Committee of the UNHCR Programme', 1 *International Journal of Refugee Law*, 1989, pp. 285–318

UNHCR, 'An Overview of Protection Issues in Western Europe: Legislative Trends and Positions Taken by UNHCR', 1 *European Series*, 1995, 3

14   Early warning and prevention: the United Nations and Rwanda

Howard Adelman[1]

Introduction

Purportedly, refugees have a right to return to their home countries. In reality, when refugees are the products of ethnic conflict, the right of return is denied. If the refugees do not find another secure status in another state, they frequently become refugee warriors determined to return home by the use of force. Force begets force. In the ensuing conflict, the ethnic cousins of the refugees within the country are victimised and, in the extreme, ethnic cleansing and genocide begin to be employed to 'purify' the country. This produces more refugees. If the refugee warriors win, many more refugees are produced, this time from the other ethnic group. The result is regional destabilisation as well as an enormous loss of life. Whether or not refugees have rights, realistic and effective actions by the international community are imperative. The events in Rwanda should not be emulated.

This chapter begins with a puzzle. Presumably, the United Nations and all our multi-lateral institutions were created, at least in part, to prevent another holocaust.[2] Yet an extremely large well-publicised

---

[1] This chapter is based on research undertaken for the report by myself and Astri Suhrke, *Early Warning and Conflict Management: Genocide in Rwanda* (Danish International Development Agency (DANIDA), Copenhagen, 1996).

[2] This statement is not self-evidently true. The UN was founded to develop a system to protect one state against the aggression of another and thus correct the failures of the League of Nations (see Geoffrey Stern, *The Structure of International Society* (Pinter, London, 1995), p. 204, section 14.3 entitled, 'The United Nations: Learning the Lessons'). The UN's mandate was a universal extension of the Concert of Europe after the Napoleonic Wars in which the great powers would be the self-appointed guardians of a stable international political order. The involvement of the UN in the internal affairs of states is perceived to be a deviation in the post-Cold War world from the UN's primary stress on inter-state order (see Thomas G. Weiss (ed.), *The United Nations and Civil War* (Lynne Rienner, Boulder, CO, 1995)). Though all of the above is true, this confuses the structure of the UN with its normative goals. The opening words of the UN Charter are 'We the peoples of the United Nations . . .'. It is a peoples' charter, not a charter of states. The Charter goes on 'to reaffirm faith in fundamental human rights, in the dignity and worth of the human person, the equal rights of men and women and of *nations* large and small and to establish conditions under which justice and respect for the obligations arising

genocide[3] was carried out in 1994 in an economically poor and militarily weak Third World country, Rwanda, while UN troops were present. Further, the legal government *and* the rebel army in the Arusha Accords had jointly given the UN responsibility for protecting civilians and disarming non-military personnel who were largely responsible for actually carrying out the mass murders.[4] This chapter outlines the information, communication, structural and other factors that undercut the UN's ability to intervene in and stop the genocide in Rwanda.

UN peacekeeping in Rwanda

This chapter is too brief to outline the historical events as they unfolded in Rwanda. Instead, I begin with the Arusha Accords[5] signed on 4 August 1993 between the Rwandese Patriotic Front (RPF – the Tutsi-led[6] rebel

footnote 2(*cont.*)

from treaties and other sources of international law can be maintained' (emphasis added). See Chadwick F. Alger, 'The United Nations in Historical Perspective: What Have We Learned About Peacebuilding', in *The United Nations and a Just World Order* (ed. Richard A. Falk, Samuel S. Kim and Saul H. Mendlovitz, Westview, Boulder, CO, 1991), pp. 88–9.

[3] The 1948 UN Convention on the Prevention and Punishment of the Crime of Genocide (78 UNTS 277) defined genocide as 'any of the following acts committed with intent to destroy, in whole or in part, a national, ethnical, racial or religious group', not only by killing, but by causing bodily harm or producing conditions which would have the same results or prevent reproduction. Even the forcible transfer of children from one group to another was considered to be an act of genocide. *Cf.* Frank Chalk and Kurt Jonassohn, *History and Sociology of Genocide: Analysis and Case Studies* (Yale University Press, New Haven, 1990), pp. 44–9. See also Frank Chalk, 'Definitions of Genocide and Their Implications for Prediction and Prevention', in *Remembering for the Future* (ed. Yehuda Bauer *et al.*, Oxford University Press, 1988), pp. 39–58.

[4] The agreement was communicated in a formal letter dated 14 June 1993 signed by the Permanent Representative of Rwanda and addressed to the UN on behalf of both the government of Rwanda, and the Rwandese Patriotic Front (RPF). The letter dealt with the stationing of what was called a neutral international force (NIF). In Section B dealing with its 'security mission', this force was given a mandate to '1. Guarantee overall security in the country and monitor, in particular, the way in which the authorities and competent bodies maintain public order . . . 3. Help to ensure the safety of the civilian population.' See United Nations, *The United Nations in Rwanda, 1993–1996* (United Nations, New York, 1996), Document 16, p. 166.

[5] A detailed analysis can be found in Bruce Jones, 'The Arusha Accords', in *The Path of a Genocide: The Rwanda Crisis from Uganda to Zaire* (ed. Howard Adelman and Astri Suhrke, Transaction Books, Trenton, NJ, 1999).

[6] It should be noted that the present government resents such descriptions in its interest in defining Rwandese nationalism solely in Rwandese or state terms and not in ethnic terms. Thus, the fact that the RPF consisted of a majority of Tutsis is an accident. Phrases like 'Tutsi-dominated' and 'Tutsi-led' are considered as objectionable as if Major-General Romeo Dallaire, the Force Commander of the UN Assistance Mission to Rwanda (UNAMIR), were to be described as a Quebecois coming from a French-Canadian-led government. This example was actually used in the protests of government leaders to some of the phrases used in the 1995 Emergency Evaluation Report when presented to them in Kigali, September 1996.

army which invaded Rwanda on 1 October 1990) and the Hutu government of Rwanda. The local African leadership of the surrounding countries, led by the Tanzanians and supported by European, US and UN
diplomats, helped the Hutu moderates within Rwanda and the Tutsi-led
invading army to forge an elite coalition based on a military power pact as
the foundation for a peace agreement.

It should be noted that invasion by refugees in exile is against the 1969
Convention of the Organisation of African Unity (OAU) Governing the
Specific Aspects of Refugee Problems in Africa,[7] which in its preamble
affirms that the signatories are 'determined to discourage' refugees from
using their status for subversive activities (paragraphs 4 and 5). Article 3
deals in its entirety with 'Prohibition of Subversive Activities', prohibiting
refugees from engaging in subversive activities against any OAU member
state (article 3(1)), and requires that the host states undertake to 'prohibit
refugees residing in their respective territories from attacking any State
Member . . . by use of arms, through the press, or by radio' (article 3(2)).
To ensure that these conditions are met, article 2(6) advises that, 'for
reasons of security', refugees shall settle 'at a reasonable distance from the
frontier of their country of origin'. These provisions are unique to African
regional instruments in international refugee law.[8]

Thus, the reordering of Rwanda was not based on a civil society of individuals, associations, professionals, intellectuals, trade unions etc., even
though the goals of the Arusha Accords were to rebuild the political structures and the economy by reconnecting the political structures with all
the elements of the society. The peace agreement spoke the language of a
new civility in public affairs, a new regime of participation and inclusive-
ness, but the arrangements operated on the old rules of elite accommodation and compromise dictated by the force of arms.[9]

The power agreement relied on external actors, namely a neutral

---

[7] 1001 UNTS 46.

[8] More generally, the OAU Charter expresses 'unreserved condemnation' for subversive
activities on the part of neighbouring states or any other state (article 3(5)). The 1981
African Charter on Human and Peoples' Rights (21 ILM, 1982, p. 58) states unambiguously that 'territories [of signatory states] shall not be used as bases for subversive or terrorist activities' against another party (article 23(2)b).

[9] The pattern described is not unique to Rwanda. See Donald Rothchild, 'Ethnic
Bargaining and State Breakdown in Africa', 1 *Nationalism and Ethnic Politics*, 1995, 1, pp.
54–72. For more particulars on Rwanda, see Colette Braeckman, *Rwanda, histoire d'un
génocide* (Fayard, Paris, 1994); Rony Brauman, *Devant le mal: Rwanda un génocide en direct*
(Arléa, Paris, 1994); Jean-Pierre Chrétien, 'Hutu et Tutsi au Rwanda et au Burundi,' in *Au
coeur de l'ethnie* (ed. J. L. Amselle and E. M. Bokolo, La Découverte, Paris, 1985), pp.
129–66; Alain Destexhe, *Rwanda: Essai sur la génocide* (Complexe, Brussels, 1994);
Catherine Newbury, *The Cohesion of Oppression: Citizenship and Ethnicity in Rwanda
(1860–1960)* (Columbia University Press, New York, 1988); and Gérard Prunier, *The
Rwanda Crisis: History of a Genocide* (Columbia University Press, New York, 1995).

international military force, to provide the security in the transition period to oversee both a drastic reduction in the armed forces and military integration. Both sides, in an unprecedented step for antithetical forces forging peace, came together to New York to lobby for UN support for the deployment of peacekeepers. The peacekeepers arrived late (though rapidly by UN standards) to support the usual compact of elite accommodation, but without the commitment of the extremists, the Third Force,[10] who opposed the accommodation. Further, the peacekeepers were ill-equipped, under-funded in general and not provided with operational funds until 4 April 1997, six months after they were deployed and two days before the Arusha Accords were sabotaged.[11] The UN Assistance Mission to Rwanda (UNAMIR) was composed of a very uneven combination of troops ranging from well-trained and well-equipped Belgian troops to very poorly provisioned Bangladeshis. It was never supplied with the requisite armoured personnel carriers (APCs)[12] and helicopters to provide an intimidation backup force. The USA, in particular, 'nickelled and dimed' the new force into impotence.[13] Consequently, it was never supplied with the tools to do a job even under the apparently idealistic conditions of the Arusha Accords.

The greatest weaknesses of the peacekeepers, however, were their mandate and the interpretation given to the terms of engagement by headquarters. The Arusha Accords required UNAMIR to act to protect internal security, in particular to help protect the civilian population. However, with the debacle of Somalia hanging over their heads, the members of the Security Council and the Department of Peacekeeping Operations

[10] The Third Force is sometimes used as a general term applicable to all the extremists. More particularly, the Third Force referred to Akazu, literally 'the little house', the immediate inner circle around President Juvénal Habyarimana and his wife, but also the Impuzamugambi, meaning 'single purpose', the militia organised by the Coalition for the Defence of the Republic (CDR), the extremist political party organised in 1992 and allied with extremist elements in Habyarimana's party, the National Republican Movement for Democracy and Development (MRNDD), 'Network Zero', the death squads apparently run by Akazu, and Kangura, the extremist newspaper dedicated to be 'the voice which seeks to awaken and defend the Hutu'.

[11] For example, the UNAMIR Administrative Officer never received either money or any independent spending authority; given the need to buy food, water and fuel on a cash basis, these bureaucratic procedures were a nightmare. The Bangladeshi troops evidently never did get paid.

[12] In fact, before 6 April 1994, UNAMIR managed to obtain seven Russian-made APCs from Mozambique, but without any keys to access the motors, without any spare parts and without any manuals that anyone could read. As a result, within two weeks, six of the seven APCs could no longer operate as self-propelled vehicles.

[13] See Milton Leitenberg, 'The Case of Rwanda: US and UN Actions Result in Escalation of Genocide and Higher Costs', in *Contemporary Genocides: Causes, Cases, Consequences* (ed. Albert J. Jongman, Interdisciplinary Research Programme on Root Causes of Human Rights Violation (PIOOM), Leiden, 1996), pp. 131–40.

(DPKO) interpreted this mandate in a very restricted way, limiting UNAMIR to a supportive role. The Rwandese army and the *gendarmerie* were given primary responsibility for maintaining security, even though the army was heavily infiltrated by extremists who exercised effective control.[14]

UNAMIR was deployed as if it was a peacekeeping force between two competing armies without recognising that it was also a force designed to provide security for a new elite coalition against those who opposed the coalition and whose strength and power reached deep into the army and the *gendarmerie*. At the same time as UNAMIR was deployed, the Third Force was strengthened by the overthrow and assassination of the newly elected Hutu president in Burundi in October 1993. This weakened UNAMIR immediately after it was deployed, as it had to allocate part of its forces to the south of the country on a front that was not even contemplated when the force was set up. The events in Burundi strengthened the appeal of the Third Force in the Rwandese population. UNAMIR was not in a position of strength when the coup came on 6 April 1994.

This inadequate, under-funded and improperly mandated force was then faced with genocide. Between the decision to deploy and the commencement of the genocide, did the UN fail to revise any of the following: its mandate, its terms of engagement, the ways its troops were deployed, the numbers of troops, the equipment provided etc.? Were these actions or inactions taken because the UN could not and did not anticipate a genocide, and was taken off-guard by the unexpected? Or did the UN, the US and European governments know about the Third Force, its ideology and plans? If so, when? And why did the information not influence the role assigned to the peacekeepers and the way they were equipped?

Early warning: the information available

From 7 to 21 January 1993, at the invitation of local human rights groups[15] and as part of the International Commission of Investigation on Human Rights Violations in Rwanda sponsored by international human rights organisations,[16] eleven experts from eight different countries

---

[14] See Joan Kakwenzire and Dixon Kamukama, 'The Development and Consolidation of Extremist Forces in Rwanda', in Adelman and Suhrke, *The Path of a Genocide*.

[15] The invitation came from a coalition of Rwandese human rights associations known as the Liaison Committee of Associations in Defence of Human Rights in Rwanda (CLADHO).

[16] The investigating team was sponsored by four different human rights organisations, the Fédération internationale des droits de l'homme (FIDH) in Paris, Africa Watch in New York, Washington and London, the International Centre for Rights of the Person and of Democratic Development (CIPPDD) in Montreal, and the Inter-African Union of Human Rights (UIDH) in Ouagadougou.

investigated allegations of human rights violations by the Rwandese government and the RPF. The human rights organisations provided the most accurate record of Rwanda's deteriorating human rights situation.

Just after the Commission of Investigation arrived in the Rwandan capital, Kigali, President Major-General Juvénal Habyarimana rejected a power-sharing agreement signed in Arusha on 9 January 1993, suppressed opposition protests and slaughtered members of the Tutsi minority. This was serendipitous, but it meant that the report was regarded by the 'experts' on Rwanda as taking events out of their historical context. The slaughter might have been part of a continuing pattern of political bargaining, an isolated event, and not genocide. The resumption of the formal peace talks in March, at the very same time that the human rights report was officially released, also helped push that report into the background. Thus, although this particular commission was the first to use the designation 'genocide',[17] the report was ignored.

It stated: 'The majority of the victims have been members of the minority group, the Tutsi, and they have been killed and otherwise abused for the sole reason they are Tutsi.' The report continued:

While the casualty figures established by the Commission are significant, they may be below the threshold required to establish genocide . . . These technical matters aside, the tragic reality is that for the sole reason of belonging to the Tutsi group, many Rwandans are dead, have disappeared, have been seriously injured or mutilated, have been deprived of their property, or have had to flee their homes and been forced to hide or live in terror.[18]

When the peace process resumed again in March 1993, the warnings of dire consequences of a failure to bring about peace, however, had been loud and clear. On 11 March, Hervé Ladsous, the Permanent Representative of France to the UN, announced in the Security Council his country's concern with the security risk and the grave and escalating humanitarian crisis in the area.[19] UN senior staff and the members of the Security Council were told in no uncertain terms in an informal briefing *after* 1 April that an urgent UN response was necessary 'since a resump-

[17] The report of the International Commission of Inquiry on Human Rights Violations in Rwanda (1993) (hereinafter, the 'FIDH Report') was widely circulated. The Belgian government, for one, took it so seriously that it temporarily recalled its ambassador from Kigali. The report documented the involvement of the government in what was described as systematic killings directed against the Tutsi, and estimated that about 2,000 persons had been murdered in 1990–2. Briefing reporters on its finding, the Commission used the term 'genocide' to describe the killings. This claim was retracted in their official report published in March because of fear that such a designation would be considered hysterical.   [18] FIDH Report, p. 29.
[19] *Cf.* Agnès Callamar, 'French Policy in Rwanda', in Adelman and Suhrke, *The Path of a Genocide.*

tion of hostilities could lead to a massacre and a humanitarian disaster'.[20]

The report which the then UN Secretary-General, Boutros Boutros-Ghali, received from his goodwill mission in March 1993 seemed to confirm these conclusions. If the situation were not to be resolved peacefully in a way which safeguarded political participation, ensured a broad-based government and provided protection for human rights as a necessary ingredient, a large massacre could be expected. Macaire Pédanou, the head of the goodwill mission, tried to convince the Secretary-General that the roots of the conflict ran very deep, with strong passions and long memories on both sides, at the same time as both sides genuinely seemed to want to resolve the situation through peaceful negotiations. It was a situation that called for deft management and a firm commitment with sufficient resources.

These views were echoed by the Secretary-General of the OAU and the Tanzanian mediator. There was a consensus by everyone well informed about the situation that a disaster of massive proportions could, and probably would, follow a failure to resolve the situation by peaceful means, though no one expected or prophesied a genocide. The minister of defence in the Rwandese government, at that time a moderate, fled in July 1993 in fear for his life from threats from hardliners after he had tried to disarm the militias.

Other events seemed ominous. Warnings even came directly from the government *after* the Arusha Accords were signed in August. Both Habyarimana and Colonel Kanyarengwe, chair of the RPF, warned the UN reconnaissance mission that, in the absence of an international neutral force after 10 September 1993, there would be a political vacuum during which time paramilitary groups in the country would have an opportunity to cause trouble.

Thus, much was known in general *before* UNAMIR was deployed. These fears were confirmed after deployment. Jacques-Roger Booh-Booh, appointed as the Special Representative to Rwanda on 12 November 1993 by the UN Secretary-General, was warned by the RPF that elements in the government were adamantly opposed to the Arusha Accords and would stop at nothing to derail the process. Booh-Booh confirmed the RPF alert and was able to warn the Secretary-General at the end of November that a local, though small but influential, minority

---

[20] It must be said that the French fear was largely directed at the resumption of hostilities by the RPF, with the bloodbath expected as revenge for the resumption of hostilities. On 6 April Ladsous sent a new missive to the Security Council complaining that the military withdrawal was not progressing as agreed, and that the political talks were deadlocked. France again reiterated the urgency of the situation and urged the UN to take emergency action, specifically by sending a force to monitor the Rwanda–Uganda border.

was determined to derail the peace process and promote an atmosphere of distrust and apprehension. He envisioned their goal as creating a situation which would lead to the resumption of the hostilities. He did not portray their aim as genocide. Slaughters were thought to have been perpetrated for political purposes. Major-General Romeo Dallaire, Force Commander of UNAMIR, confirmed that the massacres were part of an organised conspiracy.[21]

Words reinforced facts. The new minister of defence expressed open hostility to UNAMIR. All the President would do or say was that the minister did not represent the views of the government; Habyarimana took no steps to dismiss this extremist minister. By the end of December 1993, Booh-Booh and Dallaire both recognised that a powerful, subversive Third Force was operating in Rwanda. It was a ruthless, well-organised, well-equipped and centrally directed group of terrorists, which had already killed sixty civilians in and near the demilitarised zone separating the RPF forces in northern Rwanda from the government army in the west, south and central areas of the country. Not only was there a conspiracy to overthrow the peace accords, but a very influential part of the army was involved in the conspiracy.

On 11 January 1994, Dallaire sent UN headquarters in New York the most prescient and clearest warning of all. The highest level of informant, a top-level organiser of the *interhamwe* militia itself, told Dallaire that a plan was in place. If any swearing-in took place of a new Broad-Based Transitional Government (BBTG), deputies would be assassinated, a few Belgian soldiers would be killed to provoke the only formidable force in UNAMIR to withdraw, and the RPF would be instigated into resuming war, while 1,400 *interhamwe* in a camp outside Kigali were readied to spread insecurity throughout the city. The Tutsi in Kigali had been registered and listed for extermination. Teams of forty *interhamwe* were organised within Kigali to kill them. The planned rate of killing was 1,000 every twenty minutes. Assassinations were no longer of the order of a political tactic, but were clearly genocidal. In addition, Dallaire was informed of the location of weapons caches.

This information was all included in the most important document providing the warning, a cable from Dallaire to the DPKO in New York in January 1994 indicating that arms were being collected and hidden, that an incident was planned to kill Belgian troops and instigate their withdrawal, that names were being collected from Kigali in order to exterminate all the Tutsis in the city. In addition to other information provided by

---

[21] These communications, as with all other communications between UN officials, are not included in *The United Nations and Rwanda 1993–1996*. They were read as part of the research for Adelman and Suhrke, *Early Warning and Conflict Management*.

Dallaire, an unofficial intelligence unit of the Belgian military provided Belgium with additional information, supporting the evidence for a planned genocide and attesting to the authenticity of the source for the information.[22] A Human Rights Watch Arms Project Report of January 1994 was sent to the UN in February and confirmed the existence of this Third Force, designated ironically as 'little house' or 'Akazu'. So the UN had plenty of early warnings that an effective and dangerous force was in a position and intended to destroy the peace and initiate a large-scale genocide.

Direct observations

By 7 April 1994, the day after the plane carrying President Habyarimana crashed, the UN knew that it was the Presidential Guard who, throughout the night, had assassinated the moderate ministers and the Prime Minister, Agathe Uwilingiyimana, and murdered the ten Belgian peace-keepers protecting her. UN personnel had directly witnessed the latter incident. One day after the plane crash, it was impossible not to know who was criminally responsible for destroying the government and disrupting the peace process.

On 12 April, Willy Claes, then Belgian Minister of Defence, told

---

[22] See Adelman and Suhrke, *Early Warning and Conflict Management*. Since the publication of that report, the new official history by the UN on its response to the genocide in Rwanda (*The United Nations and Rwanda, 1993–1996*) has been published. How does that report handle the matter of the cable? Originally, in our interviews with Secretariat officials, the existence of any such information was denied. Now, they admit to its existence (para. 84) but play down its significance by stating that 'such situations and alarming reports from the field' are not uncommon, while omitting any reference to the uncommonly high rank of the informant. In reality, the document was so uncommon that the report was placed in a special Black File at UN headquarters. What action did the UN Secretariat take? It denied the request of the Canadian Force Commander to test the validity of the report by looking for the hidden arms caches in several locations specified by the informant. The official record concedes this and also admits that the UN insisted that the army and the *gendarmerie*, which were the *loci* for the planned genocide, were asked to look for the hidden arms caches. If this were not enough, the official record now compounds its errors by shifting the blame to its own Force Commander, stating that Dallaire asked for permission to 'mount a military operation, using overwhelming force, to address the issue' (para. 85). From a review of the documents and other interviews, Dallaire made no such request. Further, the report goes on to shift responsibility onto its executive body to which it is responsible. In New York, the Secretary-General now tells us: '[M]y Special Advisor briefed the Security Council on the reports that had been received from UNAMIR.' No evidence of a briefing about the cable was found by ourselves, our team, or subsequent independent researchers who have reviewed the evidence. Security Council members told us explicitly that they were never briefed about the cable. Further, this current version of the official UN history belies their initial denial that the cable existed, their initial dismissal of its dubious value once they were confronted by the fact that it was in our possession, and even their current attempt in the official report to insist that it was but one of many alarming reports.

Boutros-Ghali that the Belgians would be withdrawing their troops. Belgium advised the total withdrawal of the remainder of the UN force.[23] By 14 April France, contrary to most popular perceptions, opposed a complete withdrawal of UNAMIR, and feared the consequences of the instability that would result. Further, France was quite convinced that the carnage of civilians would spread from Kigali to the rest of the country and even to Burundi. The United Kingdom concurred that a total withdrawal would be disastrous. Even the USA seemed to support this stance at that time, though they had already been committed to total withdrawal of the UN peacekeepers. In the US view, UNAMIR had no business in Rwanda if there was no peace to keep; a domestic conflict was not a threat to international peace and security.[24]

By mid-April, the UN Special Rapporteur on Human Rights, Bacre Waly Ndiaye, noted that several thousand civilians had been killed because they were moderates, human rights activists, or simply because they were Tutsis. There were many other reports of even larger numbers. For example, the 14 April report on humanitarian assistance to Rwanda was clearer and more unequivocal. It stated that there were 20,000 unburied bodies in Kigali alone, and that these people had been slaughtered at the hands of bands of civilians, the militia, the *gendarmerie* and the Presidential Guard. UNAMIR was perceived by the humanitarian agencies as representing a stabilising factor.

The UN knew without a doubt that the hardliners were now in charge in Kigali. They knew about the actions that the Presidential Guard had already committed. They knew that the interim government was unacceptable to the RPF, and that the RPF would not sign a cease-fire until the massacres stopped. Most importantly, within two weeks of the plane crash, the UN knew 'ethnic cleansing' was in effect and escalating in scale and scope just in front of the RPF advance. The militias showed no respect for the Red Cross (six patients being evacuated by a Red Cross ambulance were slaughtered in front of Red Cross personnel) or the UN.

In other words, the UN knew that a genocide was underway before it made the decision to reduce UNAMIR to a token force.

Communications

If there was more than sufficient information, was the problem that the information had not been communicated adequately? The members of

[23] See the letter from the Permanent Representative from Belgium to the UN dated 13 April 1994 in *The United Nations and Rwanda 1993–1996*, Document 44, pp. 258–9.
[24] See Michael N. Barnett, 'The UN Security Council, Indifference and Genocide in Rwanda', 12 *Cultural Anthropology*, 1997, pp. 551–78.

the Security Council do not seem to have been fully briefed on what headquarters had learned from the Field Commander and the Representative of the Secretary-General. At the other end of the spectrum, the field operation did not have the means (radio or newspaper) to communicate to the population for which UNAMIR was intended to provide security.

UNAMIR had not received either what it requested or required. The problem was not because of miscommunication, at least in terms of technical inadequacies. On 7 April, the Secretariat reported that they had lost touch with Booh-Booh, but this was not the case. It is not clear whether this misreporting was deliberate or simply a breakdown in communications between different parts of the UN headquarters, for headquarters was continuously and fully updated on events in the field. The UN DPKO told the Security Council that UNAMIR was unable to function; in fact, though limited and stretched to capacity in what it was doing, UNAMIR had demonstrated that it could protect itself, attempt to negotiate, and protect civilians within the limits of its capabilities. Further, though securing the airport became a major concern following the withdrawal of Belgian troops, it was more a problem of timing until Ghanaians troops had been redeployed from the demilitarised zone. It was also a contingency problem for the future, for there were no immediate threats against the airport.[25] DPKO contended that UNAMIR was in danger, when all evidence contradicted this assessment except as a prospective possibility; only Belgian troops had been targeted.

Why was there such a different view at the UN headquarters in New York compared to that in the field? The inability of the peacekeepers to obtain an armoured company and five helicopters (which were part of the equipment needed by the UN reconnaissance mission to help provide security for civilians) directly affected communications between the field and headquarters and between headquarters and the Security Council, for it influenced the interpretation given to the communications provided. For example, if Dallaire sent a message depicting how bad the situation was, to reinforce his argument that he needed additional equipment to protect civilians, the very same information was used by headquarters to support a recommendation for withdrawal if the Security Council would not authorise a change in mandate for a more robust peacekeeping operation.

What was UNAMIR to do? Monitoring the Uganda border and

[25] Interviews with Dallaire in 1995 for Adelman and Suhrke, *Early Warning and Conflict Management*. *Cf.* also Jacques Castonguay, 'In Search of a New Cease-Fire', in Adelman and Suhrke, *The Path of a Genocide*, for a discussion of Dallaire's proposal for security areas more generally known as 'safe-zones'.

occupying the demilitarised zone in order to separate the two parties to the conflict became a moot issue when the RPF resumed fighting following the coup and assassinations. Kofi Annan, at that time Under-Secretary-General for Peacekeeping Operations, first posed the problem in terms of two dichotomous choices: remaining and reassessing the mandate and the capabilities of UNAMIR to fulfil its mandate; or total withdrawal. In other words, UNAMIR should either shift from peace-keeping to peacemaking or get out. The option of simply protecting civilians was never presented.

On 14 April, two options were put before the Security Council meeting by the UN Secretariat: the maintenance of the *status quo* in the interim or immediate total withdrawal.[26] Maintaining the *status quo* was not interpreted as including the protection of civilians. The focus had been on extricating foreigners and then on making sure the UN force itself could get out. UNAMIR was increasingly focused on self-protection, and the reconsolidation of the Ghanaian forces from the demilitarised zone. UNAMIR was also asked to supply protection for a new Humanitarian Assistance Cell, which was desperately needed to prevent the spread of disease and the real danger of an epidemic.

The DPKO claimed that troop contributors were anxious to pull out. In fact, Ghana was committed to staying, and the Bangladeshi troops, the prime force guarding the stadium, were sitting on the fence awaiting clear direction from the UN, though they were clearly unwilling to engage in peacemaking.[27] Concern was expressed that UNAMIR would be perceived as abandoning the civilians already under UNAMIR protection – which is exactly what happened when Belgian troops left – yet DPKO claimed that civilian protection was not within the UNAMIR mandate while also reporting that Dallaire was protecting civilians. Dallaire had consistently interpreted the protection of civilians as being within the mandate, given both the terms of the Arusha Accords *and* the provision in the UN mandate that UNAMIR was responsible for contributing to the

---

[26] In the letter dated 13 April 1994 sent by Boutros-Ghali to the Security Council, the Secretary-General indicated that, if the Belgian troops were not replaced by 'another, equally well-equipped contingent' or if the Belgian government did not reconsider its decision [both highly unlikely eventualities at that time], UNAMIR's position was considered untenable, and Dallaire was ordered to draw up withdrawal plans (see *The United Nations and Rwanda 1993–1996*, Document 45, p. 259).

[27] The fact that they were not committed to withdrawal can be seen in their letter to the UN dated 21 April 1994 when the decision had been made to withdraw. In that letter they indicated a clear understanding of the dangers, but a willingness to stay if the parties to the conflict did not target them and if they received proper equipment to defend themselves. Failing that, they were willing to withdraw to a neighbouring country in order to be ready for a quick return. See *The United Nations and Rwanda 1993–1996*, Document 49, pp. 265–6.

general security in Kigali. The debate was really about the terms of engagement and how civilians were to be protected, whether passively or pro-actively. There were many other examples of miscommunication and misunderstanding.

The UN Task Force, led by Annan, then Under-Secretary-General for DPKO, and Iqbal Riza, Assistant DPKO Secretary-General, on 21 April recommended that the Secretary-General issue a strong and unequivocal recommendation that UNAMIR be withdrawn. The Secretary-General put three options before the Security Council, but did not recommend the third option, total withdrawal. The first option, 'an immediate and massive reinforcement of UNAMIR', represented a Chapter VII operation under the UN Charter[28] to authorise the UN force to coerce the opposing parties into a cease-fire, and was a virtual non-starter given the predisposition of the permanent members of the Security Council. Further, the killing of civilians was attributed to 'lawlessness' and not a centrally organised conspiracy, and its cessation was connected to the resumption of a cease-fire.[29] The second option, of a drastic reduction in the force, was clearly the only real option. No option was presented to use (or possibly enhance) the existing force to protect civilians.

The Security Council decided total withdrawal was unacceptable and instead maintained a token force to enable the UN to be in a position to reinstate the cease-fire. The UN was instructed to pursue the chimera of a cease-fire, when everyone knew and had been told that the final 'red line' had been crossed and that it was now a fight to the finish. Thus, the UN withdrew peacekeepers and abandoned civilians under their protection when the UN knew a genocide was underway.

Structural problems

Early warning is not only a matter of accurate and adequate information and its precise transmission. It is also a question of the decision-makers having a structure in place to process, analyse and interpret that information, develop strategic alternatives, and make decisions based on the analysis provided and the strategic options available. This problem was more serious than gaps, breaks or distortions in the lines of communication.

Both the field and headquarters lacked an independent body or team, not involved in operational functions, charged with responsibility for gathering, analysing and interpreting information. Within headquarters,

---

[28] Chapter VII of the UN Charter concerns Action with Respect to Threats to the Peace, Breaches of the Peace, and Acts of Aggression (articles 39–51).

[29] See 'The Special Report of the Secretary-General on UNAMIR', UN Doc. S/1994/470, 20 April 1994 in *The United Nations and Rwanda 1993–1996*, pp. 262–5.

a tiny staff was charged with running twenty peacekeeping and observer missions around the world, a fourfold increase since the term of Javier Pérez de Cuéllar. Since several of the conflict areas were 'hot spots' at the time – Bosnia, Haiti – Rwanda had to compete for the attention of the decision-makers. Further, preparing options for the Security Council was led by DPKO rather than the Department of Political Affairs (DPA), partly because James Jonah had left his position as Under-Secretary-General for Political Affairs in charge of peacemaking in Africa and the Middle East a few months earlier, and partly because the Secretary-General was travelling from eastern Europe to Bonn, Geneva and Madrid during this crisis period. The Security Council never received a paper fully outlining the situation, the implications of different scenarios, the available capacities and the options available with the various pros and cons attached. The Secretariat was not equipped to provide the appropriate analysis, nor did it operate in a professional manner given the personnel and information at hand.

The most serious problem, however, was the constitution of the executive body. Put simply, it was not an executive body, but a political body made up of rings of influence. The USA was in the centre. In the next ring were France and the UK. In the third ring could be found Russia and China. The fourth ring consisted of Western countries that favoured the strengthening of the UN and included New Zealand, which held the presidency during the crisis period. Finally, the fifth ring consisted of the non-aligned members, which at the time were led by Nigeria. Nigeria, supported by New Zealand in the presidency, was the country which persistently raised the issue of the Security Council's obligation to protect civilians.

The fact is, the Security Council lacked any coherence to enable it to respond to an emergency. Further, its most powerful member is the UN's weakest supporter. Even before May 1994 when the US President issued a presidential directive which severely restricted US support for UN peacekeeping operations, US support was limited. If the most powerful member of the executive body remained fundamentally sceptical about the functions of that body and unwilling adequately to support them, that alone influences how senior UN staff place options before the Security Council.

Nevertheless, none of the above is sufficient to explain why the DPKO failed to place before the UN Security Council, at least as an option, the maintenance of the operation with some minor reinforcements of troops and equipment in order to enable UNAMIR to protect civilians without interposing itself between the two warring armies. It can be argued that such an option would be unrealistic and would inevitably lead to a clash between UNAMIR and the Rwandese army. Largely because of the war and the imminent defeat of the army, as well as the subsequent experience with Operation Turquoise,[30] I happen to believe that such a risk in the case of Rwanda was minimal. In any case, the protection of civilians should have been a clear option put before the Security Council with the merits and demerits, as DPKO saw them, clearly spelled out. No such proposal came before the Security Council. Somehow, the organisation of the Security Council and the UN Secretariat does not seem to encourage a free flow of information and a full analysis of options in its highly charged political atmosphere.

Shadows

In the indicator models of early warning, a distinction is made between situational variables and underlying structural elements, such as the shortage of land, the demographic density of Rwanda, and ethnic divisions that have previously been politicised, all of which created conditions ripe for violence. Situational variables, such as the assassination of the Hutu president of Burundi in October 1993, are circumstances which can be exploited to allow gangs of unemployed youths to be recruited, indoctrinated and trained for committing violence. These structural and situational variables existed on the national, regional and international level and were well known to all the parties involved. Uniquely, in this case, even the event that would trigger a massive slaughter was known, namely the political implementation of the Arusha Accords, though the incident that would be used to sabotage that implementation was unknown to all but the few conspirators. These factors, however, did not determine the result. They merely provided the conditions which facilitated such results.

In the end, genocide is the result both of human decisions to commit the acts and of human decisions which fail to prevent the act from happening. In this case the latter decisions were not simply the products of structural and situational variables, but were very much influenced by previous events (which I term shadows) that haunted the decision-makers, by random circumstances, by patterns of action and response, and by the timing of coincident events and actions. In addition to more distant shadows, such as events in the former Yugoslavia and preconceptions about traditional peacekeeping that seemed to blind the decision-

---

[30] Once the genocide spread throughout the countryside, it became much more difficult to provide protection. See Gérard Prunier, *The Rwanda Crisis*, p. 292, where he noted that the Tutsis they could help were those in large concentrations as opposed to those spread throughout the countryside or who had fled to the countryside.

makers to the realities facing them and the real options available, the Rwanda crisis was shadowed by four African situations which I list in increasing importance.

The first was the Ugandan shadow in which the events leading to the assumption of power by Yoweri Museveni from Milton Obote in 1989, and the subsequent events within Uganda which directly influenced the decision of the refugees to return to Rwanda by force, their ability to do so, and the perception of that return as one sponsored by a foreign country. The second shadow was the 1993 Arusha Accords, for the inertial force and importance of the peace accords so preoccupied almost all the outside players that they permitted the growing organisation of the extremists intent on undermining the peace to slip into the background. Even after 6 April, the momentum of the Arusha Accords was so great that the major focus, after the extrication of UN civilians, was the reinstatement of a cease-fire and the peace accords. Yet only a very little analysis indicated that their resurrection was highly unlikely given the new players at the table, their programme, and the response to them by the RPF. The third shadow was Somalia which haunted decision-makers at the UN and led the US government to view the Rwandese operation through the Somali lens, resulting in a propensity to follow the Belgian advice and withdraw almost entirely from Rwanda.

The fourth and most important shadow was the one overhanging Rwanda itself – Burundi. The presidential and legislative elections in June 1993 in which Melchior Ndadaye, a Hutu, was elected President, probably gave a boost to the peace process. On the other hand, the attempted coup and Ndadaye's assassination in October 1993 not only strongly reinforced the suspicions and claims of the extremists within Rwanda, but created a weak southern flank for UNAMIR; to monitor events in the south, peacekeepers had to be drawn from Kigali, the demilitarised zone, and the Ugandan border. These 'shadows' were critical, but they were deeply affected by three very different temporal factors.

Coincidence

Luck and contingent circumstances are very important elements which are unpredictable and yet often play a critical role in influencing events and responses to developments. A majority of concurrent events had negative consequences on Rwanda; some of the more immediate and proximate serendipitous factors that coincided were:

1. the arrival of the International Human Rights Commission during a slaughter in January 1993;

2. the publication of the Human Rights Report just when the peace initiative had been renewed;
3. the peace negotiations and elections in Burundi in June 1993;
4. the Arusha Accords and the slaughter of US citizens in Somalia August 1993;
5. the publication of the UN Human Rights Report when the Peace Accords had just been signed; and
6. the arrival of Dallaire in Rwanda at the time of the coup in Burundi in October 1993.

The Arusha Accords were a relief in relation to other immediate crises. Among these were the 500,000 Sudanese at risk of famine, the massacre of the bus passengers at Afula in Israel in April 1994, the security and safety of the UN troops around Gorazde in Bosnia-Herzegovina, and Russian opposition to the application of the term 'ethnic cleansing' to events in Prijedor and Banja Luka in Bosnia-Herzegovina. At the same time as the situation was particularly tense in Kigali in March 1994, the UN was preoccupied with crises in Russia, Angola, Bosnia, Burundi, El Salvador, Georgia, Haiti, Liberia, Nagorny-Karabakh, Somalia, South Africa, Tajikistan, Eritrea-Sudan, Mozambique and Hebron. The clamour from these crises was overwhelming, so it is a wonder anything was heard.

Timeliness

Another critical factor which influenced events considerably was the timeliness of decisions and actions. Among the conditions related to conflict management, timing is one which managers can affect. The indication in the Rwanda crisis is that the timing factor was not well handled in New York, though the response time of the peacekeepers themselves seemed to be exemplary.

Let me list one which was critical, though in context is very explicable. The Secretary-General could not and was not authorised to send troops to Rwanda until an agreement was in place, and then only when the Security Council had authorised the deployment after receipt of a full feasibility and operational report. The agreement to have an international neutral force was reached in Arusha on 6 June 1993, two months before the Accords themselves were actually signed. The Secretary-General had to locate a force commander, which he did in two weeks. When Dallaire was contacted in the latter part of June, he had to wind up and transfer his military responsibilities in Canada to someone else. By July, he was ready to be briefed and begin preparing for what he might need. When the Arusha Accords were signed, he immediately prepared to take a team to

Kigali, and by the end of August had concluded his reconnaissance mission. A detailed report had to be prepared and appear in both English and French. By the third week of September it was ready. It had to compete for attention and priority with Haiti; Haiti won. The report had to be studied by the various departments of the UN and submitted to the Security Council.

It is no surprise that a decision on deployment took until 4 October, almost one month after the deadline for deployment set at Arusha had passed, and three months after the initial word had been received that the parties to the conflict had agreed on the deployment of a neutral UN force. Then, the troops had still to be recruited. Further, it was a phased deployment, with the second phase contingent on a review. Eight months were to lapse between the decision in early June 1993 to have a neutral international force and the full deployment of that force.

Toward a comprehensive explanation for failure

The explanation for the failure of the international community to intervene in the genocide in a country where it would have been easy to stop with relatively small military means and where the legal authority already existed to allow the peacekeepers to protect civilians, cannot be assigned to money. After all, the international community, one year after the genocide, had already spent six times the sum it would have cost to prevent it, even without including all the costs in subsequent years. In attempting to be 'penny wise' as a result of pressure from a US government suspicious of the UN, the USA and the UN could be said to have been 'pound foolish'.

A second explanation for the failure to heed warnings or respond expeditiously is located in history, in the determination by the high-level staff at the UN and the US government not to experience a repetition of the situation in Somalia. However, if Somalia scared the UN and the major powers, Burundi scared the Hutus in Rwanda. The Kantian 'good guys' were too mesmerised by the success and promise of the Arusha Accords to make adequate contingency plans for those hurt by the Accords.[31]

In addition to money and ghosts, either as devils or angels of deliverance, which haunted the peace process, structural elements are part of the explanation. For example, the Security Council is not an executive body but a series of concentric rings of coalitions. The UN lacks a singular executive body with any cohesion or unity. Further, in addition to all the

---

[31] Stedman calls them 'spoilers'. See Stephen Stedman, 'Spoiler Problems in Peace Processes', 22 *International Security*, 1997, 2, pp. 5–53.

other humanitarian and diplomatic responsibilities, the head of the institution now has peacekeepers all over the world with a very small headquarters staff. These few bureaucrats are required to administer a military operation within a host of bureaucratic procedures that would drive anyone mad. The UN lacks a standby rapid deployment force to deal with emergencies. It lacks any uniformity in equipment and training (for example, when the ten Belgian paratroopers were arrested by the Presidential Guards in April 1994, the local lieutenant's message had to be relayed through three incompatible sets of communication equipment to report to the Force Commander). The UN peacekeepers lack any formal intelligence-analysis capacity independent of operations, both in the field and at headquarters, so that the pieces of information that filter in can be assembled to undertake an intelligence analysis from which alternative strategies can be developed and weighed. In other words, there is simply no early warning system in the UN, though the UN Integrated Regional Information Network (IRIN) and ReliefNet now serve as a foundation for an early warning system by distributing information.[32]

The UN seeks to control and manage in the most Byzantine bureaucratic system imaginable – lest it leave itself open to any possibility of accusations of corruption and mismanagement by its members. This is one reason why the UN did not delegate the peacekeeping task to the OAU through a supply of equipment, training and resources, even though it was the OAU which could be credited with the series of diplomatic breakthroughs in the peace process. The UN insistence on management and control came from a body that not only lacked any capacity for a rapid deployment force itself, but was unable to provide adequate material support to its own peacekeepers.

Normative factors

All these factors, including many of the other factors already cited and many more, which space precludes from detailed mention here, *explain at one level* why the UN did not intervene to prevent and stop the genocide. They do not explain the *ethical* failure. There was a gross failure to implement international legal norms on genocide. The systems for the implementation of norms governing civilian protection, like those with respect to the norms governing the solution of refugee problems, may be inadequate.

This is true of the norms governing the treatment of refugees. For

---

[32] For example, the IRIN updates in the Great Lakes region of Africa can be obtained by e-mail by contacting irin-cea-updates@ocha.unon.org

example, in refugee matters, countries of origin are obliged to allow their nationals the right to be repatriated.[33] States may not permit invasions of other states from their territories. These norms are not always compatible, either in principle or in practice. Thus, norms affirming the right of refugees to return, and norms against using military force from outside the country to enforce that right, seem to be at odds in practice.

However, no similar ambiguity existed with respect to the strictures against intervention in the internal affairs of Rwanda and the legal right and moral obligation to intervene to stop the mass slaughter of civilians according to the Genocide Convention. There is an obligation *not* to intervene in the internal affairs of sovereign states *except* in cases of genocide.[34] At a deeper level, the key problem was not one of conflict management or even early warning: it was a normative problem. We have norms to which most countries subscribe, but these same countries do not see their duty as being to ensure that these norms are implemented.

Conclusion

The least important problem in Rwanda was an absence of information or lack of communication about the potential disaster from the field. The absurdity of the wealthy West and the UN not adequately responding to a 'low-tech' genocide in a small, poor country when information was available in advance, and then responding by withdrawal when the genocide was underway, and finally taking months to re-enter when the genocide

---

[33] These norms also include the problem of refugees exercising their 'right of return' through armed force in the case of the OAU Convention on refugees, which, in that respect, differs from other instruments of international refugee law. Article 12(2) of the African Charter on Human and Peoples' Rights states: 'Every individual shall have the right to . . . return to his country. This right may only be subject to restrictions provided for by law for the protection of national security, law and order, public health and morality.' The same right is affirmed in article 13(2) of the 1948 Universal Declaration of Human Rights (42 *American Journal of International Law*, 1949, Supplement 127), though it is not qualified as in the African Charter, while article 12(4) of the 1966 International Covenant on Civil and Political Rights (6 ILM, 1967, p. 368) is similar. For a more general analysis of the ethics of refugee repatriation, see Howard Adelman, 'Refugees: The Right of Return', in *Group Rights* (ed. Judith Baker, University of Toronto Press, 1994), pp. 164–85.

[34] Parties to the Genocide Convention have the legal right and the moral obligation under international law to investigate and to take measures to halt genocide and punish the perpetrators. While some UN bodies determined by early May 1994 that a genocide was taking place in Rwanda, powerful individual member states equivocated. The US State Department and the US National Security Council instructed US spokespersons in June to claim only that 'acts of genocide may have occurred'. See Douglas Jehl, 'Officials Told to Avoid Calling Rwanda Killings "Genocide"', *New York Times*, 10 June 1994, p. A8. Further, the Justice Department interpreted the Genocide Convention narrowly as permitting states to intervene, but not obligating them to do so.

became known throughout the world, is not satisfied by the 'rational' explanations provided. Rational systems are intended to enable a body to respond to unforeseen events and contingent factors in the light of what was already known. Instead, in this situation, the shadows and contingent factors scared the decision-makers. The fact that top decision-makers acted in response to ghosts and accidents rather than rational deliberation or accepted norms requires a deeper level of explanation best left for further analysis.

Bibliography

Adelman, Howard, 'Refugees: The Right of Return', in *Group Rights* (ed. Judith Baker, University of Toronto Press, 1994), pp. 164–85

Adelman, Howard and Astri Suhrke, *Early Warning and Conflict Management: Genocide in Rwanda* (Danish International Development Agency (DANIDA), Copenhagen, 1996)

(eds.), *The Path of a Genocide: The Rwanda Crisis from Uganda to Zaire* (Transaction Books, Trenton, NJ, 1999)

Braeckman, Colette, *Rwanda, histoire d'un génocide* (Fayard, Paris, 1994)

Brauman, Rony, *Devant le mal: Rwanda un génocide en direct* (Arléa, Paris, 1994)

Chrétien, Jean-Pierre, 'Hutu et Tutsi au Rwanda et au Burundi', in *Au coeur de l'ethnie* (ed. J. L. Amselle and E. M. Bokolo, La Découverte, Paris, 1985), pp. 129–66

Destexhe, Alain, *Rwanda: Essai sur la génocide* (Complexe, Brussels, 1994)

Leitenberg, Milton, 'The Case of Rwanda: US and UN Actions Result in Escalation of Genocide and Higher Costs', in *Contemporary Genocides: Causes, Cases, Consequences* (ed. Albert J. Jongman, Interdisciplinary Research Programme on Root Causes of Human Rights Violation (PIOOM), Leiden, 1996), pp. 131–40

Newbury, Catherine, *The Cohesion of Oppression: Citizenship and Ethnicity in Rwanda (1860–1960)* (Columbia University Press, New York, 1988)

Prunier, Gérard, *The Rwanda Crisis: History of a Genocide* (Columbia University Press, New York, 1995)

Rothchild, Donald, 'Ethnic Bargaining and State Breakdown in Africa', 1 *Nationalism and Ethnic Politics*, 1995, 1, pp. 54–72

United Nations, *The United Nations in Rwanda, 1993–1996* (United Nations, New York, 1996)

Part 4

The European regime

15 The impetus to harmonise: asylum policy in the European Union

Elspeth Guild

Introduction

In the first paragraph of the preamble of the European Community (EC) Treaty can be discerned the seeds of the fundamental divergence in political perspective of the member states which in turn finds specific expression in the policies of the European Union (EU) on immigration and asylum in respect of the third country nationals. The preamble states: 'Determined to lay the foundations of an ever closer union among the peoples of Europe.'

This first expression of political intention commences with the word 'determined' which implies opposition, and is equally the first word to be found in the EC Treaty. As Professor Weiler has argued, there is a fundamentally elusive quality to the objective of an ever closer union among the peoples of Europe.[1] Implicit in the formulation of the expression 'ever closer' is the recognition that the actual union itself may never be achieved or indeed may not even be desired. Further, the use of the plural 'peoples' is a clear recognition of diversity which itself may be seen as an advantage or an insurmountable obstacle to union.

The conflict, apparent in the preamble, perhaps provides a background to the lack of clarity which characterises the development of policy in many areas of EU activity but may also be seen as a paradigm for the confusion prevailing in asylum policy.

This chapter outlines the process leading to increased co-operation among member states on asylum policy. Starting with the impetus to harmonise provided by the free movement provisions of the Single European Act,[2] it examines the problems surrounding intergovernmental moves to conclude conventions between the member states, as evidenced by the experience of the Dublin Convention,[3] and charts member states'

---

[1] W. G. Hart Legal Workshop, 1996.   [2] OJ, 1987, L169.

[3] Dublin Convention Determining the State Responsible for Examining Applications for Asylum Lodged in One of the Member States of the European Communities, OJ, 1997, C254; and 30 ILM, 1991, p. 425. Entered into force for twelve of the EU member states on 1 September 1997, for Austria and Sweden on 1 October 1997 and for Finland on 1 January 1998. See also pp. 318–22 below.

increasing preference for non-binding instruments. The provisions and shortcomings of the five key European instruments concerning asylum (the three 'London Resolutions',[4] the Resolution on minimum guarantees for asylum procedures[5] and the Joint Position on a harmonised definition of the term 'refugee'[6]) are analysed in some detail.[7] Finally, the new direction embarked upon since the signing of the Treaty of Amsterdam[8] in October 1997 is shown as providing an enhanced role for the EC institutions, although prospects for asylum seekers being able to gain protection from persecution in the EU remain poor.

The impetus to harmonise

The origins of the European Union are deeply set in economic policy. The purpose and reason for the existence of the three initial treaties is and always was irrevocably to bind member states together through the integration of their national economies.[9] The strategy was to set limited and specific economic objectives as steps towards the long-term political objective of European Union.[10] The weakening of political will towards the project in the late 1970s and early 1980s was manifested in endless wrangling over contribution rates of the member states and in particular the United Kingdom. The EC institutional response during the term of Jacques Delors as President of the Commission was to face squarely the fact that the common market had not materialised and to commence the 1992 single market project, under which physical, technical or fiscal barriers to trade among the member states were to be removed.[11]

The political commitment to the creation of a single market was formalised with the adoption of the Single European Act in 1987. This inserted article 7a into the European Economic Community (EEC) Treaty, which describes the internal market as 'an area without internal frontiers in which the free movement of goods, persons, services and capital is ensured'. This single market was to be achieved by 31 December 1992.

Even at this stage, however, alarm bells were ringing in the interior ministries of those member states where the emphasis of the phrase 'an ever closer union among the peoples of Europe' was found in the

---

[4] Note from the General Secretariat of the Council to the Asylum Working Party on the *Compilation of Texts on European Practice with Respect to Asylum (March 1996 Update)*, 4464/1/95, Rev. 1.   [5] OJ, 1996, C274/13.   [6] OJ, 1996, L63/2.
[7] For broader discussion of instruments adopted at this inter-governmental level, see chapter 17 of this volume.   [8] OJ, 1997, C340/01, 37 ILM, 1998, p. 44.
[9] Derrick Wyatt and Alan Dashwood, *European Community Law* (3rd edn, Sweet and Maxwell, London, 1993), pp. 4ff.   [10] *Ibid.*, p. 4.
[11] Paolo Cecchini, *The European Challenge, 1992, the Benefits of a Single Market* (Gower, London, 1988).

differentiation of peoples and the uncertainty of the goal of union.[12] The question was how to achieve the goal of abolishing barriers to trade between the member states while maintaining control over the movement of people. This conundrum found expression in a Political Declaration on the free movement of persons attached to the Single European Act which stated that in promoting free movement of persons, no action should 'affect the right of Member States to take such measures as they consider necessary for the purpose of controlling immigration from third countries, and to combat terrorism, crime, and the traffic in drugs and illicit trading in works of art and antiques'.[13]

Even before the Single European Act came into force, a first meeting of ministers responsible for immigration was held in London in the second half of 1986.[14] While the ministers confirmed their commitment to the promotion of the free movement of persons in accordance with the Act, doubts were already being raised as to the compatibility of the abolition of internal frontier controls with the aim of controlling immigration of third country nationals. Therefore, from the commencement of the 1992 project to complete the single market two sets of competing concerns may be identified which are particularly relevant to the subsequent harmonisation of asylum policy in the EU.

First, there was the conflict between the member states' genuine desire to abolish intra-EC obstacles to trade and the concerns of interior ministries to maintain control over third country nationals entering their territory. Secondly, the ambition of some member states to achieve a union among the peoples of Europe contrasted with the objective of other member states to move towards the objective but not to arrive. For instance, the approach of the UK government to some extent might be described by the adage 'it is better to travel hopefully than to arrive'.

The Palma Document

The Report to the European Council by the Co-ordinators' Group, Note on the Free Movement of Persons, the so-called 'Palma Document',[15] was produced

[12] Demetrios G. Papademetriou, *Coming Together or Pulling Apart? The European Union's Struggle with Immigration and Asylum* (International Migration Policy Program, Carnegie Endowment for International Peace, Washington DC, 1996), p. 24.
[13] General Declaration on articles 13–19 of the Single European Act 1987.
[14] This was the first formal meeting of interior and justice ministers of the member states in their new capacity as 'ministers responsible for immigration'. Previous meetings had taken place informally. See Papademetriou, *Coming Together or Pulling Apart?*
[15] The Palma Document, *A Report to the European Council by the Co-ordinators' Group, Note on the Free Movement of Persons* reprinted in Elspeth Guild and Jan Niessen, *The Developing Immigration and Asylum Policies of the European Union* (Kluwer Law International, The Hague, 1996), p. 444.

at the request of the European Council to establish the measures necessary for creating an area without internal frontiers.[16] It was adopted by the Council in June 1989 and has been described as the Community's internal frontier-elimination master plan outlining a dual strategy of first strengthening checks at the external frontiers of the EC and then abolishing internal border checks.[17]

At this critical initial point in time the dispute as to the competence of the member states and that of the Community in respect of free movement of persons was already recognised. A political decision was taken *not* to address the issue but to seek to make progress on a practical level. The wisdom of such a compromise may well be questioned as the failure to deal with this fundamental aspect has bedevilled all future work relating to the abolition of border controls and so to the harmonisation of asylum policy.

The Palma Document specifies that the achievement of an area without internal frontiers would involve the approximation of national laws and their rules of application and scope, collaboration between national administrations and a prior strengthening of checks at external frontiers. To this end a set of legal, administrative and technical instruments was needed to harmonise the grant of asylum and refugee status. This common policy, based on the member states' obligations pursuant to their accession to the 1951 Geneva Convention Relating to the Status of Refugees and the 1967 New York Protocol,[18] focused on five aspects:

1. the acceptance of identical international commitments with regard to asylum;
2. the determination of the state responsible for examining the application for asylum;
3. simplified or priority procedures for the examination of clearly unfounded requests;
4. the conditions governing the movement of the asylum seekers between the member states; and
5. a study of the need for a financing system to fund the economic consequences of implementing the common policy.

Inter-governmental co-operation

The forum chosen for developments in the field of immigration and asylum as flanking measures to the creation of the single market was inter-governmental. This choice was the direct result of the conflict

---

[16] *Ibid.*   [17] Papademetriou, *Coming Together or Pulling Apart?*, p. 37.
[18] 189 UNTS 137 and 606 UNTS 267 respectively.

apparent in the Palma Document as to the legal effect and scope of article 7a of the EC Treaty creating the single market. Between 1986 and 1993, the year of entry into force of the Treaty on European Union (TEU),[19] the only venue for discussing the harmonisation of asylum law in the EU was inter-governmental, although within this inter-governmental context there was a proliferation of different groups looking at different aspects.[20] This in itself was a source of criticism, in particular from the European Parliament which was effectively excluded from any participation in the debate.

By the end of this inter-governmental phase of co-operation, immigration and asylum-related issues were under consideration in the following EC fora:

1. the Trevi Group set up in 1976 to co-ordinate efforts against terrorism and extended in 1980 to include illegal immigration and asylum flows which included four subgroups: (i) terrorism; (ii) police co-operation; (iii) serious crimes and drug trafficking; and (iv) policing and security implications of the Single European Act;

2. the Ad Hoc Group on Immigration which grew out of the Trevi Group in 1986 (without replacing it) which was charged with responsibility for developing common policies on immigration and asylum; it had six subgroups: (i) asylum; (ii) external frontiers; (iii) false documents; (iv) admissions; (v) deportation; and (vi) information exchange;

3. the Horizontal Group on Data Processing, the primary function of which was to produce the European Information System designed to combat serious forms of crime and strengthen external border controls and police co-operation in fighting illegal immigration networks through the exchange of information; and

4. the Customs Mutual Assistance Group, charged with the co-ordination of customs and other technical information exchange and maintenance issues in order to strengthen external border controls.[21]

Each of these groups was in one way or another intricately involved in the 1992 project. Without the objective of the abolition of internal border controls the need (or as some would have it, the excuse) for such groups would not have materialised and many of them would not have existed. One difficulty with inter-governmental groups of senior officials is that once established they are difficult to abolish.

Accordingly, the impetus to harmonise European asylum policy was a

---

[19] OJ, 1992, C224.

[20] Guild and Niessen, *The Developing Immigration and Asylum Policies*, pp. 31ff.

[21] António Cruz, *Schengen, Ad Hoc Immigration Group and Other European Intergovernmental Bodies in View of a Europe Without Internal Borders* (Churches' Committee for Migrants in Europe, Briefing Paper No. 12, June 1993).

by-product of an economic imperative to create a single market. This political will expressed in the late 1980s and early 1990s to create a genuine single market by abolishing obstacles to trade among the member states was spearheaded by the Commission under Delors. In view of what was at stake, the Commission opposed and prevented the derailing of the 1992 project by the concerns of interior ministries in some member states, which were anxious to retain control over the admission of third country nationals generally and asylum seekers in particular. Instead, that aspect of harmonisation necessary to achieve the single market was allowed to be hived off into an extremely active intergovernmental limbo which has subsequently blocked the abolition of internal frontier controls, one of the goals of the project, while at the same time has catapulted European policy into a downward spiral of harmonising asylum policy to the level of the lowest common denominator across the Union.

The Dublin Convention and the shortcomings of the convention approach

The tension between the Commission and the member states regarding competence for third country nationals found specific expression in the action brought before the European Court of Justice by the member states against the Commission as regards a consultation procedure on immigration laws in 1985.[22] This resulted in an uneasy truce whereby the Commission took no further action in respect of immigration of third country nationals and left the field open, without prejudice to its competence, to the member states.

The Dublin Convention was the first fruit of the member states' intergovernmental efforts to co-ordinate, if not harmonise, asylum policy within the Community. Signed on 15 June 1990 and effective since 1 September 1997, the Convention is designed to identify which member state has responsibility for examining an asylum application and to ensure that only one state determines any application. In other words, in preparation for the abolition of internal frontiers, the Convention was envisaged as a system to prevent asylum seekers from applying for asylum in more than one state, either simultaneously or consecutively, by taking advantage of unrestricted access to the territory of all the member states once within one of them.

The underlying principle of the Convention was to establish a system

---

[22] C-281, 283-5 and 287/85, *Germany and Others v. EC Commission* [1988] 1 CMLR 11; [1987] ECR 3203.

of responsibility based on the asylum seeker's residence or, in the absence of residence, where the asylum seeker had entered the EU. Therefore, an asylum seeker who entered the EU over a land border in Germany who was not in possession of a visa or residence permit for any member state and who applied for asylum in France would, subject to countervailing circumstances, have his or her asylum application determined in Germany and would be returned to that state for the purpose.

In the development of the EU's asylum policy, the Dublin Convention can be seen as setting the framework which has since been elaborated and provides the theoretical foundation of all subsequent work. The underlying premise is that an asylum applicant ought to seek asylum in the first safe country to which he or she arrives and that country must accept responsibility for determining the application.[23] Exceptions to this principle are only permitted under article 3(4) on the basis of the presence of very close family members who have been recognised as refugees in another state or a voluntary choice by the state to accept responsibility for the individual, that is, by issuing a residence permit or visa or by an indication that, even though not liable under the first state rule, it will accept responsibility.

In administrative terms this policy relieves all but the initial host state of any responsibility to consider the substantive merits of an asylum application. The most difficult task for any administration in the determination of an asylum application is the assessment of the risk of persecution and the credibility of the individual. By removing this aspect from the equation in all cases except those where the state is itself the first state to which the asylum seeker came, the procedures for determining asylum applications, in theory, ought to speed up substantially. This may be perceived as a way of reducing the administrative burden of asylum applications faced by some states, in particular those with small numbers of asylum applicants arriving directly from persecution at their borders.

The initial consequences of this approach were, first, a perception by the member states that controlled access to their territory from third countries was critical as each state was responsible for the substantive determination of all asylum applications from persons who first arrived in their state. In the process, the state also became responsible for caring for the asylum seeker, an expense shouldered with increasing unwillingness by some member states. This responsibility, in turn, fuelled the adoption

---

[23] See chapter 13 of this volume on the question of the asylum seeker's right to choose the country of his or her asylum.

across Europe of liability on carriers, particularly airlines, for bringing persons without proper documentation to their territory.[24]

Secondly, those member states sharing extensive land borders with third countries were likely to receive the most numerous applications for asylum which would require a substantive determination. In the light of events in central and eastern Europe in 1989–90 and the very substantial land borders with third countries of what was soon to be the largest member state, the policy was refined further to include the conclusion of readmission agreements with third countries bordering on the member states on a bilateral basis.[25]

Turning to the wider consequences of this policy, it may be valid to suggest that it introduced a new form of territorial limitation on the right to seek asylum. Just as the 1967 Protocol lifted the original territorial limitation of the Geneva Convention so that it could apply to refugees wherever arising in the world and as a result of whatever circumstances, so now the EU is developing a new form of territorial limitation. According to new thinking which began with the Dublin Convention and was refined and developed in the subsequent inter-governmental measures (see below), asylum seekers must apply for asylum in the first safe state in which they arrive and stay there. This will usually be a state in the region, most often on the borders of the state where they fear persecution. Any subsequent effort to flee farther afield will result in their return to that first state. Therefore for the refugee him or herself, there is in fact a territorial limitation on the right to apply for asylum. Whichever state he or she first arrives in will be the state where he or she must remain unless a fear of persecution in that state can be substantiated.

This limitation may be less conclusive than that which appeared in the Geneva Convention as originally drafted in that it relates to the individual circumstances of the applicant. However, as a very substantial number of asylum seekers are unable to flee directly from their own state to the state where they would wish to seek refuge and therefore travel to a neighbouring state before embarking on a more distant flight, the consequences are nonetheless territorial. This consequence is clearer where there are no direct flights from the country of origin to any member state where the asylum application is made. Increasingly the suspension of direct air links

[24] António Cruz, *Shifting Responsibility: Carriers' Liability in the Member States of the European Union and North America* (Trentham Books and School of Oriental and African Studies, Stoke-on-Trent, Staffordshire, 1995); and Frances Nicholson, 'Implementation of the Immigration (Carriers' Liability) Act 1987: Privatising Immigration Functions at the Expense of International Obligations', 46 *International and Comparative Law Quarterly*, 1997, pp. 586–634.

[25] Recommendation concerning a specimen bilateral readmission agreement between a Member State of the European Union and a third country, OJ, 1996, C274/20.

with countries in turmoil has the consequence of trapping asylum seekers from those counties in the third country cycle, since in order to flee they must travel, even in transit, to a third state so that when they arrive in the EU their asylum applications will generally be ineligible for determination on the merits, as in most cases there will be a safe third country to which they can be returned.

Returning for the moment to the Dublin Convention which constitutes the first step towards this policy, the weakness clearly lies in the differential rates of recognition of refugees from the same country by different EU member states. While there may be a certain random quality as to where an asylum seeker ends up applying for asylum, that choice may be critical to whether or not his or her asylum application is likely to be successful or not. The statistics on recognition rates among the member states still vary substantially in proportion to the numbers of applications received by each state. This may indicate a difference in sympathy of different member states towards asylum seekers from various countries, though it is not uncommon to hear officials involved in asylum processing complain that the problem really lies in the fact that their state receives the 'wrong type' of asylum seekers.

The second injustice is in relation to the adequacy of procedures and appeal mechanisms. So long as the legal protection of asylum seekers and the rights of appeal against refusal of their asylum applications continue to vary among the member states, let alone outside the EU, the system of sending asylum seekers back to the first safe country they reached on fleeing persecution may result in real detriment to their chance of finding protection from persecution.

In other words, without equivalence in the way in which asylum applications are determined and in judicial remedies with a supervisory appellate structure to ensure consistency across the member states (and any other states to which asylum seekers are sent) the protection against *refoulement*[26] to which the signatory states of the Geneva Convention have adhered may not be fulfilled.

The problems of lack of consistency in asylum determination and access to procedural remedies have been at least partially remedied by the Amsterdam Treaty which gives a competence to the Community to adopt measures on, *inter alia*, minimum standards with respect to the qualification of nationals of third countries as refugees, and minimum standards on procedures in member states for granting or withdrawing refugee status (article 73k of the Amsterdam Treaty) and a duty to adopt such measures within five years of entry into force of the Treaty. However,

---

[26] Geneva Convention, article 33.

in-built into the solution are two checks: first there are opt-outs in the form of protocols for the UK, Ireland and Denmark which will only participate in the new provisions on asylum in the Treaty if they choose to opt in. Secondly, the power of the European Court of Justice to give guidance to national courts on the interpretation of the new provisions on asylum is limited. Only courts of final instance may seek the guidance of the European Court of Justice (article 73p of the Amsterdam Treaty).

Indeed, the Dublin Convention is also likely to be the subject matter of a new Community measure, which must be adopted within five years of entry into force of the Amsterdam Treaty. However, initial experiences on the application of the Dublin Convention indicate that, without effective and enforceable common standards on the definition of asylum and protection, its application is resulting in unequal treatment of refugees across the Union.[27]

Member states' use of less-binding instruments: the London Resolutions

Not long after the signing of the Dublin Convention it became apparent that the convention format was a particularly cumbersome way of dealing with approximation and harmonisation in the fields of asylum and immigration. This is not least because of the political sensitivities which 'ring fence' the field.

Where harmonisation is sought through the medium of a convention signed by all of the parties and then presented to their parliaments, there is no scope for the parliaments when debating the draft convention realistically to propose amendments to it. One of the shortcomings of the Dublin Convention as identified by some parliaments, (most notably the Dutch parliament) is the lack of a judicial dispute resolution mechanism. The only means of amendment is by way of a protocol. Therefore national parliamentary participation is limited to placing conditions, to wit the conclusion of a protocol, on its approval. The Dutch and Belgian parliaments long refused to ratify the Convention without an additional protocol giving jurisdiction to the European Court of Justice to adjudicate on disputes not only between the parties to the Convention but also on references from national courts in the context of individual appeals.[28] However, the political pressure on such recalcitrant parliaments is intense

---

[27] Steve Peers, *Mind the Gap! Ineffective Member State Implementation of the European Union Asylum Measures* (Immigration Law Practitioners' Association and Refugee Council, London, May 1998).

[28] Professor Dr K. Groenendijk, *Immigration Law Practitioners' Association Update*, September 1996.

and in the case of the Dublin Convention both eventually ratified it. In this case the position which was taken was primarily a matter of principle on democratic and judicial accountability of the harmonisation of asylum policy in the EU. To this extent the conflict could hardly be more fundamental to the constitutional balance of the member states and the Union. It was less a battle over the contents of the new European asylum policy.

The lesson, however, has not been lost on the member state governments. Clearly, in such a sensitive area as asylum policy the convention mechanism was not particularly appealing. Since 1990 only one further convention has been put forward among the member states in order to harmonise asylum policy.[29] Instead, the next step in this process was the creation of new hybrid measures the legal status of which has never properly been clarified but which are entitled Resolutions, Conclusions, Decisions and Recommendations.[30] The first three of these new forms of measure relating to asylum were adopted by the European Council on 30 November 1992 variously, the Resolution on manifestly unfounded applications for asylum, the Resolution on a harmonised approach to questions concerning host third countries and Conclusions on countries in which there is generally no serious risk of persecution.

The two Resolutions are peculiar documents in format in that they contain mandatory language and dates by which implementation is to be achieved and yet lack any legal structure for their adoption or implementation. As they are not part of Community law they have not been subject to the legislative process of the EC Treaty. Nor are they classic forms of inter-governmental agreements as they do not require ratification nor are they accompanied by any enforcement mechanism. This then leaves these measures in a legal limbo. They only acquire a legal identity if transposed into national law. This means that national parliaments are *prima facie* entitled to participate actively in the formulation of law in the sensitive area of asylum and are not being requested, by their executives, to rubber stamp conventions already signed as in the case of the Dublin Convention.

What is lost, however, is consistency and coherence of implementation

---

[29] Both the Convention on the Establishment of a European Police Office (Europol Convention), OJ, 1995, C316/01, which was opened for signature in July 1995 and entered into force on 1 October 1998 following completion of the member states' ratification process on 12 June 1998, and the EU Extradition Convention, OJ, 1996, C313/12, which was opened for signature in September 1996, are not directly related to asylum. The European Automated Fingerprinting Recognition System (EURODAC) Convention, agreement on a final text of which has yet to be concluded (see also chapter 17 of this volume) is more accurately an asylum Convention but the ratification process has encountered similar delays to the Dublin Convention.

[30] See also chapter 17 of this volume.

and application. The laws of the member states purporting to implement the principles of the measures will inevitably vary substantially from one member state to the other depending on the political issues of the day in any one state. It may be argued that a similar situation obtains in respect of those EC Directives which leave a substantial margin of appreciation to the member states as to how they wish to implement them so long as their objective is achieved. However, as regards Community law, the member states receive assistance from the Commission in respect of any proposal to implement and, following the transposition of a Directive into national law, the European Court of Justice has jurisdiction over interpretation and is frequently called upon to adjudicate on the interpretation of a Community Directive in the light of national implementing measures.

There is no mechanism in respect of the inter-governmental measures on asylum whereby action can be taken to enforce their implementation or require a member state to adapt its legislation. Notwithstanding the existence of an implementation date in some of the measures these are in fact toothless lions in that the measures themselves, without any clear legal force and without any administrative structure to supervise and ensure implementation, in effect, constitute no more than gentlemen's agreements.

Turning to the substance, the three measures adopted at the London Council Meeting in 1992 provide an interlocking web designed to screen out and determine rapidly asylum applications coming within two primary categories:

1. those of asylum applicants who have passed through a third country outside the EU before travelling to the member state; and
2. those of asylum applicants from countries which have been determined safe according to a nationally determined 'white list'.

The mechanism by which this is achieved is the Resolution on manifestly unfounded applications for asylum. According to paragraph 1 of the Resolution, an application for asylum should be regarded as manifestly unfounded, *inter alia*, because it comes within the ambit of the Resolution on host third countries or (at the option of the member state) because the applicant comes from a country designated in accordance with the Conclusions on countries in which there is generally no serious risk of persecution.

According to paragraph 3, where an asylum application is alleged to be manifestly unfounded, a decision on the application should be taken within one month and the completion of any appeal or review procedure should take place as soon as possible. Appeal or review procedures may be more simplified than those generally available in the case of other rejected asylum applications. Under paragraph 4 of the Resolution the only procedural guarantee to which an asylum seeker is entitled is that the decision will be taken by a competent authority at an appropriate level, who is fully qualified in asylum and refugee matters and that the applicant *should* be given the opportunity for a personal interview with a qualified official empowered under national law before any final decision is taken.

In accordance with the Resolution on a harmonised approach to questions concerning host third countries, it is specifically stated in paragraph 1(d) of that Resolution that, if an asylum applicant cannot, in practice, be sent to a host third country, only then should the provisions of the Dublin Convention apply. Therefore the principle of sending people beyond the member states' border is to take priority over the Dublin Convention system of selecting a state within the territory of the Union responsible for determining an asylum application. The Resolution on host third countries requires in paragraph 2 that the host third country must fulfil four criteria:

a) In those third countries, the life or freedom of the asylum applicant must not be threatened, within the meaning of Article 33 of the Geneva Convention.
b) The asylum applicant must not be exposed to torture or inhuman or degrading treatment in the third country.[31]
c) It must *either* be the case that the asylum applicant has already been granted protection in the third country or has had an opportunity, at the border or within the territory of the third country, to make contact with that country's authorities in order to seek their protection, before approaching the Member State in which he is applying for asylum, *or* that there is clear evidence of his admissibility to a third country.
d) The asylum applicant must be afforded effective protection in the host third country against *refoulement*, within the meaning of the Geneva Convention.

While these principles, in theory at least, ought to provide an asylum seeker with some protection against being sent to a host third state which he or she does not consider safe, in practice, in the implementation of the Resolution these requirements have not necessarily made their way into national law and therefore are not necessarily justiciable.[32]

This is one of the weaknesses of the measures at the moment. If they were in fact Community law then the applicant, in seeking to establish that a third country is not safe, could rely directly on the Resolution (if formulated in accordance with existing Community law) in order to

---

[31] No reference is made, though, to article 3 of the European Convention for the Protection of Human Rights and Fundamental Freedoms, 213 UNTS 221; ETS 5, article 3 of which states: 'No one shall be subjected to torture or to inhuman or degrading treatment or punishment.'

[32] For examples of the application of the 'safe third country' principle in EU states, see Danish Refugee Council, *'Safe Third Country' Policies in European Countries* (Copenhagen, 1997); and Peers, *Mind the Gap!*

defeat a claim by the member state that he or she should be returned there. In particular, the requirement that the asylum applicant be afforded effective protection against *refoulement* would be a particularly valuable protection for the applicant where he or she feared that the host third state would send him or her on to another state or the state of origin without an appropriate and adequate determination of the asylum claim.

It is interesting to consider this point again in the context of the Resolution on minimum guarantees for asylum procedures which was adopted by the European Council on 20 June 1995. Specifically, if the minimum guarantees for asylum procedures agreed by the member states as applicable where one member state is required to consider substantively the asylum claim, then the equivalent minimum guarantees for asylum procedures must apply in a host third country if it is to be considered safe for the return of the asylum seeker there.

Completing the structure: measures under the 'third pillar'

After the adoption of the three London Resolutions in 1992 there was something of a lull in the adoption of inter-governmental measures relating to asylum. Instead, the member states focused their attentions on adopting Resolutions, Recommendations and Conclusions in other areas, most notably, expulsion, family reunion, access to employment, self-employment and students.[33]

In the light of the civil war in the former Yugoslavia a Resolution was adopted in June 1993 on certain common guidelines as regards admission of particularly vulnerable persons from the former Yugoslavia.[34] This Resolution is of interest in that it marks a departure for the member states prescribing that admission ought to be granted to certain groups rather than defining which groups should be excluded. Nonetheless the Resolution does again present difficulties as regards its compatibility and interface with the Geneva Convention.

This hiatus in activity on asylum also marked the period between the signature and the belated entry into force of the TEU in November 1993 which finally provided a constitutional basis for the inter-governmental co-operation in the field of asylum which had until then been taking place in a legal limbo.

The TEU has most frequently been described as a temple structure.

[33] See texts in Guild and Niessen, *The Developing Immigration and Asylum Policies*; Richard Plender, *Basic Documents on International Migration Law* (2nd edn, Martinus Nijhoff, The Hague, 1997), Parts VII and VIII.

[34] *Compilation of Texts on European Practice with Respect to Asylum.*

Community law, the binding law of the EC Treaty, constitutes the 'first pillar' of the Union. A 'second pillar', Title V of the TEU, provides a constitutional basis for the political co-operation on a Common, Foreign and Security Policy (CFSP). The 'third pillar' of the temple structure, Title VI, provisions on co-operation in the fields of Justice and Home Affairs, finally provided a constitutional structure within the Union for the co-ordination and harmonisation of asylum law, although the 'third pillar' retained its inter-governmental character. In the 'third pillar', asylum policy is identified in article K.1 as a matter of common interest. Article K.2 requires that matters be dealt with in compliance with the European Convention on Human Rights and the Geneva Convention but provides that the 'third pillar' is without prejudice to member state action regarding the 'maintenance of law and order and the safeguarding of internal security'.

According to article K.3(2), all action taken under the 'third pillar' is executed by the Council on the initiative of any member state or of the Commission as regards asylum policy. This is a fundamental difference from the EC Treaty where only the Commission has a right of initiative. The member states' history, through inter-governmental co-operation, of directing the harmonisation of asylum policy has encouraged the Commission to keep very much in the background. It might even be said that the Commission has left the member states to sink or swim in Title VI on their own. Certainly the first independent assessment of results has been less than glowing.[35] The European Parliament was in effect marginalised from the activities under Title VI in that under article K.6 its only participation was through enforcement of the duty on the Presidency to consult the European Parliament on principal aspects of the activities. Even this duty on the Presidency appeared more honoured in the breach than the fulfilment. For instance, the 1995 Resolution on minimum guarantees for asylum procedures must be considered a principal aspect of the activities of the 'third pillar'. Yet, according to the European Parliament's rapporteur on the Resolution:

The first point of criticism concerns the way in which the Resolution was drawn up. The fact that the European Parliament was not consulted on the substance of this Resolution seems to be totally at variance with Article K.3 of the Maastricht Treaty, since the Resolution touches on the core of asylum policy and therefore automatically comes under the 'principal aspects of activities' of the Council.[36]

---

[35] Reflection Group's Report to the Intergovernmental Conference, Brussels, 5 December 1995, SN520/95 (Reflex 21), p. 16.

[36] Hedy d'Ancona, *Draft Report on the Council Resolution on Minimum Guarantees for Asylum Procedures to the European Parliament*, 30 April 1996, DOC-EN/PR/296/296703; PE 217.481.

Further, the competence of the European Court of Justice was limited in the TEU to the 'first pillar' with a power under article L to extend it to conventions adopted under the 'third pillar'. Accordingly, there was no power to make a reference to the European Court of Justice as regards the clarification of any measure adopted in the 'third pillar' other than a convention with specific provisions for doing so.

The power given to the Council as regards asylum policy was limited to the adoption of Joint Positions and the promotion, using the appropriate form and procedures, of any co-operation contributing to the pursuit of the objectives of the Union, the adoption of Joint Actions insofar as the objectives of the Union can be attained better by Joint Actions than by member states acting individually; and, without prejudice to article 220 of the EC Treaty, the drawing up of conventions (article K.3(2)). Accordingly, there was no specific provision in Title VI for the member states to continue to adopt Resolutions, Recommendations and Conclusions in the field. Nonetheless, this is exactly what has happened.

Within the 'third pillar' a very clear example of diverging political will as to the meaning of the 'ever closer union among the peoples of Europe' can be discerned. On the one hand there is a clearly stated intention to harmonise immigration and asylum policy in order to achieve the objectives of the Union and specifically the single market. This intention perhaps results from the political perspective of those member states which are normally classed as federalist in approach. On the other hand, the intergovernmental nature of the 'third pillar' and its lack of real power or integration into the Community structure may be seen as the uneasy compromise with those member states whose interpretation of an ever closer union is focused on striving rather than achieving. It is within this context that the Resolution on minimum guarantees for asylum procedures and the Joint Position on the harmonised application of the definition of the term 'refugee' in article 1 of the Geneva Convention were adopted.

The Resolution on minimum guarantees for asylum procedures

Turning to the substance of the Resolution on minimum guarantees for asylum procedures it is first important to note that asylum applications which are determined to be manifestly unfounded in accordance with that Resolution are to be dealt with in accordance with the procedure contained in that Resolution. It is only 'subject to the principles laid down therein' that the Resolution on minimum guarantees applies.

Several features of the Resolution on minimum guarantees are of particular interest. First, paragraph 3 states that regulations on access to the asylum procedure are governed by individual member states' legislation and are not the subject of harmonisation in accordance with the Resolution. As access to the asylum determination procedure has become an increasingly disputed area[37] the Resolution does not assist either the member state governments or applicants and their advisers in this regard. As regards the procedures themselves, several important guarantees are included in the Resolution including the right to the services of an interpreter where necessary, the right to an examination of the asylum application by a fully qualified official and to have it decided individually, objectively and impartially, and the right to be informed of the procedure including access to the office of the United Nations High Commissioner for Refugees (UNHCR) or other organisations working on behalf of UNHCR. The applicant is also entitled to a personal interview before a decision is taken.

In the European context, a right of appeal with suspensive effect is perhaps the most important procedural guarantee which is increasingly under attack in the member states.[38] Paragraph 8 of the Resolution provides that 'in the case of a negative decision, provision shall be made for an appeal to a court or a review authority which gives an independent ruling on individual cases'. This is supplemented by paragraph 17 which states:

Until a decision has been taken on the appeal, the general principle will apply that the asylum seeker may remain in the territory of the Member State concerned. Where the national law of the Member State permits a derogation from this principle in certain cases, the asylum-seeker should at least be able to apply to the bodies referred to in paragraph 8 . . . for leave to remain in the territory of the Member State temporarily during procedures before those bodies, on the grounds of the particular circumstances of his case; no expulsion may take place until a decision has been taken on this application.

This provides a very important remedy for the asylum seeker. However, it is limited to those cases where a substantive consideration of the application is undertaken by the member state. It does not apply to applications deemed manifestly unfounded because there is a safe third country or because the applicant comes from a country in which there is in general terms no serious risk of persecution. Paragraph 19, which permits the derogation from paragraph 8 in respect of manifestly unfounded asylum applications, provides that the member states 'may exclude the possibility of lodging an appeal against a decision to reject an application if, instead, an independent body which is distinct from the examining authority has already confirmed the decision'.

---

[37] Immigration Law Practitioners' Association conference on Safe Countries of Origin and Safe Third Countries, London, 8 July 1996; see also chapter 13 of this volume.
[38] For example, the UK Asylum and Immigration Act 1996.

Even where the member state does allow a right of appeal against a manifestly unfounded asylum application, paragraph 21 of the Resolution on minimum guarantees permits the member state to dispense with suspensive effect of the appeal right. However, in such cases the member state should at least guarantee that the decision on the application is taken at a high level and that additional sufficient safeguards ensure the correctness of the decision (these include the same assessment, before the execution of the decision, by another authority which must be of a central nature and must have the necessary knowledge and experience in the field of asylum and refugee law).

In her report to the European Parliament, Hedy d'Ancona of the Committee on Civil Liberties and Internal Affairs has criticised the legal status of the Resolutions:

> Another point of criticism concerns the ambiguity surrounding the legal status of the Resolution. According to paragraph 31 of the Resolution Member States will 'strive to bring their national legislation into line with' the principles enunciated in the Resolution by 1 January 1996. But this wording is too loose to enable it to be interpreted as meaning that the Resolution is legally binding. The legal consequences for Member States failing to offer asylum seekers these minimum guarantees after 1996 or in any future legislation remain ill defined.[39]

Furthermore, the interrelationship between the Resolution on minimum guarantees and that on manifestly unfounded asylum applications is not clear. Specifically, where an asylum application is held to be manifestly unfounded on the basis that there is a safe host third country to which the asylum applicant can be returned, the safety of that country must equally be determined by reference to the asylum procedures and appeal rights in force there. As the EU member states have determined the minimum procedural guarantees which must apply to a substantive determination in the member state of an asylum application so, where an asylum applicant is to be returned to a third country in order for that country to be determined as safe, the asylum procedures there must meet the same criteria as contained in the Resolution on minimum guarantees. In other words, if the member states are entitled to dispense with the procedural guarantees contained in the Resolution because the asylum seeker can be sent to a third country to have his or her asylum application determined there, then, in order for that decision to be valid, the third country's procedures must fulfil the criteria of the Resolution, since otherwise the asylum seeker would be denied access to a procedure characterised by the minimum procedural guarantees considered safe by the member states.[40]

---

[39] D'Ancona, *Draft Report*, p. 10.   [40] See also chapter 13 of this volume.

In light of the above legal argument regarding host third countries and minimum guarantees for asylum applications, an anomalous position then obtains as regards the return of asylum seekers to their country of origin where that country has been held to be one in which there is generally no serious risk of persecution in accordance with the Conclusions adopted on 30 November 1992. Paragraph 8 of the Resolution on manifestly unfounded applications for asylum permits an application to be categorised as manifestly unfounded in a variety of circumstances, including where the country is determined by the member state in question to be one in which in general terms there is no serious risk of persecution. Asylum applications determined to be manifestly unfounded on this ground and therefore excluded from the Resolution on minimum guarantees will not get the benefit of the procedural guarantees in any country as the applicant will be returned to the country of origin whence he or she alleges a fear of persecution. No attempt appears to have been made to reconcile this problem.

Joint Position on the harmonised application of the definition of the term 'refugee'

The final step, so far, in the harmonisation of substantive European asylum policy is the Joint Position on the harmonised application of the definition of the term 'refugee' in article 1 of the Geneva Convention which was adopted on 23 November 1995 and formally approved on 4 March 1996. The Joint Position attempts to harmonise member states' differing interpretations of the refugee definition contained in the Geneva Convention. It is a somewhat anomalous instrument in that, while it recognises the priority of the Geneva Convention and accepts that the UNHCR *Handbook*[41] is a valuable aid, the Joint Position goes on to deviate substantially from the recommended interpretation of the Convention by limiting important aspects of the scope of the Convention.

UNHCR, in a press release on the Joint Position, advised that it 'has serious reservations about the new European Union Resolution which it believes erodes refugee principles and could leave large numbers of refugees without adequate protection'.[42] In particular, UNHCR's main concern is that the Joint Position:

will allow states to avoid recognising as refugees people persecuted by 'non-state agents' – such as rebel groups or extremist organisations. This interpretation

[41] UNHCR, *Handbook on Procedures and Criteria for Determining Refugee Status* (Geneva, re-edited 1992).
[42] UNHCR Press Release, 'UNHCR Expresses Reservations over EU Asylum policy', 24 November 1995.

creates an anomalous situation in which someone targeted by the government in a civil conflict could gain asylum abroad, but not an equally innocent civilian persecuted by the opposition, as has been the case with many Algerians. If governmental authority collapses altogether – as has happened recently in Somalia or Liberia – no-one might qualify for refugee status.[43]

The requirement in paragraph 5 of state persecution is only one of the aspects of the measure which limits the application of the Geneva Convention. Another example is persecution on the grounds of political opinions. The Joint Position requires in paragraph 7.4 that the applicant must show that the authorities know about his or her political opinions or attribute them to him or her. Accordingly, where the person has not yet come to the attention of the authorities, he or she would not qualify for refugee status even though the political opinions of the person would invariably result in persecution once known or attributed.

A further example concerns the 'internal flight alternative' (where a person's fear of persecution relates to one part of the country, he or she may reasonably be expected to seek refuge in another part of the same country,[44]) which is now ostensibly tied to the definition of a refugee by virtue of the Joint Position. Paragraph 8 reads:

Where it appears that persecution is clearly confined to a specific part of a country's territory, it may be necessary, in order to check that the condition laid down in Article 1A of the Geneva Convention has been fulfilled . . . to ascertain whether the person concerned cannot find effective protection in another part of his own country, to which he may reasonably be expected to move.

Yet, the UNHCR *Handbook* provides:

The fear of being persecuted need not always extend to the *whole* territory of the refugee's country of nationality. Thus in ethnic clashes or in cases of grave disturbances involving civil war conditions, persecution of a specific ethnic or national group may occur in only one part of the country. In such situations, a person will not be excluded from refugee status merely because he could have sought refuge in another part of the same country, if under all the circumstances it would not have been reasonable to expect him to do so.[45]

Accordingly, the Joint Position may be seen as an attempt by some state parties to the Geneva Convention to limit unilaterally the scope of the Convention in contrast to the position which has been taken by UNHCR.

---

[43] *Ibid.*

[44] See Hugo Storey, 'The "Internal Flight Alternative" (IFA) Test and the Concept of Protection', in *Current Issues of UK Asylum Law and Policy* (ed. Frances Nicholson and Patrick Twomey, Ashgate, Aldershot, 1998), pp. 100–32; Hugo Storey, 'The Internal Flight Alternative Text: The Jurisprudence Re-examined', 10 *International Journal of Refugee Law*, 1998, pp. 499–532.   [45] UNHCR *Handbook*, para. 91.

The impetus to harmonise and the Treaty of Amsterdam

However, with the signing of the Amsterdam Treaty in October 1997 much is about to change, assuming that the Treaty is ratified and enters into force as signed. The fundamental difference of perspective among the member states as to the implications of article 7a of the EC Treaty has now crystallised. Twelve of the fifteen member states have agreed to the 'Communitarisation' of asylum policy within the EC Treaty. Three (Denmark, Ireland and the UK) have negotiated protocols which position them outside the common provisions but permit them to opt in on specific measures.

The new Title IV which has been created transfers into European Community competence responsibility for:

1. the criteria and mechanisms for determining which member state is responsible for considering an application for asylum submitted by a third country national in one of the member states (in other words, the subject matter of the Dublin Convention);
2. minimum standards on the reception of asylum seekers in the member states;
3. minimum standards with respect to the qualification of third country nationals as refugees (in other words, the subject matter of the Geneva Convention and the UNHCR *Handbook*);
4. minimum standards on procedures in member states for granting or withdrawing refugee status (the subject matter of the Resolution on minimum guarantees);
5. minimum standards for giving temporary protection to displaced persons from third countries who cannot return to their country of origin and for persons who otherwise need international protection (a subject of particular relevance following the crisis in the former Yugoslavia);[46] and
6. promoting a balance of effort between member states in receiving and bearing the consequences of receiving refugees and displaced persons (otherwise known as burden sharing or responsibility sharing, an issue of particular interest to Germany).

In terms of the constitutional consequences of these changes, on the positive side of the balance, the European Parliament will be entitled to consultation in respect of measures taken. This should ensure the measures adopted have much greater transparency and political legitimacy. On the negative side, the powers of the European Court of Justice in respect

---

[46] For further discussion of the concept of temporary protection, see chapter 16 of this volume.

of this new Title have only been established in truncated form. Only courts of final instance in the member states will have the power to refer any question on the interpretation of provisions in measures adopted under this new chapter. However, an interesting new power has been included: the Council, the Commission or a member state may seek a ruling from the European Court of Justice on a question of interpretation of a measure in this area. This new power, if used intelligently, for instance by the Commission, could compensate for the loss of the reference power to lower courts in the member states.

Conclusions

The harmonisation of the asylum policy in the European Union, although a product of the 1992 single market project, has laid bare some fundamental contradictions in the European Union. The choice of a non-justiciable, 'soft law' route to harmonisation is the result of the deep political divide among the member states between those which seek to achieve an actual union of the member states and those which wish to travel the road but never arrive.

In terms of the content of the harmonisation measures, the member states have implemented a policy which aims to return asylum seekers to the first country through which they travel in their flight from persecution for their asylum applications to be determined there. Additionally, it introduces a concept of a safe country of origin and, in respect of applications falling within both of these two categories, dramatically limits procedural rights and guarantees. To this extent the member states appear to be introducing a quasi-territorial limitation on asylum in that these policies, when combined with mandatory visa requirements and carrier sanctions, severely inhibit the flight of refugees from persecution.

Finally, the move towards a harmonised interpretation of the definition of refugee is resulting in a unilateral breaking of ranks by the member states from the accepted interpretation of the Geneva Convention produced by the Executive Committee established under the Convention and the UNHCR.

Clearly, however, the Treaty of Amsterdam has shifted the balance of power between the member states and the Community in the field of asylum policy fundamentally and irretrievably in favour of the latter. The possibility of individual action by member states will become ever more restricted as the new Community powers are exercised. What this will mean for asylum seekers remains a matter of deep concern. On the one hand there is a real chance for the member states to revitalise their commitment to the Geneva Convention and the protection of refugees through Community measures. There is further power now for the Community to take measures to protect persons at risk of torture, inhuman and degrading treatment, or punishment,[47] who increasingly constitute the majority of persons in need of international protection as the threshold for recognition as a refugee has risen. On the other hand, if the trend towards harmonisation at the level of the lowest common denominator as regards the assessment of asylum applications, which was apparent in the inter-governmental process and subsequently within the 'third pillar', is carried over into Community measures which will be binding on the member states, the prospects for refugees seeking asylum in the EU may be very grim indeed.

Bibliography

d'Ancona, Hedy, *Draft Report on the Council Resolution on Minimum Guarantees for Asylum Procedures to the European Parliament*, 30 April 1996, DOC-EN/PR/296/296703; PE 217.481

Cruz, António, *Schengen, Ad Hoc Immigration Group and Other European Intergovernmental Bodies in View of a Europe Without Internal Borders* (Churches' Committee for Migrants in Europe, Briefing Paper No. 12, June 1993)

> *Shifting Responsibility: Carriers' Liability in the Member States of the European Union and North America* (Trentham Books and School of Oriental and African Studies, Stoke-on-Trent, Staffordshire, 1995)

Danish Refugee Council, *'Safe Third Country' Policies in European Countries* (Copenhagen, 1997)

Guild, Elspeth and Jan Niessen, *The Developing Immigration and Asylum Policies of the European Union* (Kluwer Law International, The Hague, 1996)

Nicholson, Frances, 'Implementation of the Immigration (Carriers' Liability) Act 1987: Privatising Immigration Functions at the Expense of International Obligations', 46 *International and Comparative Law Quarterly*, 1997, pp. 586–634

Papademetriou, Demetrios G., *Coming Together or Pulling Apart? The European Union's Struggle with Immigration and Asylum* (International Migration Policy Program, Carnegie Endowment for International Peace, Washington DC, 1996)

Peers, Steve, *Mind the Gap! Ineffective Member State Implementation of the European Union Asylum Measures* (Immigration Law Practitioners' Association and Refugee Council, London, May 1998)

Wyatt, Derrick and Alan Dashwood, *European Community Law* (3rd edn, Sweet and Maxwell, London, 1993)

---

[47] Article 3 of the European Convention on Human Rights as interpreted by the European Court of Human Rights. See chapter 4 of this volume.

16   A new asylum regime in Europe

Danièle Joly

A new asylum regime is being formulated within the context of a profound all-embracing economic, political, social and ideological crisis in
the developed world. This chapter argues that the paradigm has changed
from a regime implementing a selective but integrative policy of access
and full status recognition paired with full social rights and long-term
settlement, to one which maximises exclusion, undermines status and
rights, and emphasises short-term stay for refugees. This is concomitant
with a more comprehensive approach to asylum issues. Temporary protection is a cornerstone of the new regime in the making.[1]

Parameters of the 'old' asylum regime

At the end of the Second World War, the presence of millions of refugees
in Europe brought the question of asylum onto the political agenda of the
international community. During that period, what I refer to here as the
'old regime' began to come into existence (see Table 16.1). The historical
circumstances which presided over its formulation are twofold: the
Second World War and the Cold War. Events leading up to the Second
World War and the war itself generated widespread guilt throughout
Europe, as a result of the atrocities carried out against millions of victims
of fascism and Nazism, many of whom were refused permission to enter
and obtain asylum in other European countries. As a consequence, the
notion of refugee was influenced by the social realities of the time to
include those categories who had suffered persecution under Nazi and
other fascist regimes.[2] In addition, the beginning of the Cold War was
marked by the political supremacy of the USA in the Western world,
pitted against the Warsaw Pact countries.[3]

---

[1] I understand 'regime' to include legal instruments, policies, established practices and
ideology governing refugees' access to asylum and their treatment in the host society.
[2] James C. Hathaway, 'The Evolution of Refugee Status in International Law: 1920–1950',
33 *International and Comparative Law Quarterly*, 1984, pp. 348–80.
[3] Kim Salomon, *Refugees in the Cold War* (Lund University Press, 1991).

The 1951 Geneva Convention Relating to the Status of Refugees[4] arose from this conjuncture, awarded a special treatment to 'political refugees' and, through a universal definition, stressed the individual rather than the group. It was thus designed to accommodate refugees from communist states with the result that international law on refugees reflects not only 'the conscience of the world' at a particular point in history but also the global balance of power and the political climate of the time. A measure of consensus had to be attained which took on board different national interests, but also the social forces at work, including the labour and communist movements. As a result, not only are notions of individual liberty enshrined in the Geneva Convention but also those of social rights and standards of treatment. The question of asylum was not merely formulated in terms of entry but also of status and protection. Moreover, this period coincided with an economic boom and liberal European migration policies designed to meet labour shortages. In the 1970s, the trend in asylum law was a liberal one,[5] incorporating the principles of the Convention and the 1967 New York Protocol (which applies the Convention without temporal or geographic limitation),[6] although communist bloc countries did not initially ratify these instruments. By February 1999 there were 137 states party to the 1951 Convention and/ or the 1967 Protocol.[7]

The regime that developed in the wake of the Second World War prevailed until approximately the end of the 1970s. It is difficult to give it more precise historical limits as it was neither born nor ceased overnight. We are dealing with a regime being constructed and thereafter dismantled over time. The main characteristics defined here are in a sense those of a type and do not dwell on the many variations in its implementation by different countries.

Instruments and status determination

Under this 'old regime' the Geneva Convention became the main instrument governing the status of persons in need of protection in Europe and the majority of asylum seekers became Convention refugees. A key characteristic of the Convention is that it offered a universal definition not tied

---

[4] 189 UNTS 137.
[5] Gilbert Jaeger, 'Comparative Asylum and Refugee Jurisprudence and Practice in Europe and North America', in *Asylum Law and Practice in Europe and North America* (ed. Jacqueline Bhabha and Geoffrey Coll, Federal Publications Inc., Washington DC, 1992), pp. 1–8.   [6] 606 UNTS 267.
[7] The temporal and geographical limitation has now been lifted by all parties to the Geneva Convention (including most recently Hungary on 8 January 1998), except for the Democratic Republic of Congo (Zaire), Madagascar, Malta, Monaco and Turkey.

Table 16.1 *The 'old' and 'new' asylum regimes of the European Union*

	Old regime	New regime
Instruments and status determination process	1951 Geneva Convention	Geneva Convention residual Several other instruments
	A binding instrument	Guidelines
	A liberal interpretation of the refugee definition	Strict interpretation of the refugee definition
	A universal definition	No universal definition
	Individual determination	Group determination
	Non-refoulement	*Non-refoulement*, but return is main objective
Procedure and access	Easy access to host country	Difficult physical access to host country
	Ready access to asylum procedure	Impeded access to (short or 'fast-track') procedure
	Access to procedure after crossing own national border	Access to procedure possible outside host country
	Successive applications in different European countries possible	Impossible to apply in more than one country
Standard of protection in reception countries	Majority gain Convention status and rights	Majority receive non-Convention status and rights
	All have travel documents and identity papers	Not all have travel documents
	Social rights as nationals	No social rights on a par with nationals
	Permanent stay	Temporary stay
	Programme and facilities promoting integration	No programme and facilities promoting integration
	Favourable attitudes by host governments, media and population	Hostile attitudes by host governments, media and population
	Asylum seekers seen as future refugees	Negative presumption towards asylum seekers
Scope of protection	In-country reception only	Comprehensive approach
		Internationally protected zones

Table 16.1 (*cont.*)

	Old regime	New regime
		Reception in region of origin
		Burden-sharing discussed
		Root causes action in country of origin
		Aid for reconstruction and return of refugees
		Protection in host country as well
Institutional actors	Individual government decisions on Convention or other status	Inter-governmental agreements on harmonisation
	Limited government discretion (sovereignty limited by Geneva Convention and Protocol)	Individual governments have more discretion on asylum decisions
		UNHCR enhanced role in Europe. Other institutional actors interested including European Parliament, European Commission, OSCE, Council of Europe, NGOs

to time or place and replacing the nationality or group-based criteria in force before the Second World War. The criteria of this definition are precisely defined and cover persons in need of protection outside the borders of their country of nationality or habitual residence on account of a well-founded fear of persecution for reasons of race, religion, nationality, membership of a particular social group or political opinion.[8] These criteria were drawn up to cater for the refugees resulting from the Second World War, of which there were still 1 million in Europe in 1947,[9] and for those who could be anticipated as fleeing from the Warsaw Pact countries.

One central feature of the Convention is that it is a binding instrument: states party to the Convention are bound to grant refugee status to persons who come under its remit. They do not have any discretion on

---

[8] For further analysis of these issues see Part 1 of this volume.
[9] M. J. Proudfoot, *European Refugees: 1939–52* (Faber and Faber, London, 1957).

this matter and their status must be determined according to the merits of their case. In reality many other factors were influential in asylum decisions which favoured some groups of refugees at the expense of others, but this was not enshrined in legal instruments until 1980, except in the USA.[10] What was officially the prerogative of states was the decision to grant territorial asylum.

Individual determination was the practice in European states. It is implicit, although not stipulated, in the Convention. However, in exceptional cases a kind of *prima facie* group determination took place with a favourable presumption (such as the Hungarians in 1956 and Chileans and Vietnamese in the 1970s). A liberal interpretation of the criteria for refugee definition gave full scope to the subjective element (the 'well-founded fear' as set out in article 1A of the Geneva Convention). The asylum seeker enjoyed the benefit of the doubt and was presumed genuine until it was determined that he or she did not meet the Convention criteria. The prohibition of *refoulement* under article 33 of the Convention was mandatory and was generally accompanied with the recognition of status, so that these two articles tended to coincide or were deemed to do so.

Although a long-term or permanent authorisation to stay was not stipulated under the Geneva Convention, it became the practice in Europe that the granting of refugee status was accompanied by permanent stay (and while the cessation clause of article 1C could be invoked this was not generally envisaged as a concrete possibility).

It was established that access to protection was only possible after the crossing of the host state's borders, but there were generally no obstacles in the shape of visas or sanctions on carriers to reaching the reception country. Once in a country of asylum, the procedure for the determination of refugee status was readily available without restrictions, either on or after arrival. Furthermore, it was possible to apply successively in different European countries.

Standard of protection in reception countries

Until the middle of the 1980s asylum seekers and refugees benefited from favourable presumptions, positive reception and settlement programmes. Refugees were provided with travel documents and identity papers, allowing them the possibility of travelling across borders without problems. Moreover, as most European countries were party to the 1977

---

[10] See the 1965 amendment to the Immigration and Nationality Act (3 October 1965, Pub. L. No. 89-236, 79 Stat. 911 (1965)), which included as qualifying for refugee status those fleeing a communist country or a communist-dominated country or area.

Strasbourg Declaration on Territorial Asylum,[11] Convention refugees could cross borders. They generally enjoyed social rights and the right to work on a par with nationals of the country of reception and they were entitled to family reunion. Asylum seekers were considered future refugees.[12] The assumption and practice was that a right to remain permanently was granted. This was often concomitant with early programmes and facilities for integration in the national collectivity which were promoted by the receptive attitudes of governments, media and native populations. Even where other statuses were initially granted, for the benefit of refugees who needed protection but did not meet the Convention definition, the quality of protection approached that of Convention refugees.

Institutional actors involved in debate and decision

However, there were still a number of controversial areas which non-governmental organisations (NGOs) and scholars raised, such as the lack of harmonisation and the existing discrepancies among and within European countries. Those discussions took place within non-governmental institutions. There was no such discussion of harmonisation at European governmental or inter-governmental level. Decisions on status were taken by individual governments and there was no systematic co-ordination or exchange of information between governments. Nevertheless, the latter did not have total discretion on decisions to grant refugee status, as their sovereignty was superseded by the Geneva Convention and the 1967 Protocol. All western European states were parties, though Italy maintained the geographical limitation until 1990.

The new asylum regime

The regime described above no longer prevails in Europe, having been replaced by an asylum regime which has been in the making for the last decade under the influence of two sets of circumstances (see Table 16.1).

By the end of the 1970s economic recession had replaced economic expansion and the closure of Europe's borders, which had begun in the middle of the 1970s, continued. This coincided with a substantial increase in the number of asylum seekers reaching western Europe: the

[11] Council of Europe, Committee of Ministers, Declaration on Territorial Asylum.
[12] Claude Guillon, 'Evolution des dispositifs d'aide aux demandeurs d'asile et aux réfugiés', in Actes du Colloque, *Les réfugiés en France et en Europe: Quarante ans d'application de la Convention de Genève 1952–1992*, 11–13 June 1992 (Office français de protection des réfugiés et apatrides (OFPRA), Paris, 1992), pp. 279–92.

number of applications for asylum in western Europe rose almost every year from 1983, when there were 73,700 applications to reach a peak of 692,380 in 1992.[13] Meanwhile, the perspective of a Europe free of internal borders entered the public scene with the 1987 Single European Act and then the 1992 Treaty on European Union. The unequal distribution of refugees led the 'northern' countries to get together in order to tighten up policies for 'fear' that asylum seekers might enter the European Communities (EC) through southern Europe and migrate freely to the north.[14] At this time 80 per cent of asylum seekers in the EC were received by France and Germany. This generated intensive activity at inter-governmental level. At the same time the character of refugee movements reaching Europe changed with a greater proportion comprising 'humanitarian' refugees who could not be accommodated under a strict interpretation of the Geneva Convention definition.

At the end of the 1980s a momentous upheaval shook Europe with the collapse of the Berlin Wall and the dismantling of communist regimes: the Cold War was over. While eastern European frontiers opened for their nationals, western European countries closed theirs as the numbers of both actual and potential asylum seekers from those regions increased dramatically. By 1993 applications from European nationals made up 65.2 per cent of applications made in Europe;[15] moreover, no ideological gain any longer warranted their acceptance in a post-Cold War era. Tragic ethnic conflicts generated a mass movement of refugees in Europe on a scale unheard of since the Second World War and its aftermath. Meanwhile, values of solidarity were replaced by individualism and protectionism in reception countries.[16] Before convergence and harmonisation became prevalent, several western European countries took individual initiatives to introduce measures to control the arrival and acceptance of asylum seekers. These initiatives were in turn emulated by others. The contours of the new asylum regime were drawn over this long period, but it is the introduction of temporary protection which tilted the balance and resulted in a qualitative change. The main features of the regime are now clearly defined and are examined below.

This new European regime may be defined by its content, its form and

---

[13] Secretariat of the Intergovernmental Consultations on Asylum, Refugee and Migration Policies in Europe, North America and Australia (IGC), *Report on Asylum Procedures: Overview of Policies and Practices in IGC Participating States* (Geneva, 1997), p. 402.

[14] Danièle Joly, 'Le droit d'asile dans la Communauté européenne', 1 *International Journal of Refugee Law*, 1989, pp. 365–79.

[15] Danièle Joly with Lynette Kelly and Clive Nettleton, *Refugees in Europe: The Hostile New Agenda* (Minority Rights Group, London, 1997), p. 13.

[16] Grete Brochman, 'Immigration Control, the Welfare State and Xenophobia Towards an Integrated Europe', 18 *Migration*, 1993, pp. 5–25.

the actors driving it. It is characterised by five concepts: restrictions and non-integration (content), selective harmonisation and the development of a reactive comprehensive approach (form), and governmental control (actors).

Restrictions

The restrictionist trend which evolved throughout the 1980s and 1990s is now fully fledged with an arsenal of measures designed to ensure the reduction of asylum seeker and refugee numbers both at national and European Union (EU) level. Germany and France, which were also the main recipients of asylum seekers in the 1980s, have circumscribed the right of asylum previously enshrined in their constitutions. Physical access has been made difficult by the introduction of transit and visitor's visas, combined with carrier sanctions. These moves have been strengthened by the provisions of the 1990 Schengen Convention[17] which include provisions on such matters as visas, carrier sanctions and trafficking in aliens. Access to the asylum procedure is limited by the creation of airport international zones, by the first country of asylum rule, and by readmission agreements with countries of transit. Restrictions are also imposed by resort to another status (temporary protection) which frequently cannot be received in conjunction with an application for asylum under the Geneva Convention. In the EU, the possibility of applying for asylum is limited to one single country responsible for the examination of the application and no other, as stipulated in the 1990 Dublin Convention.[18] Access to the full procedure is hindered on procedural or substantive grounds by the drawing up of fast-track or short procedures and the coining of concepts such as manifestly unfounded applications or countries where there is generally no serious risk of persecution,[19] which determine who will come under such accelerated procedures. As a further curtailment, the EU Council of Ministers added to the Treaty of Amsterdam,[20] which was signed in October 1997, a Protocol which defines other member states as safe countries of origin for asylum purposes and states that applications for asylum from nationals of one member state in another member state will only be considered or declared admissible in very

---

[17] 30 ILM, 1991, p. 84, entered into force 1 September 1993 and implemented from 26 March 1995.
[18] 30 ILM, 1991, p. 425; and OJ, 1997, C254, entered into force 1 September 1997. For further details see chapter 15 of this volume.
[19] For further details see chapters 15 and 17 of this volume.
[20] OJ, 1997, C340/01; 37 ILM, 1998, p. 44.

limited circumstances.[21] This Protocol creates a precedent for other regions of the world by linking the legal right of asylum to the political and economic alliance of neighbouring countries.

Finally, the interpretation of the Geneva Convention definition has been narrowed and curtailed. It has been argued that excessive emphasis is laid on the wording at the expense of the spirit of the Geneva Convention.[22] Higher standards of proof of persecution are demanded, the only recognised agent of persecution is the state, and applications from asylum seekers where so-called internal flight alternatives exist may be rejected.[23]

The result of this is that less than 10 per cent of applicants obtained Convention status in western Europe in 1995 and 1996.[24] The protection from *refoulement* derived from article 33 of the Geneva Convention is derived under increasingly contrived interpretations of articles 3 and 8 of the 1950 European Convention on Human Rights and Fundamental Freedoms[25] or article 3 of the 1984 Convention Against Torture and Other Cruel, Inhuman or Degrading Treatment or Punishment.[26] Instead of a universal definition, negative and, more exceptionally, positive group determination is adopted. Countries in which there is generally no serious risk of persecution are related to the drawing up of lists of safe countries of origin, nationals of which are confronted with a presumption that their claim is unfounded when they apply for asylum. Temporary protection applies group determination in a positive sense but with a strictly defined brief, restricted to specific events, times and places. Temporary protection introduces a qualitatively different approach which negates the premise of the Geneva Convention.

A June 1993 Resolution of the Council of (Immigration) Ministers[27]

---

[21] Protocol on asylum for nationals of member states of the European Union, OJ, 1997, C340/103. A declaration regarding this Protocol was, however, made by Belgium. See also European Council on Refugees and Exiles (ECRE), *Analysis of the Treaty of Amsterdam in so far as it Relates to Asylum Policy* (London 1997); Nicholas Blake, 'Asylum and Security', *Justice in Europe*, 1997, 2, p. 2.

[22] Frédéric Tiberghien, *La protection des réfugiés en France* (2nd edn, Economica, Paris, 1988); Anne Chemin, 'Des juristes contestent les restrictions au statut de réfugié politique', *Le Monde*, 19 April 1988.

[23] EU Joint Position on the harmonised application of the definition of the term 'refugee' in Article 1 of the Geneva Convention, OJ, 1996, L63/2. For a more detailed discussion of these issues see chapter 15 of this volume.

[24] IGC, *Report on Asylum Procedures*, pp. 418–19.   [25] 213 UNTS 221.

[26] UN Doc. A/RES/39/46. For further details on both of these Conventions see chapter 4 of this volume.

[27] Resolution on certain common guidelines as regards the admission of particularly vulnerable groups of persons from the former Yugoslavia, adopted by Council of (Immigration) Ministers on 1/2 June 1993, in Note from the General Secretariat of the Council to the Asylum Working Party on the *Compilation of Texts on European Practice with Respect to Asylum*

first established a criterion for protection based on the area of origin, that is, 'particularly vulnerable persons from the former Yugoslavia'. It set out further qualifications on two grounds:

1. those who 'have been held in a prisoner-of-war or internment camp and cannot otherwise be saved from a threat to life or limb; are injured or seriously ill and for whom medical treatment cannot be obtained locally; are under a direct threat to life or limb and whose protection cannot otherwise be secured; have been subjected to sexual assault, provided that there is no suitable means for assisting them in safe areas situated as close as possible to their homes'; and

2. those who 'have come directly from combat zones within their borders and who cannot return to their homes because of the conflict and human rights abuses'.

This does not mean that European countries fail to receive or accept refugees any longer or that they openly renege on the Geneva Convention. As a result of conflicting pressures they continue to pledge their support to the institution of asylum and quote the Geneva Convention in official texts (such as the Schengen and Dublin Conventions). They also grant some form of status to a number of asylum seekers. In particular, the *non-refoulement* clause is exercised even when applicants do not obtain Convention status but ought not to be returned to their country of origin, as testified by the proportion of refugees who have been granted a variety of lesser statuses. In Europe as a whole the number of asylum decisions resulting in full Convention status has been overtaken from 1992 onwards by the number refused refugee status but given some form of alternative leave to remain. To the latter must be added all the persons receiving temporary protection not included in asylum application statistics.[28] *Non-refoulement* thus retains its authority as an established principle of international law, independently of, and beyond, the Geneva Convention criteria.[29]

Non-integration

The qualitative change which has taken place is noticeable in the general attitude of governments, media and host populations which now tend to

(March 1996 Update), 4464/1/95, Rev. 1, pp. 141–4. At their meeting in London on 30 November–1 December 1992, EC ministers responsible for immigration had agreed a Conclusion on people displaced by the conflict in the former Yugoslavia (Council Secretariat, Press Release 10518/92 (Presse 230)) which set out a slightly less full set of criteria.

[28] UNHCR, *The State of the World's Refugees: A Humanitarian Agenda* (Oxford University Press, 1997), pp. 208–14.

[29] Guy S. Goodwin-Gill, '*Non-Refoulement* and the New Asylum Seeker', 26 *Virginia Journal of International Law*, 1986, pp. 897–918.

be hostile to refugees and asylum seekers: racism and xenophobia are rampant. Politicians' declarations, electoral responses to asylum, and criminal acts against refugees all testify to this.[30] All types of refugees, whether *de jure* and *de facto*, are affected and the discrimination they suffer turns them into prime targets of exclusionary societal processes. Conditions of reception are often designed adversely with the clear purpose of deterring arrivals or applications. This includes detention, limitation of freedom of movement, reduced or no welfare benefits, and limited rights to education or work. Each country tries to outbid the next in the exercise of 'humane deterrence' to ensure that they do not 'attract' too many asylum seekers.

Asylum seekers suffer from a negative presumption. One could almost say that they are considered guilty until they prove themselves innocent (of being 'fraudulent') and this is their responsibility. A programme of non-integration is also implicit in the measures applied to non-Convention refugees in most of the European countries. With the absence of early programmes or facilities for integration and with authorisation to stay being for a limited period of time, they generally do not enjoy social rights (whether social benefits, the right to work, or the right to family reunion) on a par with nationals. The quality of protection is inferior. They have to fend for themselves and if they achieve a satisfactory solution to their plight and some form of authorisation to stay, this is almost despite the host society. Moreover, even after obtaining authorisation, they are not always provided with identity or travel documents. As a result a marginalised group in a semi-legal situation is created.

Refugees under temporary protection schemes are a prime example of the existence of programmes precluding integration into the host society. Temporary protection status does not include measures towards integration; on the contrary, reception facilities sometimes evidence a policy of deterring integration. For instance, in Denmark those afforded temporary protection were kept in a camp where they were not taught the host country's language and where children were educated in the language of their country of origin.[31] Those granted temporary protection do not generally receive the same level of rights as Convention refugees; and in particular temporary protection does not lead to family reunion or the grant of identity papers. Even the United Nations High Commissioner for Refugees (UNHCR) initially requested a lesser standard of treatment

[30] Danièle Joly with Clive Nettleton and Hugh Poulton, *Refugees: Asylum in Europe?* (Minority Rights Group, London, 1992), especially pp. 117*ff*.
[31] Grete Brochman, *Bosnian Refugees in the Nordic Countries: Three Routes to Protection* (Oslo, 1995), p. 21.

for this category than that to which Convention refugees are entitled.[32] Moreover, the length of stay is limited by the very status which stipulates return as the main objective and is seen as the only durable solution associated with temporary protection status. This tends to disempower those groups and hamper their contribution to host societies, thus exacerbating hostile perceptions of them by the host society.

A significant body of literature examines the whole area of reception and settlement policies and programmes in the shape of practitioners' reports or scholarly writings.[33] It generally finds room for improvement in all the major areas considered (reception centres, employment, housing, education, health, and social and cultural rights). However, the current developments towards a non-integrative approach still need to be researched and their implication for the societies of reception investigated. Those receiving temporary protection are placed in a totally different league, and it is this very rationale underpinning reception policies which is being called into question by NGOs such as the European Council on Refugees and Exiles (ECRE) and many scholars.

Selective harmonisation

Paradoxically, whereas harmonisation is the fashionable term nowadays, it could be argued that asylum policy in Europe has become more disparate rather than more harmonised. On the one hand, the largest proportion of refugees do not come under the Geneva Convention but are processed under a great variety of procedures. The Geneva Convention becomes a residual instrument protecting refugees in Europe; Convention status is limited to a small percentage of asylum applicants, less than 10 per cent in 1996.[34] The majority of asylum seekers gain lesser statuses. These are disparate and without consistency, for example, *de facto* refugee status (F-status) as opposed to Convention refugee status (K-status) in Denmark, *Duldung* (tolerated status) in Germany, or exceptional leave to remain in the United Kingdom.

With temporary protection, a new status enters the scene and is implemented through a variety of instruments in European countries. Several instruments may lead to the granting of some sort of protection either

[32] UNHCR, *A Comprehensive Response to the Humanitarian Crisis in the Former Yugoslavia* (International Meeting on Humanitarian Aid for Victims, 1992).
[33] Danièle Joly and Robin Cohen (eds.), *Reluctant Hosts: Europe and its Refugees* (Gower Press, Aldershot, 1989); Ana Escalona and Richard Black, 'Refugees in Western Europe: Bibliographic Review and State of the Art', 8 *Journal of Refugee Studies*, 1995, 4, pp. 364–90; Shaila Srinivasan, *An Overview of Research into Refugee Groups in Britain During the 1900s* (4th International Research and Advisory Panel Conference, Oxford, 5–9 January 1994).   [34] IGC, *Report on Asylum Procedures*, pp. 418–19.

directly or indirectly: recommendations from UNHCR documents, the European Convention on Human Rights, the Convention Against Torture, and in-house guidelines (which, for example, in Sweden until recently permitted the granting of protection to deserters and war resisters).[35] Despite their exclusionary effects, both the Schengen and Dublin Conventions include 'discretion' clauses which enable governments to grant protection for 'humanitarian reasons' (Dublin Convention, article 9) or for reasons relating to national law (Schengen Convention, Chapter 7, especially article 32).

Further, EU instruments concerning asylum have been negotiated at inter-governmental level and the resulting Conclusions and Resolutions are not legally binding, unlike the Geneva Convention. Indeed, many of these instruments are implemented in widely varying ways in national legislation.[36] Where reception and settlement are concerned, the lack of harmonisation is even more blatant with no measure so far being passed at EU level on these questions. Thus far a discussion on the conditions of reception of asylum seekers has not yet yielded concrete results, although the Treaty of Amsterdam states in Title IIIa, article 73k(1)(b), that the Council shall within a period of five years after its entry into force adopt 'minimum standards on the reception of asylum seekers in Member States'.

At the same time as this process of so-called harmonisation, asylum has been projected onto the public agenda and has generated intense activity among European governments. The Schengen and Dublin Conventions (to be complemented by the stalled Convention on the Crossing of External Borders[37]) were accompanied by a good number of Resolutions, Conclusions, Recommendations and Joint Actions,[38] which are either directly related to asylum or which apply to immigrants in general but have an impact on refugees. Harmonisation also involves information gathering and sharing at EU level through the Centre for Information, Discussion and Exchange on Asylum (CIREA), the Centre for Information, Discussion and Exchange on the Crossing of Frontiers and Immigration (CIREFI) and through computerised information systems. The prevalent trend is what has been termed harmonisation to the level of the lowest common denominator.

Commentators have attempted to minimise the importance of this harmonisation. It has been argued by Cornelis de Jong[39] that each country

---

[35] For further details see chapter 3, p. 68 above.

[36] See also chapter 15 of this volume; Steve Peers, *Mind the Gap! Ineffective Member State Implementation of the European Union Asylum Measures* (Immigration Law Practitioners' Association and Refugee Council, London, 1998).   [37] OJ, 1994, C11.

[38] For details see chapter 17, pp. 359–71 below.   [39] See pp. 371–2 below.

would in any case copy the restrictive measures of its neighbour and that harmonisation initiatives make little difference to this development. I would like to disagree with this proposition. The whole process of harmonisation measures at EU level creates a momentum which is not comparable to individual countries imitating each other; it creates a critical mass which accelerates and expands the convergence. In the first place, one feared consequence is that asylum seekers will be diverted to third countries, which in turn are driven into a 'copy-cat' stampede to follow suit with equivalent measures. This process has created a pole of attraction so that non-EU states are eager to join initiatives such as the Dublin Convention. In addition and more importantly, the impact of measures adopted at EU level goes beyond their actual implementation at national level because they assume a normative value. This extends not only to the countries of central and eastern Europe[40] but also to Australia, Canada and the USA, as revealed by their discussions in the Inter-Governmental Consultations on Asylum, Refugee and Migration Policies in Europe, North America and Australia (IGC).

It may be more appropriate to speak of a selective harmonisation. The measures that have been prioritised and were introduced deal primarily with Convention refugees. The Schengen and Dublin Conventions and most of the 'soft law' instruments adopted deal with the state responsible for assessing asylum claims, with aspects of the procedure to process applications, or with the interpretation of the Convention definition. As noted above, these measures all lead to reductions in the number of recognised refugees. The positive guidelines introduced for the treatment of refugees from the former Yugoslavia can be explained by the desire to deny them full Convention status, as shown by instruments concerning temporary protection for those from the former Yugoslavia cited above.[41] Many of the persons concerned could, according to UNHCR,[42] have claimed Convention status. Other EU initiatives control the number of asylum seekers reaching reception countries and gaining access to the full procedure, and organise their being sent back.[43] Further, the Resolution on minimum guarantees for asylum procedures[44] excludes entire categories of cases, while non-Convention refugees and reception issues have

---

[40] See, for instance, '3rd International Symposium on the Protection of Refugees in Central Europe, 23–25 April 1997, Budapest', 3 *European Series*, December 1997, 2, in which EU measures provide the context for the development of asylum policy in the region.

[41] See note 27, pp. 344-5 above.

[42] UNHCR, *Position du HCR sur la question de l'application de la Convention de Genève aux demandeurs d'asile en provenance de l'ex-Yougoslavie* (Paris, 2 December 1992).

[43] These initiatives include visa policies, carrier sanctions, readmission agreements with third countries and the 1992 London Resolutions. For further details see chapter 15 of this volume.   [44] OJ, 1996, C274/13.

not yet been broached seriously by the EU despite repeated requests by a number of non-governmental organisations.[45]

A comprehensive approach

While this array of restrictive measures demonstrated EU member states' great reluctance to accept more refugees, a major crisis exploded on its doorstep in the former Yugoslavia. After procrastinating the EU yielded to the pleas of UNHCR and accepted refugees from the region on a temporary basis. In the last analysis it proved impossible for the EU to ignore totally the war in the former Yugoslavia and its masses of displaced people resulting from massacres not seen in Europe since the Nazi period. *Realpolitik* led UNHCR to come up with a scheme which EU states were prepared to consider.[46] This solved their dilemma. The major protagonists in the formulation of temporary protection in Europe were thus UNHCR and the EU. Other bodies such as ECRE and Amnesty International also had views and attempted to influence the course of events but with less efficiency.[47]

UNHCR called an international meeting on humanitarian aid for victims of the conflict in the former Yugoslavia on 29 July 1992 and proposed a comprehensive response. The conflict was raging and there were already hundreds of thousands of displaced people. Temporary protection constituted one of seven components in this comprehensive plan. The basic elements of temporary protection as presented at that meeting were as follows:

It should include, at a minimum, admission to the country where such protection is being sought, respect for the principle of *non-refoulement* and basic human rights (the elements of which are further outlined in [UNHCR's Executive Committee's Conclusion No. 22 (XXXII) 1981 on protection of asylum seekers in situations of large-scale influx]) and repatriation when conditions so allow in the country of origin.[48]

In addition, governments, UNHCR and NGOs have pledged their support for a more comprehensive approach. What is not so clear is what this means and different sources disagree as to its content.[49] A broad

[45] See, for instance, ECRE and Amnesty International, 'ECRE and Amnesty International Believe New EU Minimum Guarantees for Asylum Procedures are Insufficient' (Press Release, 10 March 1995).
[46] See also chapters 9 and 10 of this volume for further details concerning the role of UNHCR in the former Yugoslavia itself.
[47] ECRE, *Position on Refugees from the Former Yugoslavia* (1996).
[48] UNHCR, *A Comprehensive Response to the Humanitarian Crisis in the Former Yugoslavia*, p. 4.
[49] Danièle Joly and Astri Suhrke, *Asylum: Changing Concepts and Practices* (International Union for the Scientific Study of Population (IUSSP), Committee on South–North Migration, Barcelona, 1997), pp. 7–10.

interpretation includes early warning, pre-emptive action and generally focusing on the root causes of refugee movements. What was implemented was a limited version which I call 'a reactive comprehensive approach' because it took place *after* the crisis had erupted and when refugee movements were already arriving on western Europe's doorstep.

This approach includes a variety of initiatives aimed at tackling the refugee crisis, which mostly took place in the country and region of origin. It comprises internationally protected zones in the area producing refugees (the so-called 'safe havens' in Bosnia-Herzegovina and Iraqi Kurdistan) and humanitarian corridors. Reception in the region of origin is not new in the developing world where the vast majority of the world's refugees are, but this has now also been introduced in Europe in a big way. Thus, the EU and international institutions assisted countries outside western Europe and the former Yugoslavia in receiving and settling refugees. This formula is considered by states as an important strategy deserving of international discussion and blueprints.[50] Action in countries of origin is directed towards social and economic development, preventing human rights violations and in particular conflict resolution.[51] One case in point is the 1995 Dayton Accords. Return forms part of the comprehensive approach. The importance of a good return programme is unanimously accepted.

More generally, the Conference on Security and Co-operation in Europe (CSCE)[52] promotes the creation of programmes to assist the return in dignity not only of refugees but also of foreigners who do not qualify for permanent immigration.

Even at the beginning of the decade some EU countries had already begun organising return programmes for refugees or asylum seekers. Germany in 1990 prepared a reintegration and re-emigration plan for asylum seekers, such as Sri Lankans.[53] Other instances are those of countries taking back their own nationals in return for financial compensation from the host country, as between Italy and Albania, and Germany and Romania.[54] Scandinavian countries have set up return programmes for Chilean refugees: in 1992 the Norwegian government introduced a programme for the repatriation of refugees, building on the previously established support scheme for Chilean refugees which includes benefit

[50] IGC Secretariat, *Working Paper on Reception in the Region of Origin* (Geneva, 1994).

[51] See also chapters 10 and 11 of this volume.

[52] CSCE, Office for Democratic Institutions and Human Rights, *CSCE Human Dimension Seminar on Migration, Including Refugees and Displaced Persons, Consolidated Summary* (Warsaw, 20–23 April 1993).

[53] German Federal Ministry of the Interior, *Report by the Inter-Ministerial Working Group on a 'Refugee Concept'* (Bonn, 1990).

[54] Philip Muus *et al.*, *Reception Policies for Persons in Need of International Protection in Western European States* (UNHCR, Geneva, 1993).

payments, a travel grant, health insurance for one year, development aid
in the society of origin beneficial to the whole local society, and a two-year
period for returnees to change their mind if they could not make good in
their home country (as long as they had a settlement permit).[55] Similar
programmes are being set up for former Yugoslavs in other Scandinavian
countries. Aid for reconstruction and the monitoring of satisfactory treatment on the return of refugees form part of the package for returnees to
the former Yugoslavia. Good will on the part of countries of origin to
accept the return of refugees was to be one of the criteria for the granting
of reconstruction aid to states of the former Yugoslavia by the EU.[56]
Unlike Convention refugees, those granted temporary protection can
thus fall under forcible repatriation orders and some countries such as
Germany have set out to implement this.[57]

A number of fora and documents insist on the safeguards which need
be an integral part of a return programme. ECRE emphasises that states
should grant to a returning refugee the legal right to return to the host
country for a six-month period.[58] This measure in fact seems to constitute an incentive for the refugees to attempt a return. ECRE also
stresses the need to support the 'voluntary return of refugees to their
homes so long as they may do so in safety, dignity and with the means to
live'.[59] As stated here, mere security is not deemed sufficient: dignity is
also becoming a *sine qua non* of return in the discourse of agencies and
individuals concerned with the interests of returning refugees. This
involves a complex combination of conditions which pertain to the
legal, material and emotional domain. In a normative document,
Hathaway sets out the general premises underpinning a successful repatriation.[60] A set of guidelines is also advanced by Walter Kälin, who
writes:

Repatriation will not succeed if it is not yet safe and feasible to return . . . [It] may
be seriously hampered if refugees are not encouraged to explore, without penal-
ization the feasibility of return. Finally, repatriation is meaningless without reinte-

[55] Brochman, *Bosnian Refugees in the Nordic Countries*, p. 45.
[56] *Migration News Sheet*, No. 152/95-11.
[57] See, for instance, 'Germany: CSU Takes Hard Line', 5 *Migration News*, August 1998,
which reported: 'There were about 350,000 Bosnians in Germany in December 1995
when the Dayton peace agreement was signed. Since then, about 190,000 have returned,
including 60,000 in 1998. About 2,000 have been deported (500 from Bavaria) [and thus
in effect forcibly repatriated] and 9,000 were accepted as refugees in the US, Canada,
and Australia. The remaining Bosnians, 90 per cent of whom are from the Serbian-ruled
Republic Srpska, are expected to return now that the German school year has ended.'
[58] ECRE, *Position of Refugees from the Former Yugoslavia* (1996).   [59] *Ibid.*
[60] James Hathaway *et al.*, *Towards the Reformulation of International Refugee Law: A Model for
Collectivised and Solution-Oriented Protection* (consultative workshops, London and
Washington DC, 4 and 11 October 1996).

gration, and reintegration requires careful bridge-building between returnee and stayee communities.[61]

The return phase of the temporary protection saga in the former Yugoslavia is undoubtedly a pivotal one. On the one hand, return is seen by some as the acid test of temporary protection.[62] On the other, it is not at all straightforward as the map of the homeland has *de facto* changed and a good number of refugees cannot gain access to what was their former place of residence.[63]

Governmental actors

Western European governments and the EU are the main institutional actors determining the traits of the new regime. Inter-governmental agreements govern and inform policy decisions in Europe, whether under the Schengen and Dublin Conventions or via the numerous inter-governmental Resolutions and Conclusions on asylum. Under the Treaty of Amsterdam, however, twelve of the fifteen EU member states have agreed to the 'communitarisation' of asylum policy whereby the European Commission, the European Parliament and the European Court of Justice gain (limited) powers in this field.[64]

In addition, a phenomenon of globalisation involves the whole of the industrialised world in discussions on asylum through the Inter-Governmental Consultations. Moreover, individual governments have more discretion on decisions determining status, and are breaking away from the influence and control of international instruments.

However, these bodies do not enjoy a completely free rein in their decisions. Another characteristic of the new regime is that the prominence of asylum issues on the political agenda has brought a considerable number of national and international institutions into the debate. UNHCR enjoys an enhanced role in Europe but its greater involvement as an adviser to the EU and the expanded brief of its action seems to entail more accommodation with governments.[65] Other actors, although less influential, are taking an active part in the debate on refugees: the European Parliament,

---

[61] Walter Kälin, *Towards a Concept of Temporary Protection* (study commissioned by UNHCR, 1996), p. 15.

[62] Secretary of the Inter-Governmental Consultations quoted by the then ECRE General Secretary, Philip Rudge, in an interview with the author, 21 November 1995.

[63] See, for instance, UNHCR, *A Regional Strategy for Sustainable Return of Those Displaced by the Conflict in the Former Yugoslavia* (paper for presentation to Humanitarian Issues Working Group, 26 June 1998, and as presented to the Steering Board of the Peace Implementation Council, 9 June 1998).

[64] ECRE, *Analysis of the Treaty of Amsterdam* (1997). For further details see chapters 15 and 17 of this volume.   [65] See chapter 11 of this volume.

the European Commission, the Organisation for Security and Co-operation in Europe (OSCE, the successor to the CSCE), the Council of
Europe and actors emerging from the organised sectors of civil society,
such as Amnesty International, ECRE and other NGOs.[66] These derive
their persuasive strength from the moral grounds they stand on, as demonstrated in France by the 'sans-papiers' episode, which concerned some
145,000 illegal immigrants (including rejected asylum seekers) without
papers, some 430 of whom had occupied and been evicted from a church
in Paris in March 1996.[67] The government eventually agreed to examine
their cases and as a result by the end of May 1998 the position of around
half of those affected had been regularised.[68]

On each of the aspects outlined above it is possible to find differing
views and interpretations according to the institutional and social actors
involved. Fundamentally, there is a tension between, on the one hand,
those who have a more liberal interpretation of the institution of asylum
coupled with a greater concern for human rights in countries of origin,
while promoting the integration of refugees into the host community and,
on the other hand, those who want to restrict asylum and integration.

What is presented here represents two poles and there are varying
points in between. There may even be contradictions within a single
government or non-governmental body. There is also a struggle for
influence taking place which results in compromises. This chapter has
outlined the predominant features of the regime without developing all
the nuances and compromises which exist at every stage.

Conclusion

The EU, or more precisely several of its member states, have been a
driving force for the establishment of a new asylum regime in Europe.
This initiative is motivated by two interrelated factors: the desire to
tighten immigration controls in order to contain immigrant populations
(some politicians have spoken of 'zero immigration'[69]); and the determination to regain complete sovereignty over national borders or at least
shared sovereignty over EU borders. This explains why the Geneva
Convention and its potential beneficiaries have become the main target of

---

[66] See Danièle Joly, *Haven or Hell: Asylum Policy and Refugees in Europe* (Macmillan,
Basingstoke, 1996).
[67] 42 *Keesing's Record of World Events*, 1996, p. 41011.
[68] Philippe Bernard and Nathaniel Herzberg, 'La moitié des demandes de régularisation
des sans-papiers seront rejetés', *Le Monde*, 31 May 1998.
[69] For instance, in June 1993 the then French Interior Minister Charles Pasqua said that
'France has been a country of immigration but no longer wants to be one' and announced
a target of 'zero immigration': 39 *Keesing's*, 1993 p. 39527.

an intensive EU effort. Manifestly, such a goal could only be attained through the harmonisation of policies and this is a major feature of the new regime. States did not dare renege on the Convention for fear of an uproar from organised sectors of civil society and international institutions. The chosen strategy was thus to clip its wings and reduce its scope as much as possible through inter-governmental agreements and a battery of EU Resolutions, Recommendations and Conclusions.

However, it was clear that protection could not be abandoned totally and that many refugees could not be returned to their place of origin. *Ad hoc* statuses were thus implemented, but the prevalent xenophobia and the anti-immigration rhetoric of governments made it difficult to offer integration in the host society. The result is that, despite being allowed to remain, non-Convention refugees are often left in limbo. Temporary protection solved the dilemma for governments: protection was granted, but for a limited period with return as the only outcome envisaged. The question of integration did not have to be posed and family reunion did not become an issue. Moreover, the instruments adopted to govern temporary protection took the form of guidelines on an EU level, thus furthering the harmonisation process without impinging in any way on national sovereignty, as has been stressed by the Inter-Governmental Consultations.[70]

If keeping people out or limiting their right to stay was a priority, other strategies had to be adopted to accompany stricter border controls. This was evidenced by the conflict in the former Yugoslavia and temporary protection measures for those displaced as a result of the conflict there. Action to put an end to the conflict in countries producing refugees was a *sine qua non* for stopping outflows and allowing returns. Protection *in situ* and in close proximity to the conflict zone became necessary, as well as help towards reconstruction and the reception of returnees. Finally, and reluctantly, burden-sharing came to the fore. Such a comprehensive approach only became possible as the end of the Cold War facilitated international co-operation.

These changes represent a substantial paradigm shift for Europe from unco-ordinated liberalism to harmonised restrictionism. The lead in the formulation of this new regime rests firmly in the hands of the European Union (with the encouragement of UNHCR) and constitutes a challenge to the whole ethos of asylum and protection worldwide.

---

[70] IGC Secretariat, *Report on Temporary Protection in States in Europe, North America and Australia* (Geneva, 1995).

Bibliography

Brochman Grete, 'Immigration Control, the Welfare State and Xenophobia Towards an Integrated Europe', 18 *Migration*, 1993, pp. 5–25

European Council on Refugees and Exiles, *Analysis of the Treaty of Amsterdam in so far as it Relates to Asylum Policy* (London, 1997)

European Council on Refugees and Exiles and Amnesty International, '*ECRE and Amnesty International Believe New EU Minimum Guarantees for Asylum Procedures are Insufficient*', (Press Release, 10 March 1995)

German Federal Ministry of the Interior, *Report by the Inter-Ministerial Working Group on a 'Refugee Concept'* (Bonn, 1990)

Goodwin-Gill, Guy S., '*Non-Refoulement* and the New Asylum Seeker', 26 *Virginia Journal of International Law*,1986, 4, pp. 897–918

Guillon, Claude, 'Evolution des dispositifs d'aide aux demandeurs d'asile et aux réfugiés', in Actes du Colloque, *Les réfugiés en France et en Europe: Quarante ans d'application de la Convention de Genève 1952–1992*, 11–13 June 1992 (Office français de protection des réfugiés et apatrides (OFPRA), Paris, 1992), pp. 279–92

Hathaway, James C., 'The Evolution of Refugee Status in International Law: 1920–1950', 33 *International and Comparative Law Quarterly*, 1984, pp. 348–80

Joly, Danièle *Haven or Hell: Asylum Policy and Refugees in Europe* (Macmillan, Basingstoke, 1996)

Joly, Danièle with Lynette Kelly and Clive Nettleton, *Refugees in Europe: The Hostile New Agenda* (Minority Rights Group, London, 1997)

Joly, Danièle and Astri Suhrke, *Asylum: Changing Concepts and Practices* (International Union for the Scientific Study of Population (IUSSP), Committee on South–North Migration, Barcelona, 1997), pp. 7–10

Muus, Philip, *et al.*, *Reception Policies for Persons in Need of International Protection in Western European States* (UNHCR, Geneva, 1993)

Salomon, Kim, *Refugees in the Cold War* (Lund University Press, 1991)

Secretariat of the Inter-Governmental Consultations on Asylum, Refugee and Migration Policies in Europe, North America and Australia (IGC), *Working Paper on Reception in the Region of Origin* (Geneva, 1994)

Report on Temporary Protection in States in Europe, North America and Australia (Geneva, 1995)

UNHCR, *A Comprehensive Response to the Humanitarian Crisis in the Former Yugoslavia* (International Meeting on Humanitarian Aid for Victims, 1992)

17   Is there a need for a European asylum policy?

Cornelis D. de Jong

Introduction

In December 1991, at the Maastricht Summit which approved the Treaty on European Union,[1] the European Council adopted an ambitious work programme aimed at the harmonisation of the asylum and immigration policies of European Community (EC) member states.[2] Those participating in the negotiation of this work programme must have believed that it would be possible to set up a common European asylum and immigration policy in a relatively short period of time, since the programme clearly indicates that its subjects should be dealt with between its adoption and the entry into force of the Treaty on European Union, although 'if necessary, this work must be continued after that date'.[3]

However, when one considers the results of the harmonisation process between 1992 and 1997, there is still no common European asylum and immigration policy. Several non-legally binding instruments have been adopted, but they contain many safeguard provisions making it possible for member states to maintain divergent national policies. It is also questionable whether the instruments reflect the European tradition of respect for human rights and social justice as required by the work programme.[4]

After a short description of the priorities laid down in the 1991 work programme, supplemented by the suggestions made by the European Commission in its 1994 Communication on Immigration and Asylum

[1] OJ, 1992, C224. The Treaty on European Union established 'three pillars' of the Union: the first involved the traditional European Community institutions and two other pillars where co-operation was essentially inter-governmental. These related to common foreign and security policy (the 'second pillar') and justice and home affairs issues (JHA, the 'third pillar'). See also chapter 15, pp. 326–8 above.   [2] Document WGI 930.
[3] *Ibid.*, pp. 4–5. For a general outline of these developments see, for example, Elspeth Guild and Jan Niessen, *The Emerging Immigration and Asylum Policy of the European Union* (Kluwer Law International, The Hague, 1996); and Demetrios G. Papademetriou, *Coming Together or Pulling Apart? The European Union's Struggle with Immigration and Asylum* (International Migration Policy Program, Carnegie Endowment for International Peace, Washington DC, 1996).   [4] WGI 930, p. 16.

Policies,[5] this chapter recalls the instruments adopted by immigration ministers and, since 1 November 1993, by the Justice and Home Affairs (JHA) Council of Ministers in the field of asylum. In particular, it considers to what extent these instruments represent real harmonisation efforts and meet the criteria of respect for human rights and social justice.

Having concluded that there still is not a common European asylum policy, the final part of the chapter focuses on the question whether, under the present circumstances and in light of the new provisions of the Treaty of Amsterdam,[6] such a common policy is still desirable and, if so, what the priorities should be.

The state of play

The 1991 work programme lists the following six areas as representing necessary subjects for harmonisation, although it is mentioned that the list is not exhaustive and may be supplemented in the light of discussions:[7]

(a) application and implementation of the Dublin Convention;
(b) harmonisation of substantive asylum law:
   – unambiguous conditions for determining that applications for asylum are clearly unjustified;
   – definition and harmonised application of the principle of 'first host country' [also known as 'host third country' or 'safe third country'];
   – common assessment of the situation in countries of origin with a view both to admission and expulsion;
   – harmonised application of the definition of a refugee as given in article 1A of the 1951 Geneva Convention Relating to the Status of Refugees;[8]
(c) harmonisation of expulsion policy;
(d) setting up a clearing house;
(e) legal examination (examination of the problem of guaranteeing the harmonised application of asylum policy);
(f) conditions for receiving applicants for asylum.

The 1994 Communication of the Commission mentioned above lists the following supplementary subjects:

(g) taking action on migration pressure:
   – improvement of the collection of accurate information on migratory flows into the European Union and their causes;
   – consideration of the establishment of an 'observatory' for migration;
   – definition of actions to be taken in order to tackle root causes of various types of migratory movements (human rights policies, humanitarian assistance, security policy, etc.).

---

[5] COM(94)23 final, 23 February 1994.
[6] OJ, 1997, C340/01; 37 ILM, 1998, p. 44, signed 2 October 1997.
[7] WGI 930, pp. 8–9.   [8] 189 UNTS 137.

(h) development of minimum standards for fair and efficient asylum procedures;
(i) elaboration of a Convention on manifestly unfounded asylum applications and the implementation of the host third country principle;
(j) harmonisation of policies concerning those who cannot be admitted as refugees, but whom member states would nevertheless not require to return to their country of origin in view of the general prevailing situation in that country;
(k) harmonisation of the schemes for temporary protection;
(l) development of a monitoring system for absorption capacities and creation of a mechanism which would make it possible to support member states who are willing to assist other member states faced with mass influx situations; similarly to support projects of member states of third transit countries faced suddenly with new pressures.

The remainder of this section contains a comparison of the outcome of the harmonisation process so far with the list mentioned above.

Application and implementation of the Dublin Convention

The Dublin Convention entered into force on 1 September 1997, seven years after it had been signed.[9] Upon entry into force of the Convention, a meeting of the Committee provided for in article 18 of the Convention was convened. Immediately thereafter, several application measures were adopted, based on the instruments listed below. These had been politically agreed by immigration ministers or by the JHA Council before the entry into force of the Convention, but only the Committee could grant them legal effect:[10]

1. general guidelines for implementation of the Convention (immigration ministers, 11/12 June 1992);
2. calculation of periods of time in the framework of the Convention (immigration ministers, 30 November 1992);
3. conclusions on the transfer of asylum applicants under the provisions of the Convention (immigration ministers, 30 November 1992);
4. standard form determining the state responsible for examining an application for asylum (JHA Council, 20 June 1994);
5. form of a *laissez-passer* for the transfer of an asylum applicant from one member state to another (JHA Council, 20 June 1994);

---

[9] Convention Determining the State Responsible for Examining Applications for Asylum Lodged in One of the Member States of the European Communities, OJ, 1997, C254; 30 ILM, 1991, p. 425. Entered into force for twelve of the EU member states on 1 September 1997, for Austria and Sweden on 1 October 1997 and for Finland on 1 January 1998.
[10] All except the last of these instruments are listed in Note from the General Secretariat of the Council to the Asylum Working Party on the *Compilation of Texts on European Practice with Respect to Asylum (March 1996 Update)*, 4464/1/95, Rev. 1.

6. text on means of proof in the framework of the Dublin Convention (JHA Council, 20 June 1994); and

7. Conclusions concerning the practical implementation of the Dublin Convention (JHA Council, 27 May 1997).[11]

Despite the adoption of all of these measures, one cannot say that the implementation of the Dublin Convention has been successful to date. One of the main problems is that many asylum applicants do not carry valid travel and identity documents with them, which makes it difficult, if not impossible, to prove that the applicant entered the Union via another member state. Especially in cases where applicants have entered the Union illegally, it is often very difficult to transfer responsibility given the lack of evidence concerning the travel route.

The adoption of a system for the exchange and comparison of the fingerprints of asylum applicants, the European Automated Fingerprinting Recognition System (EURODAC), may improve this situation, but it presupposes that the person concerned lodges an asylum claim in the first member state he or she reaches upon entering the Union. These days, many of those entering the Union illegally do not apply for asylum in that member state but continue their travel directly to their preferred member state.[12] EURODAC would only help to cover such cases if member states were to include in EURODAC, not only fingerprints of asylum applicants but also of illegal immigrants. Although a proposal to this effect was tabled in May 1998 and the JHA Council agreed on the desirability of such an inclusion, it may still take some time before all technical, legal and financial aspects are appropriately dealt with to make the conclusion of a separate EURODAC Convention possible.

There are other problems relating to the application of the Dublin Convention. No consensus has been reached, for example, on its applicability with regard to those cases where the events necessary for determining the responsible state have taken place before 1 September 1997. Several member states argue that the Convention only applies to cases where all of these events have taken place after its entry into force: if the asylum applicant entered the Union illegally before 1 September 1997, these states argue, the Convention is not applicable.

A more fundamental problem relating to the structure of the Convention itself is the question as to whether its system of responsibility-sharing leads to a balanced division of responsibility among member states. The main philosophy behind the Convention is that states are

---

[11] OJ, 1997, C191/27.
[12] On the issue of an asylum seeker's right to seek asylum in the state of his or her choice, see chapter 13 of this volume.

responsible for (external) border controls: each member state is therefore, in principle, responsible for all asylum applications of persons who cross the external border of their territory, be it legally or illegally. Ultimately, such a system would lead to the situation, where peripheral states can be responsible for most of the asylum applications. In my opinion, the existing implementation problems should be attributed, at least in part, to the fact that member states with extended external borders are increasingly worried about the consequences of the system as such.

Although, therefore, important steps have been taken to follow up the 1991 work programme in this respect, much remains to be done, especially in the field of the necessary implementation measures. In the longer term, it cannot be excluded that the criteria contained in the Convention will be questioned by those member states with extended external borders.

Harmonisation of substantive asylum law

This subject undoubtedly represents one of the hard core areas. It should be seen together with subjects (h) on fair and efficient asylum procedures, (i) on a proposed Convention on manifestly unfounded asylum applications, and (j) on the status of those who do not qualify as refugees, but cannot be expected to return to their country of origin in view of the general prevailing situation in that country. Related to the last-mentioned subject is also the harmonisation of the schemes for temporary protection, included as subject (k) above.

A large number of instruments have been adopted in these areas:[13]

1. Conclusions on countries in which there is generally no serious risk of persecution (Immigration Ministers, 30 November 1992);
2. Resolution on manifestly unfounded asylum applications (Immigration Ministers, 30 November 1992);
3. Resolution on a harmonised approach to questions concerning host third countries (Immigration Ministers, 30 November 1992);
4. Resolution on certain common guidelines as regards the admission of particularly vulnerable groups of persons from the former Yugoslavia (adopted by Immigration Ministers, on 1–2 June 1993);

---

[13] The first four of these documents are to be found in the *Compilation of Texts on European Practice*. See also Guild and Niessen, *The Emerging Immigration and Asylum Policy of the European Union*; and Richard Plender, *Basic Documents on International Migration Law* (Martinus Nijhoff, The Hague, 1997), sections VII and VIII. See also chapter 15 of this volume.

5. Guidelines for joint reports on third countries (JHA Council, 20 June 1994);[14]
6. Conclusions concerning circulation and confidentiality of joint reports on the situation in third countries (JHA Council, 20 June 1994);[15]
7. Conclusions concerning procedures for drawing up joint reports on the situation in third countries (JHA Council, 20 June 1994);
8. Resolution on minimum guarantees for asylum procedures (JHA Council, 20 June 1995);[16]
9. Joint Position on the harmonised application of the definition of the term 'refugee' in article 1 of the Geneva Convention of 28 July 1951 relating to the status of refugees (JHA Council, 4 March 1996);[17]
10. Resolution on unaccompanied minors who are nationals of third countries (JHA Council, 26 June 1997);[18] and
11. Decision on monitoring the implementation of instruments adopted concerning asylum (JHA Council, 26 June 1997).[19]

As far as the relevant subject matter is concerned, these instruments cover most of the ground, with the exception of the difficult area of the harmonisation of policies concerning those who cannot be admitted as refugees, but whom member states would nevertheless not require to return to their country of origin in view of the general situation prevailing in that country (subject (j)). At first sight, it is, therefore, not entirely illogical to conclude, as the Council did,[20] that most of the work programme has been implemented.

However, a closer examination of the adopted texts may easily lead to a questioning of this rather optimistic conclusion. None of the adopted texts is legally binding and no provision has been made for ensuring their uniform application. Since neither the Commission, nor the European Court of Justice has any special role to play in watching over the application of these instruments, states remain completely free to interpret them in whatever manner they deem justified. Even though each member state is politically bound fully to implement the instruments, it is utopian to believe that the implementation measures will be the same in all member states.

A closer look at the contents of the various instruments brings out a tendency towards progressively less harmonisation. The instruments adopted in 1992 are sometimes criticised,[21] as they deal with the more

[14] OJ, 1996, C274/52.   [15] OJ, 1996, C274/43.   [16] OJ, 1996, C274/13.
[17] OJ, 1996, L63/2.   [18] OJ, 1997, C221/23.   [19] OJ, 1997, L178/6.
[20] See, for example, the Report on the Completion of the Maastricht Programme on Asylum, of 1993.
[21] See, for example, Guy S. Goodwin-Gill, *The Refugee in International Law* (2nd edn, Clarendon Press, Oxford, 1996), p. 346; and UNHCR Regional Office, Brussels, *Review of the Implementation of the 1992 Resolutions in the EU Member States* (March 1996). For further details see also chapter 15 of this volume, pp. 322–6.

restrictive aspects of the asylum procedure, but I would not agree with such criticisms. Although the introduction of accelerated procedures for manifestly unfounded asylum applications is certainly a measure restricting the rights of certain asylum applicants, it does not, in itself, diminish the chances of refugees to be recognised as such. More importantly, the London Resolutions contain a long series of conditions which should ensure that this is the case.

In the Conclusions on countries in which there is generally no serious risk of persecution, it is, for example, stated that:

An assessment by an individual Member State of a country as one in which there is generally no serious risk of persecution should not automatically result in the refusal of all asylum applications from its nationals or their exclusion from individualized determination procedures . . . The Member State will nevertheless consider the individual claims of all applicants from such countries and any specific indications presented by the applicant which might outweigh a general presumption.[22]

The Conclusions, therefore, do not undermine the right of every asylum applicant to have his or her claim examined on an individual basis. If one were to criticise the Conclusions, the argument should, in my view, be based on a different aspect, that is, the lack of real harmonisation. The Conclusions do not even establish a political obligation to introduce the concept of countries in which there is no serious risk of persecution, but leaves this as 'a national decision'. Not surprisingly, no attempt has been made to establish a European list of such countries, since not all member states wish to apply this concept. Neither has the periodic review of the major elements of assessment, as suggested in the final paragraph of the Resolution on manifestly unfounded applications for asylum,[23] taken place.

Although this latter Resolution is sometimes seen as a restrictive instrument, it actually contains important rights for the asylum applicants concerned. For example, it stipulates that each decision will be taken by a competent authority at the appropriate level fully qualified in asylum or refugee matters and that, amongst other procedural guarantees, the applicant should be given the opportunity for a personal interview with a qualified official empowered under national law before any final decision is taken. Another positive element of the Resolution is the fact that it tries to give an exhaustive description of the various grounds for concluding that an application is manifestly unfounded.

The same holds for the Resolution on a harmonised approach to questions concerning host third countries. It would be wrong to consider this a

---

[22] Conclusions on countries in which there is generally no serious risk of persecution, para. 3.   [23] Resolution on manifestly unfounded applications for asylum, para. 12.

restrictive Resolution, as it lays down a large number of conditions that must be fulfilled before a member state may conclude that there is a host third country.[24] For example, the criteria in paragraph 2 of the Resolution spell out that in the host third country the asylum applicant should not be threatened with persecution, torture or inhuman or degrading treatment, should have the opportunity to seek protection and must be afforded effective protection against *refoulement*. The member state which wishes to apply the host third country concept, therefore, takes upon itself the responsibility for having verified all of these elements. If, for example, the asylum applicant has reason to believe that he or she may not obtain effective protection against *refoulement*, the concept cannot be applied.

Turning to the more recent instruments, the picture becomes less positive. It seems as if member states have become less willing to engage in a real harmonisation process. In this respect, the negotiation of the Resolution on minimum guarantees for asylum procedures is typical. During the first half of the discussions, the emphasis was put on minimum guarantees. Thereafter, however, member states compared these guarantees with their national legislation and, as it turned out, exceptions had to be made for the procedures concerning manifestly unfounded asylum applications and applications lodged at the border. This reflects the tendency among member states to seek confirmation of national legislation through European instruments, whereas the political commitment to harmonise requires a certain readiness to give up particular national practices in favour of a European approach. This lack of real harmonisation is also reflected in the five interpretative declarations issued by various member states.[25]

On substance, it seems in itself justified to formulate different minimum guarantees for manifestly unfounded asylum claims, as in these cases accelerated procedures are normally applicable. However, it is questionable whether the exceptions formulated in the Resolution on minimum guarantees are in conformity with the conditions set out in the London Resolutions referred to above, despite the explicit reference in paragraph 18 of the Resolution to these conditions. For example, the requirement that a decision be made 'by a competent authority fully qualified in asylum or refugee matters' does not automatically apply to asylum applications lodged at the border, if the ground for rejection of the asylum application is based on the host third country principle. It is also unclear whether in such cases the right to 'a personal interview with a qualified official' is guaranteed. I base these conclusions on the deroga-

---

[24] See also chapter 13 of this volume.
[25] These are to be found in the Council minutes, although they are not published as such.

tion from paragraph 7 provided for by paragraph 25 of the Resolution on minimum guarantees.

As far as the fairness of the harmonisation process is concerned, it is not too difficult to conclude that member states have not used the opportunity to agree on minimum guarantees of a higher level than those prevailing nationally. The idea of Europe as a whole being less sensitive to migration pressures than individual member states and thus being able to be more liberal than individual member states, has therefore lost much of its meaning (this view maintained that the fear of 'pull' factors would be of lesser importance for the EU as a whole than has, for instance, been the case for the Netherlands following Germany's tightening of its asylum laws). In November 1996, the European Parliament adopted a Resolution concerning the Council's Resolution on minimum guarantees for asylum procedures.[26] Contrary to the Council, the European Parliament is of the opinion that the guarantees should have been formulated in a less restrictive manner. In particular, the Parliament calls for better guarantees concerning the appeal procedure and requests the recognition of the right of every asylum applicant to have access to a judicial authority in order to request temporary leave to remain during the appeal procedure. It appears to me that, even if such a measure may no longer be realistic at national level, it merits consideration at European level. On the one hand, the restoration of this right would significantly improve the quality of the (accelerated) asylum procedures; on the other hand, it is not very likely that individual member states will be faced with a substantial increase in the number of applications as a result of this measure.

One of the more recently adopted instruments is the Joint Position on the harmonised application of the definition of the term 'refugee' in article 1 of the Geneva Convention. The effect of this instrument is severely limited, however, since in its introductory provisions it is clearly stated that:

These guidelines shall be notified to the administrative bodies responsible for recognition of refugee status, which are hereby requested to take them as a basis, without prejudice to member states' caselaw on asylum matters and their relevant constitutional positions.

This means that judges should not use the guidelines as a source of inspiration and that in cases of conflict between existing case law and the guidelines, the national authorities should not implement the guidelines. In my opinion, this is a most unfortunate provision that questions the harmonisation principle itself. On substance, I would describe the Joint Position as representing a higher level of harmonisation than the

---

[26] OJ, 1996, C362/270.

Resolution on minimum guarantees for asylum procedures. It reflects the prevailing tendencies in literature and jurisprudence and in some areas it even takes relatively liberal stands. In this respect, I would point to the link between persecution and violations of human rights (paragraph 4); to the reference to disproportionate sentences (paragraph 5.1.2); to the broad definition of the concept of religion as including theistic, non-theistic and atheistic beliefs (paragraph 7.2); and to the open-ended definition of social group (paragraph 7.5).

Apart from procedural aspects and the interpretation of the term 'refugee', decisions on asylum applications are primarily determined by the appraisal of the situation in the country of origin. Even though the Council has adopted several Conclusions on the drawing up of joint reports on the situation in third countries, as yet no such systematic reporting has come about. In the past, initiatives to request the competent 'second pillar' bodies to prepare joint reports failed to produce satisfactory results, since the time-consuming procedures meant that the reports were often out-of-date and lacked the necessary detail. In recent years, asylum experts have discussed their personal appraisal of the situation in a number of countries of origin in the context of the Centre for Information, Discussion and Exchange on Asylum (CIREA), also known as the clearing house on asylum.[27] So far, these discussions have not resulted in new joint reports that can be used in national asylum procedures. Under the Irish presidency of the Council in the second half of 1996, discussions were begun on how to improve these procedures, but it is doubtful whether the effectiveness of CIREA can be greatly enhanced under the prevailing institutional arrangements.

Finally, the issue of temporary protection has been discussed primarily with respect to displaced persons from the former Yugoslavia. Although in 1997 the Commission submitted its long awaited proposal for a joint action on temporary protection,[28] the discussions so far are far from promising. Much confusion persists on the notion of temporary protection itself, its relation to the Geneva Convention and on the necessary burden-sharing provisions.

In summary therefore, the harmonisation of substantive asylum law has so far produced only instruments which are not legally binding. There appears to be a tendency towards less harmonisation instead of more harmonisation. The discussions on related issues of temporary protection and the harmonisation of policies concerning those who cannot be admitted as refugees, but whom member states would nevertheless not require

[27] Established subsequent to the Decision establishing the clearing house (CIREA), Immigration Ministers, 30 November 1992 (SN 2836/93 (WGI 1505)).

[28] COM(97)93 final, 5 March 1997.

to return to their country of origin in view of the general situation prevailing in that country, have not yet produced any tangible results. The more recent instruments generally represent a lower level of harmonisation than the earlier ones.

Harmonisation of expulsion policies

This next item of the 1991 work programme, concerning the harmonisation of expulsion policy, has been dealt with in the broader context of the fight against illegal immigration in general. My observations are therefore limited to noting that no special arrangements have been elaborated for rejected asylum applicants, even though there is a general tendency among member states to increase practical co-operation efforts in this area.

Legal examination

This issue has always been considered highly sensitive. Even in 1991, it had to be carefully worded, since earlier explicit references to the competence of the European Court of Justice were not acceptable to all delegations. Since the entry into force of the Treaty on European Union, the position of the Court in the fields of Justice and Home Affairs has been strengthened, as an opt-in provision has been adopted introducing the competence of the Court in the context of the Europol Convention for those member states which agree to it.[29] Since there is no 'third pillar' convention on asylum or immigration policies, no comparable step could as yet be taken in this domain. With respect to the Dublin Convention, however, the Netherlands submitted a proposal for an optional Protocol, which would provide for the Court's competence in interpreting the Convention. As of August 1998 this proposal is still under examination.

Article 68 of the consolidated EC Treaty (incorporating the changes made by the Treaty of Amsterdam, hereafter referred to as 'EC Treaty')[30] stipulates that the Court shall have jurisdiction to give preliminary rulings, *inter alia*, with regard to measures adopted by the Council on asylum, on refugees and on displaced persons. The Court shall only have jurisdiction, however, in a case pending before a court or a tribunal of a member state against whose decisions there is no judicial remedy under national law, if the court considers that a decision on the question is necessary to enable it to give judgment. In addition, the Council, the Commission or a member state may request the Court to give a ruling on

---

[29] OJ, 1995, C316.   [30] See also chapter 15 of this volume.

a question of interpretation of the relevant part of the Treaty or of acts of the institutions of the Community based thereon. Access to the Court is therefore limited and it should be added that these provisions do not necessarily apply to Denmark, Ireland and the UK.

Conditions for receiving applicants for asylum

These vary widely among member states and therefore even the 1991 work programme recommended a careful, step-by-step approach. Successive presidencies have nevertheless tried to elaborate an instrument on this subject. As it became clear that consensus could only be reached on rather meaningless texts, these efforts came to an end. Instead, the theme is being dealt with through conferences and by projects based on budget line B5–803 concerning the reception of asylum applicants and displaced persons. Eventually, the co-funding of projects submitted by member states could turn out to be the most effective way of bringing the harmonisation process forward in this area: the reception conditions are highly dependent on the available national budgets. By increasing the possibilities for EC funding, the right incentives could be given to member states to improve reception conditions, whenever necessary, and, even more importantly, to maintain relatively high standards even in times of mass influxes.

The harmonisation of reception conditions has not been tackled yet, although it might become possible, through increased Community funding, to provide the right incentives for member states to introduce or maintain the right level of reception of asylum applicants and displaced persons.

Burden-sharing

Reception, admission and expulsion procedures can pose a heavy burden on national budgets, especially in situations of mass influx. The ever-imminent danger is that national governments facing such budgetary implications may be tempted to deal with 'asylum' as a major 'problem'. In extreme situations, this may have the unforeseen effect of promoting certain xenophobic, anti-asylum tendencies. If there is one area where Europe could help national governments, it would seem to be the area of burden-sharing. If governments knew that they could rely on EU financial and possibly technical assistance when facing a gradual or sudden increase in the number of asylum applications or in the number of displaced persons in general, they would probably feel more confident in addressing such gradual or instant crises. As indicated above, the harmonisation of reception conditions would, in my opinion, also be greatly facilitated by effective burden-sharing mechanisms.

So far, the Council has adopted two instruments relating to burden-sharing:

1. Resolution on burden-sharing with regard to the admission and residence of displaced persons on a temporary basis (25 September 1995);[31] and
2. Decision on an alert and emergency procedure for burden-sharing with regard to the admission and residence of displaced persons on a temporary basis (23 November 1995).[32]

Despite their ambitious titles, these instruments do not provide criteria for physical burden-sharing, that is, for the sharing of the case load involved, and only pay lip-service to financial burden-sharing. In any case, their scope is confined to mass influx situations, which means that they do not apply under 'normal' circumstances. The main thrust of the instruments is the expression of the principle of solidarity on the one hand, and the creation of a rapid decision-making mechanism to deal with mass influx situations on the other.

Although the instruments therefore put a certain pressure on member states to find fair solutions in case of mass influx situations, the lack of precise criteria for physical burden-sharing implies that member states will have to deal with each situation on its own merits. Although it is conceivable that member states will find fair solutions, it is in my view far more likely that in such crisis situations no consensus will emerge with respect to burden-sharing. I base my pessimism in this regard on the lack of any operational criteria for burden-sharing arrangements and on legal and moral considerations concerning the question whether it is acceptable to transfer asylum applicants from one member state to another against their will and for the sole reason of burden-sharing. If it appears impossible to set out a detailed burden-sharing arrangement under 'normal' circumstances, one must be a real optimist to expect any such agreement to be reached in crisis situations.

Migration pressure

Finally, the 1994 Communication mentions the need for action on migration pressure. This is what is commonly called the 'root causes approach'. During the informal JHA Council in Thessaloniki, in May 1994, ministers appeared quite positive with respect to these suggestions and it is therefore surprising that no follow-up action has ever been taken in this

---

[31] OJ, 1995, C262.   [32] OJ, 1996, L63/10.

respect. Admittedly, the subject matter does not fall entirely within the ambit of the 'third pillar', but this can hardly be seen as an excuse for the present state of inertia.

The only steps forward taken thus far have to be attributed to the Commission itself. Its services commissioned a number of studies which together seem fully to cover the field of root causes. The first measure identified in the Communication concerns the consistent and permanent collection of relevant information on root causes. In the case of refugees and displaced persons, this would amount to the collection of information on human rights violations and on political, social, religious or other conflict situations which may prompt a substantial number of persons to flee their country of origin.

In this regard, two Commission initiatives are particularly relevant: first, the Commission took the initiative for a pre-feasibility study followed by a feasibility study with regard to the possible creation of a European Migration Observatory. Although neither the European Parliament nor the Commission any longer support the idea of creating a separate observatory, the Commission has indicated that it would seek to integrate this function into its own service. Secondly, a study has been made of the migration aspects of the crisis in the former Yugoslavia and lessons to be learnt from it. One of the elements that was completely missing at the time concerns the availability of rapid, verifiable and relevant information on the number of people who might flee their country of origin, the routes to be taken in that regard and the potential countries of destination. Had there been some kind of early warning mechanism, ministers responsible for immigration and asylum policies might have been better prepared to deal with what turned out to be a mass influx situation. More generally, the more time a country has to prepare for a mass influx, the better it can provide decent reception facilities. Also, more time is then available for discussing possible burden-sharing arrangements. One can only hope that the Commission will make the results of this fascinating study available as soon as possible.

The interaction between asylum and immigration policies on the one hand and foreign and security policies on the other has not yet been dealt with by the Council. This hardly comes as a surprise, considering that even the necessary arrangements for the collection of relevant data have not yet been put in place. Again, the Commission's study concerning the migration aspects of the crisis in the former Yugoslavia may demonstrate the potential of an integrated approach in this regard. In this context, may suffice to say that this area is indeed full of potential and that it should constitute a priority especially during relatively quiet periods, in order to be better prepared in case of any future crisis situations.[33]

Apart from some preparatory work undertaken by the European Commission, no progress whatsoever has been made with respect to the development of a root causes strategy.

The future

It would be too easy and politically unrealistic to conclude that, since the 1991 work programme and the 1994 Communication have not been fully implemented, the future work of the JHA Council should be simply to fill up the remaining gaps. As for the 1991 work programme, this may have been heavily influenced by the asylum crisis at the time, and perhaps what was valid in 1991 may no longer be desirable in the new millennium. The 1994 Communication has never been formally adopted by the Council, although the latter committed itself to considering the Commission's suggestions with a view to including them in the yearly or multi-annual work programmes, whenever appropriate.

In my opinion, it is far more sensible to look at the existing situation in the Union and the member states and to reflect once again on the need for legally binding harmonisation in conformity with Europe's traditional respect for human rights and for the principle of social justice, briefly called 'real and fair' harmonisation.

Most European governments are of the opinion that they have succeeded in overcoming the 'asylum' crisis. Each member state has adopted new asylum legislation introducing accelerated procedures for manifestly unfounded asylum applications and reducing the accessibility of the asylum procedure at its borders. In most, but not all, member states, the number of asylum applications has indeed dropped considerably.[34] Developments at the European level may have inspired some governments to take these measures, but I doubt if the situation would have been much different, had no European instruments been adopted.[35] Since European instruments generally reflect the lowest common denominator,

---

[33] For a more detailed analysis of the possibilities in this regard, see my article 'Elements for a More Effective European Union Response to Situations of Mass Influx', 8 *International Journal of Refugee Law*, 1996, pp. 156–68.

[34] See, for instance, Intergovernmental Consultations on Asylum, Refugee and Migration Policies in Europe, North America and Australia (IGC), 'Statistics: Asylum Applications in States Participating in the Intergovernmental Consultations, 1983–96', 9 *International Journal of Refugee Law*, 1996, pp. 483–6; IGC, *Report on Asylum Procedures: Overview of Policies and Practices in IGC Participating States* (IGC, Geneva, 1997), pp. 402–8; and UNHCR, *The State of the World's Refugees: A Humanitarian Agenda* (Oxford University Press, 1997), pp. 290–2. [35] For a contrary view, see chapter 16, pp. 348–9 above.

the outcome of European 'harmonisation' corresponds with the automatic process of copying one's neighbour's existing, more restrictive legislation. This certainly is not what was meant by fair harmonisation, but perhaps the concept of 'fairness' itself has evolved since 1991?

In my opinion, the 'ethical' considerations of the 1991 work programme, as well as of the 1994 Communication, calling for harmonisation at a more liberal level have not lost any of their value. If it was possible to formulate such principles at the peak of the asylum crisis, it is difficult to understand why they are not as valid in times of relative stability. Perhaps, a more general discussion of the principles underlying the national asylum policies of member states should have been organised in order first to reach a consensus on the general level of harmonisation, before actually adopting the relevant resolutions and instruments. Had this been done, different approaches might have come to the fore demonstrating that member states interpret the notion of real and fair harmonisation quite differently.

There are a number of principles which, in my view, should be valid for all member states, since they constitute the heart of the concept of 'asylum'. In accordance with article 14 of the Universal Declaration of Human Rights, 'everyone has the right to seek and to enjoy in other countries asylum from persecution'.[36] When this article was drafted, of course, the idea of 'asylum' being used as a route to obtain immigrant status, in the event of all other doors being closed, was never given serious consideration. Just as in case of the 1951 Geneva Convention, the authors had in mind individual cases of those persecuted by Nazi regimes during the Second World War or by communist regimes during the Cold War. Even today, however, there still exists consensus in theory that every 'real' refugee should be protected. If this is the case, would it not then be useful to reconsider the accessibility of asylum procedures for such individual refugees?

In particular, I am concerned with procedures at the border. The Resolution on minimum guarantees for asylum procedures leaves the possibility open that border guards without the necessary expertise in matters relating to asylum can apply the concept of first host country. This means that the asylum applicant who argues that he or she also has a well-founded fear of persecution in the first host country may face rejection of his claim by an authority lacking the necessary expertise. In addition, the negative decision of the border guard may be communicated to the asylum applicant orally, instead of in writing.

To a lesser extent, one may also wonder whether the Resolution fully

---

[36] 42 *American Journal of International Law*, 1949, Supplement 127.

respects the basic principles of refugee law in cases of manifestly unfounded asylum applications. If no suspensive effect follows from appeal procedures, the fate of the asylum applicant basically depends on the decision of one competent authority. No matter how well prepared or accompanied by (administrative) checks, as required by the Resolution, I doubt whether this really excludes the possibility of error, especially when there is a high volume of applications.

Review of the Resolution on minimum guarantees for asylum procedures

As a first proposal for further work in the field of asylum, I would therefore call for a review in particular of the Resolution on minimum guarantees for asylum procedures to examine whether all of the provisions of this instrument reflect fair harmonisation as called for in the 1991 work programme.

Further, it may be true that under the present circumstances member states feel confident that they can handle the current number of asylum applications, but how many of the rejected asylum applicants actually return to their country of origin? I would not rule out the possibility of the asylum and immigration policies of member states collapsing in the coming years, for the following three reasons.

In the first place, no real solutions have been found for the return of undocumented asylum applicants, whose claims have been rejected. If there is no certainty as to the nationality of the persons concerned, it is difficult for the alleged country of origin to take them back. Return policies thus become part of foreign policy, as they require complicated negotiations with such countries of origin. Although enough leverage may sometimes be created to force those countries to co-operate, more often than not this will not be the case. In the longer term, a dialogue based on mutual respect will be required. However, countries of origin will then point out that, apart from possible brain-drain effects, their economies generally profit from remittances returned by their nationals who are residing legally or illegally in the Union. In practice immigrants tend to transfer considerable amounts to their families in their country of origin. Moreover, emigration may reduce pressure on a tight labour market in the country of origin. Negotiations with countries of origin could therefore become quite interesting from a policy perspective. In return for a more co-operative attitude *vis-à-vis* readmission requests from member states, countries of origin could bargain for financial and other support to compensate for the loss of remittances and for help with the reintegration of the persons concerned. Similarly, these countries might request more liberal immigration policies in order to create the possibility of their nationals acquiring technical, professional and educational skills during their stay in the Union, which they could subsequently bring back with them upon return to their country of origin.

In the second place, the application of the host third country principle will become ever more difficult in view of the enlargement process of the Union. Once the central European states and the Baltic states have entered the Union, this principle will have to be applied *vis-à-vis* Russia, Ukraine and other neighbouring states (including Mediterranean countries). It is by no means certain that these countries meet all of the requirements (for example, Russia has indicated on many occasions that it simply does not have the resources to apply the Geneva Convention fully and Turkey has entered a geographical reservation to the Geneva Convention, applying this instrument solely to European asylum applicants). Even if future member states were prepared to consider these countries as safe third countries, it remains highly unlikely that countries such as Russia would be prepared to relieve the pressure of asylum claims from the EU.

In the third place, as explained above, the principles underlying the Dublin Convention are not beyond dispute. The more successful the application of this Convention becomes, the more complaints about its effects will be heard.

In the end, for these three reasons, member states may be faced with a situation whereby rejected asylum applicants cannot be sent back to their country of origin, nor to any transit state.

Treatment of rejected asylum applicants

A second proposal for further work therefore relates to the entire set of issues involved in dealing with rejected asylum applicants. Eventually, the problems involved in their return may be of such importance that a fundamental reconsideration of asylum and immigration policies may be required.

In addition, the number of asylum applicants in member states is still highly imbalanced. Germany still receives by far the largest proportion of the reduced number of asylum applicants in the Union. Although enough attempts have been made to make the concept of burden-sharing operational, the adopted instruments relate to situations of mass influxes and not to the present, 'normal' situation. In any case, physical burden-sharing, that is, the transfer of responsibility for the examination of asylum applications from one member state to another will need a firm legal basis, since it may set aside the criteria of the Dublin Convention. It is also difficult to see how physical burden-sharing fits in with one of the basic concepts of refugee law subscribed to by states, that is, that the asylum applicant should lodge his or her claim in the first country of arrival (derived from article 31(1) of the Geneva Convention), upon which the Dublin Convention purports to be based.

If physical burden-sharing is not feasible in the foreseeable future, it is all the more surprising that no follow-up has taken place to the Commission's suggestion in its 1994 Communication to develop a 'monitoring system for absorption capacities'. This suggestion is related to the further proposal for the creation of a mechanism of financial support for member states facing mass influx situations. More generally, however, financial burden-sharing is an idea that could work positively both in terms of 'normal' reception conditions and of reception in case of mass influxes. As harmonisation of reception conditions for asylum applicants, other than at the level of the lowest common denominator, may have severe budgetary implications for a number of member states, a European fund covering (part of) the costs involved in setting up and running decent reception facilities could play a most useful role. Against this background, the initiative taken by the European Parliament to create a separate budget line on positive action for refugees[37] may prove to be most timely and can indeed serve as the basis for gradual and increasing Community financing of reception costs.

Financial mechanisms to assist the reception of asylum seekers

A third proposal for further work relates to the need to create a financial mechanism that will help individual member states in creating and running decent reception facilities both under 'normal' circumstances and in mass influx situations.

The need for legally binding instruments

Fourthly, further thought needs to be given to the need for legally binding instruments together with a more professional monitoring system concerning the implementation of existing instruments. It may be that the non-legally binding instruments adopted thus far are implemented in a uniform fashion, in which case there is no real need for further action. However, the preliminary findings of the United Nations High Commissioner for Refugees (UNHCR) and the European Council on Refugees and Exiles (ECRE), which closely monitored the

[37] B5.803.

implementation of the 1992 London Resolutions, seem to indicate that in practice there are important differences between member states.[38] If this is already the case for these relatively clearly worded, instruments, there is little reason for optimism about the uniformity of implementation of the more recent, and more vaguely worded instruments.

In this respect, it is important to note that article 63 of the EC Treaty requires that, within a period of five years after the entry into force of the Treaty of Amsterdam, the Council shall adopt:

(1) measures on asylum, in accordance with the Geneva Convention of 28 July 1951 and the Protocol of 31 January 1967 relating to the status of refugees and other relevant treaties, within the following areas:
   (a) criteria and mechanisms for determining which Member State is responsible for considering an application for asylum submitted by a national of a third country in one of the Member States,
   (b) minimum standards on the reception of asylum seekers in Member States,
   (c) minimum standards with respect to the qualification of nationals of third countries as refugees,
   (d) minimum standards on procedures in Member States for granting or withdrawing refugee status;
(2) measures on refugees and displaced persons within the following areas:
   (a) minimum standards for giving temporary protection to displaced persons from third countries who cannot return to their country of origin and for persons who otherwise need international protection,
   (b) promoting a balance of effort between Member States in receiving and bearing the consequences of receiving refugees and displaced persons.[39]

This means that, after the ratification and entry into force of the Treaty of Amsterdam, the Council will have to proceed quickly with the adoption of legally binding instruments in practically all of the areas previously covered by non-legally binding instruments. However, since the decision-making process over this period will still be based on consensus and taking into account that the EC Treaty frequently refers to minimum standards, one should not be optimistic with regard to the level of harmonisation. It is to be feared that consensus will only be reached, as in the past, on the level of the lowest common denominator. Worse still, some of

---

[38] See UNHCR, 'An Overview of Protection Issues in Western Europe: Legislative Trends Taken by UNHCR', 1(3) *European Series*, September 1995; UNHCR Regional Office, Brussels, *Review of the Implementation of the 1992 London Resolutions in the EU Member States*, 1996; ECRE, *'Safe Third Countries': Myths and Realities* (London, February 1995). See also Steve Peers, *Mind the Gap! Ineffective Member State Implementation of European Union Asylum Measures* (Refugee Council and Immigration Law Practitioners' Association, London, May 1998).

[39] According to the last para. of article 63, measures mentioned in para. 2(b) are not subject to the five-year period.

the more innovative and liberal elements of the early resolutions on asylum may have to be sacrificed under pressure of time and the need to reach a consensus.

The only positive development is that the Amsterdam Treaty unambiguously states that legally binding instruments are required and that the application of these instruments will be monitored by the European Commission, in accordance with the traditional 'first pillar' procedures. Eventually, the European Court of Justice may also provide binding rulings which could further enhance the harmonisation process. Finally, therefore, the monitoring of the implementation of the adopted instruments should result in the elaboration of legally binding instruments, as required by the EC Treaty.

Conclusion

Eight years after the adoption of the work programme, the EU finds itself at a crossroads. It is clear that with the adoption of non-legally binding instruments most subjects of the work programme have now been dealt with. For some, this may be enough: based on this non-legally binding framework, in their view, practical co-operation should flourish and determine the future agenda. For others, such as the author of this chapter, much higher aspirations are called for, in order finally to engage in 'real and fair' harmonisation. Although the EC Treaty requires the adoption of legally binding instruments within five years of the adoption of the Treaty of Amsterdam, whether this will bring about real progress towards such a level of harmonisation will depend heavily on the prevailing political climate. Since decision-making during this initial period will still be based on consensus, one cannot be too optimistic as to future developments in this regard.

Apart from this legislative work, the emerging crisis concerning the return of rejected asylum applicants will require a major international debate on the basic principles underlying our asylum and immigration policies. Such a debate cannot take place without the presence of and active participation by the major countries of origin and transit. This is a fascinating development with unprecedented challenges to the restrictive nature of member states' policies.

Finally, the development of an effective root causes strategy should now be firmly taken in hand. Considering the efforts already undertaken by the Commission in this regard, it seems logical that any such initiative should come from that institution, although every member state should of course feel free to increase the necessary pressure. An 'inter-pillar' dialogue is essential in this respect. Although present arrangements do not make it easy to establish such a dialogue, the Committee of Permanent Representatives (COREPER) has already created a number of horizontal, 'inter-pillar' working groups. As soon as the Commission submits concrete ideas for the development of an effective root causes strategy, it seems perfectly legitimate to create a special horizontal working group for the discussion of these ideas.

Bibliography

Amnesty International, *Europe: The Need for Minimum Standards in Asylum Procedures* (Amnesty International EU Secretariat, Brussels, 1994)

Bunyan, Tony, *Key Texts on Justice and Home Affairs in the European Union* (Statewatch, London, 1997)

Bunyan, Tony and Frances Webber, *Intergovernmental Co-operation on Immigration and Asylum* (Briefing Paper No. 19, Churches' Commission for Migrants in Europe, Brussels, 1995)

Guild, Elspeth and Jan Niessen, *The Emerging Immigration and Asylum Policy of the European Union* (Kluwer Law International, The Hague, 1996)

JUSTICE, *The Jurisdiction of the European Court of Justice in Respect of Asylum and Immigration Matters* (JUSTICE Position Paper, London, 1997)

Papademetriou, Demetrios G., *Coming Together or Pulling Apart? The European Union's Struggle with Immigration and Asylum* (International Migration Policy Program, Carnegie Endowment for International Peace, Washington DC, 1996)

Peers, Steve, *Mind the Gap! Ineffective Member State Implementation of European Union Asylum Measures* (Refugee Council and Immigration Law Practitioners' Association, London, 1998)

Plender, Richard, *Basic Documents on International Migration Law* (Martinus Nijhoff, The Hague, 1997)

Index